Vasily Grossman
and the Soviet Century

Vasily Grossman

and the Soviet Century

Alexandra Popoff

Yale

UNIVERSITY PRESS

NEW HAVEN AND LONDON

Published with assistance from the foundation established in memory of Calvin Chapin of the Class
of 1788, Yale College.

Yale University Press books may be purchased in quantity for educational, business, or promotional use. For
information, please e-mail sales.press@yale.edu (U.S. office) or sales@yaleup.co.uk (U.K. office).

Set in Fournier MT type by IDS Infotech Ltd.
Printed in the United States of America.

Library of Congress Control Number: 2018955015

ISBN 978-0-300-22278-4 (hardcover : alk. paper)

A catalogue record for this book is available from the British Library.

This paper meets the requirements of ANSI/NISO Z39.48–1992 (Permanence of Paper).

10 9 8 7 6 5 4 3 2 1

His daring, his frankness were drawn from his very despair.
So was his revolt.
—Elie Wiesel, *Souls on Fire*

Contents

Illustrations follow page 114

Preface and Acknowledgments

In 2014, during the International Grossman Conference in Moscow organized by the Study Center Vasily Grossman in Turin, I first realized that the legacy of this writer equally concerns scholars from Russia, Italy, Germany, England, and the United States. During the conference I discussed this book with Robert Chandler, the major translator of Grossman's works into English. I am grateful to him for permission to quote his translations of Grossman's prose and for the encouragement and expert advice he offered upon reading my manuscript. I also want to thank the author and literary scholar Joshua Rubenstein for his valuable comments. This book is more accurate owing to the contributions of Peter Crane, author and historian, whose suggestions were both meticulous and insightful.

I want to thank Ekaterina Korotkova-Grossman, who shared stories about her father. Our conversations at her Moscow apartment, which Grossman had visited, had special meaning. In Baden-Baden, Germany, I interviewed the writer's stepson Fyodor Guber, a major surviving witness of Grossman's life. I am thankful to Guber and his wife, Irina Novikova, for answering my queries and for permission to use letters and photographs from their archive. Irina, who was with Grossman during the confiscation of *Life and Fate* by the KGB, shared this and other stories. The couple's daughter, Elena Kozhichkina, who accommodates Grossman's library and memorial study at her Moscow apartment, spoke fascinatingly about her grandmother, Grossman's second wife. Elena's meticulous descriptions of Grossman's original study are employed in this book.

I am indebted to Maria Loboda (Karpova) and her sister Lyudmila Efremova, both of whom met Grossman in adolescence. The Loboda family risked their safety preserving the final draft of *Life and Fate* for three decades. (This was a portion of the writer's archive the KGB never found.) Maria's stories and her mother's unpublished memoir shed light on Grossman's sources; photographs from their family archive were also invaluable.

My thanks go to Alexander Zelinsky for permission to reproduce the previously unpublished photograph of Grossman from Kornely Zelinsky's private archive. I owe thanks to Natalya Zabolotskaya, the daughter of Grossman's friend the poet Nikolai Zabolotsky, for clarifying information that led me to discover Grossman's major source on Ukraine's famine. Her blunt refusal to speak about Grossman, her family's neighbor, was also illuminating. It revealed the depth of emotion over her mother's affair with the writer in the 1950s.

I'm indebted to Elena Surits for sharing her recollections of Grossman, who was her parents' closest friend; to Tatyana Sharapova, who told of her meeting with Grossman and his genuine interest in people and their stories; to Arnold Sharapov, who recommended literature indispensable for this book; to Elena Makarova, for permission to reproduce photographs of her stepfather (and Grossman's close friend) Semyon Lipkin. I'm also grateful to the Russian journalist and director Elena Yakovich, who told of how in 2013, during the shooting of her biographical film about Grossman, the FSB (the successor to the KGB) finally released the "arrested" manuscripts of *Life and Fate* to the public domain.

My deepest thanks go to the Memorial International, a Russian human rights organization in Moscow; to the late historian and human rights activist Arseny Roginsky, with whom I discussed parts of this book; to Irina Shcherbakova of Memorial International, who recommended literature on Stalin's repressions; and to Svetlana Fadeeva, who suggested using the drawings of Thomas Sgovio, former Gulag inmate, American artist, and author of *Dear America! Why I Turned against Communism*. Tatyana Goryaeva, director of the Russian State Archive of Literature and Art, and other curators of this archive have accommodated my research over the years. I am equally grateful to curators of the V. I. Dahl State Museum of the History of Russian Literature (State Literary Museum) for permission to reproduce Grossman photographs from their rich collection. My special thanks go to Alexei Nevsky, the museum's deputy director; Vasily Vysokolov, head of the photo department; and Evgeniya Varentsova, head of the manuscript department, who accommodated my research concerning the final draft of *Life and Fate*.

I am indebted to my husband, Wilfred, for his editing, shared interest, and unfailing support for my book, which took years to produce. And I'm grateful to my editor at Yale University Press, Jaya Chatterjee, and copy editor

Robin DuBlanc, for their faith in my project and hard work. Finally, this book would have been impossible without grants from the Canada Council and the Saskatchewan Arts Board.

A number of important translations and studies have become available in the West within the last decade or two. These include Frank Ellis's *Vasily Grossman: The Genesis and Evolution of a Russian Heretic* and Carol and John Garrard's biography *The Bones of Berdichev: The Life and Fate of Vasily Grossman*. Robert and Elizabeth Chandler have made superb translations of *Everything Flows*, a collection of Grossman's short prose, *The Road*, and *An Armenian Sketchbook*. Having brought *Life and Fate* to the English-speaking reader, Robert Chandler is also about to launch his translation of the novel *For the Right Cause* (it will appear under Grossman's original title, *Stalingrad*). Antony Beevor's remarkable book *A Writer at War* explores Grossman's writings and the notebooks he kept as a war correspondent. The author's expert commentaries deepened my understanding of "a writer at war."

As Patrick Finney points out, the multifaceted character and richness of Grossman's work explains why historians, philosophers, political theorists, and Holocaust scholars "have turned to Grossman for the insights of unparalleled acuity and sensitivity that he offers into some of the central horrors of the totalitarian century—from the Stalinist Terror of the 1930s, to the brutal Eastern Front warfare of the Second World War, to the Holocaust."[1] Grossman's account of the war and the Stalingrad battle informed Beevor in his best-selling history *Stalingrad*. Timothy Snyder employed Grossman as a source in *Bloodlands: Europe between Hitler and Stalin*. Earlier, *The Complete Black Book of Russian Jewry* Grossman and Ilya Ehrenburg had edited appeared in English. Its publication prompted further research. Drawing from the previously suppressed archival material of the Jewish Anti-Fascist Committee, Ilya Altman and Joshua Rubenstein published *The Unknown Black Book: The Holocaust in the German-Occupied Soviet Territories*.

It would be impossible to name all the numerous scholars who have published papers that contribute to our understanding of the writer, among them Polly Zavadivker, who translated Grossman's article "Ukraine without Jews," Maxim Shrayer, who wrote articles on Grossman, the Holocaust resistance, and Soviet memory of the Shoah, and David Feldman and Yuri Bit-Yunan, who have contributed biographical studies (published in Russian).

Introduction

Vasily Grossman began *Life and Fate*, a powerful anti-totalitarian novel, when Stalin was still alive. Back then he had no prospect of publication. But after the dictator's death, when the regime admitted half truths about Stalin's crimes, there was a glimmer of hope. Despite knowing that the repressive state had not changed in essence, that Stalinists remained in control, Grossman made the daring decision to publish his testimony on the Soviet century and on Stalinism. This was the first major attempt to resurrect the historical truth along with the names of people the regime had erased from life and from the record. In *Life and Fate* Grossman put Stalinism on trial: he juxtaposed Soviet crimes against humanity with those committed by the Nazis. In 1960, two years before the world heard Solzhenitsyn's account of the Gulag, Grossman completed his exposé of the two dictatorships and the practices of slavery they established. The decision to attempt publication in the USSR was an act of desperate bravery and defiance.

Grossman's novel opens with an image of camp cities in twentieth-century Europe—a world of straight lines and identical barracks where individuality is erased: tens of thousands share the same fate. Whether they live and die in a Nazi camp or in the frozen wastelands of Russia's Far East, people are treated as the living dead.

Having likened the Gulag to the Holocaust, Grossman told the story of his entire generation, which had experienced twin dictatorships and World War II. He wanted post-Stalinist Russia to deal with its past in the manner of post-Nazi Germany. Grossman was prepared to fight for the right cause, but an editor reported him to the KGB. The secret police did not arrest the author, they arrested his novel—a greater punishment.

In February 1961 the KGB raided Grossman's apartment and the editorial offices where he had submitted *Life and Fate* and seized all typescripts and drafts. The writer was told that his book was more dangerous to the Soviet state than Pasternak's *Doctor Zhivago*, "and if it will be possible to ever publish it, then, perhaps, not for about 250 years." The main Soviet ideologist, Mikhail Suslov, compared the explosive power of Grossman's work to a nuclear bomb, thus admitting that its historical facts endangered a regime founded on fabrications.

In his appeal to the Soviet government Grossman wrote, "There is no logic, no truth in the present condition, in my physical freedom when the book, to which I have given my life, is in prison, for I wrote it, I have not renounced it, and I do not renounce it. . . . I ask for my book's freedom." The regime suppressed the truth—and Grossman's novel—for as long as possible.

The Soviet state, with its "heavy, multitrillion-ton mass," as Grossman describes it, prevailed in destroying him physically.[1] The writer died of cancer in 1964, three years after his novel's confiscation, unaware whether *Life and Fate* would ever see light. The novel was believed to have been lost or burned. But in 1980 *Life and Fate* suddenly emerged in the West. Preserved by Grossman's friends and smuggled abroad in microfilm, it was brought out in Lausanne, published across Europe (where it became a bestseller), in America, and in 1988, under Mikhail Gorbachev, it was finally released in the USSR.

Grossman never learned his readers' judgment. The confiscation of *Life and Fate* made him a banned writer: for almost three decades his name was not mentioned in the Soviet press. Long before that, however, he had been a prominent Soviet author: during World War II he reported on major battles from Moscow and Stalingrad to Berlin; his articles and fiction alike were read widely. By the late 1940s his books had sold over 8 million copies in the USSR and were published abroad. In the West he is still remembered as a Soviet war correspondent, the author of a famous 1944 article, "The Hell of Treblinka."

One of the first accounts of the Holocaust, "The Hell of Treblinka," was used as evidence at Nuremberg. It still surprises the reader with its clarity of analysis, insight into unprecedented genocide, and emotional power. In this article, anticipating the Nuremberg trials, Grossman presented the evidence "before the eyes of humanity, before the conscience of the whole world."[2] His perceived audience has always been the whole of human-kind. But humanity was not an abstract idea for Grossman: he had a unique ability to describe the experiences of millions in a personal way.

As a Jew whose mother was killed by the Nazis in his native Berdichev, Ukraine, Grossman felt the twentieth-century calamities most acutely. His mother had perished in September 1941, during one of the first massacres of Jews in the occupied Soviet territories. Her destiny became the strongest motivational force in Grossman's life. It prompted him to become an early chronicler of the Holocaust and was behind his determination to tell the whole truth about the global evil unleashed by the twentieth-century's totali-tarian regimes.

In 1943, in the article "Ukraine without Jews" (unpublished in Russian during his life) Grossman first elucidated the meaning of the Final Solution, describing it as the murder of a nation, of its body and soul. That same year he became involved in a unique undertaking, collaboratively collecting and editing accounts to document the lesser known Holocaust—that on Soviet soil. The resulting compendium, *The Black Book of Russian Jewry*, to which Grossman also contributed original articles, was banned in 1948 when Stalin launched a massive anti-Semitic campaign. All printed copies of this compen-dium were destroyed and the metal printing plates broken up. During Stalin's "secret pogrom," members of the Jewish Anti-Fascist Committee involved in bringing out *The Black Book* were arrested, secretly tried as "Jewish nationalists," and shot. Across the country Jews were driven out of positions of authority and preparations were made to deport them en masse. The purge was halted only by Stalin's death in 1953—events Grossman depicts in his final novel, *Everything Flows*.

Thus, Grossman had experienced anti-Semitism twice—during the war with the Nazis and back in the Soviet Union. Stalinists referred to Jews as "rootless cosmopolitans," the phrase that surfaced in every Soviet news-paper at the time. One can imagine what Grossman felt during the campaign against ethnic Jews in his home country after the war with Fascism. But while his comparison in *Life and Fate* between Stalinism and Nazism was suggested by events, he alone in the USSR had the courage to express it.

Notwithstanding their different ideologies—of race and of class—the two totalitarian systems were alike in their complete inhumanity, in their rejection of the fundamental notion that individual human lives have value. Belonging to "an inferior race" in Nazi Germany or an "inferior" class in the

USSR sealed one's destiny. As Grossman observes in *Life and Fate*, the Stalinist regime applied a "statistical method" in ferreting out class enemies: "There was a greater probability of finding enemies among people of a non-proletarian background. And it was on these same grounds—probability theory—that the German Fascists had destroyed whole peoples and nations. The principle was inhuman. . . . There was only one acceptable way of relating to people—a human way."[3]

The war and the Holocaust opened Grossman's eyes to the inhumanity of totalitarian systems. In 1946 in the article "To the Memory of the Fallen," he wrote that the millions of deaths in World War II cannot diminish the value of a single life: "There is nothing more precious than human life; its loss is final and irreplaceable." He urged Soviet writers to follow in the steps of their literary predecessors Tolstoy and Chekhov by advocating the "basic and sacred human rights, the right of each individual to live on earth, to think, and to be free." Every word in this article argued against the Stalinist regime, which considered the state paramount and its people disposable.

After the war Grossman found that all his topics became the strictest Soviet taboos. He considered himself a chronicler of events and believed, as he remarks in his Treblinka article, in his duty as a writer "to tell the terrible truth." But the truth about the war could not be told: Stalinists had created their own victorious version of events that excluded devastating Soviet losses. The Soviet press had to remain silent about a vast range of issues—from Jewish suffering during the war to Stalin's mass purges, peasant genocide, and man-made famine—that affected tens of millions in the USSR. Grossman struggled against forgetting and thus against totalitarian power while striving for freedom and historical truth.

In 1952, after three years of battling with Soviet editors, he succeeded in publishing a censored version of the novel *For the Right Cause*. This was the first part of *Life and Fate*. Structured to resemble Tolstoy's *War and Peace*, with narrative switching from global events to domestic scenes, it was intended to show how the world had changed over a hundred years. Grossman's portrayals of Mussolini and Hitler, his accurate depiction of the war from the battlefield, and the Jewish theme, coming at the height of Stalin's campaign against the "rootless cosmopolitans," were unprecedented for a Soviet writer. The main protagonist in the novel is the Jewish physicist Victor Shtrum, engaged on the Soviet atomic project. Grossman was forced to make numerous revisions, but Shtrum and a brief discussion of the Holocaust remained. In February 1953, one month before Stalin's death, the Soviet press launched a coordinated assault on Grossman and his novel. During this time Grossman endured high drama that nearly ended with his arrest. In the post-Stalinist era *For the Right Cause* became a Soviet classic, and in subsequent editions the writer restored more of his original text.

Although Grossman lived all of his adult life in a totalitarian Soviet state, he had the mentality of a man from the free world. In the early historical novel *Stepan Kolchugin*, published before the war, Grossman's protagonist argues that Russia needs a long school of democracy, of "introducing glasnost" and "all those freedoms inherent in democratic society." Over the decades his views changed, but only to become more uncompromising. In his last and most radical anti-totalitarian novel, *Everything Flows*, written after the arrest of *Life and Fate*, he declares that "there is no end in the world for the sake of which it is permissible to sacrifice human freedom."[4]

During his final years Grossman lived under the KGB's surveillance; nonetheless, he worked to complete his testimony on the Soviet century. In *Everything Flows* he investigates how the People's State, founded on promises of liberty and equal rights, became one of the world's bloodiest dictatorships. As he observes in this novel, the Bolsheviks "had no doubt that the new world was being built for the people." However, they viewed people as the main "obstacle to the building of this new world."[5] The novel's strongest indictment of the regime is made by a woman who witnessed Stalin's collectivization and the Terror Famine.

Grossman's experiences were unusually diverse for a writer. Trained as a scientist, he worked for a while as a chemical engineer in the Donbass's coal mines. This education and working experience benefited his art. As a scientist he was capable of dispassionate analysis; as an artist he would demonstrate his prodigious imagination and deep emotion. The two different sides of his personality and talent gave him a special insight into twentieth-century events.

His beliefs in democracy and universal equality were typical of a generation of idealists that was almost entirely destroyed under Stalin. Grossman's true internationalism (strikingly different from the official ideology of "friendship of Soviet peoples," which justified deportations of entire nationalities) explains his ability to depict the Holocaust, Ukraine's famine, and the Armenian genocide with equal power. His exuberant travel memoir, *An Armenian Sketchbook*, remained unpublished during his life: he refused to remove the passages in which he compares the suffering of the Jewish and Armenian nations.

Raised by a disabled mother (his parents divorced when he was still a baby), Grossman was sensitive to the plight of the most vulnerable. The theme of mother and child is prominent in his works. His 1934 story "In the Town of Berdichev," which made him famous overnight, is about a woman commissar who gives birth in Berdichev during the Russian Civil War.

Grossman perceived motherhood as a spiritual force that cannot be enslaved even by totalitarian violence. His 1955 essay "The Sistine Madonna" pictures the fate of a mother and child in the epoch of Fascism and Stalinism. He saw this painting as an everlasting work and also a contemporary symbol of suffering humanity and unconquerable human strength. The essay ends with Grossman's thoughts about humanity entering the age of atomic reactors and thermonuclear bombs—and along with it prospects of a new global war.

Because Grossman was a banned writer, his major works have appeared only after much delay. Over the years his legacy attracted attention from scholars researching totalitarianism, Ukraine's famine, World War II, and the Holocaust. His writings have become recognized as a valuable historical source, a testimony about the calamitous twentieth century. The famine chapter in *Everything Flows* informed the American-English historian Robert Conquest, who treated Grossman's material as factual in *The Harvest of Sorrow*. Conquest felt that Grossman's depiction of Ukraine's famine belonged to "the most moving writing on the period."[6] Anne Applebaum also quoted *Everything Flows* as a historical document in *Red Famine: Stalin's War on Ukraine*. Today, references to Grossman abound in books by Western authors on Soviet history, World War II, and Stalin's famine. Grossman, however, is far less known in Putin's Russia, where Stalin's popularity along with nationalism has been steadily on the rise and where the myth of a glorious Soviet past is again being revived.

We are beginning to properly examine Grossman's life and legacy only now, more than half a century after his death in 1964. The first thing to learn is that his prose hasn't aged: Grossman's ideas are essential to understanding Russia's totalitarian past and authoritarian present. His artistry, talent for apt expression, and humanity explain the everlasting and universal appeal of his prose.

1. In the Town of Berdichev

Berdichev was considered the most Jewish city in the Ukraine. Before the Revolution anti-Semites and the Black Hundreds called it the "Jewish capital."
—Vasily Grossman, "The Murder of the Jews in Berdichev"

In 1929, in the article "Berdichev—Not as a Joke, but Seriously," Vasily Grossman, aged twenty-four, described his native city as having an undeservedly low reputation. "What does the average citizen know about Berdichev? He knows nothing, except that to be born in Berdichev, to be wed there, or to live there for a year or two is something that should not be said out loud." What does Anton Chekhov's character Doctor Chebutykin (in *The Three Sisters*) know about Berdichev? The doctor exclaims—with horror—that Balzac was married in Berdichev! The anti-Semites describe Berdichev as "*their* capital."[1]

By the time Grossman wrote this article, Berdichev was no longer a center of Jewish cultural and religious life. After the 1917 Revolution it became a Soviet city with several factories and a sizable working class. Its population was predominantly Jewish, but with religious education abolished, all children were taught the standard Soviet curriculum. Rabbis teaching the Torah in heder had ended. Berdichev's artisans, once numerous, still produced their famous furniture and leather footwear, and their goods were in high demand across Ukraine and Central Asia. But commerce ceased to exist, writes Grossman: "Trade died after the Revolution." Only rows of warehouses, now empty and locked in the old part of the city, reminded one of the former prosperity and trade.

In the eighteenth and nineteenth centuries Berdichev was a big commercial center—first as part of the Polish-Lithuanian Commonwealth and second, after the Partitions of Poland, as part of the Russian Empire. Its strategic geographic location enhanced its wealth. In the 1870s the railroad was built, eventually connecting Berdichev with two main lines: Kiev-Petersburg and Kiev-Brest-Warsaw.

Berdichev was a Polish town until it was absorbed by the Russian Empire in 1793. It was assigned to the Pale of Permanent Jewish Settlement where Jews had to live after 1791 when Catherine the Great's government imposed restrictions on Jewish residence and trade. Initially, this measure aimed to protect the interests of the Moscow merchants who complained about the influx of Jewish traders from the annexed Polish territories. The decree, which came into full force in 1835, forbade Jews from leaving the Pale without special permission, which only the rich could afford, and from settling in major cities. Stretching along Russia's western and southern borders from the Baltic to the Black Sea, the Pale occupied around 472,590 square miles. Restrictions on Jewish settlement were abolished only after the 1917 Revolution, when Grossman was twelve.

Located in the middle of the impoverished southwest region of the Pale, Berdichev was head and shoulders above Sholem Aleichem's native town of Voronka and his fictional Anatevka. Jewish poverty, isolation, and overcrowding were typical for shtetls and villages in the Pale. Aleichem felt these places were "stuck away in the corner of the world, isolated from the surrounding country" and civilization. In his words, the Jewish population in the Pale was "packed as closely as herring in a barrel."[2] But Berdichev was different. In 1898 Aleichem wrote humorously to a relative: "I just returned from Paris, that is from Berdichev, and found a letter from you."[3]

Berdichev and neighboring Kiev were important centers of trade and light industry. In the early nineteenth century some companies in Berdichev even traded internationally. At some point Berdichev threatened to overtake Kiev. This motivated Alexander II in 1859 to temporarily lift the ban on Jewish settlement in the Ukrainian metropolis.[4] A monument was installed in Berdichev to the tsar, who had emancipated the serfs and permitted Jews to settle outside the Pale in agricultural colonies. Lev Trotsky's grandfather and parents were among the sixty-five thousand Jewish pioneers who benefited from the decree. They received virgin land in the Kherson province of southern Ukraine and prospered despite not having farming experience.[5]

In the 1860s, its heyday, Berdichev had thousands of merchants and artisans. Its eighty synagogues and prayer houses were organized around specific occupations: tailors, cobblers, stove makers, blacksmiths, and bakers all had separate places of worship. Berdichev's prominent Hasidic movement had been established in the eighteenth century by tsadik Levi-Yitzhak ben Me'ir. A famous fighter for justice, he called on Jewish leaders to oppose government restrictions on Jews. Elie Wiesel, who was born in Romania more than a century after Levi-Yitzhak's death, imagined him as "a powerful, invincible defender of the weak . . . ready to risk all and lose all in the pursuit of truth and justice. . . . 'The greatness of Levi-Yitzak of Berditchev?' my grandmother asked. And answered: 'He was a fighter.' "[6] Grossman and his family were not religious, but the story of Berdichev's famous rabbinical teacher was known to all.

During Grossman's childhood Berdichev still had discrete Polish and Jewish quarters; the residents spoke Yiddish, Polish, and Ukrainian. In his novel *Stepan Kolchugin* Grossman describes Berdichev's prayer houses, located in whitewashed village-type huts with thatched roofs, known in Ukraine as *mazanki*; and the older Polish section: "The town had two Roman Catholic churches and a medieval Carmelite monastery; its mighty walls and tiny windows made it look more like a fortress than the house of God."[7] In 1850 Honoré de Balzac and Eveline Hanska, a Polish noblewoman, were married in Berdichev's Church of St. Barbara.[8]

In the late nineteenth century, when most successful merchants and bankers transferred their activity to Kiev and Odessa, Berdichev's importance declined. Kiev became the magnet for the young and talented from the nearby shtetls—all those who wanted to escape the economic and cultural trap of the Pale. By the turn of the century Jewish merchants, although a minority in Kiev, controlled two-thirds of the city trade.[9] Jews owned most of the tobacco factories in Kiev, its sugar factories, and the largest tannery and wheat mill. Around this same time in Odessa, most banks were also run by Jews, as were Russia's timber and export industries.[10] Jewish banks were among the first commercial lending institutions in the Russian Empire. They stimulated Russian industrial development: Jewish businesses financed railroad construction, gold mining, oil production, river transportation, and the like. Russian industrialization of the late nineteenth century greatly benefited from Jewish investment.[11] But despite sizable contributions to Russia's economy, public life, and culture, the Jewish population continued to face legal restrictions and was treated worse than other minorities. When in the 1880s Alexander III traveled on the Southwestern Railroad, he complained to Sergei Witte, then director of the Department of Railroad Affairs, about the slow speed of the train: "I traveled on other roads and nowhere else has my speed been reduced; your railroad is an impossible one because it is a kikish (*zhidovskaia*) road."[12]

The official government policy of anti-Semitism, combined with pogroms, made Jews the "first among non-equals" in the Russian Empire.[13] Beginning in the 1880s, a wave of deadly pogroms rolled through Kiev, Kishinev, and Odessa. In 1891 some thirty thousand Jews were expelled from Moscow by the city governor, Grand Duke Sergei Alexandrovich. In Petersburg two thousand Jews were deported by the municipal government; merchants, doctors, engineers, and other professionals were driven out of the city bound in chains.[14] Because of relentless government persecution and pogroms one-fifth of the total 5.2 million Jews of the empire emigrated between 1897 and 1915, the majority to the United States.[15]

In 1897, about a decade before Grossman was born, the all-Imperial Russian census estimated Berdichev's Jewish residents at 41,617, about three-quarters of the total population. By 1929, the year Grossman published his article about Berdichev, the Jewish population had shrunk to 30,000.

Both sides of Grossman's family descended from well-to-do merchants. This background had to be concealed in Soviet days, but Grossman told the true story to his daughter Katya: "Our family was unlike the poor shtetl Jews described by Sholem Aleichem, the kind that lived in hovels and slept side by side on the floor. No, our family comes from an entirely different Jewish background. They owned carriages and trotters; their wives wore diamonds, and their children were educated abroad."[16] Grossman's uncle David Sherentsis, a medical doctor and entrepreneur, had a large medical practice and invested in construction. He built Berdichev's theater where actors from Kiev and Odessa performed Italian operas and gave readings of Aleichem's stories in Yiddish. Uncle David's private clinic, an impressive three-story building, was equipped with the city's only X-ray machine. The family lived in a two-story adjacent house—and this is where Grossman spent his early childhood and adolescence.

Grossman's mother, Ekaterina Savelievna, née Vitis, was born in 1871 and grew up in Odessa, where her assimilated family had migrated from Lithuania. Her Jewish name at birth was Malka, but she never used it. The four Vitis sisters received a European education, the second generation in the family to do so; they were fluent in Russian and French, and assumed Christian names: Maria, Anna, Ekaterina, and Elizaveta.

The family of Grossman's father, Solomon Iosifovich, engaged in the lucrative grain trade in Bessarabia, the southwestern part of the Pale that bordered Romania. Semyon Osipovich, as he would call himself in the Russian fashion, was born in 1870 in Reni (currently part of Ukraine), a town on the river Danube. He belonged to a generation that rejected their parents' way of life, their religion and traditions, and aspired to leave the Pale for good. It was a time when a growing number of Jews, overcoming government restrictions on education and professions, were becoming lawyers, doctors, and engineers. In 1886 in Odessa, Jews already comprised almost half of all of the city lawyers. In Petersburg the Jewish share of doctors and dentists reached 52 percent by 1913. And scores of Jewish artists, musicians, and writers were entering Russian culture. The government responded by imposing quotas to slow down their advance in the professions.[17] Jewish admission quotas at universities, restrictions on certain professions (for example, Jews were barred from government employment), and the existence of the Pale of Settlement drove a large number of Jews to the revolutionary movement.

Witte, Russia's minister of finance and first prime minister, would write that instead of gradually eliminating discriminatory laws against the Jews, the government only added legal restrictions. Brutal anti-Jewish government policies in the empire and the persistence of pogroms help explain why "no other nationality has produced so high a percentage of revolutionaries as the Jews."[18] The government-backed ultranationalists, such as the Black Hundreds and the Union of the Russian People, openly preached anti-Semitic violence. In 1905, immediately after the tsar's October Manifesto, which promised civil liberties, ultranationalists organized a deadly pogrom in Kiev, blaming Jews for anti-government agitation. The pogrom left dozens killed, hundreds wounded, and countless businesses destroyed. The deadliest pogroms in Kishinev, Gomel, Kiev, and elsewhere were conducted with government consent and help from the Interior Ministry, the police, and local authorities.

A painting by a Polish artist depicting the 1905 pogrom against Jews in Kiev—with the figure of Nicholas II in the background—produced a stir at a 1910 exhibition in Frankfurt. Because the emperor and the royal family were in Frankfurt, police tried to convince the exhibition organizer to remove the painting.[19] The Russian autocracy was using brutal force to implement its one tsar, one religion, and one nationality policy. While it attempted to discourage Jews from revolutionary activity, it achieved the opposite by radicalizing them.[20]

Jews would become well represented in all revolutionary parties, including the Bolshevik. The Jewish Bund, founded in 1897, became the first Social Democratic Party in the Russian Empire; it promoted Marxism in the Yiddish language.[21] Many of the prominent Jewish revolutionaries—Lev Trotsky (Leiba Bronstein), Grigory Zinoviev (Ovsei-Gersh Apfelbaum), Lev Kamenev (Rozenfeld), Grigory Sokolnikov (Girsh Brilliant)—became Bolshevik leaders close to Lenin. They had no religion and did not want to be defined as Jewish. Trotsky identified his nationality as "Social Democratic."[22]

Like thousands of the empire's Jews who became lawyers, engineers, and doctors, Grossman's parents aspired to enter the professional class. Attaining a profession was a path to equality and freedom. Ekaterina Savelievna studied in France; Semyon Osipovich graduated from the University of Bern as a chemical engineer. The couple met in Italy when they were in their thirties; the only surviving photograph of them together was taken in Turin. Ekaterina Savelievna was already married to an Italian Jew, of whom we know only that he was too jealous to be told about the affair. When she fell in love, she had to secretly escape from her husband. Breaking a marriage was a daring decision for a woman of her time and with her disability: Ekaterina Savelievna had hip dysplasia, or misalignment of a hip joint. Her marriage with Semyon Osipovich did not last: he left the family when their son was still a baby. But they remained friends and maintained regular correspondence. Although Semyon Osipovich later remarried, he never had another child. He and Ekaterina Savelievna deeply cared about their only son.

Grossman's father was active in the revolutionary underground. Europe at the turn of the century was teeming with Russian political émigrés and socialists. Marxist ideas became popular in Russia in the 1890s, and a decade later colonies of Russian Marxists proliferated in Germany, Switzerland, England, and France. In Switzerland, one could meet Georgy Plekhanov, a leading Marxist thinker and publicist who opened the First Congress of the Russian Social Democratic Labor Party (RSDLP), and Mikhail Bakunin, a prominent revolutionary anarchist. (In *Life and Fate*, the Bolshevik

Mostovskoy and the Menshevik Chernetsov, both incarcerated in a Nazi death camp, recall the days when their party was founded: "They talked excitedly about the relations between Marx and Bakunin, about what Lenin and Plekhanov had said about the hard-liners and the softs on the editorial staff of *Iskra*. . . . How warmly Engels had welcomed the young Russian Social Democrats who had come to visit him when he was a blind old man!")[23]

Grossman's father joined the RSDLP around 1903. (Toward the end of 1917 it was renamed RSDRP, Russian Social Democratic Workers Party.) During the Second Congress, which took place that year in Brussels and London, the party split into factions, and he became a Menshevik. The Bolsheviks, headed by Lenin, believed that membership must be restricted to professional revolutionaries. The Mensheviks, led by Yuli Martov (Tsederbaum), wanted the party to be more inclusive. Notably, they opposed Lenin's fanatical ambition to build socialism overnight.

In 1905, when the Mensheviks actively worked to foment unrest, Semyon Osipovich helped organize an uprising in the Black Sea Fleet in Sebastopol. Grossman would cite some of their proclamations in *Stepan Kolchugin*: "Long live freedom and democracy, long live an eight-hour working day, long live socialism."[24] The Sebastopol mutiny, which began on October 1, was led by Peter Schmidt, a hero of the Crimean War and lieutenant commander in the Imperial Russian Navy. Schmidt sent a telegram to Nicholas II stating that the fleet would no longer obey government ministers; he demanded that a Constituent Assembly be called. The uprising was suppressed and Lieutenant Schmidt executed. His name became synonymous with Russia's fight for freedom. Boris Pasternak romanticized Lieutenant Schmidt in a 1927 poem bearing his name, in which he compared his predicament with that of Christ on Golgotha.

The turbulent year of 1905 threatened the Romanov monarchy. Russia's defeat in the war with Japan and the Bloody Sunday of January 9, 1905, when government troops massacred participants in the workers' peaceful march, destroyed the regime's credibility. A wave of political terrorism, peasant unrest, and mutinies swept the empire. A general strike in early October soon after the navy uprising in Sebastopol forced Nicholas II to make concessions. On October 17 the tsar issued a manifesto promising civic freedoms and elections to Russia's first parliament, the Duma. But little was achieved in the end: Nicholas II preserved most of his autocratic powers and impeded the creation of an actual parliamentary body.

Grossman was born at the end of this revolutionary year, on December 12, 1905. His mother was thirty-four when she bore him, her first child. The family in Berdichev, Ekaterina's sister Anna (Aunt Anyuta) and uncle David, worried whether this would be a normal birth, given her age and disability. A midwife and relative, Rosalia Samoilovna Menaker, delivered the baby. In his famous story "In the Town of Berdichev," Grossman preserves the midwife's name. The story tells about how Vavilova, a woman commissar, gives birth in Berdichev during the civil war. She is somewhat older than Grossman's mother. Vavilova is billeted with the large Magazanik family in their over-crowded hut. During labor, which lasts many hours, the midwife confides to Beila Magazanik: "If you think I'd wish it upon myself to be having my first child at the age of thirty-six, then you're wrong, Beila." The baby's father, only mentioned in the story as a revolutionary and "the sad, taciturn man," is killed in the fighting long before his son's birth.[25] Grossman's father was mostly absent during his childhood. Later, his job inspecting coal mines required Semyon Osipovich to be constantly on the move. Father and son would rarely see each other. Grossman anxiously anticipated their meetings, writing to Semyon Osipovich at twenty-three: "I miss you badly, I want to see you very much; with that, whenever I think of your arrival, I imagine that I will sit on your lap as in childhood and will touch your prickly moustache."[26]

Grossman's given name, Iosif, would appear only in his official papers. Family and friends called him Vasya, since this was the name his mother liked. (His readers would know him as Vasily Grossman or Vas. Grossman, which was the way he signed his reports from the front.) Vasily was, of course, a Russian name; no Jewish boy was called that. His assimilated family belonged to a small Jewish minority in the Kiev province who claimed Russian as their first tongue. The family did not send him to heder, so Grossman learned only a handful of words in Yiddish.[27] In Petersburg, where Osip Mandelstam grew up, 37 percent of Jews gave Russian as their native language.[28] Russian was a language of the secular, larger world—and for the Jews who wanted to escape the Pale, it was the language of "the striving for freedom."[29] Mandelstam and Isaak Babel, two contemporary writers Grossman esteemed, were fluent in Russian and French. Babel helped edit and translate Maupassant's collected works into Russian.[30] Although

Mandelstam's parents had engaged a teacher of Hebrew, he (like Grossman) had no grasp of Jewish customs as a child, admitting that even the names of the holidays Rosh Hashanah and Yom Kippur jarred on his ears.[31] (But even if Grossman was not religious, he read the Bible and was influenced by the biblical tradition. He was deeply influenced by the Jewish belief in the need for compassion, in the need to love life and resist death to the last minute, in the need and obligation to remember the past and honor the dead, and in the need to bear witness.)

Ekaterina Savelievna taught French and wanted her son to master the language. In 1910, when Grossman was five, she took him to Switzerland, where for two years he studied at an elementary school in the canton of Geneva. Grossman would later read the French parts of Tolstoy's *War and Peace* without translation and recite poems by Alfred de Musset; he knew by heart whole pages of Alphonse Daudet's *Lettres de mon moulin* and of Guy de Maupassant's *Une vie*, which was also his mother's favorite reading. But he absorbed more than just language. Two years in Geneva introduced Grossman to Western values, including the respect for individual rights and freedoms he later believed essential.

Their return to Berdichev in 1912 was memorable to Grossman, and he would describe it in *Life and Fate*. The Jewish boy David, who shares Grossman's date of birth and other autobiographical details (except that he would perish in a Nazi death camp) recalls returning to Berdichev with his mother:

> It had been night when he and his mother arrived at the station. In the moonlight they had walked down the cobbled street, past the white Catholic church—where a niche in the wall housed a rather thin, bowed Christ, about the height of a twelve-year-old, his head crowned with thorns—and past the teacher-training college where his mother had once studied. A few days later, on Friday evening, David saw the old men walking to the synagogue through the clouds of golden dust kicked up by the barefooted footballers on the wasteland. There was a heart-rending charm in this juxtaposition of white Ukrainian huts, squeaking well-handles and the ancient patterns on black-and-white prayer-shawls.[32]

David reads Russian and Ukrainian literature—Pushkin, Tolstoy, poems by Taras Shevchenko—as well as physics textbooks, which Grossman read in childhood and adolescence. A better picture of Grossman as an adolescent emerges from his 1935 story "Four Days" in which he portrays himself in Kolya, the doctor's teenaged son, who is never seen without a book.

"Four Days" gives a good picture of growing up in Uncle David's "peaceful and plentiful home." It was a hospitable place where guests were treated like family, where health was a priority, where children were loved, and where many people would sit down to dinner—even in troubled times of civil war. The family never surrendered its love of traditional Jewish food (something Solomon Mikhoels jokingly described as "gastronomic nationalism"); Grossman would mention gefilte fish in *Life and Fate*.[33]

His uncle and aunt had two sons—Peter and Victor—who were about his own age; however, Grossman repeatedly portrayed himself in his prose as the doctor's only child. As apparent from this story, he was ashamed of his uncle's wealth. This was typical for a revolutionary-minded youth: Trotsky rejected his family's "acquisitiveness, the petit-bourgeois outlook and way of life."[34] Kolya, Grossman's alter ego, is annoyed by his father's "petty-bourgeois" views and dreams of escaping with the Bolshevik commissars sheltered in the doctor's house during the civil war.

The doctor's domineering wife in the story is a replica of Aunt Anyuta, who supported and fed dozens of needy families in Berdichev. An overwhelming majority of the Jewish population in Kiev province suffered from poverty and disease. Uncle David provided free medical help, but it was Aunt Anyuta who threw herself wholeheartedly into philanthropy. Grossman admired his aunt's disdain for material possessions and her strong character: almost tyrannical in her generosity, she would burst into her husband's office demanding money for charities.[35] Describing his uncle and aunt in the story, Grossman writes: "Maria Andreevna had a character of steel, and the doctor knew that no power in the universe could force her to change, so he silently endured poor folk, who dined in the kitchen; the parcels she sent her nephews and nieces; and the commissars who, after coming for an X-ray, unexpectedly moved into the pantry."[36]

In the story, the doctor complains that a Rothschild's fortune would not be enough to pay for all the destitute his wife feeds and clothes; she retorts that she would not be seen refusing a single person. Everyone in the house sympathizes with the commissars, with the exception of the doctor, who demonstrates sound judgment: "I only want to know one thing: why is it that during the revolution, which is made for the happiness of all, it is the children, the old people, and all those innocent and vulnerable, who suffer most?"[37] The doctor's question is left unanswered. Grossman did not want his family to read the story, but in 1935 his cousin Victor brought it to Berdichev. Uncle David and Aunt Anyuta were offended by the portrayal of their household and their nephew's occasional mockery, as in the scene where the doctor, standing on tiptoe, kisses his big wife on the neck.

In summer 1914, on the eve of the Great War, Grossman and his mother moved to Kiev where he would attend realschule. The curriculum was modeled on European secondary schools, emphasizing a practical approach to education. Here Grossman's love of sciences would blossom, but the year he arrived, he had to attend a preparatory class. The proportion of Jewish students in realschule was smaller than in most gymnasia.[38] While studying in a Christian school, Grossman would be subjected to anti-Semitic gibes, much like Trotsky, who attended St. Paul's realschule in Odessa. Trotsky's associate Yuli Martov, who studied in the same school, recalls how his geography teacher had asked him to name Russia's capital before it was moved to St. Petersburg. Martov answered correctly that it was Moscow. What was it before Moscow? Martov replied that Russia's ancient capital was Kiev. The teacher, pretending to be surprised, remarked that he expected Martov to say it was Berdichev.[39] Jews were the largest religious minority in Kiev. But before they could be accepted at universities and gymnasia, they had to petition authorities for permission to live and study there—even if this was only for a period of exams. This discriminatory regulation remained in place until the 1917 Revolution.[40]

In *Stepan Kolchugin*, Grossman's half-Jewish protagonist, Sergei Kravchenko, arrives in Kiev to study not long before the Great War.[41] Coming from a mining town in the Donbass, he is impressed with the big European city of half a million and the "grandiose" Bezakovskaya Street lined with three-story hotels. The hero's sense of novelty and delight as well as his dream of becoming a scholar reflect Grossman's sentiment upon entering a larger world. There was a sense of the future in Kiev, a major European city with many schools, gymnasia, and universities, of which St. Vladimir's University and the Polytechnical Institute were among the best in Russia.

Sergei Kravchenko's story line in the novel is autobiographical: he is another bookish boy and a doctor's only son. The relationship with his mother, a powerful force in his life, is sensitively portrayed. Grossman's mother loved this novel, writing in April 1941 that she became "attached" to its main characters, Sergei Kravchenko and Stepan Kolchugin; they had become dear to her, and she wanted to know what would happen to them next.[42]

In Kiev, where he remained until early 1919 (and to which he would return near the end of the civil war in 1921), Grossman made friends that lasted all his life. Among them was Semyon, or Syoma Tumarkin, a Jewish boy from Poltava province in Ukraine who would become a celebrity mathematics professor. His older and more famous brother, Lev Tumarkin, would serve as dean of the Moscow University Department of Mechanics and Mathematics. Later Grossman would meet both of them in Moscow. While in Kiev's realschule, he shared a double desk with Syoma. His other close friend, Vyacheslav Loboda, a sensitive and musical boy of Ukrainian ancestry, was two years older. His father, Ivan Loboda, was a teacher of Russian language and literature in Kiev's gymnasium no. 2. Grossman used his friend's last name (but not his portrait) in *Stepan Kolchugin*. Vyacheslav Loboda, a future educator and school inspector in Chukotka, the Far East, became an important source for Grossman about Ukraine's famine and the Gulag. Grossman would also trust him to keep a copy of his banned novel, *Life and Fate*. Also in Kiev, Grossman would meet his first love and future wife, Anna Petrovna Matsyuk, a pretty, free-spirited Ukrainian girl from a Cossack family in Chernigov.

Grossman's early obsession with science is apparent in his prose. Both Sergei Kravchenko and Kolya in the story "Four Days" are child prodigies who read volumes on theoretical physics, chemistry, acoustics, and mathematics. Kolya thinks about atoms and molecules immediately upon waking up. His curiosity drives him to plow through textbooks on geology, astronomy, paleontology, and evolutionary biology; he relishes Darwin's *On the Origin of Species* and *The Voyage of the Beagle*. Kolya also reads the first part of *Das Kapital* (in Russian), taking copious notes, although without much understanding. (Translated in 1872, *Das Kapital* was permitted by Russian censors who mistook it for an economics tract.) Like Kolya, Grossman dreamed of making ground-breaking discoveries; his unshakable faith in his own genius would amuse him later on. Kolya agonizes over his future career but never doubts that he is destined for greatness: "He was deeply concerned whether he should dedicate himself to science and give humanity a new Theory of Matter or should join the ranks of communist fighters. . . . Should he become a Newton or a Marx? This was not a trifling question, but Kolya, despite his erudition, was unable to resolve it."[43] In *Stepan Kolchugin* Grossman projects his aspirations of becoming a scientist even onto the young proletarian, Stepan, who reveals a great capacity for learning and perseveres in chemistry.

In the fall of 1914, despite mobilization for war, life in Kiev continued at a leisurely pace. Trams were running; theaters, museums, schools, and universities remained open. But the musical repertoire for operas and concerts began to reflect the general anti-German sentiment: Wagner, Beethoven, and Schubert were banned, and Goethe's *Faust* was performed in Gounod's operatic version.[44] At the start of the war patriotism ran high. In August Kiev's main street, Kreshchatic, was swamped with patriotic crowds marching with portraits of the emperor and empress, and Russian and Serbian flags. Many thought at the time that the war was to defend Russia and Serbia. Ethnic strife was abandoned. In *Stepan Kolchugin*, describing a pro-government demonstration in Kiev, Grossman writes that Jews marched "with the Tsar's portrait, with flags and scrolls of the Torah; old men with their traditional beards next to the 'Union of Russian People.' "[45] The spectacle of Jews joining the same patriotic demonstration as ultranationalists was especially striking after the Beilis affair, Russia's Dreyfus case; the story of how it was instigated in Kiev and concluded there during a highly publicized 1913 trial will be discussed later.

At the outbreak of war, thousands of the empire's Jews enlisted, many believing they would be granted equal civil rights. But the opposite happened. Although over half a million Jewish soldiers served in the Russian Army, the authorities accused the Jewish population in the Pale of supporting the Germans. Beginning in March 1915, hundreds of thousands of Jewish civilians from the western borderlands, where much of the fighting took place, came under suspicion and were forced to leave their homes with a day's notice. They were deported eastward into the Russian interior, either on foot or in freight trains.[46]

Russia had entered the war with optimism and unity: differences were forgotten, and strikes, which had involved 1.5 million workers before the summer of 1914, ended abruptly.[47] Students volunteered for the front; women and girls joined the Red Cross. The State Duma declared unconditional support for the war, boosting the tsar's confidence in the outcome. Nicholas II expected a brief and victorious war, a "repetition" of something that had "happened during the war of 1812" with Napoleon.[48] But only months later the patriotic mood subsided. In 1915 Russia lost its western provinces. "The sky was red at night, reminding one of the fires in Galicia, and of soldiers' blood," Grossman writes in *Stepan Kolchugin*.[49] With thousands of wounded streaming to the rear, Kiev became a hospital city. Public buildings, shelters, and gymnasia were converted to accommodate hospital beds. Factories switched to wartime production, their main workforce comprised of women, boys, refugees, and prisoners of war.[50]

During Grossman's years in Kiev the memory of the Beilis affair was alive. The ordeal began in spring 1911 when just before Easter a Christian boy, Andrei Yushchinsky, was killed by criminals. The murder was blamed on Mendel Beilis, the Jewish manager of Kiev's Zaitsev brick factory. His only connection to the case was that the victim's body was found near his factory. Nonetheless, Beilis spent two years in prison while the affair dragged on. Much like the Dreyfus case in France, the Beilis affair divided Russian society. The authorities put pressure on the prosecution. The minister of justice, Ivan Shcheglovitov, ensured that the case went to trial as a blood libel. Meantime, ultranationalists distributed leaflets, claiming that Jews had committed a ritual murder.

Russian authorities had previously used blood libel to incite pogroms, including one of the worst in Kishinev in April 1903. A local right-wing paper, encouraged by the authorities, published an article accusing the Jews of the ritual slaughter of a Christian boy, although it was known that the boy's uncle had committed the murder. The Kishinev pogrom stirred protests around the world and among Russian intellectuals; however, the government of Nicholas II did nothing to change its policies. That same year, pogroms were instigated in cities across Ukraine and Belorussia.

The Beilis trial entered history as the most infamous reemergence of blood libel in Europe since the Middle Ages. The trial was held in Kiev's Superior Court in September–October 1913 amid wide press coverage and protests across Russia, Europe, and America. Because of the publicity, the case became an embarrassment for the tsar, exposing his government's anti-Semitic policies. The defense team was made up of eminent Jewish and Russian lawyers who called respected rabbis to elucidate Jewish beliefs and practices. The prosecution included major anti-Semitic activists. Beilis was acquitted by the all-Christian jury, but government backing for the case ensured that the jurors' verdict was ambiguous, finding Beilis himself innocent but also confirming that the boy's killing had been a ritual murder.[51] As a result, the case was never put to rest. More than a century later, ultranationalists made pilgrimages to the grave of the Christian victim where in 2006 they installed a tombstone with an inscription quoting the jury verdict.[52]

During the Beilis affair Jews were randomly attacked across Ukraine and lived in terror of pogroms. In *Stepan Kolchugin* Grossman shows the factory administration in a Donbass mining town promoting right-wing publications; factory managers, many of whom were ultranationalists, spread anti-Semitic propaganda to divert workers' attention from revolutionary unrest. Also in the novel, Grisha Bakhmutsky, the son of an exiled Bolshevik, tells his cousin Sergei Kravchenko that the Beilis affair was fabricated by the government and calls Vladimir Golubev, a student leader of Kiev's Black Hundreds who first accused Beilis of ritual murder, "a fanatic of anti-Semitism." Golubev refuses to travel by train because the railroad was "built by Jews."[53] The tsar, the boy says, is in the same league with ultranationalists and the clergy.

In fact, the Union of the Russian People and groups of thugs known as the Black Hundreds were endorsed by the regime. A notorious anti-Semitic text, the *Protocols of the Elders of Zion,* was written by members of the Russian secret police, the Okhrana, and published in 1905. The *Protocols* helped incite anti-Semitic violence during years of revolutionary unrest. Although Nicholas II recognized that the work was a forgery, he kept a 1906 edition in his library.[54] Ironically, portraits of Tsars Alexander III and Nicholas II that were hung in every government office and Russian noble house were painted by Valentin Serov, a foremost portraitist of Jewish origin.

Russian intellectuals realized that political change was inevitable in their country: the masses were destitute and exploited, religious minorities were persecuted, and the tsar, in the twentieth century, retained absolute power. The country's future was a central topic of discussion in Grossman's milieu when he was growing up. "Russia! How many times Sergei repeated this word, how many times he heard it. 'Only in Russia are such things possible,' 'Russian backwardness' . . . 'Russia was behind the rest of the world by 300 years.' "[55]

The autocracy was unable to deal with the complexities of total war, and anti-government sentiment was rising. Nicholas II, who assumed personal military command, surrendered the task of governing the country to Empress Alexandra, who was unpopular because of her German origins and ties to Rasputin. At the front, there was a shortage of ammunition and incompetent commanders. Russia's losses in World War I—almost 2 million dead and close to 5 million wounded—were the highest among the countries involved.[56] Such staggering losses, the economic strain of war, growing food shortages, and inflation brought on general unrest. There were numerous strikes and their number continued to increase, culminating in March 1917 when workers at the Putilov factory, the capital's largest, went out.

The centuries-old monarchy was overthrown within days of a popular uprising in Petrograd. On March 8 bread riots began in the capital's working-class Vyborg district.[57] On March 11 the crowds became uncontrollable and poured into Petrograd's center. The police fired at the crowd, which only caused more disorder. Soldiers, instead of suppressing the riots, took the protesters' side. On March 12 the capital was in the insurgents' hands. This peaceful and spontaneous revolution was not led by any political party. Nicholas II, no longer supported by the army or the Duma members, had no choice but to abdicate. On March 15 the reign of the Romanov dynasty ended.

The "dual power" that succeeded the monarchy was comprised of the liberal ministers of the Provisional Government, the majority of whom belonged to the Constitutional Democratic Party, and of the Petrograd Soviet of Workers' and Soldiers' Deputies.[58] Alexander Kerensky, a prominent lawyer, was the only person to hold positions in both governing bodies, serving as minister of justice and vice chairman of the Petrograd Soviet. Kerensky would become the head of the Provisional Government in July.

The new government faced the daunting task of dismantling autocratic structures and beginning the transition to a socially just democratic order.[59] It gave Russia its first liberal laws, guaranteeing freedom of the press, of assembly, and of conscience. On March 22 the Provisional Government abolished all discriminatory legislation based on ethnic origin, class, and religion. All citizens received equal rights. Prince Lvov, who headed the first of the two Provisional Governments, dreamed of making Russia a parliamentary democracy and the freest country in the world. In fact, Russia became the first country to give women the right to vote. The U.S., France, Britain, and Italy immediately recognized the Provisional Government, which aspired to make Russia a modern capitalist country and a reliable Western ally.[60]

The February Revolution of 1917 introduced the freest time in Russia's history—the country's transition from slavery to liberty. Grossman, aged twelve, had a taste of freedom and equality he would never forget. In his last novel, *Everything Flows*, pondering his country's destiny and short-lived democracy, he would write: "In February 1917, the path of freedom lay open for Russia. Russia chose Lenin."[61] In fact, had Russia followed the path to democracy offered by the Provisional Government, the nation would have been spared Lenin's Red Terror and civil war, the widespread famine that ensued, and Stalin's terror and genocides.

Russian Jews, most of whom supported the Mensheviks, considered the eight-month interlude after the fall of the monarchy and before the Bolshevik coup d'état as the best time in the country's history.[62] The Mensheviks and the Socialist Revolutionaries (SR) formed the majority in the third Provisional Government. The former believed that Russia, a peasant country, was not ready for socialism and must first undergo capitalist development. Although Grossman's father distanced himself from the Mensheviks, he embraced the changes brought on by the February Revolution. When Grossman wrote *Stepan Kolchugin*, Semyon Osipovich was his main source on Russian political parties and the revolutionary movement before 1917. Although Grossman could not explicitly refer to the Mensheviks in the novel, his protagonist Lobovanov presents their views convincingly and credibly:

> Our country needs a long education in democracy, in parliamentary freedoms, raising public consciousness, and years of squeezing out a slave, as Chekhov would say. . . . Russian people need to raise a sense of dignity and confidence in themselves, an ability to think independently. . . . Russia has always been a country of painted façades, concealing illness, cholera cemeteries, alcohol abuse, and absence of political rights. This can only disappear with the dissolution of autocracy, this terrible force of Russian despotism . . . and by introducing glasnost, freedom of the press, freedom of speech, of conscience, of all those freedoms inherent in democratic society.[63]

However, the Provisional Government was unable to resolve the country's most pressing issues—ending the war and distributing land. In fact, it believed that only a permanent, democratically elected government would have the authority to resolve these matters. A national election for a

Constituent Assembly was called as a first step. But the ideas of democracy and legality could not compete with Lenin's populist promises of peace, land, and bread. As Grossman would observe, Russia followed Lenin "because he promised her mountains of gold and rivers flowing with wine."[64]

The election of a Constituent Assembly took place on the eve of the Bolshevik coup. Upon seizing power on November 7, 1917, the Bolsheviks proclaimed a socialist regime. The work of the All-Russian Electoral Commission was impeded, and results of the first democratic vote in Russia's history were suppressed. Much later, when these results were reconstructed by experts, it transpired that the Bolsheviks had come in second to the Socialist Revolutionary Party favored by peasants.[65]

Upon seizing power, Lenin promptly dismantled the legislation that had made it possible for his party, banned in Russia before the February Revolution, to return from exile. He shut down the democratically elected Constituent Assembly, launched an offensive on the liberal Constitutional Democratic Party, and began to deport and arrest the Mensheviks and Socialist Revolutionaries. In 1919 the Cheka, the Bolshevik secret police, arrested people on mere suspicion of belonging to the Left SR. By 1921 prisons were packed with arrested socialists, who were kept for months without charge.[66] In summer 1922 the first major Soviet show trial took place. Thirty-four members of the Right SR, previously imprisoned under the tsar for revolutionary activity, received death sentences (these were later commuted). *Pravda* branded them "traitorous lackeys of the bourgeoisie."[67] The Mensheviks were also continually arrested. In 1922 their party was banned. (But it did not end there: in the early 1930s Stalin hunted down even the former Mensheviks.) As Grossman would write in *Everything Flows*, for Lenin the Russian Revolution "had nothing to do with Russian freedom." Driven by his "fanatical faith in the truth of Marxism," Lenin imposed a dictatorship for the sake of the Communist ideal.[68]

On December 11, 1917, the Bolsheviks institutionalized the concept of "enemy of the people." Not long after, on December 20, the Cheka was established. By 1921 its numbers had swelled to more than 280,000 employees.[69] New revolutionary courts were set up to judge crimes committed "against the proletarian state," "sabotage," "espionage," and so on. In 1918 Lenin reintroduced capital punishment, which had been abolished by the Provisional Government, and by fall the Cheka had conducted thousands of arrests and executions.

The 1918 Soviet Constitution deprived millions of kulaks, priests, and nobles of voting rights. Branded as "former people," they found themselves outside the law.[70] By spring 1918 all non-Bolshevik newspapers across the country were liquidated. "The destruction of Russian life carried out by Lenin was on a vast scale," writes Grossman in his last novel.[71]

Acting in the name of "the dictatorship of the proletariat," the Bolsheviks unleashed the Red Terror. The decree justified arrests and executions even among striking workers.[72] In May 1918, after half a year in power, the Bolshevik government issued a decree "on the monopoly of food" that deprived the peasants of the right to own what they produced. Unable to deliver its promise of "bread," Lenin's government authorized the seizure of "surplus" grain to feed the cities. Special detachments comprising thousands of unemployed workers were sent to the countryside. Unlike what the Bolsheviks would claim, the requisitioning was not an extraordinary measure caused by civil war: the decree was issued months ahead of the war, an integral part of Lenin's plan to establish state control over production and distribution.[73] In 1918–22 ruthless grain requisitioning in the countryside, accompanied by beatings and public hangings, sparked peasant revolts; these were brutally suppressed by regular troops. Crop requisitioning destroyed the incentive to produce, so the peasants considerably reduced the area seeded. The widespread famine of 1921–22, which took 5 million lives, was largely caused by Lenin's draconian policies in the countryside.[74]

Lenin's Red Terror brought on the Russian Civil War, an apocalyptic event that, according to some estimates, claimed 13 million lives.[75] (Between 1918 and 1922 the country lost from 7 million to 14 million people in fighting, famine, and epidemics.[76] Indisputably, this loss of life was higher than the Russian death toll in World War I.) Additionally, around 2 million people were lost through emigration; the majority of those who fled to the West were the educated elite.

Throughout 1918 Grossman and his mother remained in Kiev, where they witnessed the onslaught of the civil war. (In June 1941, shortly before the Nazis occupied Berdichev, Ekaterina Savelievna wrote to Grossman's father that daily air raids brought back her memory of the civil war. "I recall how our apartment in Kiev burned down from shelling . . . and we spent that horrible year with Malina and Tinushka.")[77] Grossman's aunt Maria

Savelievna Benyash, nicknamed Malina, and her German companion, Tina, sheltered mother and son when they became homeless. This likely happened in February 1918 during the Battle of Kiev, when the Red detachments under the command of Lieutenant Colonel Muravyov bombarded the city from across the Dnieper for several days.[78] The anti-Bolshevik Ukrainian government was driven out and the city fell to the Reds.

During that year, Grossman and his mother witnessed Ukraine's nightmare politics and swift changes of power. The Peace Treaty of Brest-Litovsk, then negotiated by the Bolsheviks, compelled them to surrender Russia's territories in Poland, the Baltic States, and Ukraine. On March 2, one day before the treaty was signed, German troops entered Kiev. On April 29 a German-backed coup brought to power General Pavlo Skoropadsky, a descendant of an eighteenth-century Cossack nobleman, who pronounced himself hetman, or leader. Skoropadsky's dictatorial regime fell in December: when German troops left Kiev, the hetman abdicated and fled. Next the city was held by Semyon Petliura's nationalist forces. In early January 1919 it again fell to the Reds.

After "the horrible year" in Kiev, Grossman and his mother attempted a dangerous journey to Berdichev. Ukraine was ravaged by war and Jewish pogroms. Much of the fighting occurred within the territory of the former Pale of Settlement and around it.[79] The area became a battleground between the Red Army, led by Trotsky, and the White tsarist forces, with smaller battles fought by Ukrainian peasant armies and anarchist bands. The Jewish population was terrorized from all sides, with tens of thousands killed. Although the Reds were responsible for fewer pogroms than the White Army or Petliura's men, Semyon Budyonny's Red Cavalry was also notoriously anti-Semitic. From 1918 to 1920 over twelve hundred pogroms against Jews took place across Ukraine.[80]

Nadezhda Mandelstam, who witnessed fourteen changes of power in Kiev during the civil war, describes atrocities conducted in turns by the Reds, the Whites, and Ukrainian nationalists: "Blood flowed in every street, outside every home. Bullet-ridden corpses lying on the roads and on the pavements were a familiar sight to us all, but more than bullets we feared the indignities and tortures that could be inflicted before death." The years during the civil war were "as overwhelming as a natural disaster, and their first effect was to heighten one's sense of the present." Knowing that death might come at any time, people "learned to make the utmost of each passing

moment."[81] Grossman was in his teens when he witnessed death and devastation in Kiev and Berdichev—and first contemplated his own mortality. In
Stepan Kolchugin, Sergei Kravchenko, who volunteers for the front during
World War I, walks through the battlefield past a bomb crater and suddenly
feels "the happiness and dread of being alive on earth."[82]

Like Kiev, Berdichev changed hands fourteen times. As Grossman
explains in the story "In the Town of Berdichev," "it had been held by
Petliura, by Denikin, by the Bolsheviks, by Galicians and Poles, by Tytyu-
nik's brigands, and Marusya's brigands, and by the crazy Ninth Regiment
that was a law unto itself." The story depicts the events of the Russo-Polish
War of 1920: the Reds are driven out, and the Poles are about to enter. During
this interlude Beila's husband, Magazanik, observes: "To be honest with you
. . . this is the best time of all for us townsfolk. One lot has left—and the next
has yet to arrive. No requisitions, no 'voluntary contributions,' no pogroms."[83]

The story "Four Days," which also employs Grossman's experiences
of the time, shows murder and pillaging in Berdichev as daily occurrences:
"At dinner they spoke about the terrible day yesterday. They named the
dead, specified who was robbed and how, and drank to the health of the best
doctor in town." Everyone in the town becomes accustomed to "a terrible
human howl, full of ghastly despair and fear."[84] As the doctor explains, when
soldiers approach a house, its inhabitants and all their neighbors start
howling; this helps discourage pillaging and rape, and also serves to warn
others. Notably, portrayals of the Red commissars in the story are sarcastic.
Grossman's teenaged protagonist, Kolya, does not fully trust their promises
of a wonderful life under socialism. Similarly, in *Stepan Kolchugin* a forecast
of a socialist paradise by the Bolshevik Abram Bakhmutsky leaves Sergei
Kravchenko skeptical: he cannot imagine a life without hunger, poverty,
sickness, and working beyond strength.

After the civil war David Sherentsis's clinic was nationalized, and the
family also lost their savings to inflation. At fifteen Grossman worked as a
sawyer and studied in a unified labor school. Such coed schools were first
introduced by government decree in 1918 as part of Soviet educational
reform. Labor schools emphasized technical and industrial aspects of education and political indoctrination, almost completely excluding the humanities
from the curriculum.[85]

In 1921 Grossman returned to Kiev, entering a preparatory class of a
newly established Institute of People's Education. Universities in Ukraine

were replaced by these institutes, designed to produce teachers for upper grades and vocational schools.[86] The government had introduced universal compulsory education, and teachers were also needed for the 3 million homeless children, orphaned by the civil war.[87]

The level of education fell sharply after the revolution. The curriculum did not satisfy Grossman, who educated himself in literature and science. At fifteen he read Tolstoy, Kipling, and Conan Doyle as well as Jack London's stories about mining gold in the Klondike. His favorite book was *The Interpretation of Radium and the Structure of the Atom* by English radiochemist and future Nobel laureate Frederick Soddy. He admired the works on thermal conductivity by Austrian physicist and philosopher Ludwig Boltzmann. He also dreamed of following Dmitry Mendeleev's path to science and of discovering a new element for the periodic table: "Only his love for his mother, from whom he was inseparable his entire life, appeared to him . . . more important than university, science, professors, and glory, of which he dreamt, and of his own genius, in which he believed as unshakably as old women believe in the kingdom of God."[88]

2. From Science to Literature and Politics

I am restless. I am athirst for faraway things.
My soul goes out in a longing to touch the skirt of the dim distance.
O Great Beyond, O the keen call of thy flute!
I forget, I ever forget, that I have no wings to fly, that I am bound in
    this spot evermore.
—Rabindranath Tagore, "I Am Restless"

The civil war did not lessen Grossman's ambition of becoming a scientist, but it changed him in other ways. It made him aware of the world's violent instability and of the transience of human existence. He learned that a man can be shot for a gold watch or a pair of shoes; he saw Polish soldiers cutting the beards of elderly Jews with sabers; a neighbor who interfered was hacked to death. The latter episode is depicted in "Four Days": Kolya witnesses this scene in Berdichev at fifteen. Grossman would show the war through children's eyes in many of his works.

At sixteen, thoughts of his own mortality and the meaninglessness of existence in the face of inescapable death seemed to follow him even as he read books on astronomy. In *Stepan Kolchugin*, portraying himself in Sergei Kravchenko, an aspiring scholar, he also shows the boy's state of mind and soul:

> He possessed an excellent memory, read a lot, and his head was crammed full of quotations from scholarly works, poems, and novels, which said that the world was vast, immense; that the history of the human race was but a brief moment between two ice ages; that the universe was infinite in space and time; that everything in it was doomed to destruction; that human aspirations, thoughts,

emotions, all of people's joys and sorrows were hollow and point-less in the limitlessness of light years . . . the infinity of time, which had neither beginning nor end; that cosmic dust zooming in dark outer space . . . [contained] traces of vanished planetary systems, of extinguished suns, of disappeared worlds; that human existence had no purpose and meaning. At sixteen these thoughts got hold of him with such force that he stopped brushing his teeth and doing his homework. These thoughts gave him acute suffering.[1]

Before the onslaught of World War I Sergei Kravchenko imagines a brilliant career for himself: upon finishing university, he would travel to advance his education in Germany or England. By age twenty-four, now a respected professor, he would make his first scientific discovery: "Yes, yes, of course he will become a great man, standing on a podium and announcing: 'Gentlemen! The biggest challenge facing humanity has been resolved.' " In a more realistic mood, Kravchenko thinks anxiously about his future in Russia, a country where impoverished and illiterate masses appear to be living in the Stone Age: "His native land seemed like a desert to him popu-lated with wild tribes." Yet, Grossman's hero feels the need to share his country's destiny: "This is his native land; here was he born, here will he live his whole life, and here he will die. But how to live?"[2] Grossman's close family did not consider emigrating; he also possessed a strong sense of belonging both as a man and a writer.

As a student at Kiev's Institute for People's Education Grossman became attracted to Anna Matsyuk, a carefree and popular girl. (Her name was Ganna in Ukrainian, and she called herself Galya. In *Stepan Kolchugin* Grossman describes her in Olesya, a pretty Ukrainian girl who has poor grades in geometry and math.) "Very pretty and likable," Galya was a part of his group of friends. Their romance developed around 1922, during Grossman's second—and last—year in Kiev. Galya, whom he eventually married, described Grossman as "the wittiest young man in Kiev."[3] He was in love, but too rational to enjoy his happiness: "What a beautiful time it was, and how skilfully he was poisoning and spoiling the best days of his life with little worries, fears, and trivial concerns! . . . Now, he was seized with fear that by marrying her he will bind himself for the rest of his life, ruining his future as a scientist. Now, admiring Olesya's beauty, he felt pangs of unsatis-fied sexual desire. Now, he turned cold at a horrible thought that he would prove himself impotent at a crucial moment. Now, it would seem to him that he was not in love; it's all a mistake, she is silly, uninteresting, ridiculous, and he is ridiculous with his love, and everyone laughs at him and at her."[4] Their different ethnicity did not bother Grossman. The revolution destroyed such traditions. As he would write in the novel *For the Right Cause*, the revolutionary generation formed unions based on love, overlooking dissimilar background, blood, or language. But to become involved with a virgin without marrying her was impossible for a man of Grossman's conservative upbringing.

In 1923 he was accepted by the Department of Chemistry, which was part of the Faculty of Physics and Mathematics in the Moscow University. From Moscow, he wrote Galya that their relationship had been "childish" and that it was "all over" between them.[5] He was in a hurry to set himself free, only to discover a few years later upon meeting Galya in Kiev that their relationship was far from over.

During his first year in Moscow, Grossman became absorbed in the capital's cultural life, his new friendships, and his studies. In spring 1923 the writer Mikhail Bulgakov observed in his diary: "Life in Moscow is bustling, especially in comparison with Kiev."[6] Grossman's energy and intellectual curiosity emerge from the following passage in *Stepan Kolchugin*:

> His first winter term at university passed swiftly. Sergei read a few dozen scholarly books, which had no relevance to his curriculum, attended lectures not only at the department of physics and mathematics, but also in philosophy and psychology; went to the theater twice a week . . . went to parties and sang Ukrainian songs. . . . He slept no more than five–six hours a day; yet, there was not enough time—he wanted to see everything, to work in all laboratories simultaneously, for he was also interested in animal anatomy and physiology; he wanted to hear ten lectures a day, read numerous books not only in theoretical physics and astronomy, but also . . . [Wilhelm] Bölsche's *The Love Life in Nature*, [Ernst] Haeckel's *The Riddle of the Universe* and [works by Herbert] Spencer. . . . Sometimes he studied sixteen, even eighteen hours a day, which left no time to think independently.[7]

In the early 1920s, there was much to see and learn in Moscow. Lenin died on January 21, 1924, and for the next several days and nights, while his body lay in state in the Hall of Columns of the House of Unions, lines of people stretched through the capital. Lenin's funeral, in Nadezhda

Mandelstam's words, was "the last flicker of the Revolution as a genuine popular movement," when veneration for the leader was not inspired by terror.[8] In *Life and Fate* Grossman describes the bonfires burning in downtown Moscow to prevent mourners from getting frostbite, then the mourning procession itself: "Lenin's body had been taken from Gorki to the railway station on a peasant sleigh. The runners had squeaked, the horses snorted. The coffin had been followed by his widow, Krupskaya, wearing a round fur cap held on by a grey headscarf, by his two sisters, Anna and Maria, by his friends. . . . Lenin's comrades—Rykov, Kamenev, and Bukharin—had walked just behind the sledge, their beards white with hoar frost. From time to time they had glanced absent-mindedly at a swarthy, pock-marked man wearing a long greatcoat and boots with soft tops."[9] Stalin wore soft Caucasian-style boots; portraying him again in his 1960 story "Mama," Grossman emphasized the dictator's noiseless walk and predatory fluid movements.

Although Lenin was gone, Stalin had yet to gain supremacy. The writer Varlam Shalamov recalls that at this time, the end of 1924, intellectual freedom in Moscow was on the rise, as it had been during the revolutionary year of 1917. The Moscow University was one "boiling caldron" of debate. Nobody knew how to build a socialist state, writes Shalamov: every government measure was being put to the test for the very first time. Students debated political decisions not in fear, but with the freedom and energy the revolution had unleashed.[10] These independent-minded young people were vastly different from the later generations, which grew up indoctrinated in Stalinism.

Back in 1921, faced with a catastrophic drop in industrial production, Lenin introduced the New Economic Policy (NEP), a retreat to market methods; the NEP remained in effect for seven years. As Bulgakov reported in 1921, "It's possible to survive in Moscow only through private enterprise or through trading." Housing shortages were severe, available rooms unaffordable because of soaring inflation. Bulgakov gives a good picture of living in Moscow in the year the NEP was introduced: "The most important thing is to find the roof over our heads. . . . In Moscow they count only in hundreds of thousands or in millions. . . . And the prices are rising and rising! The shops are full of goods, but what can you buy! . . . In Moscow there is everything: shoes, cloth, meat, caviar, preserves, delicacies, everything! Cafés are opening, they are sprouting like mushrooms. And everywhere hundreds of thousands of roubles, hundreds!" In 1922, when finding a room was still close to impossible, Bulgakov reported: "The rent is going up. One and a half million for April. . . . I'm making efforts to find a room. But it's hopeless. They demand enormous sums just for telling you where to find one."[11]

The situation had not changed by 1923, when Grossman became a student in Moscow. He struggled to support himself by tutoring, working in a commune for homeless children, and with funds from his father. Semyon Osipovich had bonded with his son in Kiev where he lived for a while and had an apartment. Although Grossman's father helped him through university, the money covered only bare necessities. The biggest problem for Grossman was finding a place to sleep and to study. Unable to afford rent, he slept on the floor of his friends' apartments. Luckily, Syoma Tumarkin, Grossman's closest friend in Kiev's realschule, now lived in Moscow with his well-to-do family; he was an outstanding student at the Faculty of Physics and Mathematics. Syoma's parents doted on him and welcomed his friends to their home.

Despite hardship, Grossman would remember his student years as a blissful time. His 1962 story "Phosphorus" describes his close companions at university, among them mathematician Syoma Tumarkin; future chemical engineer Efim Kugel; historian, educator, and ethnographer Vyacheslav Loboda; and engineer and inventor Alexander Nitochkin. "I had remarkable friends—clever, energetic, cheerful, and curious about everything in the world: politics, Einstein, poetry, art. . . . We debated, read a lot, drank beer and vodka, took walks at night through the boulevards, swam in the Moscow River. . . . We sang together, fooled around, and once we got into a fight at the Patriarch's Ponds with a group of tipsy young men."[12] Grossman loved to sing and did so with deep feeling, but he had no musical ear. The best singers in their company—Loboda and Syoma Tumarkin—directed an unruly choir. Alexander Nitochkin (Nyurenberg) and Grossman had known each other in Berdichev. Alexander's parents were members of the Jewish Bund; his mother, Faina Nyurenberg (she changed her name to Nyurina), joined the Bolshevik Party in 1920. She served in the People's Commissariat for Justice and in 1934 became acting prosecutor general for the Russian Federation. Nyurina and her husband would perish during the Great Purge.

Loboda, whom Grossman befriended in Kiev, joined the close-knit company in 1925. The year Loboda arrived to study in Moscow, he and Grossman pooled their resources and rented a room, but the arrangement was short-lived. Loboda soon married and settled in No. 10 Novaya Basman-naya Street, a communal flat. Coincidentally, this was the same house where, upon his arrival in Moscow, Loboda delivered documents to Alexander Blok's uncle, employed by the People's Commissariat for Railways. Over the years Grossman visited his friend in this house where Loboda maintained a room. In the mid-1920s Loboda studied history and economics at the Moscow University. His older brother, Nikolai, had been Anatoly Lunacharsky's deputy at the People's Commissariat for Education and later served as the dean of the history department at the Moscow Pedagogical Institute. Nikolai Loboda had met Bukharin and Trotsky, and this sealed his fate. (His photo-graph with Trotsky was later destroyed by one of the Loboda brothers.) In 1928 Nikolai was accused of being a Trotskyist and exiled to Kazakhstan. Later he lived in the town of Alexandrov near Moscow, working as an accountant. But the state would not leave him alone. In 1934 Nikolai was rear-rested and dispatched to Vorkuta, the seat of Vorkutlag, one of the harshest labor camps in the Gulag, located above the Arctic Circle. This is where he was shot in 1941. His brother and Grossman's friend, Vyacheslav, escaped arrest by living and working in Chukotka, next to Kolyma, the deadliest complex of camps in the Far East. Vyacheslav Loboda and Grossman corre-sponded over the years and met during his stays in Moscow.[13]

In 1928 Gedda Surits, a future geophysicist and the daughter of one of the first appointed Soviet diplomats, Yakov Surits, married Grossman's child-hood friend, Alexander Nitochkin. Gedda's father was appointed head of the Soviet mission in Denmark in 1918.[14] He gave his daughter a Scandinavian name, Gedda. When in 1921 Surits was dispatched as an ambassador to Afghanistan, Gedda's mother refused to join him, and the family fell apart. Writer Ilya Ehrenburg, who met Surits in 1922 in Berlin, describes him as a passionate art collector who owned paintings and drawings by Matisse, Rodin, and Benois.[15] By then Surits had distanced himself from his family and remarried; Gedda, however, visited her father in Europe.[16] Grossman was a frequent guest at Gedda's hospitable downtown apartment on Tverskaya-Yamskaya Street. According to friends, he liked Gedda a great deal and flirted with her when her husband was not around. Gedda was "a bit afraid" of Grossman, who made fun of her, calling her "a lady" and "mama's girl." He liked crude jokes and told them in her presence, and her embarrassment only amused him. Her love of poetry gave Grossman another opportunity to tease her. "You love too many poems," he would say. "This is like loving many girls at the same time." In 1964 Gedda wrote a memoir in which she described her friendship with Grossman, beginning in their student years. "Vasya's nickname was 'old man.' Very slender, tall, and ironic, he seemed to hide his huge eyes behind thick glasses. Whether it was his near-sightedness or his great sense of self-worth, so typical of him throughout his life, or maybe his special, inherent to him alone, attentive attitude to people; it made him at once observant, interested and yet, a bit of an outsider, as if he was watching us from a distance during the gatherings and walks he so loved."[17]

Most of Grossman's friends managed to survive the purges and World War II. They still met in the 1960s, with the exception of Abram Perelmuter, a former Komsomol leader who had once belonged to their circle. Grossman describes him in the story "Phosphorus" in Abrasha-Abrameo, a bearded student with unruly hair who wore sandals all year round and was nick-named "Christ." Abrasha had an impressive biography: during the civil war, at fifteen, he became a platoon commander. Later he rose to senior Cheka investigator, trusted to make life-and-death decisions at age seventeen; he also served as a secretary of a provincial Komsomol organization. Abrasha did not strike Grossman as particularly fanatical; both loved practical jokes. Once Abrasha made a round of phone calls to their friends alleging that Grossman had been attacked by thugs, badly beaten, and robbed. He ended each call with a plea for help. For his part, Grossman lay half dressed and prostrate on a couch, covered with newspapers for lack of blankets. A sheet of paper, splashed with red ink and with an indecent word inscribed on it, was pasted over his forehead. The idea was to check who among their friends would first come to the rescue. Efim Kugel, the most soft-hearted of the group, arrived first with a bundle of clothes. Grossman would remember this "stupid hooligan" joke in the 1960s when after the confiscation of his novel he really needed friends to support him.

Abrasha's fate is not clear: in "Phosphorus" Grossman relates that he perished at the height of the purges in 1937. But in the novel *Everything Flows*, describing Abrasha in Jewish Komsomol leader Lev Mekler, who walked around in torn sandals, Grossman writes that he survived "all the circles of the prison and camp hell."[18] However, in this novel, Abrasha's fate is used as an element of a larger story about Jewish revolutionaries and the civil war generation.

Grossman and his friends studied for exams and spent the summers in the Moscow countryside, Cherkizovo, on the territory of a farm managed by Alexander Taratuta. His son, Leonid, was Grossman's classmate and close friend. Grossman, Nitochkin, and the Tumarkin brothers would stay in a separate cottage at this farm. "My brother's friends would usually spend a whole summer with us," recalls Yevgeniya Taratuta. "They would stay in a little wooden cottage, which housed beehives in winter to protect the bees from frost. The place smelled wonderfully of honey. [Students] would sleep on the floor, on hay. In the daytime they studied for exams and in the evenings they would make a bonfire, cook millet porridge, eat *vobla* [salt-dried fish], and listen to my father's stories. Vasya would become completely engrossed with the accounts of my father, who was Kropotkin's follower."

Yevgeniya's and Leonid's father, Alexander Taratuta, grew up in a shtetl in a poor Jewish family. He ran away at sixteen and became a revolutionary and a follower of Peter Kropotkin, the theorist of the anarchist movement and proponent of a decentralized Communist society. Taratuta ended up arrested for revolutionary agitation among the workers and spent a year in solitary confinement in the Peter and Paul Fortress in Petersburg. Sentenced to hard labor in Eastern Siberia, he managed to escape but was captured in Minsk and rearrested. This time, he was incarcerated and kept in chains for four years. Despite that, he organized literacy classes and lectures for other inmates, both criminals and politicals, and created a library with the help of the prison's priest. In 1911 he was deported to hard labor in Eastern Siberia. Before deportation the priest gave him a book of religious verse with illustrations by Gustave Doré. (This book survived, and Grossman may have seen it: he mentions Doré's illustrations in *Life and Fate*.) Taratuta escaped again before reaching his Siberian destination, which was a gold mine near Bodaibo, northern Irkutsk. In Tobolsk, on the way to Bodaibo, he met a young woman revolutionary, Agniya Markova, who organized his escape, connected him with people who helped him flee to the West, and later joined him there and married him. Upon settling in Paris, Taratuta studied languages and agronomy. He also worked as a clerk for the Louis Dreyfus Company, which traded in agricultural products. Taratuta's children were born in Paris, where the family remained until the 1917 Bolshevik Revolution. After his repatriation to Russia, Taratuta organized a farm in the Moscow countryside, supplying meat and vegetables to a neighboring orphanage; he also built an electrical generation station and a school for workers. This was his vision of a decentralized Communist society, inspired by Kropotkin's ideas. In the mid-1920s his model farm received foreign delegations and was much written about. But as Stalin tightened his grip on the country's agriculture, people with initiative were replaced with obedient state employees. Taratuta was removed from his position as farm manager. In the 1930s, traveling through the country, he was horrified by the consequences of forced collectivization and told his family and friends about famine in Ukraine, where he saw dead villages. He was arrested in 1934 and shot three years later, at the height of the purges.[19]

Taratuta's family was close to Vera Figner, the legendary leader of People's Will, the terrorist group best known for assassinating Alexander II in 1881. Figner, who had participated in planning the assassination, spent twenty years in the Schlüsselburg Fortress. Taratuta's family was so close to her that Figner even offered to adopt their daughter Yevgeniya when they were hard up. Figner first met them in France, where she traveled before the revolution, and later saw the family in Moscow. Taratuta's stories about revolutionary Populists and members of People's Will fascinated Grossman. Later in life, he even wanted to write a book about Andrei Zhelyabov, one of the chief organizers of Alexander II's assassination. (If the book had been written, Grossman could have explained, perhaps, why Zhelyabov, who was born a serf, plotted against the tsar, who abolished serfdom.) In 1881 Zhelyabov was executed along with other members of People's Will and his major associate, Sophia Perovskaya, an aristocrat.

Late in life, in a 1961 letter to Yevgeniya Taratuta, Grossman spoke of his conflicted attitude toward revolutionary terrorists: "I'm getting old, my hair is turning white, but my feeling towards members of People's Will doesn't age. . . . Although their deeds were horrible and bloody, there was something godly, saintly in them."[20] In the Soviet era these early revolutionaries were practically forgotten, not least because the topic of individual resistance to the state became taboo under Stalin. In his 1962 story "The Elk" Grossman mentions the "forgotten revolutionaries"—the Populists and members of People's Will—and the "tragic struggle they fought." The idea that revolutionary fervor is akin to religious fanaticism interested Grossman in many of his works. He addresses it in *Stepan Kolchugin* in a conversation between the Bolshevik Abram Bakhmutsky and his father, Yakov Moiseevich. "A man of great knowledge" and independent mind, Yakov tells his Bolshevik son that he relinquished their family tradition of free skepticism "and returned to the dogma and fanaticism of faith."[21]

At twenty-two, Grossman felt that the sciences no longer fascinated him as before. The narrow world of a chemical laboratory prevented him from engaging in broader issues: "*Bat'ko*," he wrote his father, addressing him typically in Ukrainian, "I've thought of how I've changed without my noticing: from about age 14 to 20, I was a passionate fan of the natural sciences, and was decidedly uninterested in anything else, imagining my future only in terms of scientific work. But now it's entirely different. . . . My interests have become transferred to social issues, and it seems to me that I'll be building my life in this sphere." He now also realized his limitations as a scholar: "Definitely, I won't become a brilliant scientist. Of course, I can easily handle routine industrial work, I'll have sufficient knowledge for this, but [becoming] a chemist—a driving force behind science, an explorer—it seems I'm not made for this."[22] He yearned for novelty and travel. Senior chemistry students were going on a tour of Germany and Switzerland; they would see Berlin, Baden, and the Rhein. "The whole thing costs 70 roubles. Of course, it's tempting, but I'll let it pass. I wouldn't go even if I had the money," he added.[23]

He dreamed of traveling, of course, but was considerate of his father, who had been sending him funds. Semyon Osipovich received a modest salary for his dangerous and exhausting work of inspecting mines. His health was deteriorating, and Grossman worried because his father continued to work even though doctors prohibited him from going down the mines. Semyon Osipovich was sending his son all he could afford, but the sums were insufficient to rent even "a corner" in Moscow. Without a permanent place he had "no opportunity to read and study at home."[24] Eventually Grossman rented an unheated room in the countryside, which he held for less than a year, but for the most part, he relied on his friends' hospitality; afraid to exhaust it, he had to make new arrangements every evening. Grossman's perennial homelessness, although he described it humorously to his father, weighed him down. As he wrote in 1928, "You know, at dusk I experience what our savage ancestor in a forest in the Stone Age experienced: having to look for shelter, I'm seized with anxiety. The ancestor was better off: he would climb a tree or crawl into a cave or a crevice; my situation in the primeval forest of a big city is worse: all cracks and caves are occupied, and I have to negotiate: 'Would you let me in for the night?' "[25]

Grossman's father admonished him for lack of industry and for going to pubs. "Now, about the pubs," Grossman argued at twenty-three. "Indeed, I visit them quite often. But there is a difference between going to a pub and being a drunk. . . . You'd say, one can become addicted. This is certainly true. But addiction may affect someone who is very miserable. . . . When I feel miserable and lonesome, I've no desire to have a drink. . . . I know you hold a different view and believe that drinking even small amounts is swinishness."[26]

During school breaks Grossman visited his mother in Berdichev. Ekaterina Savelievna suffered from a variety of ailments but disliked complaining or asking for help. When in 1925 she needed to consult doctors in Kiev, Grossman wrote his father on her behalf, asking whether she could stay in his vacant apartment. "What happened to our Kievan apartment? Is anyone living in it?" Grossman thought it would be good for his mother to get away from "Berdichev's stifling atmosphere. When I come there for a few weeks, I feel oppressed by this lousy city. And she has to live there for years, while immobilized. That's hard."[27] Berdichev, of course, could not be compared with Moscow, bustling with activity, and Grossman would now go to his native town only for his mother's sake. He wrote to Semyon Osipovich in another letter: "You're asking about Mama. She is feeling good (comparatively, of course), her leg is behaving most of the time, but her kidneys are so-so; her spiritual life is not so good: she feels lonely and sad in Berdichev, and I secretly marvel at her courage. Despite circumstances, she sustains her optimism and vitality; she gives regular lessons to students, reads a lot, doesn't give up, and carries on. . . . Only people with great spiritual resources can live like this."[28]

But it was his father's companionship he really craved. In summer they occasionally traveled to Krinitsa, a village on the Black Sea near the resort city of Gelendzhik. Founded in the 1880s by revolutionary Populists, Krinitsa had a long history of political dissent. In Grossman's day, it housed an agricultural commune of Tolstoyans, proponents of Tolstoy's teaching of nonresistance to violence.

Tolstoyan agricultural communes, which sprang up during the 1880s, were short-lived. The majority of the colonists were young city intellectuals who knew little about farm labor and were helpless in practical situations. They were inspired by Tolstoy's view of moral living, but soon discovered that many of his principles, such as complete rejection of money, property, social institutions, and sex, were unworkable. But in the early 1920s, after the civil war, the Tolstoyans formed successful agricultural cooperatives, supplying vegetables and milk to the cities. These communes were more inclusive and diverse than their earlier iterations, admitting not only proponents of Tolstoy's teaching but also anarchists, Communists, and later farmers fleeing collectivization. Tolstoyans were harassed by authorities and arrested, and by the mid-1930s their communes ceased to exist.

In Krinitsa, where Grossman repeatedly traveled in the 1920s, he met dogmatic proponents of Tolstoy's teaching. Like Tolstoy's early followers, they applied inflexible moral rules to all their affairs. This led to comic situations, which Grossman describes in *Stepan Kolchugin*: "Once, they were deciding whether it was morally good to grow tobacco for sale, and the discussion lasted fifty hours without interruption."[29] The most economical and practical choices in their region—growing tobacco and grapes—contradicted their Tolstoyan principles of abstinence from all stimulants. Grossman's attitude to Tolstoyans changed over time. In *Life and Fate* he creates the powerful character of a Tolstoyan in Ikonnikov, arrested for preaching nonviolence, first by the Communists and later by the Nazis.

In 1927, the tenth anniversary of the revolution, the Soviet Union was becoming an enormous construction site. Newspapers trumpeted the Party's ambitious projections for the First Five-Year Plan that was about to be implemented: massive economic growth was expected. The following year would see the rapid development of Magnitogorsk, an industrial city in the Urals. The country was desperately short of engineers, many of whom had fled after the revolution, so hundreds of foreign specialists were invited to direct the construction of Magnitogorsk Iron and Steel Works, or Magnitka, as it was commonly known. It was expected to outcompete even the major steel mills in the United States, such as the one in Gary, Indiana.

When, in the fall 1927, Semyon Osipovich was transferred to Donetsk (then Stalino), a mining city in the Donbass, Grossman was envious of his father, heading to the country's industrial heartland. But his father's job inspecting the mines was dangerous and thankless, and Grossman soon realized that the reality might not be as attractive as it seemed from afar. "Perhaps, you don't envy yourself," he added thoughtfully.[30] But he was eager to work as a chemical engineer in the Donbass.

The idea of socialist construction inspired general enthusiasm, to which Grossman was not immune. Yet he also recognized a gap between promises to build a bright future for the masses and their actual lives. In 1927–28 he commuted daily from the village Vishnyaki, where he rented a room, to Moscow, on a train filled with factory workers.

> Today, as I was returning home by train, the passenger car was crowded with workers, all terribly drunk (Easter is coming); I saw an old man—he was singing something in a high-pitched thin voice, "celebrating"; his face was eaten by factory dust, his gaze as still and hazy as if he were dead . . . all this made me hellishly depressed: people spend their lives in daily gruelling toil, and when a holiday comes, to which they look forward all year—Easter—they get hysterically drunk. After the "celebration," downcast and sick, they take a week to recover, and then again wait for a holiday. Gorky says, "I feel sorry for the people." Indeed, one feels sorry for them.[31]

In 1928 Grossman wrote his father about his wish to become socially engaged and dedicate himself to "literature and politics."[32] In the event, the two spheres occupied him as long as he lived. By age twenty-three he had drafted a few stories and articles, which he read to his father. Semyon Osipovich did not encourage his son's literary ambition, instead pressing him to complete university.

Around this time Grossman found a well-connected and sympathetic friend in Nadya Almaz, his older cousin. Nadya became responsible for his journalistic debut. The daughter of Elizaveta Savelievna, his mother's sister, Nadya grew up in Berdichev and was eight years Grossman's senior. During World War I she had worked in hospitals as a nurse and also became involved with Social Democratic organizations in Ukraine. In 1917 she joined the Bolshevik Party and participated in the civil war. Transferred to Moscow in 1920, she worked for trade unions and edited one of their newspapers.[33] In 1925, at the height of her career, she became personal secretary and adviser to Solomon Lozovsky, then the head of Trade Union International, the Profintern. Significantly for Grossman, Nadya had contacts in newspapers, including *Pravda*, the Party's major publication.

In 1928 Nadya gave Grossman his first paid journalistic assignment, compiling a seventy-page report for the Communist Academy, a task he handled competently and quickly. Two typists, working in turns, took his dictation in Nadya's apartment, which made him feel important.[34] In March Nadya assigned him to cover a Moscow Congress of Trade Union International. He was impressed with the scores of foreign delegates—Germans, Americans, Japanese, Indians, and Turks—"all clamoring in their different tongues."[35] As Lozovsky's secretary, Nadya liaised with various labor organizations and the Communist International (the Comintern). At her apartment Grossman would meet the Soviet elite and zealous Communists who reminisced about the civil war and dreamed of world revolution. Much later, in the novel *For the Right Cause* and its sequel *Life and Fate*, he created the character of Krymov, a Communist fanatic who joined the Comintern in 1919, simultaneously with Lenin, its founder. In *Everything Flows*, his last novel, Grossman again described the generation of true believers: "The Comintern was their youth; it was the happiest, most romantic period of their life. They now worked in offices with telephones and secretaries; they had exchanged their military tunics for jackets and ties; they traveled about by cars . . . but, in spite of all this, the days of pointed Budyonny helmets and leather jackets, of millet porridge, of boots full of holes, of the world commune and ideals of unbounded, planetary scope— those days remained the high points of their lives."[36]

In early May, Nadya arranged for Grossman to go with a group of students to Central Asia for two months. The expedition would survey economic and living conditions in Uzbekistan, visit an oil refinery in Fergana Valley, and learn about local industries—production of cotton and raw silk. Grossman was ecstatic. Fergana lay on the Northern Silk Road from China, and he was eager to visit this ancient land, once populated by Iranian and Mongolian tribes, and to hear stories even more exciting than "Arabian Nights." The passionate botanist in him dreamed of seeing "the blooming desert," wild tulips flowering in Kyzylkum in May.[37] Semyon Osipovich sent his old suit to his son, and Grossman was pleased that he was now dressed like a real "envoy."[38]

In mid-May, full of impressions, Grossman wrote his father from the ancient town of Kaunchi, near Tashkent, to describe the colorful local bazaar and camel caravans, a spectacle that seemed to come from the Middle Ages. Tashkent had been destroyed by Genghis Khan in the early thirteen century, conquered by the Russian Empire six centuries later, and was now being shaped by Soviet politics. Collectivization, women's emancipation, and educational reform were implemented here all at once. Religious instruction was banned, mosques stood empty, schools were following a Soviet curriculum, and radio had been recently introduced to advance Soviet political indoctrination. Grossman visited a large collective farm where villagers were learning to operate their first tractor. He saw vast plantations of cotton in newly irrigated prairie, heard stories about redistribution of land and water, and felt sympathy for the poor, who benefited for the first time in their lives. But the campaign for women's emancipation proceeded painfully, he reported. "Husbands frequently murder their wives for taking off burkas. Two days ago, there was a tragic case here. An Uzbek woman wanted to study, the husband wouldn't let her; she decided to divorce him. They came to the Kaunchi's Soviet, and when the divorce ceremony was over, the husband took out a knife and struck her in the heart. She died a few hours later; still a girl of seventeen. Poor thing, the women's department had promised to send her to study in Tashkent."[39]

Two months later, accustomed to eating rice pilaf and shashlik, but still suffering from heat and mosquitoes, Grossman philosophized: "By the way, it's interesting how a person gets used to everything. During my first days here I gazed with an open mouth at camel caravans, Uzbeks in their turbans and robes, and other oriental stuff, but now I've become accustomed and pay no attention to a camel or a picturesque group of oriental people sitting in a *chaikhana* [tea-drinking establishment]." He regretted that novelty wore off so quickly. And there was also "a misfortune—travel itch. From here it's only two days to China, two days to the Pamir Mountains, and two days to India, Persia, and Afghanistan, so at night I'm lying in bed sleepless. I'd want so much to see all these countries."[40]

Returning to Moscow in early July, Grossman published two articles about his expedition. His first piece, about cooperative stores established by Uzbek women, appeared in *Nasha gazeta*, the cooperative newspaper Nadya edited. A week later, on July 13, his article "Islakhat," about land reform in Uzbekistan, was published in *Pravda*. This serious debut in the country's most influential newspaper would open doors.

At the time, though, Grossman was too busy to savor his luck. Days after publishing the article, he left for Kiev to see Galya, whom he had married earlier that year. In January he had written his father that he loved Galya very much and she loved him: "If Allah wills it, perhaps, I'll marry."[41] At this point Grossman was discreet about his "Kievan exploits." There was much more to tell: when the affair took place Galya was married and expecting. Later, in a letter to his father, Grossman intimated she had had an abortion. He married Galya soon after, but the couple continued to live apart because she studied and worked in Kiev.

In summer, with income from his articles, he could afford a honey-moon. Grossman's father helped secure a room for the newlyweds at a friend's house in Krinitsa.[42] Before traveling there with Galya, Grossman asked his father to join them by the sea. Semyon Osipovich was now married to Olga Semyonovna Rodanevich, a medical doctor, and Grossman dutifully invited his stepmother as well, but she didn't come. Grossman later recalled how his father "arrived in Krinitsa, all covered with road dust, ill, and how I became awfully embarrassed when introducing Galya to you."[43]

In August Grossman took Galya to meet his mother in Odessa. Ekaterina Savelievna was staying there with relatives while taking treatment. The first meeting between his mother and his bride, the two women he loved most, was not a success. As Ekaterina Savelievna would later complain to Grossman's father, their son was irritable with her only once, "when upon his marriage he arrived from Krinitsa to see me in Odessa."[44] Both Grossman's parents disliked Galya. In 1929 Ekaterina Savelievna described her as "hysterical," weak-willed, and narrow-minded, interested only in cards and good clothes. She was upset that her son, so "critical of everyone," could not see any flaws in his wife. Ekaterina Savelievna wanted a better match for her only son. Galya was previously married, she wrote to Semyon Osipovich, and Vasya was much to blame for disrupting her life: "She was married, treated her husband well, and was already pregnant; she had to have an abortion, poor thing. She told me once: 'Vasya broke my family life' "[45] For Grossman, getting involved with married women would become a pattern.

In September Grossman reported to his father from Moscow that his article in *Pravda* had been received "very favorably" and he was encouraged to keep contributing.[46] Meanwhile, his short story about a flood (he had read it to his father in Krinitsa) was accepted by an illustrated literary magazine, *Projector*. This influential magazine was published as *Pravda*'s supplement; Bukharin, *Pravda*'s editor, was on its editorial board. Grossman was told he should not expect his story to appear soon, and it's unclear whether it appeared at all. Now that Grossman was a published writer he obtained a well-paid contract to produce a brochure about "cooperatives and women's emancipation in Uzbekistan."[47] He wrote it over two weeks in November 1929; while researching the subject, he said, he read "some twenty books and boring reports."[48]

During his sixth and final year at university Grossman had to catch up. In October 1928 he rented a room on Moscow's outskirts; the arrangement saved commuting time.[49] Grossman was studying ten hours a day—simply to put his exams behind him. Textbooks on theoretical chemistry bored him. Lectures on toxic gases were sickening: the professor savored every detail of poisonous inhalation while Grossman thought that studying poisons was "a fitting occupation for someone wicked and disillusioned by life."[50] Fed up with schoolwork, he was determined to complete university in record time.

By then most of his friends had graduated. "There's a major change in my life," he wrote his father, "my friends and I have grown apart. Only a year ago, they occupied an important place in my life; now we've become almost complete strangers."[51] His friends were engineers and scientists, while Grossman now possessed literary ambition. In January 1929 *Ogonyok* accepted his proposal for an article about Berdichev. He already had a larger literary work in mind: "I have a literary plot, which tempts me," he wrote his father, without explaining what it was.[52] A while later, he shed some light on it: "I have a grand literary project, and I'm working slowly on it, this work will . . . occupy me for at least a year. I'm not in a hurry to write; I read all sorts of things; I think—and develop a plan."[53]

That month Grossman reread Tolstoy's novella *The Death of Ivan Ilyich*. At twenty-three, he felt profoundly alone, estranged from friends and from Galya, who still lived in Kiev and whom he missed badly. Tolstoy's story about the solitude of a man dying of cancer deeply impressed him:

> What a frightening book. . . . The horror of looming, inescapable death, the whole tragedy of human solitude seems so terrifying precisely because it's commonplace; he [Ivan Ilyich] is surrounded with people who are quite indifferent to him, who're occupied with mundane matters—hanging curtains, attending theater; and Ivan Ilyich is dying, he's suffering terribly, excruciatingly, but no one is shaken by this, no one screams of fear; it is as if all of this is expected, that everyone should die like this. The most shocking thing is that everyone will die like this. Tolstoy emphasizes that it's an ordinary story, Ivan Ilyich has died. This book impressed me deeply, and I'm thinking about it all the time. Please don't laugh at me; after all, the question of life and death is most important.[54]

Tolstoy's novella spoke about the value of individual life, of the need to honor suffering and death. It made Grossman realize the great power of literature. Having witnessed suffering and death during the civil war, with thousands vanishing without a trace, Grossman found an outlet for his thoughts and emotions. As a writer he would be strongly influenced by Tolstoy.

In March he was shaken by the suicide of a young woman who shot herself not far from his rental home. "She traveled here from the city to shoot herself. It was so frightening—an early spring morning, bright sun . . . and a young girl lying dead on the white snow, her skull smashed, black hair covered in blood."[55] He always found death incomprehensible and shocking, but this girl's death seemed even more senseless because it happened in spring, when the earth was awakening to a new life.

Reading Tolstoy strengthened Grossman's ambition to become a writer. Tolstoy's interest in the human soul, his quest for a deeper meaning in life, corresponded to Grossman's urge to find a genuine calling. At the time he was hoping to combine literary pursuits with his engineering profession, to write in the evenings after work. In February, during his final exams, Grossman dreamed of graduating, starting a new life, becoming occupied with "work, new people, new places, literature."[56] He wanted to write about working people. By then he knew the difference between literary hack work, ubiquitous in Soviet magazines, and genuine literature, which concerned itself with real life.

Grossman's brief meetings with Galya followed by long months of separation were a source of heartbreak. His father teased him for being overly sentimental and "attaching himself to a woman's skirt." Grossman replied that it was not the case, that although he deeply loved Galya, their relationship was far from harmonious, which troubled him.[57] In spring 1929 Galya arranged to take her practicum in Moscow at the Ukrainian mission of the Council of People's Commissars (Sovnarkom).[58] This allowed the couple to settle together in June, if only for a period of seven months. Galya was expecting a baby, and it was with some trepidation that Grossman, still a university student receiving his father's allowances, broke the news to Semyon Osipovich: "By the way, this winter I will become a father, and you—a grandfather. I don't know whether you consider this to be good or bad. In any case, a doctor who examined Galya, said it's too late to terminate her pregnancy. Galya herself wants to keep it. Lovely, I'll have a son (what if a daughter?) How do you receive the news?"[59] Semyon Osipovich responded that if Galya loved her husband, "she must think that she'll be hanging a millstone around your neck." Grossman, offended on his wife's behalf, replied that Galya's responsibilities as a mother would be ten times more burdening than his own, and that he was putting that millstone around his neck "voluntarily." Terminating a late pregnancy was dangerous; besides, Galya's first abortion had left her with painful complications.[60]

Although a married man, soon to become a father, Grossman refused a secure, well-paid government job at the Supreme Soviet of the National Economy (VSNH). The interview was arranged for him through his father's friend Galina Flakserman-Sukhanova, an old Bolshevik who worked in the Central Committee.[61] Grossman did not regret passing up this offer, since "this bureaucratic business doesn't agree with me at all." Other vacancies— working at a sugar refinery in Kursk or a winery—did not interest him; he did not want to bury himself in the provinces.[62] When Semyon Osipovich offered to help with employment, Grossman seized the opportunity. His father worked in Donetsk at the local Institute of Pathology and Occupational Hygiene, and the Donbass was the place where things were happening. "I want to participate in life, to stop being a spectator," Grossman wrote.[63]

The First Five-Year Plan, adopted in October 1928 to begin the following year, called for rapid industrialization and emphasized heavy industry. According to the plan, Soviet industrial development had to grow by 250 percent in five years.[64] Politicians set unworkable goals, and economists were pressured to pass the unrealistic objectives. This despite the fact that more than half of Soviet engineers in 1930 lacked proper training and only 11 percent had a university education.[65] Stalin blamed the resulting problems and industrial accidents on saboteurs, who now had to be discovered among engineers and other professionals.

Attacks on the technical intelligentsia, particularly on the experts educated before the revolution, would go on for three consecutive years. During the major 1928 Shakhty trial, fifty-three mining engineers, Russian and German, faced charges of counterrevolution and economic sabotage. The trial, covered in detail by national and local newspapers, sent shock waves through the Donbass region, of which Shakhty was part. Stalin declared the defendants guilty even before the trial began. Prosecutors alleged that the engineers, a group of "bourgeois specialists," received money from the West to undermine the entire Soviet coal industry. The Shahkty trial opened in Moscow's Hall of Columns of the House of Unions on May 19, 1928, and lasted forty-one days. It was presided over by Andrei

Vyshinsky, the chief judge, who would later conduct the trials for Stalin's Great Purge. It was only the second Soviet show trial, and the imperfections in staging it prompted ridicule from foreign newspapers. Only five defendants eventually received the death sentence requested by the prosecution. But Stalin was already preparing a larger campaign: in his words, "Shakhty men were sitting in all branches of our industry."[66] The Shakhty trial was presented as class warfare, with all engineers and other experts educated before the revolution made out to be potential enemies.

Grossman's father, who worked in the Donbass, belonged to a minority of experienced and well-trained engineers. Educated before the revolution, Semyon Osipovich would now live and work under a shadow of suspicion. When in 1929 a delegation of Soviet engineers was heading to the Rhineland (Westphalia province) and Luxembourg to visit part of Krupp's industrial empire, the authorities initially refused his application. Grossman advised his father to present them with an ultimatum: either he would go or he would resign. When Semyon Osipovich prevailed, Grossman wrote happily that his father would see giant blast furnaces and steel mills in Dortmund, visit Düsseldorf, and observe a steel foundry in Essen. "The Donbass will be dwarfed in comparison with these giants, which extract mountains of coal and pour out rivers of steel. . . . I swear to god, I'd give five fingers on my left hand to see this with my own eyes."[67]

As Grossman admitted a decade later, his father influenced his choice of profession: "I recalled your letters to me from the Donbass, which you wrote in 1927–28, and thought that they played a big role in my life, in my interest in labor, in workers; actually, these letters prompted me to go to the Donbass. And I thank you for this, since my years in the Donbass became central to my life, determining my interests and literary work for a long time."[68] In June 1929 he made a reconnoitering trip to meet his prospective employer in Donetsk.

Grossman graduated in December 1929. His practicum was at a Moscow soap factory to which he commuted in a packed tram. The work involved routine calculations and lab tests—a far cry from his boyhood dream of producing synthetic protein. After nine hours at the factory, and two hours commuting each way, he would return exhausted. His dream to write after work could not be realized under these circumstances.

When he was about to receive his diploma, his parents suggested that he officially change his name. He wrote his father: "Interestingly, today I received a card from Mama, and she wrote on the same subject, using your exact words."[69] But Grossman refused "to suddenly become transformed" from Iosif Solomonovich to Vasily Semyonovich, although life could be easier for Vasily Semyonovich.

On January 23, 1930, Galya bore their daughter Katya. But the trio would never again experience family life together. Grossman, now the primary breadwinner, left to work in the Donbass shortly after his daughter was born. As he writes in the story "Phosphorus," two great forces, his romantic dream and poetry, were driving him on.[70] In a letter to his father, he cited Rabindranath Tagore's poem "I Am Restless," which best described his aspiration of finding a genuine path in life: "O Great Beyond, O the keen call of thy flute!"[71]

3. Facts on the Ground

The Donbass

The deepest and hottest coal mine in the entire USSR,
with the most dangerous concentration of gas.
—Vasily Grossman, *An Armenian Sketchbook*

As Grossman tells us in "Phosphorus," he was posted as a chemist at a gas analytical laboratory that conducted air-quality tests at a coal mine in the Donbass, Smolyanka–11. The mine's depth was 832 meters, and some of its eastern stretches were more than a kilometer underground. It was notorious for massive explosions of methane and coal dust, producing blasts "comparable with underground tsunamis."[1] Heading to the Donbass at twenty-four, Grossman romanticized danger and miners' hard toil. Mining towns resembled war zones, with wailing sirens that announced deadly accidents; the menacing glow over their metallurgical plants emitted dense, poisonous smoke.

In winter 1930 Grossman arrived in Makeevka, a mining town twelve kilometers from Donetsk (then named Stalino). With no vacant cottages available at the new settlement for administration and engineers, he was assigned a flat in the miners' village. The rundown shacks, tilting to one side and black from coal dust, struck him as a crowd of drunks on a market street.[2] In fact, there was a lot of drinking going on in this village. Grossman's lodgings—two rooms and a kitchen—were too spacious for a single man whose furniture consisted of a mattress spread on the floor and a suitcase; the latter also served him as a table. His lack of furniture, bedding, and other possessions became a source of local amusement. As he writes in "Phosphorus," women peeked through his windows to have a laugh.

Grossman missed his wife and daughter, who had returned to Kiev. He expected Galya to join him soon and spent evenings writing letters to her, but she replied sporadically and without enthusiasm. His friends were equally poor correspondents. In the evenings he was desperately alone in his empty apartment; he missed friends and his life in Moscow. In addition, he developed a toothache. With no dentists around, he dulled the pain with large doses of aspirin and chain smoking. Every morning, the tin can that served as his ashtray was overflowing with cigarette butts. Smoking also helped suppress hunger: the food in the workers' canteens was sparse; rationing had been introduced in 1929. In November of that year Stalin launched his crash collectivization campaign: communal farms had to be set up within three years across the USSR.[3] Small individual farming, the backbone of contemporary agriculture, was condemned by the Party as incompatible with socialism. An exorbitant tax imposed on individual farmers was meant to squeeze them out: when a peasant paid it, he would immediately be presented with a higher tax. This was the beginning of the violent assault on traditional agriculture. Such Party policies would trigger an exodus from villages and widespread famine. In winter 1930 there was already no bread to be found in Donetsk or elsewhere in Ukraine, even if people were willing to pay.

The country was also living through Stalin's rapid industrialization, the centerpiece of the First Five-Year Plan. In 1929 Stalin had announced: "We are going full steam ahead toward socialism through industrialization, leaving behind the age-long 'Russian' backwardness. We are becoming a land of metals . . . automobiles . . . tractors."[4] Stalin's industrialization was fueled by coal: it was just as essential to the Soviet Union as it was during the industrial revolution in the West more than a century earlier. Working conditions in Soviet mines were similar to those described by Zola in his 1885 novel *Germinal*, which depicts the exploitation of white slaves in a mining town in northern France. In Soviet days, coal mining remained a dangerous occupation in which a miner faced death from explosions, fires, and inhaling coal dust.

Smolyanka–11, which Grossman inspected in 1930, was unventilated and unmechanized. Ventilation was accomplished only through the system of trap doors. Coal was extracted with picks and shovels: miners, lying on one side or kneeling, worked at the coal face with a pickaxe. A hurrier, harnessed to a tub of coal that could weigh six hundred kilograms, would crawl with it through the narrow mine tunnels, helped by thrusters, who pushed the tub from behind, delivering the load to the pit bottom. From there, horses, stabled permanently underground, would pull a train of tubs to the mine shaft. Under such conditions, Soviet miners were pressed to work overtime to fulfill the Party's unrealistic quotas for the Five-Year Plan. Grossman would attempt to describe what he saw in *Glückauf*, his first novel about miners.

Grossman's job was to measure the concentration of methane and other poisonous gases exhaled at the mine face. The coal had been formed by decaying vegetable matter, the gigantic trees and ferns of a primeval swampy forest existing hundreds of millions of years ago. Coal was the vestige of this plant life, which had once dominated the planet and contained the energy of the sun that had nurtured it. The greenhouse gases—carbon monoxide and methane, also known as marsh gas—were responsible for massive explosions in mines.[5]

The concentration of methane at Smolyanka–11 exceeded all limits. Safety standards were nonexistent: there was no air circulation in the hot mine, where the temperature reached thirty-four degrees Celsius and the humidity 100 percent. In such conditions a miner could work only for twenty minutes or so. Coal was saturated with gases, "like a sponge with water," writes Grossman in *Glückauf*. The light from safety lamps was blocked by fine particles of coal dust. This dust could also fuel spontaneous combustion. In the novel, Grossman describes conditions in the hottest and deepest stretch of the mine, more than a kilometer underground: "The air here was more static than swamp water. It stuffed lungs, like wet and hot cotton wool, weakened the body, bound movement, invited sleep. . . . After working for a while, everyone would lie down to rest. But rest would bring no relief. Your head would spin, you wanted to sleep, and the longer people rested, the less they felt like getting up or stirring. Silence, heavy like air, like millions of tons of rock hanging overhead, oppressed them."[6] A variety of lung problems, from silicosis to miners' asthma, the condition Grossman developed at Smolyanka–11, were caused by coal dust. In *Glückauf* he portrays himself in the character of a bespectacled engineer who arrives with his bright projector lamp to sample air quality in the mine's cramped, hot, and dark front line. The work of safety inspectors who measured concentrations of poisonous gases and dust was not respected; miners met them grudgingly: "You'd better measure our grief." Sometimes inspectors were abused as "freeloaders."[7]

Grossman's 1936 story "The Safety Inspector" tells of a middle-aged mining engineer fully devoted to his dangerous work. Like Grossman's father, his protagonist spends many years working in "the remotest and roughest mines." The story sheds light on the profession's risks; it explains why coal miners and especially their bosses disliked safety inspectors.

> His friends often advised him to leave his work as a safety inspector. "There's no sense to it at all; it's no good," they said, "it's the lousiest job in the mines. If the safety inspector tries to do his job, the operators get mad: . . . 'He made the men stop sorting and switched them to timbering'; 'He closed off a gaseous coal-face.' . . . And if the safety inspector stops trying to do his job, its worse: he's got to answer for men's lives with his own skin. Whatever happens, he's the first to answer for it. In a mine, anything can happen: rockfalls, cave-ins, defective cables, fires, explosions, cars running wild, ropes parting, men falling, defective timbers."[8]

Deadly explosions in mines were a reality, and so were funerals in mining towns. Although Grossman's job helped save lives, nobody saw it this way. Miners did not take him seriously, he reveals in "Phosphorus," and would laugh at him when he admired their heroic toil. In fact, the miners' back-breaking work and daily risks had little to do with glory. They did not choose their vocation: it was the only type of work in their town. Grossman would tell this in *Stepan Kolchugin*: miners began working as teenagers to replace their fathers and brothers, killed in explosions.

Grossman's first months in Makeevka were completely cheerless. A bespectacled city intellectual and Jewish, he was treated as an outsider. As he says in "Phosphorus," it was not only solitude and toothache that bothered him. During sleepless nights he kept thinking that his youthful aspirations of releasing nuclear energy and producing synthetic protein had come to nothing. His inspections of the mine and new responsibility as laboratory head at Smolyanka–11 consumed all his energy.

Although his life and work in the mining town provided material for the novels *Glückauf* and *Stepan Kolchugin*, he privately described this period as "moral death." As he intimated to his father in 1931, "There's not a single person to have a conversation with. And for us, intellectuals, it means a great deal to have a heart-to-heart talk."[9] Newspapers trumpeted the achievements of Stalin's collectivization and industrialization, while all one could see were ragged peasants fleeing villages and crowding railway stations to travel elsewhere in search of employment. Some peasants, trying to merge with the working class, sought menial jobs in mines. Nobody talked about this in Grossman's milieu: people were gossiping, discussing shortages, telling "remarkably stupid" anecdotes, and drinking "huge and senseless" amounts of vodka. "Important events were happening, but people around me— coalmine foremen, site supervisors, and the director of the mine himself— were astonishingly ignorant and small-minded."[10]

Less than a year into his employment at Smolyanka–11, Grossman developed symptoms of tuberculosis—cough, night sweats, weight loss, and fatigue. After a chest X-ray he was diagnosed with early stages of tuberculosis in both lungs. As he tells in "Phosphorus," the diagnosis struck him as a death sentence: at the time, there was no real cure for this terrible disease. In desperation, Grossman sent a telegram to Galya, who did not respond, and a letter to his closest friend, Syoma Tumarkin. Syoma spread the word and, to Grossman's joy, the kind-hearted Efim Kugel visited him in the miners' village. Grossman spared his mother the news, realizing that she "would become ill from grief."[11] In *Glückauf*, the mining engineer Lunin develops tuberculosis and dies on the job, something Grossman feared could happen to him. This novel reflects his state of mind: wooden shaft headframes look terrifying at night; cone-shaped slag heaps near the mines resemble mountains of human skulls. In the moonlight, huts in the miners' settlement "look like grave mounds."[12] Grossman saw death at close quarters. He was rescued thanks to his father: in 1930 Semyon Osipovich arranged for his son's transfer to the Donetsk Institute of Pathology and Occupational Hygiene, where he himself had formerly been employed.

Grossman's job at the laboratory of the Donetsk research institute was analyzing steel samples from the local metallurgical plant. His main problem now was boredom. "I'm not in good spirits: life is rather dull—the plant, dinner, 3 hours for reading and walking. . . . I'd very much want to write now, and I have the material . . . but I've got no time. God only knows when I'll have it." (Although Grossman often complained that he had no time to write, he proved capable of writing under any circumstances.) Life around him was grim. It struck him that nobody was free, and that, given his schedule, he had less freedom than a prisoner. Factory workers were "shackled" by labor and "various quotas and obligations. . . . I'm convinced you wouldn't find even ten workers out of forty or fifty thousand going to work at 6 am willingly and freely."[13] Grossman was unguarded in his letters: to suggest that labor in the Soviet Union wasn't joyful and free was heresy. He could pay dearly for such pronouncements. In 1923 the OGPU (the Joint State Political Directorate, which replaced the Cheka) opened and read 5 million letters and 8 million telegrams, far more than in Russia's "black offices" under the tsars.[14]

Grossman's thoughts about lack of freedom were inspired by the depressing atmosphere at the research institute, where he worked under the zealous scrutiny of Party dilettantes. Despite a shortage of qualified people, the Party persisted in harassing technical intelligentsia. On November 25, 1930, the Industrial Party trial (Prompartiya) opened in Moscow—another show trial in which top engineers, economists, and academics, educated before the revolution, stood accused of wrecking Soviet industry and transport and of conspiring against the Soviet regime. Some defendants received death sentences, later commuted to long prison terms. As in the Shakhty trial, the presiding judge was Vyshinsky. The trial caused panic among engineers and other professionals. In 1931 Grossman reported that work at his laboratory "collapsed—everyone is leaving or is planning to leave."[15] Grossman and his father belonged to a shrinking minority of experts who persevered. "You're lonesome in one coal-basin, and I'm—in another," Grossman wrote him.[16] He asked his father to keep writing: "*Bat'ko*, don't forget about me: your letters give me great joy (if there's no dressing down in them); it would be even better to see each other."[17] With the Party terrorizing engineers, professors, and scientists, their labor was disheartening.

Party policies in agriculture created disaster on a much larger scale. Collectivization was supposed to be voluntary, but in reality the state waged a war against prosperous and middle-income peasants, forcing them to give up livestock and inventory to collective ownership. A campaign against the kulaks launched in 1928 was accompanied by arrests, confiscation of property, shootings, and deportations. Stalin continued Lenin's policies in the countryside, which were responsible for the famine of 1921–22. With Stalin demanding "liquidation of the kulaks as a class," hundreds of thousands were deported to labor camps and special settlements where they were left without means to survive. The fate of those peasants who remained in villages was hardly any better: they were pressed to join kolkhozes and work without pay to meet Party quotas.

Stalin's crash collectivization was conducted without an economic plan or even administrative preparation. Peasants were told at village meetings that whoever didn't join the kolkhozes became "an enemy of the Soviet regime."[18] Grossman could learn this from *Pravda*. In 1930 it reported that women in a Ukrainian village shouted after such a meeting: "The Soviet government is bringing back serfdom!"[19] Individual farmers opposed collectivization across the USSR; in Ukraine, North Caucasus, and Central Asia the OGPU reported strongest resistance. Reluctant to work under government control, peasants slaughtered millions of cattle that otherwise would have been expropriated for the collective farms. In the coming years, excessive requisitioning of grain and other draconian measures caused widespread famine, killing an estimated 3.9 million people in Ukraine alone.[20]

In summer 1930 Gareth Jones, a young Welsh journalist who would be the first to report on the Soviet famine, arrived in Donetsk. (Founded in 1869 by the Welsh businessman John Hughes, Donetsk was initially named Hughesovka, or Yuzovka, in his honor. Hughes built a steel plant there and developed mining; his enterprises attracted Welsh immigrants to the city.) Jones, whose mother had once served as a governess in the home of John Hughes, was a recent Cambridge graduate who had majored in Russian. He had worked as a foreign affairs adviser to British prime minister David Lloyd George, also a Welshman. Jones wanted to write about the Soviet Union but had to cut short his visit to Donetsk: he had no ration cards and was able to obtain no more than a roll of bread.[21] In 1932 he returned to Ukraine, by then realizing that Soviet newspapers had lied about the country's actual situation. Arriving with his own provisions, Jones traveled on foot through the black earth region, once the richest farmland, witnessing the beginning of starvation. In spring 1933 he received permission to travel to Kharkov. But instead of going all the way, he got off the train forty miles north of the city and walked through twenty villages and collective farms. At the height of the famine in Ukraine he witnessed the impact in the Kharkov province, one of the most afflicted. On March 30, at a press conference in Berlin, Jones stated that the Soviet Union was in the midst of a major famine: "Everywhere was the cry, 'There is no bread. We are dying.' This cry came from every part of Russia, from the Volga, Siberia, White Russia, the North Caucasus, Central Asia." Several British and American publications quoted Jones's words at the press conference, and soon after the *London Evening Standard*, the *Daily Express*, and the *Cardiff Evening Mail* published Jones's articles describing his walking tour through Ukraine.[22] Stalin's government was furious. The authorities denied the existence of famine and coerced foreign correspondents in Moscow to repudiate Jones's press release. Walter Duranty, the most prominent and compliant journalist of the Moscow press corps, published an article in the *New York Times*: "Russians Hungry but Not Starving." Although Duranty was well aware that by then the famine killed millions, he used his own distinction and his newspaper's reputation to reassure the West. Meanwhile, Soviet authorities imposed a strict ban on journalists traveling outside Moscow. They even went so far as to criminalize the use of the word *famine*.[23] In 1935 Jones was kidnapped and murdered while traveling in Mongolia; he was likely killed on Stalin's orders.

Although the Soviet press was forbidden to report the famine, it was impossible to conceal the starvation of millions. The Canadian agricultural expert Andrew Cairns, who traveled through Ukraine and the North Caucasus in 1932 on behalf of the Empire Marketing Board, saw "hungry peasants, some begging for bread, mostly waiting, mostly in vain, for tickets, many climbing on to the steps or joining the crowds on the roof of each car, all filthy and miserable."[24] In 1932–33 the Mandelstams traveled to the Crimea and saw "wraith-like peasants" swollen with hunger and dying in the train stations and by the roadsides. The experiences led Mandelstam to compose his most dangerous poem, in which he called Stalin a "murderer and peasant-slayer."[25] By 1933 the Mandelstams had a good picture of the price the country was paying for Stalin's collectivization.

Grossman, who spent about two years in Donetsk and traveled through Ukraine to Russia, was also aware of the famine. Decades later in the essay "The Sistine Madonna," he described a starving peasant woman at a train station near the Ukrainian-Russian border: "I saw her in 1930, in Konotop. . . . Swarthy from hunger and illness, she walked toward the express train, looked up at me with her wonderful eyes, and said with her lips, without any voice, 'Bread.' "[26] By the time Grossman depicted Ukraine's famine in *Everything Flows* he knew the scale of the calamity from many sources, particularly his friend Loboda, who had been mobilized to conduct requisitioning and later saw peasants dying on Kiev's streets. But some of the most striking impressions would come from Grossman's own visits to Kiev in 1932 and 1933, at the height of the famine.

In summer 1931 Grossman had been granted a vacation and divided his time between Moscow, Kiev, and Berdichev. In Moscow he looked for employment. Although he was required to work at his first posting for three years, Grossman wanted to dodge this regulation. Thanks to a shortage of experts he was immediately offered positions at a mining institute and a military plant but, unsure whether his Donetsk employer would let him go, he

declined. A fortnight in Moscow restored his spirits. In a letter to his father
he joked that he had "a very good time in Moscow (e.g., drank a lot) and
enjoyed myself (since I drank at someone else's expense)."[27] All of his
friends were around, except Loboda, who had left with an expedition to
Chukotka for twenty months.

In mid-July he saw Galya in Kiev. She was living in the basement of a
communal apartment with her mother and a few dispossessed relatives who
had fled their Cossack village near Chernigov to seek shelter in Kiev.
Although Galya knew about the horrors of collectivization and the famine,
she remained pro-Soviet and referred to Stalin as "a supreme leader."[28] In
Berdichev Grossman was reunited with his mother and daughter Katya, now
eighteen months old. Galya had struggled to feed the baby in Kiev so it was
decided that Katya would stay in Berdichev where the countryside was not
devastated and one could buy milk in a village. "Katyusha talks, walks, and
sends you a bow," Grossman wrote lightheartedly to his father.[29] Katya was
growing up in Uncle David's house, as had Grossman, nurtured by his
mother and Aunt Anyuta. His aunt took Grossman to her dacha where within
a short period he put on some weight; before the age of antibiotics tuberculosis was treated with nutrition and rest, so he drank plenty of milk.

In a letter from Berdichev Grossman reported to his father that their
Moscow relative Rosaliya Grigorievna had been released from prison where
she spent seven months in connection with the Menshevik trial. Fourteen
economists, former Mensheviks, had accurately forecasted the extent of fulfillment of the Five-Year Plan and had given realistic figures for the industrial
production in 1932. Because their prognosis was half the goal set by the Party,
the experts were accused of economic sabotage.[30] Their show trial in March
1931 followed a familiar script, with the defendants confessing their "crimes."
The most prominent among them, Vladimir Groman, was the country's chief
economist and a member of the Presidium of the State Planning Committee,
Gosplan. He was forced to admit that his counterrevolutionary group in
Gosplan engaged in meddling with the Party's production targets. The prosecution asked for the death penalty for him and other leaders, but the court
came up with various prison terms. In 1931 the courts still preserved some
independence from the prosecution. For the intelligentsia reading such reports
in newspapers, the big question was—why did they all confess?

Returning to Donetsk in August, Grossman resumed his work at the
laboratory, where he was now a senior research assistant. In addition he

accepted a position as lecturer in chemistry at the local medical institute. The work atmosphere at the institute was the same as everywhere: Party people were in charge and the brightest among Grossman's colleagues were leaving.

In early winter 1931 Grossman was finally sent to treat his tuberculosis at a sanatorium in Sukhumi on the Black Sea. From the resort town of Gelendzhik to the sanatorium was a four-hundred-kilometer drive. It was unusually cold: the subtropics were hit by heavy snowfalls. Grossman was traveling with several other tubercular patients when their car slid into a ditch. They spent the night in the field, trying to shield themselves from wind, snow, and freezing rain. Grossman had a warm coat and was better off than others. The ride to the sanatorium, he thought, shortened the remaining lives of the consumptives by half.

Sukhumi, the capital of Abkhazia, "a city of mourning, tobacco, and fragrant vegetable oils," as described by Osip Mandelstam, reminded Grossman of Berdichev.[31] If one were to plant a few palms along the Berdichev streets, he joked, you'd have "a typical Abkhazian town." At the sanatorium an experienced radiologist told Grossman that he had healthy lungs; he was registered among the convalescing. Reporting the welcome news to his father, Grossman asked him to keep it confidential: his original diagnosis could come in handy. Now that he knew he had no tuberculosis he feared catching it at the sanatorium.[32] The patients were industrial workers and miners from across Russia and the Caucasus. Grossman was impressed by their courage: "Nobody can die so humbly and merrily (upon my word, merrily) as simple people, the laborers. More than half of them here are candidates to depart to another world within a year or two. Despite this, everyone giggles, laughs, and talks of anything but their illnesses. You know they're ill, gravely ill, but they're not the kind of patients who pity themselves and view the world through the prism of their own illness. But—my god—only here I understood what a terrible malady tuberculosis is. What it does to people! And it's here that I really felt frightened."[33]

"Treatment" at the sanatorium, a drafty building where the temperature hovered around seven to eight degrees Celsius, consisted of exposure to cold. There was no medical help: the head doctor, formerly a city gynecologist, had no experience with tuberculosis. Food was scarce, and patients were perennially hungry. But there was no famine in Sukhumi: provisions could be still bought at a local market. Because of snow and freezing rain, patients were confined to their rooms, where they played cards and chess. After three weeks of such life, Grossman was bored stiff, reporting that most patients could not wait till the end of their term. "Those who are leaving the sanatorium are envied, like inmates discharged from prison."[34]

While in the sanatorium Grossman had more time to read and write. Actually, he had always managed to write. In 1928–30 he had drafted some short prose and a poem, covering the pages with drawings and portraits of people around him. He recorded half-baked thoughts on various subjects: "Happiness is found in movement towards happiness. . . . It's good that people are unhappy. Had they found happiness, humanity would become extinct." (This thought could have been inspired by Tolstoy's philosophy, by his belief in continual self-perfection.) In his early twenties, Grossman made notes about art, love, death, and freedom—his perennial themes. The sketch "In a Pub" is about an old man who worked thirty years as a prison guard—still under the tsars. "I know what freedom is," says the guard. He goes on to tell about a political inmate who spent a year on death row in solitary confinement. Assigned to watch over him, the guard is surprised that the prisoner spends much time by the grid window of his jail cell: the view is blocked by a wall. "I asked him, 'Why do you stare at the window, are you expecting guests?' He says, '. . . The air is freer on the other side.' "[35] "Fate," a poem Grossman drafted in 1930, is about a ship carried toward the rocks during a storm.

Themes of inevitability and approaching one's fate reemerge in his story "Comrade Fyodor," drafted in 1931. A revolutionary and his doctor, both suffering from tuberculosis, talk about fear of dying. "Death," repeated the doctor. . . . "I could write a book about it . . . entitled, 'What frightens me about death.' You know what? Inevitability."[36] This story also deals with the 1917 February Revolution, which engrossed Grossman. The sketch "Precious Stones," also written around this time, reflects Grossman's fascination with Lenin's belief in world revolution. Lenin is described as "the greatest rebel of mankind. . . . Nobody else was so loved and feared."[37]

Grossman's early prose also deals with couples living apart. By the end of 1931, he knew that his marriage was on the rocks. In his novel *Glückauf,* drafted in 1931–32, a young German engineer, August Schwartz, thinks obsessively about his bride, Maria, in Bochum. She doesn't reply to his letters, and he is tormented by jealousy: " 'What is it?' he thought. 'It's like an illness. I must take myself in hand or I'll go mad. . . . After all, what's wrong? He's being ridiculous. He's just twenty-six.' "[38] Grossman's sketch

"A Tale about Happiness" is another story of marital separation: a young girl refuses to join her husband, posted in a remote town, because she won't live in a shack. His novellas "A Cook" and "A Story about Love" (the latter published in 1937) depict couples considering divorce.

Nearing twenty-seven, Grossman was fed up with the isolation of mining towns; he missed his intellectual milieu in Moscow and wanted to return there for good. His original TB diagnosis set him free: he attached it to his letter of resignation to his employer in Donetsk. Arriving in Moscow in July 1932, Grossman looked for work and a place to settle with Galya. But by August he knew that his marriage could not be saved: Galya had a lover in Kiev. Her infidelities were not news to Grossman and his family. Nadya, with whom Grossman was staying, may have told him about Galya's latest affair. Arriving in Kiev, he found that Galya was dating their common acquaintance Victor Baranov, who would become her third husband and Katya's stepfather.[39] Grossman's mother was relieved to learn about the breakup of the marriage. In a letter to Semyon Osipovich, she credited Nadya for weighing in: "I'll be always grateful to Nadya that she 'divorced' Vasya from Galya. She saw [this marriage] was a fiasco."[40]

Galya was Grossman's first love, and the decision to divorce her, he admitted to his father, cost him many sleepless nights. Their separation was dramatic: trying to rescue the marriage, Galya denied infidelity. Unaware of her husband's circumstances, she had come to Donetsk, from which she "bombarded" Grossman with letters. She threatened to commit suicide unless he joined her. As he wrote his father, he was "frightened by this; if she commits suicide because of me it will be horrible. But I must divorce her." Grossman asked Galya to return to Kiev, where she would not be alone. Instead she arrived in Moscow. Grossman was resolute: "Galya is not a wife to me anymore. I don't love her, it's all over, it would be impossible for us to live together as before." He wanted his father to believe that his decision to end the marriage was "very firm" and final: "Listen, old man, I imagine your green-blue eye [Grossman's father had lost one eye] staring at me with scepticism, wisdom, worry, and sad masculine doubt—you of all people would know the power of a woman and weakness of a man. So, listen, I've decided."[41]

Katya was in Berdichev with Grossman's family. Galya threatened to take her away but the plan was impractical. In summer 1932 bread lines in Kiev were half a kilometer long. People queued for hours, but even with ration cards the daily norm of bread (from two hundred to four hundred grams) was not guaranteed. The last few hundred people in line received only numbers inked on their hands to present the following day.[42] Katya would remain with her grandmother until she turned five. In August, while in Berdichev, Grossman was able to have his first conversations with his daughter: "Katysha and I talk about goats, cats, bad boys and impeccable girls and, actually, I'm surprised to discover that the lot of a single father is not painful; on the contrary, it's pleasant."[43]

That summer Grossman resumed his life and activity in Moscow, both as a writer and an engineer. He found a job as a chemist at a pencil factory and wrote a brochure about mechanization and ventilation of coal mines. While thoroughly researching his subject he read piles of technical literature, but when he took the manuscript "Mine Gases" (Shakhtiny gazy) to a Moscow publisher, it turned out that a similar book had just been released.

Nadya, his devoted cousin, continued to guide him on a literary path. The two discussed Grossman's plan of becoming a professional writer. It was now impossible to publish anything without a Party mandate. With independent publishing eliminated in the late 1920s, writers were at the mercy of state publishers and Party functionaries of Glavlit, the censorship agency. In 1932 the term *socialist realism* was coined to describe the only officially approved style for Soviet literature and art. In practice it was "a kind of hyperrealism" obliging writers to embellish Soviet life.[44] Literature was becoming fully subservient to government needs. That year writers' independence was further reduced with the establishment of the Union of Soviet Writers, a powerful organization whose staff was appointed by the Party. Soviet writers who broadcast the Party message enjoyed the prestige and prosperity an engineer could never dream of. However, Grossman was reluctant to write on "social assignment" and toe the Party line. If he did, he would inevitably "slide down to hack-work." As he wrote his father, "I decided (together with Nadya) that in order to pursue a literary career I need another profession."[45]

Helping Grossman on various fronts, Nadya arranged for his short stories and his novel *Glückauf* to be typed. The title was suggested by Grossman's father, who had visited coalfields in Germany and Belgium. (Grossman considered several titles, including "The Black and the Red," an inversion of Stendhal's *Le rouge et le noir*.) In the 1935 foreword to the novel, Grossman explained: "People in the Ruhr . . . don't say 'hello,' 'good-bye' and 'see you.' They say: 'Glückauf.' "[46] Coming up to the surface after a day's work German miners are greeted with the word *Glückauf*, which translates as "happy lifting" or literally "happy up." Grossman employed his father's impressions of the Rhineland and Westphalia. The German engineers in the novel, who install a new ventilation system in the Donbass mine, are from the Ruhr. Both are Social Democrats. The ending deals with anti-Fascist demonstrations in Germany and purges among Social Democrats in 1933.

Significantly, this novel introduces the theme of Fascism and Communism that would later occupy Grossman. The rise of these two ideologies that would soon overshadow the world was already apparent. Back in September 1923, after the Munich Putsch, which saw two thousand Nazis marching to the center of Munich, Bulgakov observed in his diary: "Our newspapers are blowing events up in every possible way, although who knows, maybe the world is really splitting into two parts—Communism and Fascism."[47] Grossman's novel mentions beatings of anti-Fascist demonstrators in Germany and arrests among Communists. The two ideologies then seemed poles apart; decades later, Grossman would perceive their similarities.

Glückauf was considered by Profizdat, the same trade union publisher that produced Grossman's brochure about women in Uzbekistan. In August Grossman was revising *Glückauf* with "a charming twenty-four-year-old female editor."[48] The editor was as vigilant as she was charismatic. Sher Nyurenberg, younger brother of Grossman's friend Alexander Nitochkin, saw the manuscript of *Glückauf* with editorial revisions. The novel was "beaten to a pulp," he writes: the editor's blue and red question marks covered the pages like black and blue bruises.[49] In the end, the novel was rejected as containing "counterrevolutionary tendencies." In the fall, Grossman appealed to Maxim Gorky, asking him to give an opinion on the book.

> The publishing house rejected my manuscript; as well, the editor was trying to persuade me that the book is written in a counterrevolutionary way. I wrote what I saw while working for three years in the mine Smolyanka–11. I wrote the truth. Perhaps, this is a bitter truth. However, truth cannot be counterrevolutionary. In our day truth and revolution cannot be separated. I fail to understand what's counterrevolutionary about my book—is it that there is drinking in the Donbass, that there are frequent brawls there, that work in a coalmine is very hard or that people, coalminers . . . don't smile 24 hours a day? . . . My second tormenting question is about the artistic side of what I've written.[50]

In addition to *Glückauf*, Grossman asked Gorky to read his short story "Three Deaths." (The title alluded to Tolstoy's early story about the deaths of a nobleman, a coachman, and a tree.) Gorky had towering authority, and a letter from him could boost a writer's career. Although Gorky received a flood of manuscripts, he read Grossman's novel and short story quickly and replied in a long letter on October 7, 1932. He was brusque: the story "Three Deaths" struck him as shallow and unnecessary. The subject of mortality had been perfectly covered by Tolstoy ("Three Deaths," "The Death of Ivan Ilyich"), Chekhov, and other Russian writers. A contemporary writer should view death only "as a biological phenomenon." The spiritual side of the story—an attempt to make the reader think about the inevitable end—was "futile, i.e., religious business, and obviously harmful as such." *Glückauf* had good material for a novel but Grossman did not rise above that material. Moreover, he spoiled his work with moralizing. "Personally, I don't see any counterrevolutionary tendencies in this novel; however, critics can understandably perceive such tendencies in the author's 'naturalism.'" (Gorky suggested the work was influenced by Zola's *Germinal*; Zola was the father of naturalism.)

Gorky, of course, was a proponent of socialist realism, which embellished reality. Naturalism was "the trade of photographers," he explained in the same letter; this method could not be applied to Soviet reality. Moreover, it "distorted" Soviet reality: "The author says, 'I wrote the truth.' He should have asked himself two questions: first—what sort of truth? And second—why?" The "dirty truth of the past" has died, and a new truth has been born. "The author can see well the truth of the past. . . . He truthfully depicted the dull-wittedness of coalminers, their drunkenness, brawls. . . . Of course, all this—is truth, but it's a very bad and tormenting truth." Gorky was teaching Grossman the ropes of socialist realism. Grossman should ask himself "why he writes? What kind of truth he asserts? . . . He is a gifted man, and should be able to resolve these questions."[51] Gorky's didactic letter was, in fact, an invitation to rewrite and resubmit *Glückauf*. Grossman would do just that. Gorky launched the careers of many writers, including that of Isaak Babel: in the 1920s his *Red Cavalry* was published with Gorky's backing.

Glückauf became the weakest of Grossman's works: the political message overshadowed his talent and originality. His revisions introduced compulsory content about the Five Year Plan and shock-work brigades toiling enthusiastically to mechanize the coal mine. He reduced the negative parts, stating in the introduction that the novel told about Soviet miners and their "happy lifting" from the depths of capitalist exploitation.[52] Although he thus watered down his message, the novel stood out for its truthful depictions. The Donbass waste was expelled into the air, making it among the most polluted places in the world.[53] There was persistent smog in Donetsk generated by the industrial enterprises there.[54] Grossman describes a multicolored haze over Makeevka—from black to green and amber. He was able to reveal some realities of the miners' town: the accidents, the pollution, the workers living two families to a single room, and the inefficiency of Soviet bureaucracy. German engineers in the novel quickly learn two Russian words: *nyet* (no) and *zavtra* (tomorrow). In contrast, other industrial novels of the time, such as Valentin Kataev's *Time, Forward,* about the construction of the Magnitigorsk Steel Mill, Fyodor Gladkov's *Energy,* and Marietta Shaginyan's *Hydrocentral,* about the building of dams, trumpeted Soviet achievements.

When the book finally came out, it sold quickly. In December 1935, during a conference of young writers in Donetsk, Babel praised *Glückauf* for its accurate depiction of mining and metal works. Among writers who attended the conference with Babel were novelist Yuri Olesha, Jewish poet and playwright Peretz Markish, and German Communist writer Willi Bredel, who emigrated to Moscow after spending a year in a Nazi concentration camp.[55]

4. Great Expectations

I dressed and walked to the party in a state of great excitement. After all, this
was a world that was new to me, the world that I was striving to enter. This
world was about to reveal itself to me from its very best side—the leading
representatives of literature, its finest flower, were due to be at the party.
—Mikhail Bulgakov, *A Theatrical Novel*

The years 1933 to 1935 were the happiest in Grossman's life: an outsider, he
was accepted by the literary world, achieved success, and met his new love.
Yet these years were anything but cloudless. He had to work hard to succeed
as a writer—while still employed as a chemical engineer at a factory. In 1933
he had his first serious encounter with the OGPU, the Soviet secret police.
He also had to fight a legal battle to remain in Moscow.

In December 1932 Stalin introduced internal passports. It was a restric-
tive measure designed to stop the influx from a countryside ravaged by
collectivization. Now a peasant trying to escape from a collective farm and
find work elsewhere needed authorization from local authorities and a
contract from a future employer.[1] Internal passports fixed peasants to the
land; the socialist state had, in fact, reintroduced the serfdom abolished by
the 1861 Emancipation Reform. But peasants were not the only ones to lose
freedom of movement. Factory workers, who had to live where they worked,
became tied down to their jobs. Had Grossman failed to escape the Donbass,
he could have ended up working there permanently.

Internal passports gave the state unprecedented power of control. One
now had to petition the authorities for a residence permit, and in major cities
this was difficult to obtain. The police could refuse applicants without an
explanation. Before the revolution Grossman, as a Jew, needed legal permis-

sion to live and study in Kiev. The revolution abolished the Pale of Settlement, but Stalin's new restrictions affected everyone in the Soviet Union.

In 1933 Grossman was working as an analytical chemist at the Moscow
pencil factory named after Sacco and Vanzetti. (The Italian-born American
anarchists Nicola Sacco and Bartolomeo Vanzetti were executed in 1927,
ostensibly for murder. Because many felt they had really been tried for their
beliefs, the case drew international attention, becoming a popular cause in
the Soviet Union, where streets and a major factory were named after them.)

Although Grossman now worked in Moscow, he had lived there permanently for only five months, which turned out to be less than required; as a result
the authorities refused to register him in the capital. After Grossman was denied
a residence permit, his supervisor at the factory dismissed him from his job as
well. Caught up in a Soviet bureaucratic nightmare, Grossman found himself
living in Moscow illegally and unable to buy food: his ration cards, issued to
him as a factory employee, were taken away. Fortunately, he was staying with
Nadya and her mother, Aunt Lisa, so he was not starving. For three months,
facing expulsion from Moscow, Grossman fought to have his case reviewed.

In *Life and Fate*, Evgeniya Shaposhnikova similarly struggles to obtain
permission in Kuibyshev (Samara), the city where her father had been a
prominent revolutionary. In lines at the police station she hears heartrending
stories of people refused residence permits. There were "daughters who
wanted to live with their mothers, a paralyzed woman who had wanted to
live with her brother, another woman who had come to Kuibyshev to look
after a war-invalid." In the eyes of the state these people were faceless peti-
tioners, not human beings. Grossman's heroine feels powerless during her
meeting with the head of the passport department, a young bureaucrat on
whose office wall hangs the obligatory portrait of Stalin.

> Evgeniya entered Grishin's office. Grishin motioned her to a chair,
> glanced at her papers and said: "Your application has been refused.
> What can I do for you?"
>
> "Comrade Grishin," she said, her voice trembling, "please
> understand: all this time I've been without a ration-card."
>
> He looked at her unblinkingly, an expression of absent-
> minded indifference on his broad young face.[2]

Like his heroine in the novel, Grossman managed to prevail: in fact,
any situation could be swiftly resolved if one had contacts in the Party. By

April, Grossman had obtained his Moscow registration, recovered his ration cards and his job, and even received a promotion.

When he assumed his troubles were over, the OGPU came to arrest Nadya. This happened on March 28: arriving at their apartment at night, the secret police conducted a thorough search and led her away. Grossman was devastated: "Why? What for? None of us can understand this, but it will be soon three weeks that she has been incarcerated in the OGPU's inner prison [Lubyanka]. We hope this is an absurd mistake and will be resolved one of these days. . . . I'm mostly concerned for Nadya's health."[3] (Nadya had a weak heart.) During their search the police interrogated Grossman about his family, factory employment, and literary work. To his surprise, they confiscated a portion of *Glückauf*. Grossman laughed it off: "I don't think they did this with the intention of getting it published. In any case, I'm extremely flattered by such attention."[4] With Gorky's protective letter, which stated that the novel was not counterrevolutionary, he had nothing to fear. At the time, Grossman was revising the novel for a cooperative publisher, MTP (Moscow Writers' Association). His new editor requested additional changes and cuts, and Grossman worked nights to revise "my long-suffering book."[5]

While most people at the time were arrested for nothing, in Nadya's case an explanation could readily be found: she had corresponded with Trotsky's associate, the revolutionary and writer Victor Serge (Victor Kibalchich). The son of Russian revolutionary populists, exiled abroad under the tsars, Serge was born in Brussels. After the revolution, he went to Soviet Russia, joined the Bolshevik Party, and started working for the Comintern. In the early 1920s he became associated with Trotsky's Left Opposition faction. Like other opposition members, he was expelled from the Party in the late 1920s. As Trotsky's disciple Serge was twice arrested. His second arrest was in March 1933, also the time when the police came for Nadya.

Long after Trotsky's Left Opposition was crushed, scores of people were still branded as Trotskyists and detained. In 1936 Serge was fortunate to be deported from the USSR after an international campaign for his release led by influential French writers.[6] His remaining family in Russia and people associated with him would all suffer: some spent decades in the Gulag.

Nadya met Serge through her association with the Comintern. During a search of her apartment the police found several letters from Serge; these letters, described as "extremely counterrevolutionary," were attached to her OGPU file.[7] In 1933 punishments were relatively mild. Accused of "anti-Soviet agitation," Nadya was expelled from the Party and sentenced to three years of internal exile.[8] In early June she was banished to Astrakhan on the Volga, from where she sent Grossman a telegram. Over the years he helped her financially and also traveled to visit her in Astrakhan. After Nadya's arrest the house management threatened to reduce the living space in her three-bedroom apartment. Grossman, remaining there with Aunt Lisa, realized they would lose one or two bedrooms. At the time most people still lived in crowded communal apartments. Cooperative housing was affordable only to the Soviet elite: in 1934 Grossman reported to his father that a two-bedroom flat would cost the enormous sum of 15,000–20,000 rubles, completely out of reach for an engineer, a doctor, or a teacher. Living space remained one of the country's most contentious issues until Stalin's death. Since it was almost impossible to buy property, some would denounce a neighbor to get an extra room. Grossman explored the subject in *Everything Flows* and in his story "Living Space," written after the war.

Grossman's job at the pencil factory drained his energy; aside from revising *Glückauf*, he could accomplish little writing.[9] The employment, however, provided material for "Ceylon's Graphite," an engaging story he published in 1935 in *Znamya*. Grossman's friend and coworker Efim Kugel served as the prototype for Kruglyak, a Jewish chemical engineer whose resourcefulness saves a fortune for his factory. As the story reveals, Soviet pencil factories depended heavily on expensive imports: "We could build Magnitogorsk, but cannot produce decent pencils. To make a pencil we need Japanese wax, *Junīperus virginiāna* [juniper growing in North America] for timber, German anilines, methyl violet."[10] Kruglyak is a true enthusiast who believes that it's unthinkable to stop production of pencils in a country that recently learned to write. If the factory runs out of Ceylon's graphite, he declares, "we'll replace it with manure, if necessary, yet the pencils will still write." In the end, he finds a valid domestic substitute for Ceylon's graphite.[11] Although Kruglyak saves millions for his factory by purchasing graphite from the Urals, he cannot afford a winter coat for himself on his salary as an engineer. Soviet salaries were meager: doctors, engineers, and teachers were barely making ends meet. A teacher's wages were half those paid to a senior OGPU employee, and the latter was also able to buy food and consumer goods at low prices in special shops. Given these benefits, an OGPU employee's pay was many times that of a teacher.[12]

In mid-June 1933 the factory sent Grossman on a business trip to Kiev, where he spent several days.[13] That spring the famine in Kiev province had been at its worst: whole villages died and houses stood empty. In Kiev Grossman saw bread lines in which people had started queuing the previous evening. He saw starving peasants who managed to get to Kiev by circumventing OGPU roadblocks. In *Everything Flows* he would draw from memory and others' accounts to describe scenes of desperation: "The peasants could no longer walk—they could only crawl. . . . Yes, I remember Kiev all right, even though I only spent three days there."[14] But only later would he analyze his impressions. It took decades to fathom the magnitude of this man-made disaster. On the surface life in the city went on as before: trams were running, and people, accustomed to the sight of starving peasants, hurried on with their affairs. There was hardly any sympathy for the peasants, who were officially accused of hoarding grain and generating food shortages. The recent campaign to liquidate the kulaks made the public insensitive to their suffering and deaths. Newspapers were silent about the famine, nobody was talking about it, and at the time Grossman did not explore his impressions and thoughts.

From Kiev he traveled to Berdichev to spend a few days with his mother and daughter Katya, now three and a half. "Katyusha has grown, has become tall, 'grown-up,' she chats about everything and romps; she recognized me; she dangles from my neck, 'this is my papa,' she tells everyone."[15] Ekaterina Savelievna looked tired and nervous: "I know it's hard for Mama to have Katyusha, but I also know she fills Mama's life."[16] Continuing his business trip, he went on to Leningrad.

Working at the pencil factory in summer was hellish. During a heat wave in July, temperatures hovered between thirty-six and forty degrees Celsius in the shade. With no proper ventilation, the air was thick with fumes from paint, varnish, and dyes such as aniline, a toxic compound used to produce indelible pencils; it smelled of rotten fish. As Grossman writes in "Ceylon's Graphite," "It was especially hard to work in stuffy factory shops: vapors from varnish and solvent filled the air with a sweet and repulsive smell; it seemed that the powerful fans were panting like living creatures: instead of chilling the air, they exhaled hot and dry breath into the workers' faces." Grossman felt drained and yearned for a respite: he lost sixteen pounds, and his asthma returned.

That summer his father was dismissed from his job at a research institute in Novosibirsk, the largest, fastest-growing industrial city in Siberia. Having recently experienced dismissal himself, Grossman advised his father not to get upset; he cited Chekhov's civil servant who consoles a friend in similar circumstances: "Take it as an atmospheric phenomenon!"[17] Grossman suggested that his father get a job in a big city like Dnepropetrovsk or at a research institute in Moscow. Semyon Osipovich, wisely, did not listen. As a former Menshevik, he thought it safer to pursue jobs in remote mining communities. Being perennially on the move and staying out of sight helped him avoid arrest. His next posting was in the coal-mining city of Leninsk-Kuznetsky in southwestern Siberia. The city was previously known as Kolchugino, the name Grossman adopted for his principal character in the novel *Stepan Kolchugin*. Semyon Osipovich would begin working there in October; meanwhile, he proposed that the two of them travel to Altai, Siberia's highest mountain range. Grossman was overjoyed: "1. I want to see a new beautiful country. 2. I want to see you. 3. I want a holiday."[18]

In September 1933 he took an express train from Moscow to Novosibirsk; from there, he and his father traveled five hundred kilometers to Biysk, near the border with Kazakhstan. They camped in the picturesque village of Chemal on the Katun River, which originated in the glaciers of Belukha Mountain. They hiked with a view of the three-peak mountain, picking edelweiss.[19] Grossman had perfect chemistry with his father, with whom he could speak of anything, from history to contemporary life and literature. Semyon Osipovich was a good storyteller, witty and ironic, and a literary connoisseur.

In the mountains father and son could talk without fear of being heard and discuss anything from Nadya's arrest to collectivization. It was the second year of the famine that devastated the grain-producing regions of Ukraine, North Caucasus, Western Siberia, the Lower Volga region, and Kazakhstan, which on a per capita measure was the most affected area.[20] Semyon Osipovich, whose postings required him to travel widely, saw crowds of fatigued men, women, and children at small rail stations. Everywhere, people could be seen trying to escape the countryside, which had been ruined by collectivization, and heading to towns in search of jobs and food.[21] In Ukraine, according to the OGPU reports, from mid-December 1932 to early February 1933, around ninety-five thousand peasants left their homes.[22] Yet the regime suppressed all information about the exodus from villages and of the famine; moreover, by 1933 people knew that it was dangerous to speak about the evidence of their own eyes.

Grossman's letters of the period are concerned with family matters and his literary career, which he wanted to pursue full-time. Although he was now assistant head engineer, he regarded his factory employment as a nuisance. "I get up at 7 a.m. . . . I work until 4. I come home directly from work and give myself to useful occupations: eating, reading, and writing."[23] Despite his grueling work at the factory Grossman produced novellas and short stories. A prominent literary magazine, *Krasnaya Nov'* (Red Innovation), accepted three of his stories. *Krasnaya Nov'*, then edited by Alexander Fadeev, had previously published such leading writers as Gorky, Mayakovsky, and Esenin; essayists included Nikolai Bukharin and Karl Radek.

In late 1933 Grossman gave a reading to an audience of well-published authors. It was his literary coming out: "Yesterday, I read three stories at a gathering of ten writers. Actually, it was not I who read them, but [Ivan] Kataev. It was my debut, and it was successful. The stories made an impact. I was criticized (by some) for lack of a definite ideological position, but everyone praised my style."[24]

In January 1934 Grossman quit his pencil factory job. Earlier, he had rationalized: "If one were to pursue chemistry, then why at the lowest level, dealing with pencils, and working ten hours a day . . . with repulsive and querulous people?"[25] His boss refused to accept his resignation until a replacement was found, and Grossman had to fight to free himself. This was his last job as an engineer. Aside from his calling to be a writer, he discovered that literary work paid much better than engineering. He no longer doubted whether it was good or bad to depend on literary income. By then he had received a generous offer from *Literary Donbass*: the magazine promised to pay him 3,000 rubles to publish *Glückauf* in two successive issues. The magazine would produce the novel simultaneously with the book, a plan Grossman found extremely welcome, since "it will give me several thousand extra readers and will allow me to live well and help Mama and Nadya for a few months."[26] *Glückauf* was now a far cry from the original version: at the last minute, the book editor slashed another seventy pages.[27] *Literary Donbass* made further revisions without consulting the author. Grossman's heart sank in April when he received the magazine with an excerpt of his novel. "The Donbass literati" had altered his text beyond recognition, he wrote. "After I read their blockhead revisions everything went dark before my eyes. The only good thing is that the rest of the Soviet Union doesn't read this magazine."[28] However, the miners loved his novel, and Grossman was happy that it became popular at Makeevka, where he had first worked as a safety engineer.

Grossman knew his first book was a compromise; as an established writer he never reprinted it. Meanwhile, he began the historical novel *Stepan Kolchugin* and was reading a lot. "I am an ignoramus. . . . I know neither history nor philosophy or literature."[29] The novel was set in the decade 1905–16. His father became Grossman's major source on the early revolutionary movement, workers' strikes, and other contemporary details. By delving into history Grossman could escape his editors' intrusions and tell a true story of a mining town, which he was denied in *Glückauf*. But few readers of *Stepan Kolchugin* would realize that Grossman's depictions of mining accidents, pollution, and miners' lives in this novel were not only historical. Conditions for Soviet miners had hardly changed, allowing Grossman to draw from his impressions of the Donbass.

The First Congress of Soviet Writers, then the biggest event in Soviet literary life, was to take place in August 1934. The congress would endorse socialist realism as the leading method of Soviet literature and art. Gorky and members of the government, such as Bukharin, were expected to give keynote speeches. Grossman's career was propelled during the months of electrifying anticipation leading up to the congress.

In April Gorky read the new version of *Glückauf* and liked it so much that he included the novel in his almanac, *The Year XVII*. The title referred to the beginning of the Soviet era: 1934 was the seventeenth year after the revolution. This issue of the almanac was scheduled to come before the congress, and Gorky was making Grossman's novel (after it had been mutilated by editors) a showpiece of Soviet writing.

MTP was producing another almanac in time for the congress. Back in winter, Grossman had submitted several of his stories to MTP, including "In the Town of Berdichev." His manuscript went to the editors Ivan Kataev and Nikolai Zarudin, known as "severe" critics. Grossman was awaiting their judgment with apprehension: "My liver was aching the entire time; I expected a dressing down." In late March Kataev and Zarudin sent a telegram to the publisher, thus informing Grossman as well: "Salutations to the splendid writer Grossman, author of 'The Town of Berdichev.' " Grossman was jubilant: "I admit the news scalded me with joy. Unfortunately, the blister is already disappearing. All of a sudden everyone became very solicitous of me, even promising to assign me to the GORT supply store for 'exceptionally trustworthy' writers. So, there it is. That's what they call recognition."[30] Grossman was referring to Moscow's special store for VIPs where notable writers, factory directors, and Party functionaries could buy food and other goods at lower prices. One's official status could be determined from one's position in the various ranks of the Soviet distribution system. Grossman's status as a Soviet writer was officially recognized when he received a pass to buy food at a restricted store. Although he was joking about it, he was also pleased that he was moving up in life.

Aside from Gorky, Grossman now had Kataev and Zarudin as advocates. They took his story "In the Town of Berdichev" to the major writers' newspaper, the *Literary Gazette*, where it appeared on April 2, spread over an unprecedented two feuilletons. There was an immediate explosion of interest: the *Literary Gazette* received a flood of response from readers and writers. The paper organized a discussion, inviting Grossman and literary critics. Opinions were poles apart: some said that "In the Town of Berdichev" "surpassed all of Babel"; others thought Grossman had made a strong beginning "like Tolstoy." Still others were critical, accusing him "of all mortal sins." All this shouting and noise left Grossman with a bad taste. He had expected a serious conversation about literature; instead, there was just "blather, squabbling, and stupid shouting."[31]

Other leading Soviet writers—Babel, Bulgakov, Gorky, and Pilnyak— had also noticed the story. Pilnyak (Boris Vogau), who gained notoriety with his 1926 novella *Tale of the Unextinguished Moon*, extended his congratulations to Grossman through the newspaper and said he wanted to meet him. (Pilnyak's novella implied that Stalin was responsible for the death of Mikhail Frunze, a major military commander in the civil war. The novella was confiscated immediately upon publication and the entire issue of *Novy mir* in which it had appeared had to be reissued with a replacement story. The work eventually secured a death sentence for its author.) As Grossman discovered later, Bulgakov expressed surprise that "it's still possible to publish something decent."[32] For Grossman, Babel's praise was particularly valuable. The writer of Russian Jewry, whose collection *Red Cavalry* became internationally famous, said that "Berdichev" was a fresh look "at our Jewish capital." (Babel served as a reporter, propagandist, and staff officer in Semyon Budenny's First Cavalry Army, where he was the only Jew among the Cossacks.)[33] Grossman admired *Red Cavalry* and read *Odessa Stories* many times.[34] "The Town of

Berdichev" reveals that *Red Cavalry* had some influence on Grossman, at least in the subject matter. Grossman's story also depicts the Polish offensive during the civil war and a Red cavalry platoon led by Commissar Vavilova.

But while Babel explores revolutionary violence and masculinity, Grossman's story delves into the feminine world to find humanity and love. "In the Town of Berdichev" was unlike anything written about the civil war: after much bloodshed, with millions dead, it was an affirmation of a single human life. Revolutionary struggle, which served as the basis for most Soviet stories and novels at the time, is left in the background. Instead, Grossman's story is concerned with human beings and their choices. It was the first to draw attention to the fate of women during the war. Commissar Vavilova becomes pregnant and stays in Berdichev for the birth. Until then nobody in her platoon regards her as a woman: "Always with her Mauser, always in leather trousers. She's led the battalion into the attack any number of times. She doesn't even have the voice of a woman."[35] Vavilova grapples to understand her new role as a mother-to-be. In her world there is no place for love, femininity, and a child. But nature proves stronger than her: although she had tried to induce an abortion many times, "the child had obstinately gone on growing, making it hard for her to move, making it hard for her to ride." The transformation of the commissar into a loving mother fascinates her hosts, the Magazanik family: " 'You wouldn't believe it,' Beila said to her husband. 'That Russian woman's gone off her head. She's already rushed to the doctors with him three times. . . . In a word, she's turned into a good Jewish mother.' " The scene of the child's birth, of welcoming a new person into the world, is revelatory: even the blind grandmother joins the family and smiles "at the great miracle. . . . She wanted to hear the voice of ever-victorious life."[36] But the Poles are advancing on the city, pushing out the Reds, and the young Bolshevik cadets stay behind to cover the retreat. As they march toward the front, Vavilova joins them to die for the revolution. The idea of personal sacrifice for the cause was a contemporary cliché, but a mother abandoning her ten-day-old baby was unheard of. Grossman made the reader see the conflict in an entirely new way. His story instantly gained international recognition: in April, within days of publication, it was translated into German.

Gorky praised the story and invited Grossman to his residence.[37] He had a great respect for the Jewish people and their historic role. Having witnessed a pogrom in Nizhny Novgorod in 1887, Gorky believed in the need to fight anti-Semitism by introducing the Russian reader to Yiddish literature and literature by Russian Jewish writers. In the essay "Russia and the Jews" he expresses admiration for the Jewish nation and "its unconquerable faith in the victory of good over evil, in the possibility of happiness on earth."[38] He goes on to say that the Jews saved the world from submissiveness with their energy "and the tireless pursuit of truth." Russians had much to learn from the Jews about getting things done: "In the matter of both personal gain and service to society, the Jew invests more passion than the long-winded Russian and, in the final analysis, whatever nonsense anti-Semites might talk, they do not like the Jew because he is obviously better, more dexterous, and more capable than they are."[39] It was, therefore, not surprising that Gorky patronized Babel, praising him as "a Soviet Gogol."[40] He also employed Babel as a reporter and staff writer in his newspaper *Novaya zhizn'* (New Life). When, after the publication of *Red Cavalry*, General Semyon Budenny attacked Babel in *Pravda*, Gorky defended the young writer. Babel expressed his gratitude by dedicating to Gorky "The Story of My Dovecot."[41]

On May 5, Grossman arrived at Gorky's residence, an impressive downtown mansion designed by the prominent architect Fyodor Shekhtel in 1902. Before the revolution, it had belonged to the millionaire Sergei Ryabushinsky, who in 1916 cofounded Russia's first automobile plant with his brother Stepan. The Soviet government assigned the mansion to Gorky after his return from abroad. Grossman's meeting with Gorky included supper and lasted an entire evening, until midnight.

> The conversation interested me a great deal. We discussed eternal subjects—humanity, love, progress, religion, happiness, science. Some of his [Gorky's] remarks struck me as novel and original. He approved of my decision to fully dedicate myself to literature, was avidly interested in my new book, which I had begun writing [*Stepan Kolchugin*], and with regards to *Glückauf* and the short stories he read earlier, he had this to say: "*Glückauf* should be more condensed, the short stories [reveal] your considerable growth." Then he smiled and said, "Actually, I don't think you really need to be told compliments." At supper, he told various Volga stories—of captains, sailors, fishermen. What can I say? Such meetings are unforgettable; they remain with you for life.[42]

Gorky considered writing an introduction to *Glückauf*, but could not do so. On May 11, his son, Max, died of pneumonia; Gorky was devastated and unable to work for a long time.[43] Max died in murky circumstances. He had been drinking with Gorky's secretary, Pyotr Kryuchkov, and was left lying on the ground on a freezing night, perhaps deliberately. Genrikh Yagoda, the future chief of the NKVD (the People's Commissariat for Internal Affairs, which replaced the OGPU), was in love with Max's wife, Timosha, and is believed to have plotted Max's death.[44]

Grossman had another informal meeting with Gorky, this time at his luxurious dacha off the Rublyovo-Uspensky highway, in the same area as the dachas of Soviet government officials. The proletarian writer lived at the former estate of the textile mogul Savva Morozov. According to Gedda Surits, Grossman traveled there with the writer Konstantin Paustovsky.[45] Later, in the story "A Young Woman and an Old Woman," Grossman would depict the dachas of senior government officials.

Gorky's endorsement boosted Grossman's career. In a few months he rose from a virtual unknown to a writer whose prose was sought by literary journals and book publishers. In April Gorky had sent Grossman's short story about traveling in Altai to the *Literary Gazette*. He also included Grossman as a contributor on two prestigious projects: the collection *People of the Second Five-Year Plan,* with Gorky and Bukharin as editors, and a book about construction of the Magnitogorsk Iron and Steel Works. Grossman's opportunities were growing daily. In the next two years, he would publish the short story collections *Happiness* (1935) and *Four Days* (1936), produce film scripts, and bring out the first volume of *Stepan Kolchugin.*

In spring 1934 he was so busy that he declined to join his father on another summer expedition to Altai. "I'm thriving," Grossman wrote him, describing his literary affairs. "The only trouble, and it's a serious and big trouble, is that I'm completely alone here. People close to me—Mama, you, Nadya—are thousands of kilometers away. But in joy as in sorrow, or, perhaps even more so, one needs close, dear people."[46] Grossman was now able to help his father financially and send some money to Galya, who was hard up. Nadya wrote frequently. She married in exile, and Grossman was pleased: "Why do you think the news is unpleasant to me?" he asked his father. "I understood how deeply alone she was, and I had been wishing she would find a way out of this condition."[47]

Even though Grossman had friends among writers, he continued to lament his solitude: "I'm alone in the city with 3.5 million people," he complained that year. A brief reunion with his father in Moscow was a welcome experience. Now sixty-four, Semyon Osipovich was inspecting coal mines in Prokopievsk, a mining city in Kuzbas, Western Siberia, and the Gulag country.[48] Grossman advised him to apply for work at the Central Council of Trade Unions or seek employment as an engineer at a Moscow factory. Grossman's stepmother, a medical doctor, could secure a job at a Moscow clinic.

Grossman also mused about taking his daughter to Moscow, of going to the zoo with her and discussing which animal is bigger—an elephant or hippopotamus. In May, he traveled to see his mother and daughter in Berdichev. Katya remembers her father's visit: "One day, the whole house came alive. 'Papa arrived! Papa!' He grabbed me and lifted me high in the air. Next, I remember sitting in my grandmother's room, on her bed. And my father, cheerful, young, is sitting opposite me in a low, tapestry-covered armchair, and reciting [Korney] Chukovsky's children's verse. He speaks loudly, quickly, energetically. And I like him so much, although I'm somewhat bewildered by the flood of words."[49]

When Grossman wrote about his loneliness, his father understood correctly that he was in the mood for marriage. As a rising literary star, Grossman's company was sought, but most of his friends were men. He had recently joined an informal literary association, Konotop. It united a number of well-known authors, editors, and literary critics: Konstantin Paustovsky, Arkady Gaidar, Alexander Roskin, Vasily Bobryshev, Andrei Platonov, and Semyon Gekht attended this group.[50] The gatherings were held at the downtown apartment of a children's writer, Ruvim Fraerman, whose wife, Valentina, served the kind of pies for which the city of Konotop had once been famous.[51] Grossman maintained close friendship with some of the writers he met at Fraerman's apartment over the years—Bobryshev, Gekht, Platonov, and Roskin as well as Fraerman.

He also befriended writers from the literary group Pereval, disbanded in 1932. Among its members were Kataev and Zarudin, who had orchestrated the publication of "In the Town of Berdichev." Grossman became particularly close to Boris Guber, a writer and poet of German descent. Guber's grandfather Edward was the first translator of Goethe's *Faust* into Russian and a friend of Alexander Pushkin. Pereval had been founded in 1923 by Alexander Voronsky, a prominent critic and Marxist, the first editor of

Krasnaya Nov'. This politically innocuous group comprised over fifty writers who recognized the importance of reflecting socialist ideology in works of literature and art; their aesthetics preceded socialist realism.[52] Nonetheless, in 1930 Pereval came under attack for leaning toward the cult of the artist rather than the Party.[53] Although Pereval members were loyal to the Soviet state, many of them, including Voronsky, who formerly belonged to Trotsky's Left Opposition, were annihilated during the Great Purge. In 1937 the NKVD referred to Pereval as "an organizational base for Trotskyists."[54]

The Pereval members had been under surveillance since 1931: a fellow writer and informer, Pyotr Pavlenko, reported on their gatherings to the secret police. As apparent from his denunciations, Guber, Kataev, and Voronsky were critical of Stalin's agricultural policies and food requisitioning. In 1931 Guber spoke about the man-made famine he witnessed in Kazakhstan. (From 1929 to 1933 1.5 million ethnic Kazakhs died of starvation after the authorities blocked their nomadic routes and requisitioned their livestock.)[55] Kataev told of grain requisitioning in the Volga region where collective farmers were left with nothing and faced starvation. Voronsky, more forthright than others, "spoke of Stalin's dictatorship, and [said] that the revolution was failing."[56] Upon entering this circle, Grossman became a political suspect as well. In 1934, at a turning point in Soviet history, his name began to appear in the informer's reports to the NKVD. That year, after Sergei Kirov's murder on December 1, Stalin launched preparations for the Great Purge. Kirov was the head of the Leningrad Party organization and his murder, the only known assassination of a Politburo member in Soviet history, would be avenged in an unimaginable scale.[57] Stalin used it as a pretext to eradicate even potential opposition. Thus, in February–March 1935, over eleven thousand "remnants of the defeated bourgeoisie" were deported from Leningrad to northern Russia. In the coming months cities were purged of "criminal and déclassé elements." The NKVD compiled lists of political suspects. including those conducting "counterrevolutionary conversations."[58]

In summer 1934 Grossman traveled with a writers' brigade to Magnitogorsk in the Urals to collaborate on a history of the largest iron and steel works in the country. "This project strikes me as very interesting. Studying the gigantic construction of the First Five-Year Plan means . . . comprehending the essence of the epoch."[59] But at the end of July, after touring the plant and meeting the workers, he no longer sounded enthusiastic about his part in the project. "The plant itself is very impressive: I couldn't imagine such mammoth blast furnaces, producing 1,500 tons of pig iron daily! Some kind of Vesuvius. I met many interesting, even remarkable people—heroes of construction. But on the whole, my impression is complex and divided because of many contradictions, often appalling. The [workers'] living conditions are very hard."[60] Grossman could not overlook that their writers' brigade, expected to produce a glorious book about industrial achievements, was lodged in apartments incomparably better than those of the workers, fed and looked after "like tsars."[61]

Grossman declined to participate in the history of Magnitka but agreed to collaborate on a book about how people were faring in the First and Second Five-Year Plans. This time his coauthors were men he trusted, Kataev and Zarudin. They would write about the workers of Russia's oldest car manufacturer. Cofounded by the Ryabushinsky brothers, the plant was now named after Stalin. The lucrative contract promised 4,000 rubles for one hundred pages of prose; in addition, the hands-on research paid a monthly stipend of 600 rubles. Beginning in November, Grossman, Kataev, and Zarudin worked at a small assembly line where they built motors. "I work at the plant. . . . It's fascinating—people and the work."[62] At the start, the writers lived in the workers' settlement near the plant, sharing a single room.[63] But Grossman discovered he could write only when he was alone, so he rented a room in Begovaya Street.

After his initial spell of success, Grossman encountered the "first pebbles" on his literary path. In September, censors at Glavlit, which held final authority over publishing, removed his short stories, already in proofs, from the literary magazine *Tridtsat' dnei* (Thirty Days). The stories were deemed ideologically unsound.[64] Undeterred, Grossman reasoned that his path was "not an easy one" and that there would be greater obstacles on it.[65] He felt a calling to become a writer, and was happy that he could strive to realize his dream.

Grossman had a great capacity for work and could handle diverse literary projects simultaneously. The first part of his novel *Stepan Kolchugin*, which he submitted to Gorky's almanac in summer, describes life in a mining town through the eyes of a boy, Stepan, whose father was killed in an explosion. This novel would become a Soviet best seller, but while editors in the almanac liked it, Gorky's response was "more than sour." Grossman was "not delighted" by the news but felt confident, deducing that it was "impossible to be liked by everyone"; he was not a cheerful good-looking blond with bright-blue eyes.[66] By then Grossman had met Olga Guber, his friend's wife, who was that kind of attractive, likable blonde. But in the fall of 1934, when he wrote this, he was so occupied at the plant that he had "no time to think of personal life."[67] The affair would not develop until the following year.

Grossman's name now appeared frequently in newspapers and magazines. Every major paper reviewed *Glückauf*; it was both praised and attacked in a lengthy article published by the *Literary Gazette*. Meantime, Grossman was writing a film script based on the novel. In 1935 he traveled to the Donbass to refresh his impressions and visited Kadievka, a mining town and "a true socialist city."[68] Kadievka would soon become famous across the country and internationally for the record of productivity set on August 31 by Alexei Stakhanov, a local jackhammer operator. During his shift Stakhanov mined 102 tons of coal, fourteen times his quota. Few contemporaries knew, however, that Stakhanov's record was meticulously planned by local Party officials and the mine's management. Stakhanov worked with two assistants, who remained obscure, and with the best tools; in addition, he was assigned the easiest stretch of the mine. The Party people made sure that Stakhanov's work proceeded without a hitch. The local newspaper editor was present on the spot to report the record.

In September, working under similar conditions, Stakhanov doubled his previous achievement. During Stalin's industrialization this fake productivity served as a propaganda tool. The Party promptly launched the Stakhanovite movement, pressing to increase output in every industry through shock work; people had to work more for the same pay. In December Stakhanov's picture appeared on the cover of *Time* magazine in the United States: during the Depression the story could not fail to impress. Stakhanov received two Orders of Lenin and became part of the Soviet nomenklatura. Summoned to Moscow, he lived opposite the Kremlin in the famous House of Government, also known as the House on the Embankment. After Stalin's death Stakhanov was sent back to the Donbass, where he died of alcoholism.[69]

The Party's unrealistic goals for the Five-Year Plans could be achieved only through such shock work. Stakhanovites were said to exceed the norms by 1,000 percent.[70] These achievements were glorified in novels and films, such as Yuri Krymov's *Tanker Derbent* and Sergei Yutkevich's *The Miners*. In *Glückauf*, Grossman describes coal miners as a gray, listless crowd, their faces "austere and apathetic"—completely unlike those exuberant crowds of Stakhanovites in contemporary pictures.[71] Actually, his film was left uncompleted: in 1936 the Soviet-German studio, Mezhrabpomfilm, which had been producing *Glückauf,* was liquidated. Had the film been launched, it would have united Grossman's work with Andrei Platonov's: the studio had contracted him to revise the script. Grossman did not travel to the Donbass for the filming.[72]

In 1935 Grossman's affair with Olga Mikhailovna Guber, or Lyusya, as he called her, became official. In summer, with money from the film script, Grossman rented a dacha in Vnukovo, near Moscow, and spent a few months there with Olga and her two young sons, Fedya and Misha.[73] In October Olga left her husband and the boys, aged four and nine, and their comfortable home in Spaso-Peskovsky Lane in the prestigious Arbat neighborhood. At first the couple stayed with Olga's sister, Yevgeniya, who also lived in the Arbat district, making it easier for Olga to visit her children. Because of the housing shortages in Moscow, Grossman was unable to secure a place of his own until 1937, when he obtained two bedrooms in a communal apartment near the music conservatory on Herzen Street (now Bryusov Lane, 2). Until then, Grossman and Olga lived with relatives at their apartments where, despite distractions, he continued to write.

In his relationships with women, Grossman, like Babel, usually sought out non-Jewish partners.[74] Like Galya, Grossman's first wife, Olga was Ukrainian. She and Guber had married in a Christian Orthodox church in the mid-1920s. According to her granddaughter Elena Kozhichkina, Olga altered her actual date of birth to appear about the same age as her first husband, Guber, who was born in 1903. She was actually five years older than Guber and seven years Grossman's senior. Guber was in love with his wife and proud of her beauty; he himself applied makeup to her long eyelashes, saying they looked like butterflies. He was not faithful to her, however; he had casual affairs. But her involvement with Grossman came as a blow and left him depressed.

Olga did not have a career and was uninterested in literature; however, she typed Guber's poetry and prose and would later type for Grossman. Strong-willed and independent, Olga loved guns and duck hunting. She had grown up on her parents' estate near Sochi, by the Black Sea. Her father, Mikhail Nikolaevich Sochevets, was an agronomist, a graduate of the Moscow Petrovo-Razumovskaya Academy. He owned a small estate with a fruit orchard, vineyard, and livestock. There, the Sochevets' seven children were raised in a lovely setting by the mountainside and the sea. In 1928, when the campaign against the kulaks was launched, Sochevets subdivided the estate to save his family from being dispossessed. His son Nikolai, twenty-one, received half the land and livestock. Nonetheless, the Sochevets family was still listed as kulaks. In winter 1930 the family (with the exception of three eldest daughters, Maria, Olga, and Yevgeniya, who lived separately) was deported to the Urals in an unheated freight train. The journey took a month; the Sochevets family survived the transport, but many others died en route. Only Olga's brother Nikolai outlived the exile of seventeen years. His incomplete university education as an economist helped him find a job as an accountant near Sverdlovsk. Upon returning to European Russia in 1947, Nikolai settled with his eldest sister Maria in Moscow.[75] Nikolai would become Grossman's close friend and a source for the novel *Everything Flows*.

Although the regime destroyed her family, Olga remained apolitical. Her main interests were mineralogy and jewelry making. A passionate collector of semiprecious stones, she made regular expeditions to the writers' colony in Koktebel to collect carnelian and other gems on beaches in the Crimea. Olga loved her stone collection more than people, her granddaughter says, and this made her completely unlike Grossman. They were opposites: she loved things—jewelry, clothes, furniture, dishes, and paintings. "She was tough, overbearing, and adamantly stubborn. . . . It was difficult to touch her heart."[76] The boys were traumatized by their mother's departure and almost two years of separation. When Olga visited, little Fedya would clutch her, screaming hysterically and begging her to stay. Misha, five years older, took it more stoically.

Olga and Guber officially divorced on May 25, 1936. Three days later Grossman and Olga registered their marriage.[77] After leaving her husband and sons to join Grossman, Olga had faced condemnation from family and friends. Grossman's mother struggled to understand how Olga could walk away from her sons. In November she wrote to Semyon Osipovich: "I'm overcome with pity for Guber and the children. What has she done . . .?! Is her feeling so deep and serious?" Ekaterina Savelievna also disapproved of her son for breaking up his friend's marriage.[78]

Grossman did not feel good about the situation either. He visited Guber, made peace with his friend, and prevailed on him to take money for the children's upbringing. In a November letter to his father Grossman sounded cautiously optimistic about his future with Olga: "Now of my family affairs. It seems the situation has improved a bit. Boris Andreevich [Guber] remains at the Arbat apartment, his life has returned to normal (relatively, of course); he works a lot; I saw him twice, we talked about everything like friends. Olga Mikhailovna and I live very well together, harmoniously. And I don't know, maybe this is for the worse, but I feel increasingly happy about our life together."[79]

5. The Dread New World

Murder in those terrible days became a duty.
—Alexander Herzen, *From the Other Shore*

All those arrested—however famous or however unknown—were innocent.
—Vasily Grossman, *Life and Fate*

Having starved and enslaved the peasantry, Stalin moved on to subjugate the entire population of the USSR, treating millions of his own people as the enemy. During the three show trials conducted in Moscow between 1936 and 1938, the entire revolutionary generation of the Old Bolsheviks was destroyed. The military purge Stalin had secretly orchestrated in 1937 stripped the Red Army of its senior commanders. The best and the brightest among writers, artists, and scientists also perished during the purges. In *Life and Fate*, Victor Shtrum laments "dozens of people who had left and never returned," among them geneticist Nikolai Vavilov, writers Mandelstam, Babel, and Pilnyak, and theater director Vsevolod Meyerhold.[1] Vavilov had built the first international seed bank of food plants and aspired to end famine throughout the world. Denounced and arrested in 1940, he died in prison of starvation, an event Grossman mentions in *Everything Flows*.

The writers' community was hit hard by the purges: of the two thousand writers who were arrested, only five hundred returned from prisons and labor camps.[2] As Mandelstam had said, "Poetry is respected only in this country—people are killed for it. There's no place where more people are killed for it."[3] Shalamov remembered that in the 1930s people received death sentences for possessing an issue of *Novy mir* with Pilnyak's banned novella,

Tale of the Unextinguished Moon.[4] Pilnyak was among prominent writers who had welcomed Grossman's story "In the Town of Berdichev." When he was arrested 1937, the police burned his papers in the yard of his Peredelkino dacha in the writers' settlement. Pilnyak's prose was translated in many countries, including America and Japan; he traveled widely and was friends with Theodore Dreiser and Sinclair Lewis. His renown and friendship with Bernard Shaw and H. G. Wells, both of whom admired Stalin's Soviet Union, did not save him from a horrible fate. Their letters to Pilnyak, along with those by Romain Rolland, Stephan Zweig, and major Russian writers— Akhmatova, Bulgakov, Pasternak, Platonov, Sergei Esenin, and Evgeny Zamyatin—were incinerated. The bonfire fueled by these letters and Pilnyak's manuscripts burned for two days.[5] In April 1938 Pilnyak was sentenced to death during a "trial" that lasted fifteen minutes.

During the Stalin era most genuine writers were forced to create works for the desk drawer. Pasternak turned to literary translation. Babel remarked that he was practicing "the art of silence." However, even his silence would come to be seen as a crime. Although Babel could not publish what he wrote, he was working productively. In the eyes of the state he was committing an offense. When his Lubyanka interrogator pressed him to explain "the real reason" for his arrest, the writer replied, "During the last few years I have not published a single major work and this might be considered sabotage and an unwillingness to write under Soviet conditions."[6] (The Lubyanka interrogators forced inmates to incriminate themselves, pressing them to explain why they were arrested. As Solzhenitsyn writes in *The Gulag Archipelago*, this was often the first question.)

After Babel's arrest, not even his family knew what happened to him. As his daughter, Nathalie Babel, writes, "He disappeared. Not a trace, not a word. He vanished. His lodgings were searched and every scrap of paper was confiscated—correspondence, drafts, manuscripts, everything. None of it has ever resurfaced. His name, his works were officially erased as though he had never existed."[7] Nobody knows how many artistic works perished in the Lubyanka furnaces. Babel's novel about the Cheka, seized during his arrest on May 15, 1939, has never been found. Twenty-four folders of his manuscripts confiscated at the time were likely destroyed. The writers' disappearance during the purges (and Pilnyak, Mandelstam, and Babel simply vanished, along with every mention of their names) filled others with dread.

Grossman's correspondence for 1936–39 does not survive except for a few minor letters. Most people were then afraid of keeping archives. In 1936 his life was uneventful, a blessing in those days. In November he completed a first volume of *Stepan Kolchugin*, a well-written historical novel that became genuinely popular. That same month his collection of short stories, *Four Days*, was reviewed in *Pravda*. The review was neither "overly negative" nor extremely positive; what mattered was official endorsement of his career.[8] *Pravda* articles were read with trepidation: they defined careers and destinies. Earlier that year the paper attacked Shostakovich's opera *Lady Macbeth* and his ballet *The Bright Stream*, the latter in a piece entitled "False Notes in the Ballet." An article with a similar title, "Superficial Glitter and False Content," condemned Bulgakov's play *Moliere*—after it was performed with resounding success.

The old two-story house on Herzen Street where Grossman settled with his family in 1937 stood opposite the music conservatory. Here Grossman would spend a decade, producing *Stepan Kolchugin*, short stories, a play, and a portion of his novel about Stalingrad, *For the Right Cause*.[9] Formerly a merchant's spacious flat with thick walls, it became communal property after the revolution; several families shared a single kitchen. Grossman and Olga occupied two bedrooms with the boys, their nanny Natalya Darenskaya, and their German governess Jenny Genrikhovna Genrikhson. In *Life and Fate* Grossman uses the latter's real name: "Old Jenny Genrikhovna was a meek, timid, obliging creature." He also describes their dwelling: the bedrooms were subdivided "by screens, curtains, rugs, backs of sofas into little nooks and corners—one for eating, one for sleeping, one for receiving guests."[10] The flat was crowded; still, it was Grossman's first real home in Moscow. Here, in the dreadful summer of 1937, he anticipated arrest, his own and Olga's; from here, in summer 1941, he would leave for the front.

In June 1936 *Pravda* published Gorky's health bulletins. Gorky was among the few Soviet writers and public figures to die of natural causes: he developed bronchial pneumonia in addition to the tuberculosis he suffered over the years. Nonetheless, his death on June 18 generated unending speculation. In 1938, during Bukharin's public trial, the former head of the NKVD, Yagoda, and Gorky's secretary, Kryuchkov, along with the doctors who treated him, were accused of murdering the writer. While these doctors were rehabilitated during the Khrushchev era, Yagoda and Kryuchkov were not, suggesting that the Party continued to believe Stalin's version of events.

Speeding up Gorky's demise would have been convenient for Stalin: he was preparing Lev Kamenev and Grigory Zinoviev's trial when the writer lay dying. The two Old Bolsheviks had been members of Lenin's first Politburo, and Kamenev was married to Trotsky's sister Olga. Gorky was Kamenev's friend, and might possibly have defended him if he had known about the press campaign to blacken his reputation in advance of the trial. So, when *Pravda* campaigned against Kamenev and Zinoviev, false issues of the newspaper were printed especially for Gorky.[11]

Since 1933, when he returned from Italy for good, Gorky had lived under surveillance. His secretary Kryuchkov, whom Yagoda recruited from the OGPU, was part of the surveillance team. The government granted Gorky a generous allowance and several mansions. Aside from the Ryabushinsky mansion in Moscow and a dacha formerly belonging to Savva Morozov, he was assigned a villa in the Crimea—where his staff consisted of secret police agents.

When Gorky died, Korney Chukovsky wrote in his diary that he was grieved by the news. "How often I misunderstood him. He was so full of contradictions."[12] This comment also reflected Grossman's attitude. In *Everything Flows* he would accuse Gorky of complicity with the regime, of keeping silence during the famine in Ukraine: "Did Gorky not know about the children stacked on the cart? . . . Or maybe Gorky did know—and kept silent, like everyone kept silent."[13] Gorky became an apologist for the regime, and was even manipulated into endorsing the Gulag with its gigantic construction sites. The White Sea Canal, known as the Belomor, employed approximately 170,000 Gulag prisoners of whom by some estimates at least 25,000 perished.[14] Working with primitive tools the inmates excavated the 227-kilometer canal and built five dams and nineteen locks. In 1934 Gorky edited a book on the Belomor construction in which he praised the OGPU in reforming prisoners: "You have done a great thing—a very great thing!"[15]

When Gorky died, mourning flags were flown across the country. As his body lay in state in the House of Unions, writers, of whom Alexei Tolstoy now emerged as the regime's favorite, replacing Gorky, stood as honor guards. Platonov, who would become Grossman's friend and whom Stalin despised and called "scum," was among them. Grossman, not yet a member of the writers' union, may have merged with the crowd. Stalin and Molotov were among the pallbearers who carried Gorky's ashes to be interred in a niche in the Kremlin Wall, an honor bestowed on only a select few. Leading the procession was Tolstoy, walking a few steps ahead of Stalin. (Count Alexei Tolstoy, the namesake of his great predecessor, was a talented but unprincipled writer. In 1923 he returned to Soviet Russia with a group of émigrés who had fled after the revolution. His historical novels, such as *Peter I* and *Ordeal*, were meant to justify repressions and flatter Stalin. In 1937 he was elected to the Supreme Soviet, effectively sharing responsibility for the regime's crimes.)

In August 1936, weeks after Gorky's death, the first of Moscow's three spectacular trials opened in the same House of Unions. *Pravda* reported daily on the proceedings of "the United Trotskyite-Zinovievite Center," or the trial of the Sixteen, in which Kamenev and Zinoviev were star defendants. Not leaving anything to chance, Stalin himself dictated the text of the charges to the procurator-general, Andrei Vyshinsky.[16] Stalin also edited the verdicts, telling Lazar Kaganovich in the Politburo to cross out superfluous words, such as "the sentence is final and cannot be appealed."[17] The defendants were charged with being part of a Trotsky-led conspiracy, murdering Sergei Kirov, secretly allying with the Gestapo, and plotting to assassinate Soviet leaders, including Stalin himself. The 350 spectators at the trial—mainly NKVD employees, foreign journalists, and diplomats—watched the show, in which the defendants resignedly admitted their "crimes." These were broken men: during preparations for the trial Stalin demanded that pressure be redoubled to achieve confessions. Prominent Soviet politicians who had been Lenin's closest associates stood disgraced. Having admitted to plotting against the Soviet state, they erased their own legacy. Their physical destruction was now inevitable.

Pravda's editor, Lev Mekhlis, discussed with Stalin how best to publicize the trial. The newspaper filled its pages with bloodthirsty articles and collective letters, demanding execution for the accused, who were presented as less than human: "The Country Denounces Vile Murderers," "Death to Kirov's Murderers!" "One Hundred and One Nights of Trotsky's and Gestapo's Spies." The editorial on August 23 read: "The Rabid Dogs Must Be Shot!" Petitions supporting the death penalty were solicited from workers' collectives as well as from artists, scientists, and writers. Among writers whose signatures were sought, Pasternak alone refused to comply. Nonetheless, his name appeared in *Pravda*'s issue of August 21 underneath the open letter by writers entitled "Erase from the Face of the Earth!" Pasternak was added to the list by functionaries of the writers' union: they needed his spotless reputation for their campaign's credibility. On August 24, five days after the start of the trial, *Pravda* came out with this headline: "The Military Collegium of the Supreme Court of the USSR Expressed the People's Will of Our Great Motherland: THE FOUL TROTSKYIST-ZINOVIEVITE MURDERERS, WHO SOLD THEMSELVES TO THE FASCISTS, ARE SENTENCED TO BE SHOT." In *Life and Fate* Grossman depicts the disgraced Old Bolsheviks standing in the House of Unions and listening to the "inhuman, sonorous" voice of Prosecutor Vyshinsky as he accuses them of plotting to overthrow the Soviet regime. Remembering this, his protagonist Krymov thinks what Grossman may have thought at the time: "Why did they all confess? And why do I keep silent?"[18] Stalin's campaigns against enemies of the people and denunciation hysteria had a powerful demoralizing effect.

Stalin, however, was unhappy with the pace and scale of the repressions. In September 1936, in a telegram to the Politburo, he demanded the replacement of Yagoda, the people's commissar of internal affairs, with Nikolai Yezhov: "We consider it absolutely essential to appoint Com. Yezhov as people's commissar of internal affairs. Yagoda was obviously not up to the task of exposing the Trotskyite-Zinovievite bloc. The OGPU is four years late in accomplishing this task."[19] A ruthless and zealous apparatchik, Yezhov had risen swiftly in his career, from a worker at the prerevolutionary Petersburg Putilov plant to influential positions in the Party. Stalin appointed him as chief of the Central Committee's Personnel Department. There, Yezhov had conducted a commission for purging the Party, worked to strengthen the loyalty of OGPU (renamed NKVD in 1934) personnel and, most recently, assisted Stalin in preparing the Kamenev-Zinoviev trial.

As the head of the NKVD, the position he held until April 1938, Yezhov conducted the Great Purge, a series of operations to eliminate all those the Stalinist leadership considered a potential threat. On July 30, 1937, the NKVD proposed Order No. 00447, directed against "anti-Soviet elements" such as former kulaks, who had already served their prison terms, surviving tsarist officials, and the like. The Politburo approved the order the next day, and on August 5 the large-scale operation was launched across the USSR. The NKVD received 75 million rubles of reserve money to cover "operational expenses" such as prisoner transport. An additional 10 million rubles was designated for the Gulag NKVD of the USSR to organize concentration camps.[20] Each region and republic was assigned quotas for arrests and executions. Local authorities were allowed to request additional quotas. With Moscow's encouragement, the initial plan for mass murder was overfulfilled. From summer 1937 to November 1938, approximately 1.6 million people were arrested, and 700,000 of them were shot.[21] This doesn't include the many unknown people who died in NKVD torture chambers and the untold thousands who perished in the Gulag from starvation and overwork.[22]

Yezhov also conducted the purge of the Red Army. Unlike civilian "enemies of the people," who were afforded public trials, the country's top military commanders had their fate decided in deep secrecy by Stalin, Yezhov, and Marshal Vorozhilov. On June 11, 1937, *Pravda* announced that eight Red Army commanders had been charged with treason and spying for Fascist Germany. On June 12, newspapers began campaigning for death penalties. By then, however, these generals had already been executed. Marshal Mikhail Tukhachevsky, credited with the modernization of the Red Army; Commanders Iona Yakir, Ieronim Uborevich, and August Kork; and Corps Commanders Eideman, Putna, Feldman, and Primakov were framed in the case of the "Trotskyist Anti-Soviet Military Organization." Within days of their execution, 980 senior officers were arrested.[23] The military purges continued in waves over several years. On the eve of World War II, Stalin destroyed the country's entire military leadership, purging between 30,000 to 40,000 senior officers and nearly all of his General Staff.[24] In 1941 Grossman would witness at the front the tragic consequences of Stalin's military purges. The dictator's responsibility for the devastating Soviet losses in World War II is a main theme of *Life and Fate*.

In June 1937 Grossman's close friends—the writers Guber, Kataev, and Zarudin—were arrested. Grossman's own life was in jeopardy: he could easily have been found guilty by association, a fate that befell thousands at the time. In *Life and Fate*, describing Moscow that summer during the height of the purges, he pictures Krymov walking past the NKVD headquarters.

> The dark, stifling streets were deserted. For all the thousands of
> people inside, the building seemed quite dead. . . . The silence was
> anything but peaceful. A few windows were lit up; you could
> glimpse faint shadows through the white curtains. . . . Krymov had

thought of the various people he knew. Their distance from him was something that couldn't be even measured in space—they existed in another dimension. No power on earth or in heaven could bridge this abyss, an abyss as profound as death itself.[25]

Guber, Kataev, and Zarudin were acquainted with Yezhov's wife, Yevgeniya (née Feigenberg), and had attended her literary salon. Among her guests were the writers Babel, Mikhail Sholokhov, and Samuil Marshak; the film director Sergei Eisenstein; the actor and director of the Moscow State Jewish Theater Solomon Mikhoels; the jazz singer and actor Leonid Utyosov (Lazar Wiessbein); and the writers of Pereval. Grossman met Yevgeniya around 1933–34 when she worked as an editor at the MTP and had attended several of her gatherings. After Yezhov was appointed head of the NKVD, his wife became unintentionally responsible for the deaths of her friends, former husbands, and lovers, including Babel.

Born into a Jewish family in Gomel, Yevgeniya had later lived in Odessa with her first husband, the journalist Lazar Hayutin. In the 1920s she married a diplomat, Alexander Gladun, and worked as a typist at the Soviet embassy in London and at the commercial mission in Berlin. As Babel would tell his NKVD interrogator, he met Yevgeniya in Berlin in 1927 and they had an affair. Later, in Moscow, she became a deputy editor of a prominent literary journal, the *USSR under Construction*, published in five languages to promote the country's image abroad; Babel was one of the contributors. Yevgeniya was a social climber; her marriage to Yezhov and her affairs with Babel as well as with Sholokhov, who was anti-Semitic, suggest she had few principles. Her union with Yezhov prompted Babel's remark, "Just think, our girl from Odessa has become the first lady of the kingdom!"[26]

A bisexual, Yezhov had affairs with both women and men, and the open marriage also suited Yevgeniya. It was her lovers and friends, however, who would pay dearly for having been close to the Soviet femme fatale. Some guests to her salon began to disappear even before Yezhov's decline. According to the NKVD's concocted account, Yevgeniya's literary salon served as a cover-up for the conspirators' plan to kill Yezhov at his own residence. In August the Pereval writers were charged with conspiring to assassinate Yezhov. Ivan Kataev was named ringleader and other writers as participants. Grossman's name was also in the NKVD report: he was allegedly invited to the Yezhov house on the night of the planned assassination. This was enough to arrest him. But during interrogations Guber denied knowing anything politically "compromising" about Grossman, which may have saved his life.[27] On August 13, 1937, the Military Collegium of the Supreme Court of the USSR, presided over by Vasily Ulrich, took twenty minutes to try Guber and to deliver a death sentence. He and Zarudin were shot that same day. Voronsky and Kataev were tormented longer and shot on August 19.[28]

Yezhov conducted operations to exterminate entire social groups. Because the state had already destroyed all apparent opposition, those now included on execution lists were former gentry and clergymen, former members of non-Bolshevk parties, and so on. Yezhov's Order No. 00486, issued on August 15, 1937, decreed that wives of "traitors of the motherland" were to be arrested and sentenced to labor camps for five to eight years. Their children of fifteen and over, being deemed "capable of anti-Soviet activity," were to be dispatched to labor colonies; younger children to special orphanages or consigned to the care of relatives. (Today we know from Yezhov's secret note to Molotov that by May 1938 the NKVD had sent 15,347 children of repressed parents to orphanages in Moscow and elsewhere in the Soviet Union.)[29] Ex-wives were not overlooked: the document stipulated that they were subject to arrest if found to have known of their former husbands' counterrevolutionary activity without reporting it.[30] Pursuant to this order, three major concentration camps for the "wives of traitors" were established in Karaganda, Mordovia, and Tomsk, where tens of thousands were sent to die.

The overworked secret police took six months after the order was issued (and after Guber's execution) to arrest Olga. In *Life and Fate* Grossman conveys his own and Olga's helplessness while anticipating arrest: "How often Victor had lain awake listening to the cars on the street! Sometimes Lyudmila had gone barefoot to the window and parted the curtains. She had stayed there for a while and watched; then, thinking that Victor was asleep, she had gone silently back to bed and lain down. In the morning she had asked: 'Did you sleep well?' 'All right, thank you. And you?' . . . How can one ever describe those nights and that extraordinary sense of both doom and innocence?"[31]

On February 7, 1938, the police arrived at Grossman's flat on Herzen Street. The NKVD agents seemed unaware that Olga and Guber were divorced. Grossman argued they could not proceed with the arrest. Apparently he was persuasive enough that the agents felt the need to consult their supervisor by telephone. They were told to proceed with the arrest. After they led Olga away, Grossman acted quickly. First he had to save Olga's sons, Fedya, six, and Misha, eleven, from being sent to special NKVD orphanages for "socially dangerous" children. As children of "enemies of the people," the brothers would have to be separated, another inhumane instruction. Guber's extended family refused to take in the boys. This was not uncommon: fearing for their safety, people distanced themselves from arrested relatives and their children, too. In some cases a grandmother would refuse to shelter her orphaned grandchild.[32] Grossman was undeterred and obtained legal guardianship from the Department of People's Education. Fedya remembers the night NKVD officials drove them in their car from the house on Spaso-Peskovsky Lane, where they had been living with their nanny, to Grossman's new flat.

Grossman appealed to many people for help and drafted letters to the government. In his letter to Yezhov he argued that Olga's case should be reviewed on the grounds that she was now his wife, not Guber's, and that the NKVD agents were unaware of this fact at the time of her detention. Grossman stressed that he and Olga had been living together since the fall of 1935 and that she made "a complete break with her former husband" long before his arrest. Quoting Stalin's maxim, "The son is not responsible for his father," he argued that a housewife and mother should not be held responsible for a former husband she had left three years earlier. "Comrade Yezhov! I fervently ask you to participate in reviewing my wife's case; I firmly believe in the humanity of our law, and hope that my wife, who during these years became my dear and loyal friend, will return to me and the children. I will await your response every hour, for I'm filled with apprehension for my wife's health and life: she suffers from a serious and complex heart disease."[33]

Grossman's letter, written in the language of the time, did not, of course, reflect his actual belief in the "humanity" of Soviet law. The Party's requirement to denounce family members was an illustration of inhumanity. By addressing Yezhov, Grossman was putting his own head in a noose. As his friend Semyon Lipkin would remark, "Only a very brave man would dare write such a letter to the main executioner of the state."[34] (That year Andrei Platonov appealed to Yezhov on behalf of his arrested son, aged 15. In 1939 Nadezhda Mandelstam sent her daring letter to Lavrenty Beria, Yezhov's successor, asking him to review her husband's case.)[35] Within weeks of his appeal, on February 25, Grossman received a summons from the Lubyanka.

On February 28, he entered the "sleepless building," "a Radiological Institute for the Diagnosis of Society," as he would later describe it.[36] His interrogator, "Comrade Vikhnich," was a junior security officer who handled cases of wives of "traitors to the motherland." Their confessions were not considered essential; Vikhnich routinely processed their cases, terrorizing women by shouting and occasional beatings. Lubyanka interrogators were often semiliterate, an additional torment for talented and complex people subjected to primitive questioning. (In 1939 Babel and Meyerhold were interrogated and tortured by Lev Schwartzmann and the brutal Boris Rodos, both elementary school dropouts.)[37]

The transcript of Grossman's interrogation shows that he did not waver. Vikhnich tried to entrap him, asking what prevented him from registering his marriage with Olga in October 1935. "Nothing prevented me. I just didn't bother." Not so, Vikhnich countered: the marriage could not be registered because Olga divorced Guber on May 25, 1936.

"Now tell me when and how much money you'd given to B. A. Guber, the enemy of the people, both through his wife and directly?" Grossman replied that he had given Guber about 2,500 rubles for the children's upkeep, but that the money "was only a loan" and had to be repaid. "Why didn't you take the children . . . to live with you?" Grossman said he had no apartment at the time. "Where are the children now?" "They live with me."[38]

Grossman left the building a free man; more surprisingly, Olga was released within a month.

Olga initially had been incarcerated within the inner prison of the Lubyanka, in a cell with only a few bunks and parquet floors. In tsarist times the main building served as the headquarters of Russia's biggest insurance company. It had a hotel inside the courtyard. In 1920, after it became the Cheka headquarters, Dzerzhinsky converted the hotel into a secret prison for so-called dangerous counterrevolutionaries and spies. The prison's large windows, now screened by metal bars, its bigger cells, and parquet floors were vestiges of the past. In *Life and Fate*, Krymov is brought into a cell "with a clean parquet floor and four bunks" in the Lubyanka.[39]

After a few weeks at the Lubyanka Olga was transferred to Lefortovo Prison, where she shared a cell with eighty women. Two months after her arrest, on April 1, 1938, she was summoned with her belongings. Olga assumed she was being sent to a labor camp. As she was led by a guard through a maze of corridors, another guard was entering with a prisoner. Olga was shoved into a niche in the wall: prisoners were not supposed to have contact. The incoming guard asked: "Where are you taking her?" "To freedom." The second guard laughed, "Happy April Fool's Day!" But this wasn't a joke: Olga was freed.

The date of her release is known from Grossman's note. He gave Olga a copy of *Glückauf* with an inscription: "Glückauf, Lyusenka! April 1, 1938."[40] Grossman considered her release nothing short of a miracle and congratulated her on a "happy lifting" from hell. Her liberation was indeed extraordinary: very few people were released at the height of the purges. Grossman was likely helped by someone at the top. Soviet premier Molotov would have been in a position to intercede, but there is no evidence to prove who helped Grossman prevail.[41]

Olga believed that she and the boys would definitely have perished if not for Grossman. The first thing she learned upon returning to their apartment was that her boys were safe.

The regime destroyed a multitude of lives and talents. During the Great Purge functionaries at the writers' union assisted the secret police in sending writers to their deaths. Vladimir Stavsky, head of the union from 1936 to 1938, denounced Mandelstam to Yezhov. In his letter of March 1938 Stavsky asked Yezhov "to help resolve the problem of Osip Mandelstam," the author of "obscene, libelous verse about the leadership of the Party and all the Soviet people." Stavsky attached a "review" of Mandelstam's poems written by Pyotr Pavlenko, the same man who had betrayed Grossman's friends, the Pereval writers."[42]

Mandelstam was arrested in May 1938 and perished in December at a transit camp in Vladivostok. The regime rewarded collaborators. Pavlenko was granted the Order of Lenin and received four Stalin Prizes, allegedly for his film scripts. The "ominous man," as Nadezhda Mandestam described Pavlenko, lived at a dacha in Peredelkino, on a street named after him.[43]

Babel's arrest became linked with Yezhov's downfall. Replaced by Beria in December 1938, Yezhov was arrested in spring and sent to the Sukhanovo special regime prison he himself had established for "particularly dangerous enemies of the people." This dreaded prison, on the grounds of a monastery outside Moscow, was equipped with a torture chamber and a crematorium.[44] In May Yezhov told his interrogators that Babel and his wife

Yevgeniya had engaged in espionage. Babel was arrested soon after Yezhov's "confession." Yevgeniya had committed suicide months earlier: knowing she was doomed, she took an overdose of sleeping pills. In early 1940 Babel and Yezhov were executed within days of each other, although Babel's fate remained unknown until 1954.

Nadezhda Mandelstam felt that Babel's "fierce curiosity" was the driving force in his life and was behind his desire to meet Yezhov and visit his household.[45] Grossman, who was never close to Babel and possibly never even met him, wondered why Babel was drawn to Yezhov and whether a rumor that he had greeted the New Year in his house was true. The poet and translator Semyon Lipkin recalls Grossman's question: "What is it— fascination with power, with people in authority?"[46]

In 1960 Grossman would write a short story about the Yezhovs and portray Babel as a visitor to their Kremlin apartment. His source for the narrative, Faina Shkol'nikova, was Yevgeniya's friend. She was also purged but survived the Gulag and returned to Moscow in 1954.

Faina inspired Grossman's splendid story "Mama" about a girl the Yezhovs adopted from an orphanage. While in reality the five-month-old baby was adopted around 1932, in "Mama" events take place at the height of the purges when Yezhov becomes head of the NKVD "and loyal comrade-in-arms to the great Stalin." In Grossman's story, the Yezhovs adopt a girl from a high-security home for "babies whose parents had been arrested as enemies of the people." Thus the child is being raised by the same man who had destroyed her family.

A Moscow orphanage is put on high alert during the visit of a senior member of Yezhov's entourage, a middle-aged NKVD officer. He comes ahead of Yezhov to ensure that the staff has picked the best-developed baby, "normal in every respect." Such selecting suggests a parallel with the Nazis. It also emphasizes the cynicism of Stalin's henchmen, who knew that a child of the "enemies of the people" was guaranteed to have good parentage.

Whether Grossman invented the identities of the girl's parents or drew on information given to him privately is unknown; in any case, he depicts a typical version of events. The baby's father, a young adviser at the Soviet embassy in London, and his lovely wife, a singer, are called back to Moscow. As was nearly everyone returning from abroad during the Great Purge, they are arrested upon arrival and liquidated. Grossman implies their tragic fate through vague images retained by the "five-month-old memory" of the baby during the final family journey from London to Russia. "And yet, without the girl knowing it, all these sounds and images—the railway station, the London fog, the splash of waves in the English Channel, the cry of gulls, the sleeping-car compartment, the faces of her mother and father bending down over her as the express approached Negoreloye Station—had managed to hide themselves away somewhere in her little head."[47] The adopted girl, named Nadya in the story, is looked after by a village nanny, a sturdy woman called Marfa Dementievna. (In the story, he used the nanny's real name but changed that of the child, whose actual name was Natalya.)

The Yezhovs entertain their guests separately and the girl soon knows that "if Father's guests were visiting, there were never any of Mama's guests." Babel arrives, naturally, in Yezhov's absence. "There was a bald man in glasses, with a smile that used to make Nadya smile too. . . . When he came in, Mama used to answer his smile . . . and say, 'Babel's come to see us!' " Yezhov was known to have been a tender father who played with his adopted daughter and spoiled her. But Grossman wondered whether a child would not sense the horrible nature of Yezhov's activity. In one of the episodes Nadya looks into her father's eyes and screams. While it is not directly explained what frightens her, later in the story the author comments: "Yezhov's gaze had frozen all of vast Russia." The following passage connects Nadya's destiny with those of tens of thousands of Yezhov's victims:

> Day and night the interrogations went on in the Lubyanka, in Lefor-
> tovo, and in the Butyrka. Day and night trains transported prisoners
> to Komi, to Kolyma, to Norilsk, to Magadan and the Bay of
> Nagaevo. Every dawn the bodies of those shot during the night in
> prison basements were taken away in trucks. Did Marfa Demen-
> tievna realize that the fate of a young adviser at the Soviet embassy
> in London, that the fate of his pretty wife, arrested while she was
> still breast-feeding her little daughter, before she had even completed
> her singing course at the conservatory—did Marfa Dementievna
> realize that these fates had been determined by the signature, at the
> foot of a long column of names, of a former Petersburg factory
> worker by the name of Nikolai Ivanovich Yezhov? He was still
> signing list after list, dozens and dozens of these enormous lists of
> enemies of the people, and the black smoke was still pushing its way
> from the crematoria of Moscow.[48]

Yezhov's arrest is described in one sentence: "And then came a day when this short man with gray-green eyes, Nikolai Ivanovich Yezhov, did not come home at all." The NKVD employees, with their "crazed eyes," conduct a night search.[49] By morning, they send Nadya to a remote orphanage in Penza. This actually happened: after Yezhov's arrest and Yevgeniya's suicide, their adopted daughter, Natalya, was sent to Penza, six hundred kilometers southeast of Moscow. Her surname was changed from Yezhova to Khayutina, and she was beaten for refusing to forget her adoptive parents. The real Natalya would remain the only person alive with good memories of Yezhov. Through her story Grossman was able to write about human destinies during an inhumane epoch.

Earlier, in 1938–40, Grossman wrote the short story "A Young Woman and an Old Woman." It reveals that he saw his contemporary Soviet society as corrupt, with an abyss separating the Party from the people. Written for the desk drawer, the story captures typical experiences of two Soviet generations. Two women, the young and the old, work together at the All-Union People's Commissariat. Their surnames—Goryacheva and Gagareva—are alike, and both speak in officially prescribed language. But their backgrounds are entirely different. The young woman has risen from being a cleaning lady in a workers' hostel to head a department in the government ministry. Her precipitous career is a surprise to her and, moreover, she wants none of her promotions. The only job she has loved and for which she willingly trained is combine harvester operator at the state grain farm in her village. During collectivization, followed by famine, her employment saved half of her family from starvation with its daily worker's ration of eight hundred grams of bread. Later, in 1937, the entire management of the state farm is swept up in arrests. Twelve people, including the farm director and the agronomist, are denounced as saboteurs and provocateurs. The provincial Party Committee promotes the denouncer, a local man, to farm director; however, he too soon disappears in the purges. This is when the young woman, at twenty-four, is forced to quit her job as combine operator to become head of the farm. Two years later an order comes for her to be transferred to Moscow, where she is given a government post she doesn't want; she attempts to protest but has to comply. A village girl, she is suddenly living the life of the Soviet and Party elite with all its trappings: "Often she had the feeling that everything was a dream—

the telephones, the secretaries, the meetings of the Presidium, the cars, her Moscow apartment, her dacha."[50] Her driver takes her on a ZIS (a luxury limousine of the kind Grossman built at the automobile plant) to a government dacha in Kuntsevo, the neighborhood where Stalin's "nearest" dacha is located. The place comes with the job, and the young woman learns that the previous occupant was arrested as an enemy of the people. All that remains of the man is a collection of pinecones he gathered on the shores of the Mediterranean. His travels to Europe were enough to frame him as a spy.

The old woman is an experienced economist. Because she is not a Party member, she cannot be promoted to head the planning department and works under her young colleague, who got the job after a crash course. The old woman's youth was consumed with revolutionary struggle and she wants to think that the sacrifices of her generation were not in vain. Her husband, also a revolutionary, served a term in a tsarist prison colony; later they lived as political émigrés in France. In 1937, two decades after the revolution, the old woman's daughter and son-in-law, an official at the People's Commissariat of Heavy Industry, are arrested and incarcerated in a Gulag. The old woman finds this hard to fathom. At night she weeps, thinking that her daughter lives in a camp barracks in Kazakhstan. But she avoids maintaining ties with her daughter for fear of being arrested by association. In fact (though the story doesn't mention this), she is lucky to be allowed to remain in Moscow: relatives of political inmates were usually deported from the city.

The young woman and the old woman travel by train to the Black Sea. They talk about the strength of socialist ideology and the might of the Soviet Army. As they discuss the Soviet-Japanese border conflicts of 1939, they use stock phrases from *Pravda*.

> "The Red Army will soon knock that out of them. This will be the last time they [the Japanese] try to get their hands on our Motherland!" said Gagareva.
> "Yes, on May Day I couldn't take my eyes off our tanks. Iron mountains—but they move fast!"
> "I didn't have the good fortune to be on Red Square myself, but I know anyway that the strength of our army lies not only in its equipment, but also in its Socialist ideology."[51]

At the Black Sea resort the young woman meets a military officer who serves in the Far East and marries him soon after. That summer he is killed in action at Khalkin-Gol, during the undeclared 1939 war between the Soviet Union and Japan. Although the Soviets have defeated the Japanese, they have suffered heavy losses, a fact that *Pravda* does not report. Yet Grossman's story has a happy ending. The old woman's luck changes from bad to good: her daughter's case is reviewed and she is expected to be released from the labor camp. However improbable, the denouement reflected a factual occurrence—the miraculous review of Olga's case and her release.

By the late 1930s Grossman had no illusions about the Stalinist regime. During the mass purges he lost friends and witnessed Olga's arrest. He read daily reports from public trials, realizing that members of the revolutionary generation that had helped Lenin create the Bolshevik Party were being tried for crimes they had never committed. He did not believe—and would state this in *Life and Fate*—that Nikolai Bukharin was a foreign spy, provocateur, and assassin.

During these years his extended family suffered, too. Uncle David, Berdichev's best doctor, was arrested in 1937 and shot. Grossman's cousin Nadya, previously banished to Astrakhan, at the time the city of exiles, was rearrested in 1936 and accused of "anti-Soviet propaganda." Nadya was dispatched to a labor camp in Vorkuta, north of the Arctic Circle, in the Komi Republic. After her term ended in 1939, she lived in internal exile in the city of Alexandrov, northeast of Moscow, beyond a so-called one-hundred-kilometer zone.[52]

Grossman's father escaped being arrested by working in Kazakhstan. During the freezing winter of 1936 he lived in a yurt; Grossman sent him warm clothes. It was a hard life for a sixty-six-year-old; however, he lived voluntarily at the edge of the Gulag, remaining relatively free.

In 1937 the former revolutionary Alexander Taratuta was shot; his family, Grossman's old friends, were banished to Tobolsk, Siberia. This was the same place where Taratuta had been deported under the tsars for revolutionary activity and from where he escaped with his wife's help. After he was shot as "the enemy of the people," his family was sent to Siberia indefinitely. In 1939 Yevgeniya Taratuta secretly returned to Moscow. An influential writer, Alexander Fadeev, through his contacts in the NKVD, helped her receive new identity papers and find employment. Gedda Surits sheltered Yevgeniya when she was hiding from authorities, and Grossman was among the writers who helped financially.

The persecution of Grossman's friend Vyacheslav Loboda was particularly revealing. After his brother was rearrested in the 1930s, Loboda spent two decades working as a school inspector and ethnographer in Chukotka. He had first traveled there with an expedition from the People's Commissariat for Agriculture, or Narkomzem. But after his brother's second arrest, he settled there permanently. Chukotka was the remotest corner of the Soviet Union, and Pevek, where Loboda raised a family, the country's northernmost town and an Arctic port. Loboda's wife, Vera Ivanovna, worked as a teacher and school principal in Pevek; their two daughters were born there. Lyudmila, the older girl, was delivered by a Gulag doctor. The area surrounding Pevek was the site of several concentration camps where prisoners mined uranium. The Kolyma labor camps lay to the south of Chukotka's border.

But even at the edge of the earth the NKVD did not lose track of him. When in 1937 Loboda took a vacation in Moscow, the police arrived at his apartment house in Novaya Basmannaya Street to arrest him. Fortunately he was out with friends. In Chukotka the local secret police, knowing he was a brother of a Trotskyist, kept him under surveillance.

The Loboda couple reviled Stalin and both were strongly anti-Soviet, which is why Grossman would later trust them to hide his manuscript of *Life and Fate*.

Vera Ivanovna (née Dan'ko) left a memoir in which she tells about her marriage to Loboda and friendship with Grossman. She grew up on a farm and was one of Grossman's sources about the course of collectivization and the Gulag. Her family, originally from the Chernigov province in Ukraine, moved to the Far East in the nineteenth century. They were among hundreds of Ukrainian settlers to whom the Russian government allotted land near Lake Khanka, close to Manchuria. They called their settlement, 180 kilometers northwest of Vladivostok, Chernigovka. After they cleared it, the land produced bumper crops of wheat, rye, buckwheat, flax, and oats. When the Trans-Siberian Railway was built, their station was named Muchnaya (Wheat Flour Station). After collectivization the name was all that remained of the former abundance.

In 1928 most of Chernigovka's seven hundred families were dispossessed as kulaks, even though they had all worked without hired help. Vera's father and uncle escaped arrest by the skin of their teeth. They were tipped off by Vera, who saw the OGPU men walking toward their house. Later the family had to separate to feed themselves. Vera, aged nine, found work as a maid in Vladivostok. This is where she saw columns of prisoners, many of them peasants. "The jail was not far from where we lived. Each evening I saw people led to jail, and in the morning and daytime—out of jail. I looked at men, most of them bearded, skimpily dressed, and thought: 'If I hadn't then spotted the OGPU and tipped off father and Uncle Misha, they would have marched in this column, too.' "

Employed by a female dentist, Vera was also responsible for obtaining bread on ration cards. This was the hardest thing of all. One had to rise in the wee hours of the morning and line up; otherwise there wouldn't be enough bread even with ration cards. Such was the impact of collectivization: bread, butter, and meat formerly produced in abundance had vanished. Even in 1940 one could not freely buy food, except fish, in Vladivostok.

After putting herself through school and qualifying as a teacher, Vera was sent to work in Chukotka. Upon her arrival the local educational administration warned her to stay away from Loboda. When she asked why, she was told he was a brother of a Trotskyist. Vera mistrusted the authorities and defied the instruction. Because Loboda was continually harassed she became his staunch supporter.

In 1940 the Chukotka authorities conducted a campaign against enemies of the people. The population of the entire peninsula was under twenty-two thousand, and inhabitants in the town of Pevek numbered only a few thousand. Still, enemies were produced. Chukotka's only university-educated people—Loboda and four other experts from the People's Commissariat for Agriculture—were denounced and faced arrest. They were saved by a local prosecutor named Solonenko. A friend of Loboda, he arrived in time from Chukotka's capital, Anadyr, to rescue the experts.

Vera was also harassed. A local NKVD officer pressed her to inform on Loboda and report their conversation. He threatened her with arrest if she didn't comply. Loboda advised Vera to go and report, which she did a few times, but in such a way that the local NKVD would lose interest.

In 1940 the two married in Moscow. The jolly wedding was at Grossman's Lianozovo "dacha" where Syoma Tumarkin, Efim Kugel, and other university friends reunited. (Beginning in 1938 Grossman spent summers in Lianozovo, northeast of Moscow, where Olga obtained half a wooden house by trading her room in the Arbat apartment. Before the war Grossman's mother and daughter Katya stayed in Lianozovo two summers in a row.)

Loboda and Vera were Grossman's eyes and ears in the country. The route from Chukotka went through the notorious Kolyma region with its capital of Magadan, and before reaching the Vladivostok transit camps one would have an overview of the Gulag Archipelago. In her memoir Vera describes "the barbed wire stretching through the entire country." In 1940 it took her a month to reach Vladivostok. From there she journeyed through the Far East and Siberia, crossing rivers by boat and traveling by train with frequent changes. In Siberia people were running after the train, begging for bread. Before reaching Moscow Vera gave away all her supplies. It struck her that not only food but even matches were sought. "This is what our dear Stalin has done," she wrote years later. "He has ruined the country. The most hardworking, the most progressive [people] rotted in Kolyma, Vorkuta, Norilsk, Kazakhstan."

In Moscow stores were extremely well stocked and people from nearby towns and villages went there to buy food. At the Yaroslavl train station in Moscow a young woman stood waiting for her train with two sacks of bread over her shoulders. The woman was so exhausted she swayed with fatigue. This image became etched in Vera's memory.

In her memoir she describes the horrendous conditions of prisoners in the labor camp. During her brief employment at Chukotka's motor depot she supervised prisoners' work. Once, while taking papers to the camp administration, she heard screams from a punishment cell: a man shouted he was freezing to death.[53] On his desk Grossman would keep a small sculpture of a freezing man made by Olga's brother Nikolai Sochevets, a former inmate.

Vera and Loboda gave him an understanding of the scope of the Gulag Archipelago. As he wrote in "Mama," "Day and night trains transported prisoners to Komi, to Kolyma, to Norilsk, to Magadan and the Bay of Nagaevo."[54] In *Life and Fate* he describes the prisoners' roll call sounding throughout Russia's north, Siberia, "over the snows of Kolyma, the Chukotsk tundra and the camps of Murmansk and Northern Kazakhstan."[55] Thus, Grossman's friends told him about the deadly gold mines of Kolyma before he had a chance to see Majdanek and Treblinka.

6. The Inevitable War

The war was raging in Europe. . . . Many radio stations
broadcast German conversation, German victory marches.
What did we know? We knew nothing. . . . There was only an intuitive
understanding that we couldn't avoid the war with Germany.
—Grigory Baklanov, "The War"

In April 1939 *Izvestia* stopped publishing the articles on Nazi Germany Ilya Ehrenburg had been sending from Paris.[1] As *Izvestia*'s correspondent, Ehrenburg had covered the recently concluded Spanish Civil War and the growing threat of Fascism in Europe; he saw the abrupt change in Soviet policy as a betrayal of the anti-Fascist cause. In early May, Litvinov, people's commissar for foreign affairs, was dismissed from his post and replaced with Molotov. Germany welcomed the move. Litvinov was Jewish and besides he sought a pact with Western powers. By appointing Molotov, Stalin opened a path to negotiations with Hitler.

With plans to attack Poland, Germany wanted to prevent the Soviet Union from forming an alliance with France and Britain. For his part, Stalin suspected the Western powers of trying to draw the USSR into a war with Germany. Secret negotiations between the Soviet Union and Germany about forming an alliance proceeded in spring and summer 1939. On August 20 Hitler sent a message to Stalin asking him to receive his foreign minister, Joachim Ribbentrop. By then the two sides had agreed about the core of the nonaggression pact, which Ribbentrop was coming to sign.

Settled on August 23, the Ribbentrop-Molotov Pact consisted of a military agreement—a commitment to refrain from "any attack on each other"— and a trade agreement. Germany would supply technology and industrial equipment to the USSR and receive in return raw materials indispensable for its military industries. A secret supplementary protocol delineated German and Soviet spheres of influence in Poland, the Baltics, and Romania. Stalin, having read *Mein Kampf*, knew about Hitler's long-term intentions to expand into Russia's territories, but thought the pact with Germany guaranteed peace, at least for the time being.[2] Hitler, however, did not abandon his plan to destroy the Communist state. On August 22, when Ribbentrop headed to Moscow, Hitler addressed his top-ranking army officers, declaring: "Poland will be depopulated and settled by Germans. Russia will share the same fate."[3]

After the pact was signed, Soviet media were prohibited from publishing negative information about Nazi Germany. On August 24 *Izvestia* informed readers that the pact put an end to hostilities between Germany and the USSR. The word *Fascism* disappeared from all speeches and Soviet newspapers. "One might have thought that Fascism itself had disappeared," writes Ehrenburg.[4] If a while earlier Soviet national papers wrote about "German aggressors" and "new tricks of fascist propaganda," now Soviet journalists were invited to expose British imperialism. The phrase "German aggressors" was replaced with "German troops in Czechia and Slovakia."[5] Once Nazi Germany became an ally, the Soviet people had to forget that Kamenev, Zinoviev, Bukharin, Tukhachevsky, and numerous others who had recently been shot for alleged ties to German "Fascists."

The alliance with Germany revealed that Stalin was unconcerned about ideological differences between Nazism and Communism. According to George Orwell and Arthur Koestler, on the day of Ribbentrop's arrival, Moscow's airport was adorned with swastikas. Soviet national newspapers published Stalin's and Molotov's photographs with Ribbentrop. In his memoirs Ehrenburg would write how this abrupt change in Soviet policy affected him: "Molotov's words about 'short-sighted anti-Fascists' jarred on me. . . . I was staggered by Stalin's telegram to Ribbentrop, which contained the expression 'friendship cemented by blood.' I reread it a dozen times, and although I believed in Stalin's statesman-like genius, it made my own blood boil. This was blasphemy. How could one compare the blood of Red Army men with that of the Nazis? And how [could we] forget the rivers of blood shed by the fascists in Spain, Czechoslovakia, Poland, not to mention Germany itself?"[6]

On September 1, within days of signing the pact, Hitler launched his attack on Poland. Twenty-five thousand civilians were killed in the bombing of Polish cities and towns. Warsaw, bombed on September 10, was the first major European city to be subjected to regular air raids.[7] The Soviet newspapers did not report German atrocities. On September 2 a short statement about German troops crossing into Poland appeared on *Izvestia*'s last page. On the same day *Pravda* quoted Hitler's speech in the Reichstag in which he claimed that Polish troops first opened fire on German territory.[8] Subsequent reports mentioned the bombing of Warsaw but not the casualties and referred to the attack as "military actions" between Germany and Poland.

Molotov's report, carried prominently by the Soviet media on September 1, asserted that the signing of the pact "between the two biggest countries in Europe" served to eliminate the threat of war between the USSR and Germany and to promote "the cause of universal peace."[9] Far from promoting peace, however, Stalin's government launched a simultaneous invasion of Poland and, soon after, an attack on Finland.

On September 17, when the Germans were bombing Lvov, the Red Army crossed the Polish frontier from the east. Molotov cynically described the Soviet invasion as a peacekeeping mission. In fact, Germany and the Soviet Union were jointly destroying Poland as a viable state. Between September 1939 and June 1941 two hundred thousand Polish citizens were killed and a million deported. Tens of thousands of Poles would die in the Gulag and in Auschwitz.[10] During April and May 1940 the NKVD conducted mass executions of Polish officers, soldiers, and civilians. Twenty-two thousand Polish citizens including 14,500 POWs captured during the invasion and incarcerated in Soviet internment camps were secretly shot in Katyn Forest near Smolensk and other places. The Katyn Forest massacre was devised by Beria and sanctioned by Stalin and members of his Politburo, a war crime they concealed and later blamed on the Nazis.

In accordance with the pact, the Soviet Union soon proceeded to annex west Belorussia, west Ukraine, parts of eastern and central Poland, and Bessarabia (part of Romania), territories with a high percentage of Jews. The war with Finland was also a result of the nonaggression pact. On November 30, 1939, the Soviet Union crossed the Finnish border, deploying almost a million troops. The Finns could deploy only a third as many tanks and aircraft, but their army had high morale and expertise. The Red Army, crippled by Stalin's purges, suffered heavy casualties in the Winter War, a taste of what was to come in 1941.

Grossman followed world events with alarm. In April 1940, after the Germans occupied Denmark and Norway, he realized that "the war entered a new, more active phase. I avidly read newspapers, await reports on the radio."[11] In May the Nazis occupied Belgium, Holland, and Luxembourg. On June 14 German troops marched through Paris. After the capitulation of France, Germany controlled much of continental Europe. Grossman and people around him realized that the Soviet Union would inevitably be drawn into the war.

Ehrenburg, who witnessed the fall of Paris, returned to Moscow at the end of July. "I was convinced that the Germans would soon attack us; the terrible scenes of exodus from Barcelona and from Paris were still before my eyes. But in Moscow the general mood seemed calm. The press said that friendly relations between the Soviet Union and Germany had grown stronger."[12] Ehrenburg requested a meeting with Molotov but was received by his new deputy, Solomon Lozovsky. While Ehrenburg spoke "about the French situation" and Germany's imminent attack on the Soviet Union, Lozovsky listened "absent-mindedly." Ehrenburg exclaimed, "Doesn't any of this interest you at all?" Lozovsky replied that the information interested him personally, "but you know we have a different policy."[13] Stalin, of course, refused to believe that Hitler would betray him.

Ehrenburg soon realized that the Soviet government did not seek correct information to help it determine foreign policy. "It turned out to be exactly the contrary—what was needed was information that would confirm a predetermined policy."[14] Lozovsky was a man of integrity but Ehrenburg felt he had no power. Both Ehrenburg and Grossman would work with Lozovsky when during the war he headed the Soviet Information Bureau and also directed the work of the Jewish Anti-Fascist Committee.

In 1940, while completing his epic novel *Stepan Kolchugin*, Grossman described the beginning of the Great War. He wrote the final parts with thoughts of a new world catastrophe fast approaching. History was repeating itself. His Berdichev character in the novel, Mark Rabinovich, argues that there is no such thing as the last war. Grossman was reading history and the philosophy of antiquity, taking particular interest in an interpretation of history as a repeating cycle of events.

That same year, when Moscow's Vakhtangov Theater proposed that he write a play, Grossman seized on the idea. He took a few weeks to draft *If You Believe the Pythagoreans*. His character Andrei Shatavskoi is an old man, a descendant of a noble family. He is a proponent of Pythagorean philosophy, believing that everything in the world and in the cosmos is part of the eternal cycle of nature. "Everything repeats itself—just think, the war, which seemed the very last to us, is again flaring up." Like Pythagoras, the great mathematician and philosopher of antiquity, Shatavskoi thinks that "all of life is subordinate to a great cyclical law. In everything, everything, in the falling yellow leaves in September, the stars, which slowly become extinguished and are reborn to become extinguished again, in the movement of planets and the eternal rebirth of youthful dreams and their expiry—the same encompassing law seems to rule everywhere."[15] The theater considered staging the play, but war interfered. In 1946, when Grossman published *The Pythagoreans,* he was savagely attacked for contradicting the Marxist-Leninist-Stalinist view of history as progressing in a straight line, for if one believes the Pythagoreans socialism is not irreversible.

In 1939–40, when *Stepan Kolchugin* was coming out in installments, Grossman's editors did not give him an easy time. From the beginning eight editors at *Znamya* magazine scrutinized his manuscript for ideological content and continually demanded changes. The novel was unconventional and, in addition, seemed to contain some heretical thoughts, as in the following passage: "I am the deepest sceptic. I don't believe that people will become better, richer, happier or kinder. . . . Yet, the Marxists believe that life will become good and noble and that all people will turn into philosophizing altruists. And I know that no forces in the world can change human nature, defined by Voltaire as *tigre-singe.*[16]. . . Wars will always exist, and always a man will remain a man. And I support the kind of social structure that liberates even the most daring, strong and skeptical mind."[17]

But Grossman was fortunate. Critics still viewed him as Gorky's protégé. An article in *Izvestia* on December 2, 1939, praised the book for its main character, a young worker who joins the revolutionary struggle. Even though Stepan Kolchugin was not a Bolshevik, the article was entitled "A Novel about a Bolshevik": this was the highest praise a Soviet critic could bestow on a novel. Grossman's readers, people of all ages and from all walks of life, valued the book because it was genuinely interesting and well written. As a schoolboy wrote, it was "a remarkable, lively, and entirely comprehensible book. . . . I shared all feelings of its characters." An engineer from Leningrad asserted that Grossman's novel rang true and was populated with "real people, not stereotyped characters, which, sadly, have become common in contemporary literature."[18]

In 1939 the country's largest film studio, Mosfilm, approached Grossman with an offer to adapt his novel for the screen, "and I had no objections. But they can't end the red tape with the proposal going through high official channels."[19] (The idea was shelved. In 1957 *Stepan Kolchugin* was finally produced by the Leningrad studio Lenfilm, but Grossman would be dissatisfied with the adaptation.)

Both volumes of *Stepan Kolchugin* were scheduled to come out in early 1941. The book was produced by the state publisher Gosizdat and by *Znamya*. At the last moment one of the censors began to doubt the novel "and was about to suggest that I begin editing it all anew. . . . They [Gosizdat] appointed a commission; it took my side, and the book was sent to the printers." Unnerved by this, Grossman found an escape in work: "I noticed that it's the best thing to work daily, systematically, without breaks."[20] Gosizdat published seventy thousand copies of *Stepan Kolchugin*, and in January the book was favorably reviewed in *Pravda*. Nominated for the newly established Stalin Prize, it was widely expected to win. Grossman was photographed, interviewed, and congratulated. According to Yevgeniya Taratuta, he received calls from newspapers already typesetting information about his win. So he made arrangements to celebrate the prize: unable to invite friends to his crowded flat, he invited them to a play and bought tickets. On the morning of the announcement his name was not on the list of laureates: apparently, it was crossed out at the last moment. Yevgeniya Taratuta recalled, "Baffled friends exchanged phone calls. But Vasya confirmed his invitation to the theater. Cheerless, we gathered by the entrance to the Theater of Revolution on Herzen Street (now Mayakovsky Theater). A dauntless Vasya stood by the entrance handing out the tickets. It was windy, light snow was falling. I remember it all—the theater entrance covered in snow, the gathering of friends, our boiling indignation, and Vasya's philosophical calm; the only thing I fail to remember is what play was performed that night."[21]

Grossman's friend Semyon Lipkin tells a similar story: "It was known that before the war Stalin himself struck out *Stepan Kolchugin* from the list of works nominated for the Stalin Prize. . . . On the night before the list of laureates was published Grossman received congratulatory phone calls from the country's major newspapers."[22] Lipkin's account has become widely quoted.[23] Other sources confirm that Stalin decided who should receive the prize established in his name. However, Lipkin's contention that Stalin referred to *Stepan Kolchugin* as "a Menshevik novel" seems inaccurate. Had Stalin really said

this, Grossman's career would have been over. Stalin's handwritten abuse
("fool," "bastard," "scoundrel") in the margin of Andrei Platonov's 1931
novella *Vprok* [Profit] about collectivization made the writer unpublishable.
In a note to the journal *Krasnaya nov'*, which printed Platonov's novella, Stalin
demanded severe punishment for the author: "A story by an agent of our
enemies, written with the goal of destroying the kolkhoz movement."[24]
Grossman would similarly have become a literary pariah had Stalin criticized
his novel. Instead, critics mentioned *Stepan Kolchugin* alongside the recently
published final part of Mikhail Sholokhov's voluminous *Quiet Flows the Don*.

Grossman still planned to write a sequel to *Stepan Kolchugin* depicting
events of the February and October Revolutions, but he produced only a few
chapters. His friend Lipkin was skeptical about the project, saying that "if
the author is truthful," his heroes' fates would not be blissful. "Grossman
made binoculars with his fingers, held them to his glasses and peered at me
with a smile. He would often make this gesture . . . when thinking his interlocutor had made a good guess. By the way, it's not incidental that the last
part of *Stepan Kolchugin* was never written."[25] In the sequel Grossman would
have had to depict different political parties that were vibrant before the
revolution and destroyed by Lenin and Stalin. His idea to conclude the book
with a story of his hero joining the Communist International was also unfea-
sible.[26] Stalin dissolved the Comintern in 1943 and after the war the idea of
workers' international solidarity was replaced with a shameful campaign
against Westerners and Jews.

In December 1940 Grossman turned thirty-five. His mother sent him a
parcel and a touching letter, saying that his birth was as memorable to her as
if it were yesterday. "I wish you health, *anima mia* [my soul], creativity; to be
content with your work (and that your readers and critics would be content
with it); to be blissful with people close to you." Referring to the title of a
children's book she wrote in German: "Du weißt nicht wie lieb ich dich hab"
(You don't know how much I love you). Ekaterina Savelievna's parcel
contained her own silver spoon—"You'll drink tea and will remember
me"—a glass holder—"Don't worry, it's not silver, I didn't spend much"—
and a toy tiger for his writing desk. "I'm also sending you my love, and I kiss
your eyes, forehead, hair, and little face." She wanted to send him a box of
apples but ran out of money: she was also sending a parcel to Nadya.[27]

Ekaterina Savelievna wrote regularly to her son, but only a few of her letters survive. Her health deteriorated, making it hard for her to get around; she called herself "a walking polyclinic." Grossman sent her money and occasional parcels. As elsewhere in the country, even basic commodities were hard to get in Berdichev. In December Grossman sent his mother some sugar, tea, and soap. "She was so glad!"[28]

Lipkin, who befriended Grossman about two years before the war, remembers him as a happy man: "He had literary success . . . interesting and intelligent friends, and a beautiful wife. 'I was amazed, how beautiful writers' wives were,' he would tell me when he and I became close, and he reminisced about his first steps in literature. He was tall, with curly hair; when he laughed, and he often laughed in those days, there were dimples on his cheeks. The look of his near-sighted eyes was remarkable—both quizzical and kind, a rare combination. Women liked him. He radiated health. I did not know then that he was afraid of crossing Moscow squares and broad streets, sharing this phobia with my other distinguished friend, Anna Akhmatova."[29] Grossman had other phobias: in 1940, when invited to a readers' conference, he declined "because of my old fear of big gatherings."[30] He also avoided public transport and never rode the subway.

In less than a decade Grossman had become a successful writer, respected by the literary world. He was closest to the writers Semyon Gekht and Alexander Roskin, both of whom reviewed his prose, and to Vasily Bobryshev, editor of the journal *Our Achievements* (Nashi Dostizheniya). Bobryshev and Roskin enlisted shortly after Hitler's attack on the Soviet Union and were killed in early fall 1941.

In 1948 Grossman wrote a tribute to Roskin, remembering him as a sensitive and talented man. He shared Roskin's love of Chekhov and French literature. A biographer of Gorky and Chekhov, Roskin also wrote extensively about American and French writers—Jack London, O. Henry, Maupassant, Prosper Mérimée, and Anatole France. Grossman had spent time with him over the years in Yalta, Crimea. Their last vacation together was in May 1941, shortly before Hitler's invasion. During this last spring of peace, they toured fruit orchards in Derikoy, a village of the Crimean Tatars. It was in a valley surrounded by mountains. The blossoming orchards on the mountainsides looked "like streams of bright lava, crawling towards the sea." The air was saturated with the scent of blooming cherry and apple trees; in this "biblical paradise" one fully experienced the joy of living. Yet, the joy of being alive contrasted with their strong awareness of approaching war. Roskin had a premonition he would be killed, remarking, "I think this is my last Crimean spring."[31] In the evenings both read newspapers, listened to radio reports, and discussed politics.

The cloudless Crimean spring was the calm before the storm. Greece was occupied; the Luftwaffe bombed the British Isles. "Europe was submerged in darkness; huge armies of steel-clad brown locusts rushed to the shores of the North Atlantic and the Mediterranean, having conquered Europe almost bloodlessly; their paratroopers landed on Crete. Perhaps, during the days when we walked in Yalta's blossoming orchards . . . and looked at the calm sea, Hitler fetched the Operation Barbarossa Plan from the secret vault of the New Reich Chancellery and circulated it among his field marshals and generals." Grossman and his friend realized that Hitler would not stop after conquering Europe. Knowing this, Roskin "linked the fate of the world with his own fate."[32] Thus, Grossman's essay about Roskin expresses the central idea of *Life and Fate*. In the first part of this novel, published under the title *For the Right Cause*, Grossman depicts the months before Hitler's attack when "in families, rest homes, and offices people discussed politics and the war. A menacing time arrived when world events and people's destinies had become linked."[33]

In his 1948 essay about Roskin Grossman purposely mentions the village of the Crimean Tatars. During the war Stalin deported entire nationalities accused of collaborating with the Nazis; among the peoples deported in 1941–44 were 905,000 Volga Germans, 191,000 Crimean Tatars, 485,000 Chechens, and 101,000 Kalmyks.[34] The village Derikoy, as Grossman remembered it before the war, ceased to exist.

In accordance with Hitler's fateful directive No. 21, signed on December 18, 1940, preparations for Operation Barbarossa were ongoing during winter and the following spring: "The German armed forces must be prepared *to crush Soviet Russia in a quick campaign* even before the conclusion of the war against England. . . . Preparations requiring more time are to be started now . . . and are to be completed by May 15, 1941."[35] Planning to defeat the Soviet Union by October 1941, the Germans concentrated 90 percent of their forces on the eastern border. Hitler remembered the lessons of Napoleon's Grande Armée and intended to occupy European Russia before winter.

On the eve of the invasion, Soviet authorities still did not permit the slightest criticism of Hitler's Germany. Stalin continued to believe that the Nazi-Soviet Pact was unbreakable and would protect him from a war; to appease Hitler he increased supplies of raw materials to Germany.[36] On May 1 Ehrenburg noted in his diary, "Everybody is talking about war."[37] A month earlier Ekaterina Savelievna shared her worry with her son that the Soviet Union would become drawn into war; she added, possibly for the censors' sake, "I'm terrified of a war, but I believe in our [government's] wise policies."[38]

Grossman must have known that his mother was vulnerable in Berdichev, a Jewish city not far from Ukraine's western border with Romania. Although the Soviet press no longer reported on Hitler's anti-Semitic policies, some information had appeared before 1939. For example, in 1936 Molotov condemned the Nuremberg laws and expressed sympathy for the people who had given birth to Karl Marx.[39] The Yiddish-language press, which was read in Berdichev, elaborated on the harassment of Jews in Germany. On November 18, 1938, *Pravda* published an editorial denouncing Kristallnacht. That year, after a rally in Moscow in response to Kristallnacht, *Pravda* published a declaration protesting "the inhuman acts of cruelty committed by the fascists against Germany's helpless Jewish population."[40]

Grossman's mother knew about Hitler's hatred of the Jews. Undoubtedly Grossman also knew this and sensed the danger she faced in Berdichev. He wanted his mother to join the family in Moscow ahead of her usual midsummer visit to the dacha, but Olga would not hear of this. As Lipkin recalls, Grossman believed that "his mother, who perished in the Berdichev ghetto, would have been alive if Olga Mikhailovna had not opposed her visiting them in Moscow shortly before the war."[41] Grossman's failure to prevail and save his mother weighed heavily on him for the rest of his life. In *Life and Fate*, depicting Olga in Shtrum's wife Lyudmila, he writes: "In his heart he reproached Lyudmila for her coldness towards his mother. Once he had even said: 'If you hadn't got on so badly with my mother, she'd have been living with us when we were in Moscow.' "[42] In his novel *For the Right Cause* Grossman tells a slightly different story: "Shtrum expected his mother to come to the dacha in early July, but war interfered."[43] After the German attack on June 22, Grossman's disabled mother became trapped in Berdichev.

The only known photograph of Grossman's parents together:
Turin, Italy, early 1900s. (Fyodor Guber's private archive.)

Grossman, seven, with his mother, Ekaterina Savelievna, 1912.
(Fyodor Guber's private archive.)

Katya Grossman as a baby in Berdichev with Uncle David Sherentsis and a relative, Natasha, 1932. (Ekaterina Korotkova-Grossman's private archive.)

Grossman's first wife, Anna Matsyuk (Galya) (*far right*), late 1920s. (Ekaterina Korotkova-Grossman's private archive.)

Grossman, a beginning writer, Moscow, 1934. (V. I. Dahl State Museum of the History of Russian Literature.)

Grossman's second wife, Olga
Guber, aged eighteen to twenty.
(Fyodor Guber's private archive.)

Fedya Guber in 1936, the year his mother
married Grossman and one year before
his father was arrested and shot. (Fyodor
Guber's private archive.)

Grossman at the Zyabrovo airfield near Gomel, about to make his first flight on a biplane, August 1941. (V. I. Dahl State Museum of the History of Russian Literature.)

Grossman interviewing a local man on the southwestern front, 1941. (Photo by Knorring. V. I. Dahl State Museum of the History of Russian Literature.)

Tvardovsky (*left*) and Grossman in Estonia, March 1941. (V. I. Dahl State Museum of the History of Russian Literature.)

Ehrenburg (*front row left*) and Grossman (*front row right*) near Kiev, 1943. (V. I. Dahl State Museum of the History of Russian Literature.)

Back row, from left: Knorring and Grossman, October 1943. (V. I. Dahl State Museum of the History of Russian Literature.)

Grossman leaning on a smashed German tank after the Battle of Kursk, July 1943. (V. I. Dahl State Museum of the History of Russian Literature.)

Grossman (*right*) in Berlin, April 1945. (Photo by Rudnyi. V. I. Dahl State Museum of the History of Russian Literature.)

Grossman (*right*) with writer Nikolai Virta in Dubulti, Latvia, 1948. (Kornely Zelinsky's private archive.)

Back row, from left: Efim Kugel, Grossman, and Semyon Tumarkin. *Sitting on a bench, from left*: Olga Guber, Faina Shkol'nikova, and Fedya Guber with the family poodle, Lyuba, 1946–47. (Maria Karpova's [née Loboda] private archive.)

Grossman with daughter Katya on a rare outing together, late 1940s. (Ekaterina Korotkova-Grossman's private archive.)

Grossman at his desk during his work on *Life and Fate*, 1950s. (Ekaterina Korotkova-Grossman's private archive.)

Ekaterina Zabolotskaya (Grossman's late love) and her husband, poet Nikolai Zabolotsky, in Begovaya village, 1956. (V. I. Dahl State Museum of the History of Russian Literature.)

Grossman in the late 1950s. (V. I. Dahl State Museum of the History of Russian Literature.)

Thomas Sgovio, *The Death Roll*. (© Memorial International.)

Thomas Sgovio, *In the Barracks*. (© Memorial International.)

Thomas Sgovio, *Summer Work*. (© Memorial International.)

Thomas Sgovio, *1/4 of a Cattle Car*. (© Memorial International.)

Grossman's friend Semyon Lipkin with his wife, poet Inna Lisnyanskaya. (Elena Makarova's private archive.)

Vyacheslav Loboda in his Chukotka house, 1961. (Maria Karpova's [née Loboda] private archive.)

Grossman in Armenia in 1961, after the arrest of *Life and Fate*. (Photo by Ryumin. V. I. Dahl State Museum of the History of Russian Literature.)

7. 1941

It is more arduous to honour the memory of
the nameless than that of the renowned.
—Walter Benjamin, "Paralipomena to
'On the Concept of History'"

Despite numerous warnings, Stalin was caught unprepared for the German invasion. Reliable intelligence of the impending German attack came from foreign governments, including the U.S. undersecretary of state, the British Foreign Office, and from Churchill himself. In June 1940 Churchill alerted Stalin to the danger of German hegemony in Europe. But as Stalin told Molotov, he did not believe that "German military successes menaced the Soviet Union's friendly relations with Germany."[1] Molotov reported these words to the German ambassador to be conveyed to Hitler. In spring 1941 there was a flow of intelligence reports to Stalin detailing deployment of German troops along Soviet western borders. A Soviet spy, the German-born journalist Richard Sorge, supplied accurate information and even gave the correct date of the German attack. Stalin dismissed these warnings as provocations, intended to lure him into war. Having received these reports exclusively, he did not share them even with his new chief of staff, Georgy Zhukov. However, the army knew about the intensified German activity near the border. Between January 1941 and the invasion in June, German airplanes flew two hundred spy missions into Soviet territory to photograph air bases. Stalin, afraid to provoke Germany, forbade his army to interfere with these reconnaissance flights.[2]

In the novel *For the Right Cause* Grossman depicts the Belorussian border city of Brest one week before the German invasion. A Nazi official working for the Repatriation Commission walks down the street wearing his SS uniform with swastika armband. An elderly Jewish woman selling seltzer water in a kiosk and a peasant driving down the street watch the Nazi official with alarm.[3] The scene conveys the Soviet unpreparedness for war and the sense of grave danger felt by civilians of the border city. It also captures the Nazi-Soviet collaboration, which the Soviet regime would later deny. Brest belonged to Poland before it was captured by the Wehrmacht in 1939. In accordance with the German-Soviet Frontier Treaty, it was then assigned to the USSR.

In June, realizing that war was unavoidable, Zhukov and General Semyon Timoshenko, commissar for defense, asked Stalin to put their troops on alert. Stalin, still in denial, responded that this would mean mobilization and war. On the eve of Germany's attack Zhukov and Timoshenko managed to persuade Stalin to issue a directive alerting troops on the frontier. By then, however, German sabotage units had cut telephone cables, so the vital alert was received only by a few.[4]

The German assault was calculated and uncontainable. On June 22, at dawn, 3.2 million German and auxiliary troops attacked the Soviet frontier along a two-thousand-mile stretch from the Baltic Sea to the Black Sea. When news of a full-scale attack came from Minsk, Kiev, and the Baltic states, Zhukov telephoned Stalin at his Kuntsevo dacha near Moscow. Zhukov recalled that Stalin was disoriented and incoherent, breathing heavily. An hour later, in the Kremlin, Stalin was still unable to grasp the situation, issuing no permission for the troops to fight. The Soviet leadership was unable to fathom the idea until Hitler's ambassador, Schulenburg, read out a diplomatic note to Molotov. "Is this a declaration of war?" Molotov asked. "Surely, we have not deserved this."[5] Finally, at noon, eight hours after the start of the war, Molotov made his radio announcement about the unprovoked German attack.

Ehrenburg, who had known earlier from foreign radio broadcasts that the Germans had concentrated huge forces on the eastern frontier, was unsurprised. On the morning of June 22, before Molotov's announcement, an acquaintance phoned him to say that the Germans had declared war and bombed Soviet towns. Ehrenburg recalls: "We sat by the radio waiting to hear Stalin. Molotov spoke in his stead; he sounded overwrought. I was surprised when he said this was a treacherous attack. Treachery implies the breaking of pledges of honour, or at least of good faith. One could hardly attribute any ideas of honour or decency to Hitler. What could anyone have expected of Fascists? We sat for a long time by the radio. . . . Moscow broadcasted gay lighthearted songs which in no way corresponded to the mood of the people."[6] That day Grossman's friends came to see him. With Roskin, who stayed overnight, Grossman had memorable conversations. He saw his friend for the last time on July 5: Roskin was leaving for the front with the People's Militia. Practically unarmed and untrained, these battalions of People's Militia were sent against General Guderian's panzer tanks and nearly all perished.

It would take Stalin until July 3, a fortnight after the invasion, to read an appeal to the nation containing the strikingly unexpected salutation "Brothers and sisters." These were desperate times. Within the first ten days the Wehrmacht advanced 350 miles into Soviet territory, jeopardizing evacuation from the westernmost regions with predominantly Jewish populations. Most were uninformed about Nazi racial policies; a German intelligence official reported from Belorussia on July 12, 1941, that the local population was unaware how Jews were treated in Germany and Poland. "Otherwise their questions as to whether we in Germany make any distinctions between Jews and other citizens would be superfluous."[7] Some Jews who had lived through the German occupation of Ukraine during World War I did not realize that the German troops of 1941 were very different from those of a generation earlier, who had earned a reputation for being humane in their treatment of civilians. By suppressing news of the Nazi anti-Semitic policies, the Soviet media had jeopardized the lives of millions of Soviet Jews in Belorussia, Ukraine, and elsewhere.

In addition, local Soviet authorities withheld information about the German advance. Dreading personal responsibility, they acted in accordance with the Party's directive to avoid "panic." And yet these authorities managed to save their own lives. In Minsk, officials fled the city at night on the eve of German occupation, abandoning the people they were supposed to protect. By June 26 escape routes from Minsk were blocked. As a result, only seven thousand of seventy-two thousand Jews in Minsk managed to escape. In Vitebsk the authorities evacuated industrial plants ahead of civilians. Still, before Vitebsk was taken on July 11, some twenty-two thousand Jews (58 percent) were evacuated or managed to flee. In Zhitomir, which fell to the Nazis on July 11, two-thirds of thirty thousand Jews were evacuated.[8]

Berdichev was occupied on July 7, two weeks after the German attack. "Waving their arms and laughing, the soldiers shouted from their vehicles,

'*Jude kaput!*' They knew that most of the Jewish population was still in the city."[9] Thirty thousand Jews lived in Berdichev before the war, writes Grossman in his article "The Murder of the Jews of Berdichev"; only one-third managed to escape before the German occupation.[10]

Evacuation from Berdichev was not organized; people were escaping mostly on foot. Those who stayed behind were the elderly, the sick, and people who had nowhere to go. Air raids in Berdichev began shortly after the German attack. On June 25, in a letter to Grossman's father, Ekaterina Savelievna described the daily bombardments of Berdichev's airport. She wondered whether Hitler would bomb civilians and what would happen to the Jews. "I believe that this scum [Hitler] particularly hates Berdichev for its Jewish population. But come what may. I don't feel lonesome or deserted." She worried about Vasya: men in his birth year, 1905, were being mobilized for war. "Will we see each other again? How do you think we should celebrate the defeat of that vermin, Hitler?"[11]

On June 26 Ekaterina Savelievna sent a card to her son. She thanked him for the money he had wired her and reported: "The night passed well. In the morning, there were air-raid warnings, and then the all-clear. So far, it's quiet. And what comes next—cannot be known. I kiss you, my dear, my darling. Give everyone my cordial greetings. Mama." On June 29, after receiving another money transfer, she wrote: "I'm very worried, whether you're still in Moscow or have left. Are you receiving my letters? . . . I feel calmer now than in the first days—one gets used to things; I now undress for the night." She wrote that she was not alone, acquaintances visited her, and neighbors brought food from the bazaar, although prices had skyrocketed. On July 1, responding to Grossman's telegram (which hasn't survived, of course), Ekaterina Savelievna wrote that his daughter Katya was safe in a summer camp. And of herself, she wrote: "I live like everyone, my dear, awaiting the latest reports, and I read newspapers; sometimes I worry a lot."[12] This was her final letter from Berdichev. But Grossman did not receive it until much later. In September he wrote his father: "I worry days and nights on end about Mama and Katyusha."[13] In October, learning that Katya and Galya had escaped from Kiev, he wrote: "I'm very happy that Katyusha was found, but this doubles my worry for Mama."[14]

In August, before leaving for the front, he sent an inquiry about his mother to central evacuation services. Almost a year later, in May 1942, the response arrived: his mother's name was not on the list of evacuees. Grossman wrote Semyon Osipovich: "I already had realized that she didn't manage to get out, but my heart sank when I read those printed lines."[15] By then he knew about the slaughter of the Jewish population in the occupied Soviet territories. When on December 30, 1941, Soviet forces liberated Kerch, Crimea, the murder of seven thousand Jews by Einsatzgruppen squads came to light. The killings were conducted during a three-day operation: people were taken to an anti-tank trench near Kerch and shot. A description of this slaughter and photographs of the corpses appeared in the Soviet press.[16]

In September 1941, while at the front, Grossman had a telling dream, which he describes in his novel *For the Right Cause*: "That night Viktor dreamed he entered a room full of pillows and sheets thrown onto the floor. He went up to an armchair that still seemed to preserve the warmth of whoever had just been sitting in it. The room was empty; the people who lived there must have left all of a sudden in the middle of the night. He looked for a long time at a shawl hanging over the chair and almost down to the floor—and then understood that it was his mother who had been sleeping in this chair. Now the chair was empty, standing in an empty room."[17] (It was indeed in mid-September that his mother perished during the massacre of twelve thousand Berdichev Jews.) Grossman heard accounts about the slaughter of the Jewish population, but could not grasp that his mother had been killed. In November 1942 he wrote to Semyon Osipovich: "I'm thinking of Mama—and still can't believe in her perishing, I can't fathom it with my soul. The real pain will not come until later."[18] Grossman was excused from military service because of ill health.[19] But like many Soviet writers and journalists, he wanted to be sent to the front as a war correspondent. In late July he approached Major General David Ortenberg at the main political department of the Red Army. Ortenberg was the editor of the army gazette *Red Star* (Krasnaya Zvezda). Grossman had no military background and lacked the appearance of a war correspondent: bespectacled and suffering from asthma, he weighed ninety kilograms. (He would quickly shed weight during the war.) Ortenberg, however, knew him as a gifted writer, the author of *Stepan Kolchugin*, and wanted him to join his team of correspondents. Because Grossman never served in the army and was not a Party member, Ortenberg assigned him the rank of quartermaster (Konstantin Simonov also received this classification). Before sending Grossman to the front, Ortenberg had him coached by a retired colonel. Upon becoming a special correspondent for *Red Star*, Grossman joined a group of leading journalists and writers, such as Ehrenburg and Simonov.

Grossman soon proved his resilience and an ability to write under any circumstances. His reports would appear two to three times a month. In summer 1942 the newspaper would publish his first novel about the war, *The People Immortal*. Highly popular at the front, it became a Soviet classic.

Official Soviet bulletins revealed little truth of what was happening at the front. Claims of Soviet gains were entirely false. It was reported, for example, that on June 22 the Red Army's antiaircraft artillery destroyed seventy-five German airplanes.[20] In reality, hundreds of Soviet planes were destroyed on the ground.[21] The Germans knew exactly where Soviet airfields were, having conducted reconnaissance before the invasion. In addition, inexperienced Red Army commanders had moved most of their planes to civilian airports near the border.[22]

Stalin's military purges had deprived the army of its senior command. Three of the five marshals, fifteen of the sixteen commanders, sixty of the sixty-seven corps commanders, and seventeen commissars had been liquidated. To replace them junior officers were swiftly promoted. At the start of the war former brigade commander Dmitry Pavlov was put in charge of the entire western front (formerly the Belorussian Military District). This key area was previously under the command of General Uborevich, who had been executed in 1937. During the first days of the German invasion, General Pavlov lost communication with his troops and "essentially did not know what was happening at the front."[23] Stalin was quick to shift blame to General Pavlov for the chaos and devastating losses. After the defeat in the Battle of Białystok-Minsk General Pavlov and his head of staff Klimovskih were called back from the collapsed western front, accused of treason, and shot.

On August 5 Grossman left for what was now called the central front, commanded by General Andrei Eremenko, who replaced General Pavlov. Grossman was traveling to Gomel, Belorussia, with two other *Red Star* correspondents, Pavel Troyanovsky and Oleg Knorring, a photojournalist. Gomel, southeast of Minsk, was captured by the Germans on June 28. "I was told how, after the burning of Minsk," remarked Grossman in his notebook, "the blind men from an invalid home walked in a long chain by the highway, tied to each other with towels."[24] His wartime notebooks contained much invaluable material that he would use in his novels. However, everything he saw that summer—chaos at the front, the Red Army's rout, officers' incompetence, and devastating losses—would later be concealed, becoming Soviet taboos. The failure of Stalin's government to prepare the country for war and to inform civilians would result in millions of lost lives.

In Gomel, the headquarters of the central front, Grossman felt deeply for the civilians who went about their lives without understanding the gravity of the situation: "Gomel! What sadness there is in this quiet green little town, in the lovely public gardens, in old people sitting on benches, in lovely girls walking along the streets. Children are playing in sand prepared for extinguishing incendiary bombs. . . . The Germans are less than fifty kilometers away."[25] At the Zyabrovsky airfield near Gomel, Grossman interviewed Lieutenant Colonel Nemtsevich, commander of the 103rd Aviation Fighter Regiment. He told about his first night of war in Western Belorussia and the regiment's "terrible, swift retreat." On the night of the invasion communications in his border town were cut; when bombardment began, officers and their families had to figure out the situation on their own. "On the eve of the war many senior commanders and generals were on holiday in Sochi. Many tank units were occupied installing new engines, many artillery units had no shells, aviation regiments had no fuel. . . . When the higher command began receiving reports from the frontier that war had begun, some [of the officers] received the following response: 'Don't give in to provocation.' "[26]

A young fighter pilot told Grossman about his first battle over Białystok. In the first hours of war and with little ammunition, he fought against several Messerschmitts. Just as he shot down one enemy aircraft his ammunition ran out. The Germans blew up his fuel tanks, including one under the seat. Soaked in burning fuel, he parachuted to what seemed like certain death. As he was hanging over water, the Messerschmitts cut his parachute straps with bullets. The pilot survived with burns and after a month in the hospital was back fighting.

Grossman returned to Gomel on a Polikarpov U-2 biplane nicknamed "maize duster." Pilots were amused to learn this was his first flight and photographer Knorring took a picture of a smiling Grossman in the open aircraft. "The flight utterly delighted me, when suddenly the plane, like a dragonfly, easily flew over the forest, the tree tops, started gliding over the river, the meadows; I sensed the wonder of having wings, an advantage of a dragonfly over a man."[27] Gomel was captured on August 19 and soon all Belorussia was occupied.

With the situation changing rapidly and communication practically nonexistent, Grossman, Troyanovsky, and Knorring avoided capture only by a combination of luck and ingenuity. They were escaping to Ukraine's northeast, driving along the road to Kiev, which would soon become the site of a Soviet military disaster. Stalin, with his decisive voice as supreme commander, rejected a defensive proposal of Georgy Zhukov, his chief of General Staff. General Zhukov, foreseeing Guderian's breakthrough and encirclement of Soviet armies near Kiev, proposed calling in eight divisions from the Far East and pulling back behind the Dnieper. Stalin issued an order to hold Kiev and the Dnieper at all cost: "Kiev was, is, and will be Soviet."[28] Zhukov was temporarily replaced with the pliant Marshal Boris Shaposhnikov, who had survived the purges. Stalin's intrusion in the military operation led to an incalculable loss of life. The Germans captured Kiev on September 18; five armies were destroyed and more than half a million Soviet troops taken prisoner.[29] Soviet POWs were savagely treated: most were exterminated during death marches and through starvation, or died in Auschwitz, Dachau, Buchenwald, and other death camps. As Timothy Snyder points out, "As many Soviet prisoners of war died *on a single given day* in autumn 1941 as did British and American prisoners of war over the course of the entire Second World War. . . . The Germans shot, on a conservative estimate, half a million Soviet prisoners of war. By way of starvation or mistreatment during transit, they killed about 2.6 million more. All in all, perhaps 3.1 million Soviet prisoners of war were killed."[30] If captured, Grossman and his companions would face certain death.

The encirclement of Soviet troops near Kiev opened the road to the capture of Ukraine. The Donbass, known as the "Soviet Ruhr" for its resources of coal, and Kharkov were occupied next. Another massive encirclement at Vyazma-Bryansk opened the road to Moscow. By October 1941, 3 million Soviet troops had become prisoners of war.[31]

Driving through Ukrainian villages, Grossman witnessed local reluctance to leave before the German advance. In fact, for many Ukrainians Stalin's collectivization and famine were only too memorable, and they awaited the Germans as liberators. Women were whitewashing their huts as for a holiday, Grossman observed. "They look at us with challenge in their eyes: 'It's Easter.' " Ukrainian womenfolk mistrusted Soviet stories of German atrocities: "The old woman said quietly: 'We've seen what's been, we'll see what comes.' "[32] Grossman sensed from conversations that these villagers were willing to work for the Germans. But Hitler's policies in the occupied territories were similar to Stalin's: provisions were seized to feed the German Army, leaving local populations starved and enslaved.

In late September Grossman was present during an interrogation of a captured Austrian motorcyclist near Bryansk. Led by an untrained intelligence officer, the questioning was a comedy of errors. The Austrian, speaking through a Jewish Yiddish-speaking interpreter who knew no German, struggled to explain that he saw a large accumulation of Guderian's panzer tanks in the region. When he finally succeeded in communicating that there were five hundred tanks "right near you," the intelligence officer dismissed the information and moved on to the next question on his printed form.[33] (At the start of the war the incompetence of Soviet officers was proverbial. The military purges had left the army without experienced senior officers; the new military staff had to be trained during the war. Countless soldiers paid for such training with their lives. In 1941 the Soviet Army suffered twenty-four thousand casualties daily, of which seventeen thousand were fatal.)[34]

The speed of the Soviet retreat was such that in three days Grossman and his companions drove through Belorussia and Ukraine, arriving in Orel, about 220 miles southwest of Moscow. There, in early October, Grossman learned from a photojournalist that hundreds of German tanks were advancing toward the city. He realized these were the very tanks the captured Austrian had been talking about. Trying to alert local officers in the operations department proved useless: they dismissed his information and continued drinking.[35] At the headquarters of the military district, a clerk told Grossman he needed a pass to get in, and passes were issued only after 10 a.m. Grossman commented: "I recognize this unshakable calmness that comes from ignorance and swiftly turns into hysterical fear and panic."[36] Grossman and his companions left Orel just before it fell to the Germans on October 3.

They raced west along the empty highway to the front headquarters, now located in the Bryansk Forest. A road without vehicles and pedestrians was frightening: Grossman described it as a no-man's-land between Soviet and German lines. In fact, they were driving two hours ahead of Guderian's panzers. From the front headquarters there was another race before the Germans sealed the route of escape. On October 4 Grossman and his fellow correspondents joined the surge of the retreating Red Army and civilians.

I thought I'd seen retreat, but I've never seen or even imagined anything like this. Exodus! The Bible! Vehicles are moving in eight rows, there's the violent howl of dozens of trucks simultaneously tearing their wheels out of the mud. Huge herds of sheep and cows are driven through the fields; these are followed by screeching horse-driven carts, thousands of wagons covered with colored sackcloth, veneer, tin, carrying refugees from Ukraine. Behind them crowds of people walk with their sacks, bundles, suitcases. This isn't a flood or a river, it's the slow movement of a flowing ocean, the width of this flow is hundreds of meters to the right and to the left. Children's heads . . . the biblical beards of Jewish elders, shawls of peasant women, hats of Ukrainian uncles, the black-haired heads of Jewish girls and women. What calm is in their eyes, what wise sorrow, what awareness of fate, of a world catastrophe![37]

Traveling in a battered Emka (a Soviet staff car) and a truck, they gave lifts to dozens of people, so Grossman appropriately nicknamed their truck "a Noah's Ark." Having escaped from the encirclement, the correspondents drove toward Tula. Grossman persuaded the others to turn off the highway and visit Yasnaya Polyana. There was "pre-departure confusion" in Tolstoy's mansion: the museum staff had packed up paintings, dishes, and books. This recalled scenes in *War and Peace* of Russian families fleeing Moscow and their estates ahead of Napoleon's advance. Grossman felt that Tolstoy's novel captured the events of 1812 with "such strength and truthfulness" that fiction became a "higher reality." The novel preserved the past in all its authenticity. Grossman also felt a connection between events of more than a century ago and the present.[38] Yasnaya Polyana soon became General Guderian's headquarters; from here he planned his advance on Moscow.

In Tula the correspondents got a direct telephone line with the editor of *Red Star*, who ordered them to Moscow. "We were seized with fervent, irrational joy. I haven't slept all night—will I really see Moscow?"[39] When they arrived, the editorial staff examined their battered Emka with its shrapnel holes. General Ortenberg scolded the war correspondents for failing to file an article "about the heroic defense of Orel." Grossman replied that there was no defense. Then, with an air of "a Roman patrician," Ortenberg ordered Grossman and the rest to return "straight to the front." The assignment was as dangerous as it was useless. The front headquarters had moved, along with the front line, and since there was no communication to advise them of these changes, Grossman and his companions were lucky to avoid capture. Returning to the newspaper, they wrote at night, keeping awake with cigarettes and strong tea; however, "the editor did not publish a single line."[40] The army gazette wanted examples of heroism while all they saw was chaos.

Moscow's suburbs were covered in barricades and anti-tank obstacles, or "hedgehogs." The Soviet government relocated to Kuibyshev, one thousand kilometers to the east. In mid-October, as government and party officials were being evacuated, general panic ensued. Roads east were jammed with cars, railway stations crowded, and stores plundered. Stalin considered leaving the capital but stayed behind after Zhukov's reassurance that Moscow would be defended at all costs.[41] Zhukov, once again in charge, was planning the Battle of Moscow.

Grossman was able to spend a few days in the capital with his father. Semyon Osipovich had moved to Moscow shortly before the war and was now staying in Grossman's apartment. Father and son talked all night; Grossman spoke about the war and his mother's fate. "Papa and I spoke of my deepest worry, but this can't be written about—it's in my heart day and night. Is she alive? No! I know, I feel this."[42] That fall Grossman's father left for Kuibyshev, joining a flow of evacuees; from there he proceeded to Central Asia.

Olga and the boys were evacuated with other writers' families to Chistopol, a town in west central Russia on the Kama River. They remained in Chistopol until after the Stalingrad battle and the turnaround in the war. Grossman's wife and children lived there side by side with the families of Boris Pasternak and Alexander Tvardovsky. During furloughs, Tvardovsky and Grossman took turns visiting each other's families in Chistopol, delivering news and parcels. On December 13 Tvardovsky wrote to his wife from Voronezh: "I was overjoyed with Vasily Grossman's arrival here; he was in Chistopol a month ago. He told me that you live there tolerably and that you don't look so bad, but even quite well. This made me very happy and calm."[43] Grossman's letters from the front were affectionate. In the fall 1941 he wrote Olga:

> My dear, my good one, I sent two letters to you. . . . And I still want to chat with you, to say how much I love you. . . . I already spent 3 days in Moscow and perhaps, will again leave for the front in 2 days. . . . What can I tell you? During the war I've seen much more, of course, than what I've seen and suffered during my whole life. It's as if I've become a different person. And in this war I

understood how much I love you. Remember, you used to tell me sometimes, "Vasya, you don't love me." Well, here I realized . . . that my love for you is the biggest thing in my life, I understood that you're more dear to me than life itself. Remember this, my love. . . . I've seen a lot of human suffering, this war is infinitely cruel. The fascists are fighting not only against men, but also against women, children, and old people—all suffer terrible, pitiless blows. I've seen burned cities, villages; I've seen so much that I'm sometimes surprised how all this could fit inside me. I believe that you and I will see each other, that I'll tell you all about what I've seen and suffered through.[44]

In November Grossman spent two weeks in Kuibyshev, sharing an apartment with Ehrenburg and other war correspondents. Ehrenburg remembers: "At night, endless conversations would begin, and in the daytime we would sit down to write. Vasily Semyonovich . . . talked a lot about the confusion [at the front] and resistance—some units fought tenaciously. . . . He talked about Yasnaya Polyana. He then started his novel *The People Immortal*; when I read it later, many pages seemed quite familiar."[45]

The decisive Battle of Moscow began on November 15 with four armies protecting the capital from four critical points. General Konstantin Rokossovsky, brought back from the Gulag at the start of the war, was in charge of the Sixteenth Army defending approaches to Moscow from the northwest. Soviet troops, fighting with fierce determination, were helped by an early and harsh winter. With temperatures of minus twenty-five to thirty degrees Celsius, German soldiers were freezing. Hitler had anticipated that his blitzkrieg would achieve victory before the onset of cold weather, and as a result, the German forces were unequipped with winter clothing and boots.[46] Supplies had to be delivered on Russian railways over a 1,000-kilometer stretch from the frontier. In early December General Guderian realized that the attempt to take Moscow had failed and that the advance had to stop while he rebuilt his army's strength. Just then, on December 5, the Soviet Army launched a major counteroffensive, using seven hundred thousand fresh troops, brought from the Far East.[47] By early January 1942, the Germans were pushed back 100–250 kilometers from Moscow.

When Grossman returned to Moscow from the front on December 20, he wrote Olga that the situation had changed, that there had been a turnaround: "Roads, fields are covered with wrecked German vehicles, [their] artillery abandoned; hundreds of dead soldiers, helmets, weapons. We are advancing!"[48] On January 1, 1942, he described the improved morale in the Red Army, "a sense of confidence and strength" in the troops.[49] He also wrote to Ehrenburg about the turning tide in the war and the transformation he observed in people: "The men seem to have changed: they are . . . full of initiative, bold. The roads are littered with hundreds of German cars, abandoned guns. . . . This, of course, is not yet the retreat of Napoleon's army but there are indications that such a retreat is possible. . . . Yes, a great change has taken place: it is as if the people had woken up."[50]

The winter of 1941–42 was one of the harshest ever in European Russia: in January temperatures dropped to minus forty degrees Celsius. In the article "Accursed and Derided" Grossman describes German troops fleeing the occupied villages near Moscow. Soldiers are bundled up in women's shawls over thin uniforms; some drag pillows and blankets stolen from villages.[51] Grossman's readers would sense his deliberate parallel with *War and Peace* and Tolstoy's descriptions of Napoleon's Grande Armée retreating from Moscow in late fall and winter. The familiar scenes in Tolstoy's novel picture French soldiers suffering from frostbite and bundled up in women's coats and shawls.

The victory in the Battle of Moscow demonstrated the blitzkrieg's failure. Germany now faced the protracted war it had expected to avoid. Grossman wondered whether Russian troops were capable of prevailing in a long campaign: "In war I observed only two attitudes towards events: either extraordinary optimism or complete hopelessness. Transitions from optimism to gloominess are swift, easy, and abrupt. There is nothing in the middle. Nobody thinks that the war is for long, that only hard unrelenting work, month after month, will lead to victory. . . . There are only two feelings: first—the enemy is destroyed; second—the enemy cannot be destroyed."[52] During the Battle of Stalingrad he would observe yet other traits of the Russian character—patience, resilience, and ability to withstand unthinkable hardships.

8. The Battle of Stalingrad

The outcome of this battle was to determine the map of the post-war world,
to determine the greatness of Stalin or the terrible power of Adolf Hitler.
For ninety days one word had filled both the Kremlin
and Berchtesgaden—Stalingrad.
—Vasily Grossman, *Life and Fate*

In winter 1942 Grossman was dispatched to the southwestern front to cover
operations of the Thirty-Eighth Army southeast of Kharkov. The front line
ran through the Donbass region and at one point came within fifty kilometers of Donetsk, where he had worked as a mining engineer. Here Grossman
visited a division consisting entirely of coal miners. They told him they were
unafraid of German tanks: working in a mine was more frightening. Some
miners recognized him from a portrait in his recently published book and
referred to him simply as Stepan Kolchugin. "They know me well in the
army," he wrote his father in February. "They meet me well wherever I
come, and I often see my book in foxholes and in bunkers."[1]

That winter he was constantly on the move, traveling through the
region on trucks, by sleigh, and in open planes, interviewing aviators, artillerists, and tank troops. Once he drove out in a snowstorm to an airfield near
Svatovo, twenty kilometers from the village where he was stationed. His
driver lost the road, and the car got stuck in a field. Luckily, a passing tank
detected them and drove them back. Grossman joked in a letter to his father
that he got to ride on a tank. "I'm well and there's much work. . . . Remember,
a while ago you reproached me (and quite reasonably) for not traveling
enough. . . . Now I have made up for this—there will be enough trips and
impressions for the entire writers' union."[2]

Some of his strongest impressions that winter came from fighter pilots he interviewed. They told him how they worked in pairs and how the character of a pilot could be known from the movement of his machine. He was impressed with their spirit of comradeship and their remark that a fighter pilot's life is as short as a child's shirt. On a bright winter day he observed an air battle over a village, recording his impressions in a notebook: "Terrible sights—birds with black crosses, birds with stars. All the terror, all thoughts, all the fear of a human mind and heart are in these last moments of a machine's life. . . . They were fighting low, just above the tops of the roofs. One of them hit the ground. Five minutes later—another one. A man died in front of their eyes, a very young man, very strong, he so wanted to live. . . . A dead pilot lay all night on a beautiful hill covered with snow: it was very cold and the stars were very bright. At dawn the hill became completely pink, and the pilot lay on a pink hill."³ In *Life and Fate* Grossman used his character sketches of these pilots, employing some real names to commemorate their short lives. The image of the dead pilot on a pink hill also surfaced in the novel. Grossman tells the story of this young lieutenant's life and love, remarking, "How many of them were forgotten in the unforgettable time."⁴

That March Grossman observed that, compared to the previous fall, the spirit in the Soviet troops was on the rise: "Now it's entirely different. There is faith, joy, light."⁵ This impression was based on many meetings, interviews, and a night trip with the artillerists to the village of Zaliman: "Night. Snowstorm. Trucks, artillery. They are moving in silence. At a junction someone's hoarse voice: 'Hey, which is the road to Berlin?' Laughter."⁶

Grossman kept worrying about his family, scattered around the country. His father was now in Samarkand, Galya and Katya in Tashkent, Central Asia. With Olga and the boys in Chistopol, Grossman communicated mostly through the German governess, Jenny Genrikhovna, who remained in Moscow. Letters from the capital were delivered promptly, unlike the mail from Chistopol, in the Tatar Autonomous Republic. "I work a lot, and work is interesting," he wrote his father. "I'm in good spirits. I only worry about people close to my heart. . . . And I often dream of Mama; what happened to her, is she alive?"⁷

As a war correspondent Grossman was privileged to access information of all kinds. He read divisional war diaries from which, in addition to the various incidents and examples of heroism his editor requested from him, he copied down reports concerning the mood of the troops, stories of desertion, and so on. Grossman knew about the NKVD's Special Detachments assigned to every army division. The NKVD units, later known as SMERSH (the acronym for "death to spies"), investigated traitors, deserters, and ferreted out "anti-Soviet elements" in the army. Soldiers were arrested on mere suspicion of impending desertion or self-harm and sent to military tribunals. Grossman was impressed with the courage of a Jewish commissar, Mordyukhovich, who managed to save a soldier in his artillery battalion from being shot. One of his bravest soldiers, a worker from Tula, was falsely accused of deserting. Sentenced to death by a military tribunal, he was taken to a forest to be executed, but survived due to a misfire and ran away. Later the soldier secretly returned to his battalion. The commissar, who knew he was innocent, kept him in hiding for five days while pleading for his case to be reviewed. Due to the commissar's energy and persuasiveness, the case went before the army commander, who canceled the death sentence.

Also from divisional diaries Grossman learned about soldiers in penal battalions, the so-called *shtrafniki*. These men, whose lives had been spared by military tribunals, were positioned on the front lines during an attack. Some 422,700 men served in these battalions during the war and few survived: they received the most dangerous assignments and the worst ammunition.[8] Grossman saw some of these doomed men and described their frostbitten faces, torn greatcoats, and terrible coughs. Many soldiers in penal battalions were former Gulag inmates who chose the front lines over death from starvation in Siberian labor camps.

Interrogations of German POWs revealed Hitler's brutal treatment of his troops. That winter Grossman was present during interrogations of captured German soldiers who spoke about Hitler's order to take "not a step back from the captured territory." The prisoners said the order was read out to them along with death sentences for deserting.[9] On July 28, 1942, during the German summer offensive, Stalin introduced a similar order, No. 227, known as "Not One Step Back." Stalin's directive read: "Panic-mongers and cowards should be exterminated on the spot!"[10]

After a year and a half in the army, now fully adapted to his work as a war correspondent, Grossman reported to his father: "Sometimes it feels that I have always traveled around in trucks, slept in sheds and half-burned huts, and that I never had a different sort of life. Have I dreamt it, perhaps? . . . I've become a real soldier: I swear like one, and my voice has become hoarse from tobacco and a cold."[11] Flying on open planes in winter, Grossman developed bronchitis. He needed a respite and asked his editor for a leave. Having collected a mass of material, he wanted to produce a short novel about the summer and fall of 1941.

In April, during "a relative lull at the front," Grossman arrived in the offices of *Red Star* in Moscow. When he requested a two-month leave to produce a short novel, Ortenberg readily agreed. Grossman had developed a good reputation: his reports were avidly read, boosting the newspaper's popularity. While in Moscow he signed a contract for a small book of wartime writings. This helped his finances: he sent money to his father, Galya and Katya, and also planned to take a portion of the publisher's advance to his family in Chistopol. On April 10 Grossman set out for Chistopol to write the novel.

His misadventures began after he arrived by train in Kazan. While he slept there at the station, the money he was taking home was stolen. From Kazan he had to travel 140 kilometers southeast. But the roads turned into mud and the only way to get to Chistopol was on foot, so Grossman set out through the fields. On the way—it took him three days—he was also robbed of the food he was taking as a present to his family. Maria Tvardovskaya, Grossman's Chistopol neighbor, describes his ordeal in a letter to her husband: "Today, Grossman walked here all the way from Kazan. He came on foot, since there's no transportation. He walked for three days. . . . His greatcoat was stolen near Moscow. In Moscow he received a new one. . . . He took a train. In Kazan, they stole all of his money—around three thousand rubles, so he went on foot with just a loaf of bread for the road. But even this was lost to a companion, who volunteered to help carry Grossman's things. Half of his things consisted of other people's parcels. . . . So, he was out of luck. However, he delivered other people's parcels. My parcel was also intact. I immediately lent them [the Grossmans] 500 rubles."[12]

Arriving in Chistopol empty-handed, Grossman found that Olga had turned "from a very stout woman to an utter skeleton," weighing just forty-four kilos. Because of her condition she had been relieved of her grueling work on a collective farm and when Grossman arrived was working at a cooperative for the disabled. Teenaged Misha, now the family's main bread-winner, worked as a truck driver.

Grossman took the loss of money lightly but bad luck seemed to follow him. Soon after he arrived in Chistopol the family was robbed during the night while everyone was sleeping. Grossman had gone to listen to the news at a neighbor's house and failed to lock the door. In the morning the family discovered that the house had been looted and all their winter coats stolen. When the news spread in the writers' colony Pasternak arrived to donate his new woolen coat. Olga later spotted a woman selling their belongings in the market and was able to recover some of them.

In Chistopol Grossman worked at a mad pace to meet his deadline. He read chapters of the new novel to local writers, all of whom praised his work highly. Grossman believed they liked it not because his work was so good but because the state of contemporary prose was extremely bad.[13] In the evenings, sitting under a blooming apple tree and enjoying tranquility, he was already anticipating his return to the front. He recalled a general's remark that correspondents are the bravest people in war: they have to go back and forth between the rear and front line, and a transition from peace to war is the hardest thing.

In May Grossman learned about a massive encirclement of Soviet armies near Kharkov. The disaster was brought on by Stalin's interference with strategies of the General Staff. Acting against his generals' advice to build up strength, Stalin insisted on an immediate offensive. Making deals with individual commanders, he backed Marshal Timoshenko's proposal to recapture Kharkov in May. This campaign and the Soviet offensive at Kerch, which Stalin also supported, failed badly. At Kharkov thousands of Soviet troops were killed and at least 237,000 taken prisoner. At Kerch, a further 176,000 men were lost.[14] The Soviet Army was again in retreat.

In his new novel, *The People Immortal*, Grossman depicts similar events of a year before. History was repeating itself. In 1942 the Germans launched their second summer offensive, and the Red Army was again fighting its way out of encirclements. The subject matter of Grossman's novel was timely. He wrote to honor the courage and sacrifice of ordinary soldiers and officers who managed to prevail in impossible situations; the stories he tells were meant to boost the morale of Soviet troops in 1942. The central idea is reflected in the title: it was the people's war, fought for liberation, and Grossman commemorates those who sacrificed their lives to win freedom. He compares Red Army soldiers to the revolutionaries who died for universal equality.[15] Grossman's novel stood out for its focus on the individual, his knowledge of the realities of war, and his ability to portray a broad panorama of events.

Drawing from his notebooks, Grossman tells the story of a courageous brigade commissar, Nikolai Shlyapin, who assembles remnants of his

Ninety-Fourth Rifle Division in a Belorussian forest, turning demoralized soldiers into guerilla fighters. Eventually, he establishes communication with the regular army and leads hundreds of people—soldiers and civilians, including Jewish refugees from Minsk—to safety. This man told Grossman his story in September 1941; shortly afterward he was killed in battle.

The novel also includes the story of Major Babadzhanian's heroic regiment. In September 1941, while at the Bryansk front, Grossman learned about an unequal battle led by the 395th Rifle Regiment. Consisting of 120 soldiers, the regiment fought heroically to slow down the advance of Guderian's Second Panzer Group. Vastly outnumbered, Babadzhanian's fighters were covering the army's withdrawal. Most of them perished. Upon learning this, Grossman wanted to write about the regiment and interview its commander at the time, but the political department considered the task too dangerous. Later Grossman was told that Babadzhanian had been killed, so when describing his death in the novel, he leaves the commander's name unchanged. But in 1944, during the liberation of Ukraine, Grossman unexpectedly met his hero. Babadzhanian had read the novel and laughed that he was killed prematurely.

Grossman wanted the nation to know its heroes who fought with great courage. Most of them died unknown: at the start of the war entire divisions were wiped out, and soldiers remained in the fields and forests where they fell. In 1941 Grossman was struck by the fact that the Red Army had no funeral teams. Thousands of soldiers, to whom Russia owed its salvation, were left unburied. Grossman saw occasional makeshift signs: names written in ink were gradually washed away by snow and rain. In his articles and his next novel, *For the Right Cause*, he would write about the need to remember the fallen.

In *The People Immortal* he was the first to show the massive retreat of the Red Army at the start of war, a topic no other Soviet writer dared to raise. He pictures "the exodus"—thousands of troops, heavy artillery, and refugees fleeing Belorussia and Ukraine. The spirit of the army during those dreadful days is captured in an image, "the grey dust of retreat." (Grossman would use this illustration again in his reportage later that year.)

The chapter "Death of the City" portrays the destruction of Gomel that he witnessed in August 1941. "Some scenes became etched in his memory forever. A man ran out of the house shouting, 'Fire, fire!' Upon seeing an enormous fire all around, he fell silent, sat on the pavement, and remained still." A young woman stands in the square with a girl's corpse in her arms. "A wounded horse lay at the street corner. Her dark, suffering, crying pupil was like a live mirror, reflecting the flames of burning houses."[16] In Gomel, an ancient city, Grossman depicts the destruction of world civilization. The idea is projected through the death of an old lawyer, killed while trying to save his precious library, which holds the *Annals* by the Roman historian Tacitus.[17]

Also in this novel Grossman predicts the defeat of Fascism. He envisions future historians poring over German military maps to determine who gave orders to commit mass murder and destroy cities and towns. More important, Grossman contemplates a version of the Nuremberg trials: "A day will come when the tribunal of the great nations will begin its hearing." He expresses his belief that the German nation will become horrified by its war crimes and will denounce Fascism.[18] However, in this first novel, written for his newspaper, Grossman could not provide an in-depth look at the war.

In June 1942 he submitted the two-hundred-page manuscript to his editor at *Red Star*. Ortenberg read it "in one gulp" and summoned Grossman at night to embrace him and to announce that he would publish the whole work without cutting. In July the paper began publishing the novel in daily installments. It appeared in eighteen successive issues and was avidly read at the front. As Ortenberg would later remark, "Nothing of the kind was written since the war began. And even after the war literary historians regarded *The People Immortal* among the most significant works of the period. . . . The novel told about courage, selflessness, and tenacity—today's hot topics."[19] This novel would become a Soviet classic and would be republished many times.

While *Red Star* was printing installments, Grossman essentially moved into the editorial office, remaining there past midnight to read proofs. He dreaded editorial revisions, which compromised his accuracy, and looked over Ortenberg's shoulder as he made changes.

In mid-July Grossman wrote his father: "I'm happy with success, the newspaper has an enormous audience."[20] He worried about the work's reception in the army but discovered upon returning to the front that everyone "from top to bottom" welcomed his book. The last installment was published on August 12 and soon after Grossman wrote his father, "Your parental heart would have rejoiced if you'd known and seen how they met me in the army after the novel's publication. My dear, my affairs could not have been better—success, recognition, but I feel heavy, heavy at heart. I passionately want to help all of my loved ones, and to gather you all together. I'm tormented by the thought of Mama's fate."[21]

On August 23 the Luftwaffe bombed Stalingrad, dropping tons of incendiary and demolition bombs and reducing the city to rubble.[22] That same day Grossman and his fellow correspondents drove to the front. Grossman was about to chronicle the most decisive and bloodiest battle of all World War II. The combined casualties of the Stalingrad battle—killed, injured, and captured—would total 2 million.

The Battle of Stalingrad would determine the outcome of the war. Actually, the initial version of the Germans' Operation Blue aimed only at seizing the oil fields in the Caucasus. The task of General Paulus's Sixth Army was to advance toward Stalingrad but not to capture it. But on July 9 Hitler ordered two simultaneous operations—capturing Stalingrad and pushing toward the Caucasus. Hitler believed Russian resistance was waning, that Stalin had exhausted his resources and manpower. When presented with intelligence reports showing that Stalin could still assemble a quarter of a million troops north of Stalingrad and half a million in the Caucasus, Hitler was furious. Much like Stalin, he placed ideology above military expertise, declaring: "We need National Socialist ardor now, not professional ability."[23] (*In Life and Fate* Grossman has General Paulus telling his chief of staff, General Schmidt, that there is something "senseless and unnecessary" in the order to capture Stalingrad.)[24] For Hitler the victory at Stalingrad, the city named after his rival, held symbolic significance.

For Stalin this city represented his Bolshevik past, the defense of Tsaritsyn he had organized during the civil war.[25] Considering Stalingrad to be his own city, he would not allow even the thought of its capture. Like Hitler, Stalin intervened at the operational level to override opinions of his General Staff. When by a stroke of luck plans for the early phase of Operation Blue got into the Russian hands, Stalin dismissed the intelligence as a ploy by Hitler.[26] He believed that the Germans' real intention was to attack Moscow, not to establish themselves on the Don River and head out to the Caucasus oil fields. When the Germans began their summer offensive, pushing south, Soviet troops had to be hastily repositioned. Stalin's interference in military affairs again translated into tens of thousands of lost lives. General Eremenko, the commander in chief of the Stalingrad front, would tell Grossman, "We had positioned our troops stupidly. . . . We were just feeding soldiers [into the battle]."[27] Both Stalin and Hitler would remain indifferent to the human cost, pouring hundreds of thousands of troops into the Stalingrad battle. Both dictators introduced brutal repressive measures to fight desertion. Grossman's comparison between Hitler's and Stalin's regimes in *Life and Fate* was inspired by such similarities.

In *Life and Fate*, Lieutenant Colonel Darensky, a staff officer from Front Headquarters, referring to Stalin's order of July 28, "Not One Step Back," remarks that countless lives were lost because of a fear of disobeying. "There was one place where the Germans were mowing our men down by the hundred. All we needed to do was withdraw over the brow of the hill. Strategically, it would have made no difference—and we'd have saved our men and equipment. But the orders were 'Not one step back.' And so the men perished and the equipment was destroyed."[28] In Stalingrad alone, Soviet military tribunals sentenced thousands to death for allegedly retreating.

Stalingrad was a thousand kilometers from Moscow, and it took Grossman and his companions almost five days to drive there over poor roads and with overnight stops. Everywhere in towns and villages Grossman saw that women had become the main workforce. "In villages—women's realm," he observed in his notebook. Women shouldered the entire work in the rear, he continued; they drove tractors, produced bread, toiled in factories, made airplanes and shells. "A woman feeds us, she arms us. And we, men, handle the other half of the work—we fight. And we fight badly. We have retreated to the Volga."[29] In villages Grossman observed young women being sent to the army. The army was short of manpower, so women with military or medical training were being drafted. "A tragic emptiness in the villages. Girls are driven away, they cry, their mothers are crying—daughters are taken for the army."[30] Russian losses in the war were concealed but by driving through villages one could see the countryside had become depopulated.

A total of seventy-five thousand women and girls drafted from the Stalingrad area would participate in the battle. Women staffed anti-aircraft and artillery batteries that fought against the Luftwaffe and German tanks. Nurses, working under enemy fire, brought wounded soldiers from battle. At Stalingrad women worked as telephone operators, machine gunners, mortar operators, snipers, and pilots. Three Stalingrad air regiments were entirely female. Women were also driving tanks at Stalingrad.[31] In "Volga-Stalingrad," his first sketch from the besieged city, Grossman describes anti-aircraft installations operated by young women. Artillery men who fought beside them told Grossman these women battled courageously and on one occasion halted the advance of a panzer division.

Arriving in late August, Grossman found Stalingrad in ashes and jotted down his impressions in his notebook. "Stalingrad has burned down. . . . It's dead. People are [hiding] in basements. Everything has burned down. The walls of houses are hot, like bodies of people who have died in a terrible heat and haven't gone cold yet." Civilians who lived through the horror of German carpet bombing seemed "half-insane": there were "many laughing faces."[32] The heat from the burning city was so intense it melted iron and glass. Stalingrad resembled the ancient city of Pompeii, destroyed by the violent eruption of Mount Vesuvius "on the day when it was full of life." The sight brought back the memory of Gomel after bombardment. "Sunset on a square. Strangely beautiful and frightening: a light pink sky looks through thousands and tens of thousands of empty sockets of windows and roofs. . . . Bombing again, bombing of the dead city."[33] These images would appear in "Volga-Stalingrad" and in the novel *For the Right Cause*, where he compares the death of a city to a dying child, the latter a far greater loss: "Houses were dying, like people die. . . . Thousands of buildings were blinded, and shining scales of smashed glass covered the sidewalks. . . . The enormous city was perishing in smoke, dust, fire, and amidst the rumble, which shook the sky, water, and ground. It was a horrible sight, but still more horrible was to see a six-year-old child squashed by a fallen beam, his glance growing dim in death. There is power, which can resurrect huge cities from the ashes, but no power in the world is capable of lifting the light eyelashes over the eyes of a dead child."[34]

At least forty thousand civilians were killed during the bombardments of Stalingrad.[35] The exact number of civilian casualties is unknown because the city was swamped with refugees; the actual death toll is believed to have been greater. Stalin did not give consent to evacuate civilians, viewing this as a step to surrendering Stalingrad. For the same reason he did not permit relocating factories from the city.[36] As Grossman states in "Volga-Stalingrad," the three major factories—the Stalingrad tractor factory, the Red October steel factory, and the Barrikady weapons factory—continued to work during nights of bombardment. Tanks produced by the Barrikady were driven from the factory floor to the front line. In "The Stalingrad Front," his last piece about the battle, Grossman shows the human cost of maintaining factories until the last. He describes six hundred people—factory workers and their families—overwintering in the hold of a single barge, waiting to be evacuated across the Volga. Grossman pictures an exhausted new mother who gave birth to a son "on the dirty damp boards" of the hold.[37] In *Life and Fate*, he would depict this woman in Vera Shaposhnikova, a nurse at a local hospital who falls in love with a fighter pilot, a young lieutenant, Viktorov; his plane is shot down over a village.

A large industrial city, Stalingrad stretched for sixty kilometers alongside the steep west bank of the Volga. Soviet troops received their supplies and reinforcements from the east bank. Correspondents' headquarters were also on the east shore. Further to the southeast lay the steppes of Kazakhstan, reminding one that the war had reached deep into the country. The Luftwaffe relentlessly bombed the vital river crossing to the city, where the Volga was about one and a half kilometers wide. During Grossman's first journey to Stalingrad the ferry, full of vehicles and people pressed together, stalled in the middle of the river. All they could do was watch as a German Ju-88 dropped a bomb. "A huge spout of water, straight, light blue. The feeling of fear. There isn't a single machine gun at the crossing, not a single anti-aircraft gun. The quiet, bright Volga seems as terrifying as a scaffold."[38]

During the battle the wounded were evacuated from the west bank on barges towed across by tugs and on fishing boats. Grossman was told how a trawler took a direct hit with all seventy-five wounded soldiers on board drowning. Limited evacuation of civilians was conducted between August 24 and September 10, 1942. Grossman likely knew that the last official evacuation over the Volga turned tragic. Shortly after an overloaded steamer left the dock it was hit by a bomb and sank. A crowd of women and children who had despaired that they were left behind watched the tragedy from shore.[39] In the novel *For the Right Cause* Grossman describes the evacuation of an orphanage. As the ship leaves the dock, air raids begin. Much as in Grossman's dreadful crossing, the engine stalls and the vessel is marooned in the middle of the river. The most vulnerable and the sick are swiftly loaded onto a lifeboat, presumably headed for safety. But then the crew manages to restart the engine and, while sailing ahead, passengers watch the children in the lifeboat perish when a bomb hits it directly.

Later that fall Volga crossings were made at night. Men from the river-transports battalion told Grossman how they adjusted to Luftwaffe attacks. The Germans had a rigid timetable, they claimed: the Luftwaffe operated from 9 a.m. to 5 p.m., "as if it were a regular job." So a crossing could be made between 6 in the evening and 4:30 in the morning.[40]

On September 13 the German Sixth Army launched a major assault on Stalingrad, smashing Soviet defense lines and advancing within two hundred meters of the Volga. The following day the Germans occupied the dominant height over the city, the Mamaev Kurgan. From this hill their artillery could fire at the river landing. On Stalin's personal order General Alexander Rodimtsev's Thirteenth Guards Rifle Division was rushed to Stalingrad. Because of Stalin's pressure the soldiers had to cross the Volga in daylight and charge up the steep bank under fire. As Rodimtsev told Grossman, one of the barges was destroyed and forty-one men in it perished. In his sketch "The Battle of Stalingrad" Grossman re-creates the moment when soldiers from the rifle division were boarded on the barges, sensing that "the enemy was everywhere"—in the sky, on the opposite bank, and under their feet. "The air was unbearably transparent, the blue sky unbearably clear, the sun seemed mercilessly bright, and the flowing hazy water deceptive and unreliable."[41] Grossman analyzes the psychological condition of young men facing death—and then proceeds to relate the heroic exploits of the Thirteenth Guards Rifle Division, which became internationally known for its daring operation in Stalingrad.

In September and October furious fighting erupted in the industrial part of the city. General Chuikov's Sixty-Second Army was pushed back to the Volga where it occupied a thin strip along the west bank. Soldiers approaching Stalingrad thought they were entering hell. After one or two days in the besieged city they would say the place was "ten times worse than hell."[42] A soldier who lasted three days in Stalingrad was considered an old-timer.[43] After a day of intense bombardment the Sixty-Second Army would evacuate two thousand to three thousand injured soldiers.

Realizing that Germany's military successes depended on firepower and coordination between tanks, infantry, artillery, and aircraft, General Chuikov adopted a practice of keeping close to the enemy. This strategy limited German air and artillery support. Chuikov ordered his troops to dig their trenches not far from the Germans' (occasionally they were only twenty meters apart), making it difficult for the Luftwaffe to distinguish between the two.

Because of its proximity to enemy lines, Chuikov's Sixty-Second Army was often resupplied by air. U-2 biplanes, flown by female pilots, dropped provisions at night. The pilots would switch off their engines and silently glide over Soviet positions. To guide them the defenders lit oil lamps on the bottom of their trenches. In *Life and Fate* Grossman relates an incident he heard of during the war. A Soviet company commander, named Khrenov, forgets to light his lamp; suddenly he hears an angry voice from above, calling him by name and exclaiming, " 'You sod, why didn't you give us any lights?' Khrenov had felt first amazed, then terrified. How could someone up in the sky know his name?"[44] (*Khren* translates as "horseradish" as well as "old sod.") He then looks up and notices a U-2 biplane.

This proximity of the Soviet and German positions created absurd situations Grossman would successfully explore in *Life and Fate*. During heavy bombardment, a German and a Soviet soldier hide in the same pit—without realizing it at first. When the bombardment ends, the two stare at each other—no longer as enemies but as two human beings. "As Klimov staggered to his feet, he saw a German soldier lying beside him. . . . They looked at one another in silence, two inhabitants of the war. The perfect, faultless, automatic reflex they both possessed—the instinct to kill—failed to function. . . . Klimov and the German reached the surface. They both looked round—one to the East, one to the West—to see if any of their superiors had noticed them climbing quite peacefully out of the same pit. Then, without looking back, without a word of goodbye, they set off for their respective trenches, making their way through the newly ploughed, still smoking, hills and valleys."[45] Grossman did not invent this: General Chuikov told him that during air raids of Stalingrad Soviet and German soldiers would hide in the same holes.

Stalingrad was the site of some of the fiercest fighting of the entire war: streets and apartment blocks changed hands many times. Chuikov relied on close-quarter combat, for which the German infantry was not trained, and on surprise attacks by small groups, which wore out the enemy. Soviet troops anchored their defense lines in factories and multistoried apartment buildings, turning them into fortresses with snipers inflicting heavy casualties.

Crossing to the west bank at night, Grossman interviewed two famous snipers—Vasily Zaitsev, credited with killing 225 enemy soldiers, and Anatoly Chekhov, a nineteen-year-old sniper and namesake of the famous writer. Grossman accompanied Chekhov on a mission. They climbed a broken staircase of a crumbled building and from there, leaning against the wall and hiding in its shadow, the sniper watched the street and the opposite building occupied by the enemy. When it was quiet, they could even hear German conversations. For several days and nights Grossman looked at the world through the sharp eyes of this young sniper to produce the sketch "Through Chekhov's Eyes." Seeking humanity in the hell of Stalingrad, Grossman tells how a boy who loved books and geography is transformed into a merciless destroyer by the logic of war. Observing the young sniper, Grossman felt he was immune to fear: it was absent in him as it is absent in an eagle. In this sketch Grossman goes on to discuss courage, a topic often talked about in war. He coins an aphorism to echo Tolstoy's famous opening in *Anna Karenina*: "Every brave person is brave in his own way."[46]

Courage did not come naturally to Grossman: he overcame his phobias and picked dangerous assignments to gather material at the front lines. As he writes in the novel *For the Right Cause*, he had seen two kinds of war correspondents: those who collected information at the front and those who obtained it from generals' headquarters. Reporters who traveled with army units were usually late in filing their articles and did not send the material their editors wanted. In contrast, correspondents who gathered information secondhand could wire it on time. Besides, headquarters information was always positive, which is why it was eagerly received.[47] When Leonid Kudrevatyh, *Izvestia*'s special correspondent, asked Grossman why he traveled to the front lines, he replied: "In order to write about the Stalingrad battle, one needs to be there, on the Volga's right bank, among those who are fighting in the ruins, by the shoreline. Unless I'd go there, I'd have no moral right to tell the story of Stalingrad's defenders."[48] But Grossman was drawn to the epicenter of events even before he became a war reporter.

In a 1943 letter to Olga he observed that "when I worked in the Donbass, I worked at the hottest and most dangerous mine, Smolyanka–11, and when it was time to go to war, I found myself in Stalingrad—and I thank my destiny for this."[49] Letters from home arrived late. In August 1942 Olga reported a tragedy: teenaged Misha was killed in an accident during military training. Sixteen boys were assembled in the yard of a military registration office for instruction. Through someone's negligence they received a real shell, not a dummy; when it exploded all sixteen were killed. Pasternak, always first to help out, dug Misha's grave at the Chistopol cemetery.[50] In September, upon receiving Olga's letter, Grossman wrote to comfort her:

> My dear and sweet Lyusenka . . . I see a lot of grief around. . . . I see
> women who lost their husbands and children; I see women whose

little children were killed in a bombardment. . . . Try to be strong, my joy, don't give up, you have Fedya and me, and you have [our] love and a purpose in life. . . . I took a letter from a soldier who was killed; it was written in a child's scrawl: "I miss you badly. Come at least for an hour, so I could see you. I'm writing this and tears are pouring. Come, Daddy." This little letter moved me to tears, and it was so painful to see this fallen daddy. There is much, much grief in the world, my darling, and . . . it's easier to deal with grief when sharing it with the entire people.[51]

Olga would become fixated on her grief, and her inability to sympathize even with Grossman's loss of his mother would create a gulf between them. For Grossman his personal tragedy was overshadowed at this time by the tragedies of others he was witnessing daily. He kept thinking of the little girl's letter and of her slain father. In the sketch "Stalingrad's Troops" he quotes the letter in full, remarking that perhaps the soldier had read it "sensing he'd be killed; a crinkled page remained lying on the ground next to his head."[52]

In October the Germans intensified their attacks, trying to smash pockets of resistance on the west bank. Chuikov told Grossman how he narrowly escaped death. His headquarters on the Volga's steep bank were built below oil storage tanks, believed to be empty. They were actually full of fuel. On the night of October 2 the Germans hit the tanks with incendiary bullets, causing a massive explosion that engulfed Chuikov's headquarters with burning oil. Forty of his staff perished but he was dragged out alive. Grossman recorded Chuikov's story: "Oil was flowing in streams to the Volga. . . . The Volga was in flames. We were only some fifteen meters from the river's edge. . . . A fountain of smoke eight hundred meters high. All this stuff was flowing with roaring flames down to the river. They dragged me out of the river of fire and we stood on the water's edge until morning."[53] In *Life and Fate* Grossman employs the account to create a powerful scene:

It seemed impossible to escape from the liquid fire. It leaped up, humming and crackling, from the streams of oil that were filling the hollows and craters and rushing down the communication trenches. Saturated with oil, even the clay and stone were beginning to smoke.

The oil itself was gushing out in black glossy streams from tanks that had been riddled by incendiary bullets; it was as though sheets of flame and smoke had been sealed inside these tanks and were now slowly unrolling.

The life that had reigned hundreds of millions of years before, the terrible life of primeval monsters, had broken out of its deep tombs; howling and roaring, stamping its huge feet, it was devouring everything round about. The fire rose thousands of feet, carrying with it clouds of vaporized oil that exploded into flame only high in the sky. . . .

It was surprising how quickly the soldiers managed to find a path to the bank. Some of them then made two or three journeys to the flaming bunkers, helping the staff officers to the promontory where, between two streams of fire flowing into the Volga, a small group of men were standing in safety.[54]

Stalingrad's defenders felt that Hitler had sent his leading forces here.[55] And in Stalingrad the main thrust fell to the northern industrial area where the Sixty-Second Army was holding onto a strip around three factories. In "The Axis of the Main Offensive" Grossman describes Colonel L. N. Gurtiev's 308th Rifle Division of Siberians defending the Barrikady factory during the worst days in October when the Germans launched a heavy air and ground assault. Colonel Gurtiev assigned two regiments to defend the factory and a third to hold the flank and the deep ravine. The defenders called the ravine the "Gully of Death" because the division was "expected to stand to the death."[56] Preparing for aerial attacks, the Siberians dug deep narrow trenches, which reduced exposure to bomb fragments. On the first day the regiments endured eight hours of intense bombardment by German Stukas, dive-bombers equipped with wailing sirens for psychological effect. All through the night the factory was shelled with mortar and artillery fire. In the morning they had to resist attacks of panzers and infantry.

The defense of the Barricady factory lasted one month. During this time, on top of incessant air raids, the battered Siberian division fought off 117 panzer and infantry attacks. "There was a terrible day when German tanks and infantry attacked twenty-three times. And all twenty-three attacks were repelled," writes Grossman. The division, according to his estimate, had endured 320 hours of severe bombardment by the dive-bombers. "With this roar of explosions one could deafen humanity; with this fire and metal one could burn and destroy an entire country." But the defenders "did not break down, did not lose their minds and hearts, but became still stronger."[57]

On top of it all, Chuikov ordered the battered division to make daily counterattacks against the German positions. The idea was to wear out the enemy; the strength of Russian soldiers was not considered. Markelov's regiment of Colonel Gurtiev's Siberian division accomplished what was beyond human endurance: charging under fire, it advanced a kilometer. "Only here they know what a kilometer means," writes Grossman. "An iron wind lashed at their faces, but they were still advancing. And again, the enemy became seized with superstitious fear: were people really attacking them, could they be mortal? . . . Yes, they were simple mortals, and few of them survived."[58] (These words, with no credit to Grossman, are engraved on a wall of the memorial complex on Mamayev Kurgan, the site of the bloodiest battles in Stalingrad. All the engravings in the memorial complex are uncredited except for Stalin's utterings. Stalin's bust is exhibited in the mausoleum.)[59]

After a massive bombardment on October 14, the Fourteenth Panzer Division of General Paulus's Sixth Army launched an assault on the Stalingrad tractor factory. The tanks smashed into the factory and a fierce battle ensued inside for every workshop. The defenders fought "in hellish, unheard-of conditions," Grossman writes.[60] In *Life and Fate* he describes the ground and air assault on the tractor factory:

> The ensuing bombardment was quite without respite; any gap in the unbroken wall of noise was immediately filled by the whistle of bombs tearing towards the earth with all their iron strength. The continuous roar was enough to shatter your skull or your backbone. . . . Several times he was knocked off his feet; he fell to the ground no longer knowing what world he lived in, whether he was old or young, what was up and what was down. . . . This explosion of violence seemed too extreme to continue for long. But there was no let-up; as time went by, the black cloud only thickened, linking the earth and the sky still more closely. . . . Time no longer flowed evenly. It had gone insane, tearing forward like a shock-wave, then suddenly congealing, turning back on itself like the horns of a ram."[61]

A Luftwaffe pilot describes Soviet resistance as superhuman: "I cannot understand how men can survive such a hell, yet the Russians sit tight in the ruins, and holes and cellars, and a chaos of steel skeletons which used to be factories."[62] On the night of October 15, 3,500 wounded were evacuated from Soviet positions on the west bank. As General Chuikov told Grossman, "We were living by the hour, by the minute."[63]

Around this time, on September 27, Sergeant Pavlov of the Thirteenth Guards Division and his storm group seized a four-story house, turning it into a fortress on the front lines. Although a small episode in the battle, the defense of Pavlov's house became a symbol of Russian determination not to give in. But facts about the defenders were distorted by Soviet propaganda. It was claimed that Pavlov and his small group resisted artillery and mortar fire, beating back German attacks for fifty-eight days (or as long as Pavlov remained in the house). In reality there were seventy to a hundred combatants and two other commanders who continued to hold the house for three and a half months, until January 10, 1943.

The defense of "Pavlov's house," one of the most glorious episodes of the Stalingrad battle, is re-created in *Life and Fate* in Grekov's house number 6/1. Heroic defenders of the house know they are doomed and this knowledge liberates them from fear—of both the Germans and the NKVD. The fighters speak about Stalin's purges and the kolkhozes, which they hope will be liquidated after the war. Krymov, the political commissar, is sent to Grekov's house to "stamp out . . . the anti-Soviet spirit." Grossman's belief that the war was fought for freedom is apparent from the dialogue between the commissar and Grekov. The latter implies he wants freedom from both Fascists and Communists.

> "Freedom. That's what I'm fighting for."
> "We all want freedom."
> "Tell us another! You just want to sort out the Germans."[64]

In "The Axis of the Main Offensive" Grossman commemorates ordinary participants in the battle—soldiers, officers, and medical orderlies, girls from Tobolsk, Siberia, who volunteered for the front after high school. All but three out of eighteen were killed, so Grossman lists them by name. He interviewed the survivors, learning how these girls treated the wounded under fire and carried them out to safety.[65]

Beginning in September, General Zhukov, now the commissar of defense, and General Alexander Vasilevsky masterminded a massive counteroffensive known as Operation Uranus. It aimed to encircle General Paulus's Sixth Army and Fourth Panzer Army on a two-hundred-mile front near Stalingrad. A force of 1 million was being assembled on the steppes to the north and south of the city to conduct a "deep penetration maneuver." Launched on November 19, the operation would turn the tide of the battle.

The Red Army attacked the weak German flanks, manned by the less motivated Third Romanian Army. By November 23 two spearheads of the Red Army had penetrated deep into the flanks, completed the encirclement of the two German armies, and linked up at the town of Kalach, west of Stalingrad. Grossman watched the beginning of the Soviet advance from an observation post. After an initial artillery onslaught, Soviet tanks drove swiftly over the hills, with infantry troops sitting atop the tanks or following on the run. He saw flashes of gunfire through the mist. Later he drove through the battlefield, littered with corpses of Romanian and Russian soldiers, and thought about the children orphaned on both sides of the conflict.[66]

Published on November 28, "On the Roads of the Advance" describes the turning tide of the battle. The Volga, partly covered with ice, is carrying barges full of Romanian prisoners in skimpy greatcoats and tall white hats. The body of a Soviet sailor is stuck to the ice, as if the dead man "did not want to leave the Volga where he fought and died."[67]

In mid-December the Volga was frozen solid and supplies were delivered to Stalingrad over an ice road. Grossman ventured to the west bank on foot. The journey was hazardous and had to be made at night: there was still fighting in the industrial part of the city, but the bursts of machine-gun fire and the bangs of explosions were no longer frantic. They resembled the din of a peaceful plant, the sound of steam hammers pounding steel bars. The Luftwaffe no longer bombed the city. German armies were encircled, their food and ammunition dwindling. But Stalingrad was still a dangerous place, and battles between snipers were ongoing. Grossman saw the city in December, not long before its liberation on February 2, and describes it in an expressive piece, "The New Day":

> The morning comes, and the sun rises in the clear frosty sky over Stalingrad. . . . The sun shines on the heaps of rusted metal, the sturdy military and factory metal, bent by the force of explosions. . . . The winter sun shines on mass graves, on self-made monuments. . . . The dead sleep on the hills, near the ruins of factory workshops, in gullies and ravines; they sleep in places where they fought. . . . Sacred land! One wants to remember forever the new city of the triumphant people's freedom, which rose amidst the

ruins. . . . Yes, soldiers won back the sun, they won back the daylight, the great right to walk on Stalingrad's land under the blue sky without bending over; they won the day. Only Stalingraders know the price for this victory.[68]

Grossman's inspiration for the piece may have come from the famous refrain in Erich Maria Remarque's pacifist novel about World War I, *All Quiet on the Western Front*: "Monotonously the lorries sway, monotonously come the calls, monotonously falls the rain. It falls on our heads and on the heads of the dead up in the line, on the body of the little recruit with the wound that is so much too big for his hip; it falls on Kemmerich's grave; it falls in our hearts."[69] He also might have been inspired by Ecclesiastes: "The sun also ariseth, and the sun goeth down."[70] (Biblical references, both open and hidden, are scattered throughout Grossman's works. This can be seen, for example, in his depiction of the Soviet retreat as an exodus.)

In mid-November Grossman wrote Olga from Stalingrad: "What I see here can indeed inspire the world's admiration. The world has never known such courage, such stamina. One needs to bow down to the people who sacrifice their lives with such simplicity, in fierce battles that go without respite day and night. These are harsh and sublime days; I'll never forget them as long as I live. It seems to me that I've never felt so deeply as I do now."[71] In December, after three months amid death and devastation, Grossman was drained physically and emotionally. He asked his editor for leave: he was exhausted by three months of tension in Stalingrad and wanted to visit Moscow in January.[72] That month he produced another three sketches about Stalingrad. His piece "Military Council" describes his meeting with Chuikov, who spoke of how he nearly died when his headquarters were engulfed with burning oil, of bombardment shaking his bunker so hard that chairs and tables had to be nailed down, as if the military council was on a stormy sea or "in the epicenter of a powerful earthquake."[73]

The sketch "The Stalingrad Forces" was drawn from Grossman's trip to the west bank in December. He visited Colonel Nikolai Batyuk's division, which defended one of the factories in the industrial part of the city. Observing the factory ruins, Grossman realized what the defenders had gone through. The concrete walls and ceiling were breached with direct hits by demolition bombs weighing more than a metric ton. Steel bars and framework hung from holes like "threads of a fishnet" breached by a beluga whale. The factory's western wall was destroyed by long-range artillery fire, and the northern wall had collapsed. Traces of bullets and shells were everywhere. Amid the destruction hung a surviving factory sign: "Shut doors, fight flies."[74]

Divisional headquarters in the factory's deep basement were furnished with mattresses and tables from ruined buildings. Here Grossman interviewed a Chuvash battalion commander, Ilgachkin. He never ceased to remind readers about Soviet minorities, who were equally involved in the war effort. This was also important because of the ongoing deportation of minority nationalities Stalin accused of treachery. Grossman wrote to remind readers that "the brotherhood of Stalingrad's defense" had united people of all nationalities.[75] Batyuk's glorious division welcomed Grossman with "good-natured Ukrainian hospitality." The soldiers wound up a gramophone, and Grossman was overjoyed to hear Beethoven's music and his favorite Irish feast song (known in German and English as "The Deserter" or "The Evening Previous to His Execution.")[76] In "The Stalingrad Forces" Grossman writes about the great unifying power of art—Russian soldiers playing Beethoven's music in the ruins of Stalingrad. Beethoven's song knew no boundaries, bringing humanity together in a destroyed building during a bloody war. Grossman proceeds to quote the refrain in the Russian version of the song:

> My Lady Death, we beg you
> To wait outside.

Grossman comments: "These words, this simple and ingenious music by Beethoven sounded indescribably powerful here. Perhaps it gave me one of my biggest impressions of the war, for in war an individual knows many extreme and bitter emotions; he knows hatred and heartache, he knows grief and fear, love, pity, and revenge. But people in war are rarely visited with sadness. . . . And here, as never before, I rejoiced at the great power of genuine art, that soldiers, who faced death in this ruined building they have defended from the fascists for three months, listened to Beethoven's song with a solemnity of people attending a church service."[77]

Recalling his conversations with Grossman during the war, Ehrenburg writes: "He was a true internationalist and often chided me when I wrote 'Germans' instead of 'Hitlerites' or 'fascists' to describe the occupiers' atrocities: 'One shouldn't ascribe the epidemic of plague to a national character.

Karl Liebknecht was also a German."[78] But in 1943 when the two visited the Jewish settlement of Letki in the Brovarsky district near Kiev, incinerated with all its occupants, Grossman seemed to change his mind. Ehrenburg was interviewing a captured Nazi, one of the arsonists; Grossman listened in silence. A German émigré writer who was with them tried to justify the arsonists' actions. When Grossman was alone with Ehrenburg he said it was not the captured Nazi but the German writer who had caused him to reverse his opinion.[79] But as is apparent from his 1943 article "Ukraine without Jews" Grossman continued to make a clear distinction between the German people and the Nazis. Unlike Ehrenburg, he never preached revenge toward the Germans. Later, in *Life and Fate*, Grossman created the character of Lieutenant Peter Bach, a former Social Democrat, who dwells on his hatred of Hitler while recuperating in hospital near Stalingrad. Bach thinks of the Jewish contribution to German culture and science: "Einstein may be a Jew, but—forgive me for saying this—he's a genius." Bach "felt differently" from his fellow officers "about the extermination of the Jews."[80]

Ehrenburg believed that Grossman's *Stalingrad Sketches* were "the most convincing and impressive of all we've written during the war." He particularly valued "The Axis of the Main Offensive" and "Through Chekhov's Eyes," which captured the spiritual strength of ordinary participants in the battle. He wondered why Ortenberg sent him away to Elista, Kalmykia, instead of letting him remain in Stalingrad to report on the victory. Stalingraders considered Grossman more than a journalist—he was one of their own, their comrade in arms.[81]

While Grossman covered the Battle of Stalingrad during its most difficult months, Konstantin Simonov, a young popular poet, received the honor of reporting on the glorious denouement. In early 1943, when Grossman was assigned to Kalmykia, south of Stalingrad, little was happening there. In his memoir General Ortenberg claims he transferred Grossman to the southern front out of concern for his health. Although Grossman was really exhausted and unwell, suffering from a heart condition, Ortenberg does not tell the whole story. Simonov was Stalin's favorite, so it was clearly advantageous for the newspaper to have him report on the Stalingrad victory.

Leaving Stalingrad on New Year's Eve, Grossman experienced a "feeling of separation" he had never felt during the war.[82] He wrote his father that abandoning Stalingrad was like leaving a close friend behind: so many memories and thoughts were associated with the place.[83]

Grossman's *Stalingrad Sketches*, reprinted by national newspapers and occasionally by *Pravda*, brought him true popularity. In addition, his wartime writings appeared as separately printed works with a circulation of more than 1 million. In 1943 three central publishing houses (Politizdat, Voenizdat, and Sovestkij pisatel') simultaneously produced his wartime prose.[84] That year he also adapted *Stalingrad Sketches* for the documentary film *Battle for Stalingrad*. As he wrote Olga, the film was not a masterpiece, "not a Rembrandt," but he watched it with interest.[85]

Red Star took liberties in editing Grossman's articles. Annoyed with editorial changes, Grossman complained to Olga: "You should have seen how they garble my poor pieces, and not only garble them, but insert whole phrases. . . . As a rule, editors cut the endings of my sketches . . . delete the most interesting descriptions; they change titles and introduce sentences like, 'This faith and love were creating virtual miracles.' "[86] However, Ortenberg valued Grossman's prose and found it difficult to decide which paragraphs should go. Once he asked Simonov to cut twenty lines.[87]

In 1942 Grossman's novel *The People Immortal* was nominated for the Stalin Prize. The prize, however, went to Ehrenburg's novel *The Fall of Paris*. Ehrenburg heard that Stalin himself struck out Grossman's name from the list. "I don't know whether this is true, but Stalin must have disliked Grossman as he had disliked Platonov."[88] In contrast, Stalin regarded Ehrenburg highly, considering him to be his unofficial cultural ambassador. In April 1941 Stalin even phoned him to ask questions about *The Fall of Paris*.

In 1943 Grossman admitted to Olga that he was "very upset and offended by the story with the prize. But never mind, this doesn't diminish the respect I have among writers and readers. I'm asking you not to be upset. All this is now behind me and ahead is big and serious work."[89] In January 1943, during his two-week leave, Grossman began drafting the novel he initially called "Stalingrad" (it eventually appeared under the title *For the Right Cause*). Before returning to the front, he told Ortenberg that he was writing a novel about Stalingrad and had completed the first chapters.[90]

For his part in covering the battle Grossman was recommended for the Order of Lenin but received the Red Star, a lesser award. (He had been recommended for the Red Star twice before without receiving it.) In winter 1943, when he visited his family in Chistopol, his stepson Fedya rushed to congratulate him on the award. Grossman appeared almost indifferent.[91] Although he would wear the medal with pride, his thoughts were not about promotions and awards. So many people he met at Stalingrad would never see the light of day; all personal recognition paled in comparison.

In May, during a lull at the front, Grossman visited Chuikov and members of the military council of the Sixty-Second Army. The generals argued over who had made the greatest contributions to the battle: "Dissatisfaction, ambition, insufficient awards, hatred of anyone who had received greater awards, hatred of the press. They spoke of the film *Stalingrad* and cursed. . . . Not a single word about the fallen men, about memorials, about immortalizing the memory of those who never came back. Everyone is only talking about themselves and their accomplishments."[92] After the victory at Stalingrad the spirit of unity was lost: the military men were consumed with rivalry.

9. Arithmetic of Brutality

It's simple arithmetic—the simple arithmetic of brutality.
—Vasily Grossman, "The Old Teacher"

Five million Jews lived in the Soviet Union before Hitler's attack on June 22, 1941. Approximately half were slaughtered during the German occupation.[1] The invasion of the Soviet Union marked the beginning of the Final Solution. Four mobile killing units (Einsatzgruppen), whose duty was to exterminate Jews, Communist Party officials, and the Red Army's political commissars, followed the German Army into the Soviet territories. During the first six months of the invasion, almost a million Soviet Jews—mostly women, children, and the elderly, all those who could be found in German-occupied regions—were killed.[2]

On August 24, 1941, the Soviet government authorized a rally by famous Jewish intellectuals and artists. They appealed to their "brother Jews" around the world for unity and support in the face of Fascist aggression. Among the participants were the writers Ilya Ehrenburg and Samuil Marshak as well as the Yiddish poet and writer Peretz Markish. Solomon Mikhoels, the well-known actor and director of the Jewish State Theater in Moscow, spoke about Hitler's plan to annihilate the Jewish people. *Pravda* published a detailed report, and one hundred thousand copies of a transcript of the speeches, translated into English and Yiddish, were printed in America, producing an impact. That same fall, the American Committee of Jewish Writers, Artists, and Scientists was created with Albert Einstein as honorary head.

In February 1942, the Jewish Anti-Fascist Committee (JAC) was formed in the Soviet Union with Mikhoels as chair. Its primary goal was to appeal to audiences in the West to support the wartime alliance with the Soviet Union. (Four other Soviet anti-Fascist committees were also created for women, youth, Slavs, and scientists to broadcast information about German atrocities.) The Soviet Information Bureau (Sovinformburo), which supervised the JAC's activity, authorized the publication of hundreds of articles and pamphlets for audiences abroad, part of the Soviet campaign to win support for its war effort.[3]

Solomon Lozovsky, who directly supervised the JAC's work at Sovinformburo, declared at a press conference in 1942: "Hitler made it his goal to destroy the Jewish people. . . . It's no wonder that the Jews created the Antifascist committee to help the Soviet Union, the United States and England put an end to Hitler's bloody insanity."[4] At the time, authorities officially endorsed the activity of the JAC: it worked in collaboration with the Communist Party and the Soviet State Committee for Investigating Nazi Crimes.[5] A decade later, during the Cold War, Stalin would liquidate the JAC; its members were secretly tried as Jewish nationalists and shot.

In 1941–42 Soviet newspapers published reports about specific massacres of Soviet Jews. On January 7, 1942, *Pravda* carried Molotov's diplomatic statement protesting German atrocities in the occupied territories, which also referred to the massacre of Jewish civilians in Kiev. Later that year, on December 18 and December 19, respectively, *Pravda* and *Izvestia* carried their first commentaries on the Final Solution. The article in *Izvestia* appeared under the headline "On the Fulfillment of the Hitlerite Plan to Exterminate the Jewish Population of Europe."[6] This article described the deportation and massacre of Jews throughout Europe and the occupied Soviet territories.

Undoubtedly aware of these revelations, Grossman discovered even more about Nazi barbarisms as Soviet troops started liberating the occupied territories. In winter 1942 he visited Colonel Khazin's tank brigade on the southern front, later to learn that Khazin's entire family had been slaughtered by an Einsatzgruppe conducting mass executions of civilians in the occupied city of Kerch. When a local newspaper published photographs of the dead in a ditch, Khazin had recognized his wife and children. Grossman wondered what this man felt when leading his tanks into battle.[7]

When in February 1943 Grossman arrived in Elista, south of Stalingrad, the city had been burned to the ground. Elista, Kalmykia's capital, had been occupied between mid-August and the end of December 1942. Local people told Grossman that all of its ninety-three Jewish families had been murdered during the occupation.[8] (This was accurate: the city's entire Jewish population had been driven to a ravine and shot. In all, about three hundred people had perished there.)[9]

In March, attached to the Third Guards Army in the northern Donbass, Grossman traveled through the recently liberated towns of Eastern Ukraine, inquiring about the fate of their Jewish populations. That month he visited Lugansk (then Voroshilovgrad). The city had been home to eleven thousand Jews before it fell to the Germans. Lugansk was occupied from July 1942 to mid-February 1943. On November 1, 1942, several thousand Jews were led to an anti-tank trench outside the city and shot; others were killed in gas vans.[10] After visiting the city, Grossman wrote his father: "I often dream of Mama, but during this trip I dreamt of her the whole night and saw her as vividly as if she were alive. After that I was in a horrible state all day. No, I don't believe that she is alive. I travel the entire time through the regions that have been liberated from the Germans and see what these damned beasts were doing to old people and children. And Mama was Jewish. I feel a strong desire to exchange my pen for a rifle."[11]

Around then Grossman began his story "The Old Teacher," one of the first fictional works about the Holocaust. The action takes place in an unnamed Ukrainian town where Jews have lived for generations. The town is occupied on June 5, 1942, a year later than Berdichev. The fictional village of Malye Nizgurtsy is less than twenty kilometers east of the occupied town. An actual village that matches this description, Bol'shie Nizgortsy, lies twenty kilometers east of Berdichev. Grossman was undoubtedly thinking about his mother's fate when he wrote the story and made his protagonist an elder teacher, like his mother.

The Jewish residents in this town have time to flee; those who stay behind are the elderly, the sick, and the children. They face what has been termed by Holocaust scholar Lawrence Langer "choiceless choices."[12] The old teacher, Boris Rosenthal, is penniless and, like the others, has nowhere to go. At eighty-two, he is too old to endure evacuation to the Urals on a crowded freight train that would take weeks to reach its destination. On the eve of the occupation the old teacher and the town's best doctor, Weintraub, who has practiced here for forty years, know they are trapped.

"What can save us now?" Weintraub asked quickly.

"Poison. . . . Epicurus taught that, if his sufferings become unbearable, a wise man can kill himself out of love of life. Well, I love life no less than Epicurus did."[13]

As the Nazis occupy the town, its unsavory elements surface. Local volunteers, men like Yashka Mikhailyuk, a deserter from the Soviet Army, join the Nazi auxiliary police. (Although later the topic of local collaboration would become taboo, in the fall of 1943, when the story appeared in *Znamya* magazine, it was still possible to say that Ukrainians voluntarily served in Nazi police units and helped exterminate Jews.) The story mentions a Ukrainian police chief coming to the town from Vinnitsa. It tells of local Ukrainians evicting Jewish families from their homes on the eve of the German occupation. "Koryako walked up and down the yard and, with a sly grin, asked the women, 'So what's happened to our Jews? Children, old men—I haven't glimpsed a Jew all day. It's all as if they'd never existed. And only yesterday they were all coming back from the market with twenty-kilo baskets!' "[14]

The story addresses the uniqueness of the Holocaust, "the murder of a whole nation." Alone in his town to have grasped the motivation for the Germans' actions, teacher Rosenthal elucidates the Nazi theory of the master race and the "all-European system of forced labor" established in the occupied territories. Unlike the teacher, Weintraub harbors an illusion of Germans as "a cultured European people." This impression is shattered when he observes the Nazis terrorize the Jewish population and segregate them into a ghetto. As Grossman points out in the story, Soviet ghettos served mainly as places to gather the condemned before their imminent execution. The Jewish population had to be kept unaware of the looming massacre: in the story people are told they will be taken to work on farms. But Grossman believes that few were deceived: "Women, old men, little children—everyone understood what was happening." The truth comes out when German soldiers begin to barter the clothes of their victims in the market: the gossip seeps into the ghetto that instead of taking the Jewish people to work the Nazis take them "to gullies and ravines" to be shot. But the human psyche tends to reject horrible facts. "All of the Jews knew what was in store for them; they were all able to guess. But in their heart of hearts they did not believe it. The murder of the whole nation was something too terrible. Nobody could believe it."[15]

Having witnessed interrogations of captured Nazi officers, Grossman knew the details of mass executions. By 1942 Einsatzkommandos (a subgroup of mobile killing squads) followed uniform instructions. The SS officer in the story elaborates on the logistics and the most efficient ways to conduct a slaughter. For "an experienced organizer," he explains, it should take two and a half hours to kill a thousand people. The execution squad must consist of volunteers and be kept small—"not more than twenty men for a thousand Jews."[16]

Allusions to Exodus and the book of Job serve to emphasize two centers of gravity in the story—good and evil. On the eve of the Nazi occupation, Rosenthal recalls random phrases from the Bible: "Murk rose from the beds of lakes and rivers; toads swam to the surface; thistles sprang up where wheat had been planted." However, the old teacher is not religious: "His God was Life." In contrast, the Nazis devalue human life, bringing only death and destruction to the world. Despite the horrors he is witnessing, the teacher maintains his faith in humanity. Although "fated to die" during a terrible time when life is "ruled by the laws of evil," he believes that Fascism has failed in everything it is trying to achieve. The Nazis "meant to unleash hatred, but what has been born is compassion. . . . I've seen with my own eyes that the fate of the Jews has evoked only grief and compassion." (This message is inconsistent with Grossman's earlier depiction of Ukrainian collaboration with the Nazis. But perhaps Grossman was thinking of the long-term impact of the Holocaust on the world.) On the eve of the mass execution, teacher and doctor bid farewell to each other. The doctor chooses to commit suicide, but the teacher decides to "live his last bitter hour" with his people.[17]

The victims' capacity for humanity and love contrasts with the complete amorality of the perpetrators. As they are marched to the execution site, a little girl loses her family in the crowd. The teacher thinks of how to comfort her but instead the child consoles the old man: "Teacher," she says, "don't look that way, it will frighten you."[18] The idea that humanity and compassion would prevail over violence and tyranny was at the heart of Grossman's beliefs. As he writes in the story, during the war no one was "moved by blood, suffering, and death; what surprised and shook people was kindness and love."[19]

At the time he wrote "The Old Teacher" official anti-Semitism was on the rise in the Soviet Union and references to Jewish suffering were censored. According to Ehrenburg, Jewish names were deleted from his articles. After the Stalingrad victory Stalin no longer needed to play the Jewish card. Ethnic Jews were being dismissed from their posts. Grossman's editor, General

Ortenberg, was among the first to lose his job. In spring 1943 Ortenberg was summoned by Alexander Shcherbakov, the chief of the Red Army Political Department, who told him that there were "too many Jews" among his correspondents: he should dismiss some of them. "I already have," Ortenberg replied, listing eight Jewish correspondents who were killed at the front. "I can add one more—myself," he said, and walked out.[20] At the end of July Ortenberg was informed of his dismissal from *Red Star*; he was replaced by General Talensky. These were the early portents of the anti-Semitic campaign Stalin would launch after the war.

During the war Grossman encountered anti-Jewish sentiments in the Soviet Army and elsewhere; the most common was the claim that Jews did not fight. In 1941 Ehrenburg wrote Grossman that he had heard this remark from Mikhail Sholokhov. "You are fighting," Sholokhov told him, "but Abram is doing business in Tashkent." Ehrenburg was furious and called Sholokhov "a pogrom-monger." Grossman replied to Ehrenburg in November: "I think about Sholokhov's anti-Semitic slander with pain and contempt. Here on the South-Western Front, there are thousands, tens of thousands of Jews. They are walking with machine-guns into the snow-storms, breaking into towns held by the Germans, falling in battle. I saw all this. . . . If Sholokhov is in Kuibyshev, be sure to let him know that comrades at the front know what he is saying. Let him be ashamed."[21] The Soviet press rarely acknowledged Jewish participation in the war. However, even though they were a Soviet minority, Jews earned the greatest number of military medals after the three dominant nationalities—Russians, Ukrainians, and Belorussians. Approximately 150 Jews received the highest distinction during the war: Hero of the Soviet Union. Out of 450,000 Jews who served in the Soviet Army, 40 percent were killed.[22]

Grossman was yet to cover the biggest tank battle in military history. In July 1943 Hitler launched Operation Citadel, aimed at attacking Russian defense lines between Kursk and Orel. Preparing for the attack, the Germans concentrated around twenty-seven hundred tanks and assault guns and eighteen hundred aircraft. But the Wehrmacht was no longer superior militarily: the Soviet Army and the commander of the central front, Marshal Rokossovsky, amassed more tanks and aircraft in the area, and over 1 million troops. Soviet wartime production now exceeded that of Germany, with two thousand tanks and self-propelled artillery and twenty-five hundred planes manufactured each month.[23] In addition, as Grossman remarked in his notebook, the new generation of Soviet commanders fought intelligently.[24] Having learned from costly mistakes earlier in the war, they prepared effective defense lines for the battle at Kursk. In contrast to what took place in 1941, information about German military plans delivered by Soviet intelligence was now trusted. Knowing that Operation Citadel was to start on July 5, Rokossovsky launched a preemptive artillery bombardment, thus demoralizing the enemy.

In "July 1943," his first piece about the Battle of Kursk, Grossman tells about the Antitank Brigade commanded by Colonel Nikifor Chevola. Positioned at the key sector of the battle, it fired at German Tigers for three days and nights. Grossman was able to observe part of the combat:

> Black smoke was hanging in the air, people's faces were completely black. Everyone's voice became hoarse, because in this rattling and clatter one could hear words only if they were shouted. People snatched moments to eat, and pieces of white pork fat immediately became black from dust and smoke. No one thought of sleep, but if someone did snatch a minute to rest, that was usually during the day, when the thunder of battle was particularly loud, and the ground trembled, as if during an earthquake. At night, the quietness was frightening, the nerves were strained and quietness scared away the sleep. And during the day one felt better in chaos, which had become habitual.[25]

At another sector, the Ponyri station near Kursk, Colonel Shevernozhuk's multinational Antitank Gun Regiment fought fiercely for five days. Typically, Grossman describes the fellowship between soldiers of different nationalities—Russians, Ukrainians, Uzbeks, Kazakhs, Tatars, and Jews— all fighting with equal courage. In this piece Grossman mentions the Jewish battery commander, Ketselman, wounded and "dying in a pool of black blood."[26] The censors, alerted by both the Jewish name and the brutal realities of war, wanted to suppress the passage. It took Grossman's editor Ortenberg, who would soon be dismissed, much effort to have it published intact: "Vasily Grossman saw the battlefield with his own eyes. He saw destroyed enemy armour and our burning tanks and self-propelled guns. He saw our troops retreat and attack. He also saw the wounded and dead Soviet soldiers. And he believed it was dishonorable to remain silent about this."[27]

On July 12, at the end of the first week of fighting, the Soviet Army launched a counterattack near the village Prokhorovka, where over a thousand Soviet and German tanks fought a ferocious eighteen-hour battle.[28] Losses on both sides were enormous. When the German Army retreated, Grossman saw a field covered with burned-out tanks from the Waffen SS panzer divisions with ominous names such as SS Death's Head, SS Adolf Hitler, and SS Das Reich.[29] The Wehrmacht never recovered from this decisive defeat. Grossman concludes "July 1943" by stating that the Red Army is now on the offensive.

Following the army's advance in August, Grossman drove on the main highway past Tula and Mtsensk to Orel through the many villages and towns burned to the ground by the retreating German Army: "Entire regions were turned into 'desert zones.' In the area between the Desna and Dnieper rivers the Germans leveled almost all the trees to the ground. Vast regions of the Smolensk and Orel districts were transformed into uninhabited wastelands. The German forces consciously condemned residents in these areas to the greatest of suffering, to extinction by starvation, and to the bitter cold of winter."[30] In the regions between Mtsensk and Orel ruins of village *izbas*, or huts, were still smoking; old people and children were rummaging through heaps of brick, looking for things to salvage. "What a bitter and familiar sight!" Grossman exclaims in the article "Orel."[31]

The Soviet Army was advancing on the same roads as in the fall of 1941, only in the opposite direction. "We are liberating the very cities we surrendered to the Germans during the horrible August, September, and October of 1941. We are moving west in space and in time. We've now liberated Orel, Bolkhov, Mtsensk, Kharkov, Belgorod, Stalino [Donetsk], and we are back in October 1941."[32] Grossman was covering the liberation of Ukraine, his homeland. In "Ukraine," published by *Red Star* in October 1943, he writes: "How can one render the feeling, which seized us when again we saw white huts, ponds overgrown with cattail . . . tall pyramid-shaped poplars, dahlias looking out from behind wattle fences, and when the soft breath of Ukraine fanned into our faces from the earth and sky, and its land appeared before us in its indescribable beauty, in sadness and wrath, with its fertile land and black scars from fires, with its enchanting plentiful gardens; in fire and in tears."[33]

In the town of Kozary, between Nezhin and Kozelsk, wooden crosses were erected on the burned land. Kozary was one of the many settlements subjected to collective punishment by the Germans for sheltering partisans. Here 750 families were locked up in their homes and burned alive. "I saw dozens of villages around Chernigov and Kiev, burned down by the Germans as they retreated behind the Dnieper," writes Grossman. He concludes "Ukraine" with the story of an orphaned boy he met in the village of Tarasevichi near Kiev. Aged fourteen, the boy had "old, weary, lifeless eyes."[34] His parents were dead, his sister taken away to Germany; other relatives had been burned alive in a partisan village.

As Grossman was finishing the piece, he met civilians from Kiev who had slipped through the front line. They said that "German troops have surrounded an enormous grave in Babi Yar where the bodies of fifty thousand Jews were thrown at the end of September 1941" and were destroying evidence of mass murder. (While over 70 percent of Kiev's Jews had managed to escape before the German occupation, some 60,000–70,000 of them remained trapped. On September 29 and 30, 1941, the eve of Yom Kippur, 33,771 Jews were executed at Babi Yar in the deep ravines on the city outskirts.[35] The site was later used to additionally massacre tens of thousands; in all, over 100,000 perished there. The majority of the victims were Jews). In 1943 the Germans forced three hundred POWs from the Syrets camp to dig up and cremate the corpses. Gigantic bonfires burned for days; bones were crushed with large, specially designed rollers.[36] But as Grossman writes, attempting to conceal all the evidence was impossible: "Are they so mad that they really hope to erase their horrible trace? This trace is etched forever with Ukraine's blood and tears. It glows in the darkest night."[37]

Kiev was liberated on November 6, 1943, and the foreign press was brought to Babi Yar. On November 30 the Jewish Telegraphic Agency announced in London that before leaving Kiev the Germans had "emptied the graves" of tens of thousands of corpses and burned them.[38] Standartenführer (Colonel) Paul Blobel directed this top-secret operation under the code name Aktion 1005. In 1941–42 Blobel was in charge of Sonderkommando 4a, responsible for the slaughter at Babi Yar and elsewhere in Ukraine. During his testimony at the Nuremberg trials Blobel disclosed that in June 1942 the Gestapo chief, Heinrich Müller, entrusted him with "destroying evidence of the executions Einsatzgruppen carried out in the east. . . . This order was a matter of state secrecy."[39] When Soviet newspapers published information about Nazi atrocities, Himmler realized it was necessary to destroy evidence. In summer 1943 the retreating German army mobilized

POWs to remove and cremate hundreds of thousands of corpses from mass graves in the occupied territories. Blobel, who had been trained as a builder and architect, developed a machine for crushing human bodies (a photograph was presented at Nuremberg) as well as gigantic grills to incinerate hundreds of corpses each day.[40] Blobel was convicted in the Einsatzgruppen trials; he was one of the few major war criminals whose death sentence was actually carried out.

Traveling across Ukraine from east to west through regions that had had high percentages of Jewish populations before the war, Grossman found a single surviving Jewish lieutenant. He had been caught in the encirclement in 1941 and hidden by a peasant woman. Everywhere Grossman heard stories of the mass execution of Jews. In the fall he submitted to *Znamya* a lengthy article entitled "Ukraine without Jews." It was scheduled for the December issue but censors suppressed its publication. "Ukraine without Jews" was translated into Yiddish and published in two issues of *Eynikayt*, the newspaper of the Jewish Anti-Fascist Committee, on November 25 and December 2, 1943. Later the original was believed to have been lost; however, this important and powerful work survives in full in the Russian State Archive of Literature and Art.[41] As apparent from the title, the article investigates the implementation of the Final Solution in German occupied Ukraine. "Jews are silent across Ukraine. None are left in Ukraine. Nowhere—in Poltava, in Kharkov, in Kremenchug, in Borispol and in Yagotin, in none of the cities, hundreds of towns and thousands of villages will you see a young girl's black tear-filled eyes, hear the sorrowful voice of an old woman, see the swarthy-skinned little face of a hungry child. Silence. Stillness. An entire people murdered." (A German report, dated November 20, 1941, states: "There are no longer any Jews in Nezhin. . . . In the region under the command of the Orstkommandatur of Pereeaslav, there are no more Jews. The same applies to the region under the command of the Ortskommandant in Priluki." The Jewish population in these regions was murdered between November 1941 and February 1942.)[42]

Grossman, among the first to write about the Holocaust, realized that the slaughter of millions must be explained beyond statistics. Individuals cannot relate to the murder of people en masse in the same way they can to a single death. Grossman possessed a unique ability to describe multitudes with personal, individual detail. In the article he creates a moving memorial to victims by saying who they were, by listing their professions and the recognizable characteristics of old Jewish craftsmen, doctors, engineers, agronomists, grandmothers, students, and the disabled: "Dead are the violinists and pianists; dead are the three-year-olds and two-year-olds; dead are the eighty-year-old men with cataracts in hazy eyes. . . . Dead are the noisy newly born who suckled their mothers' breast until their last minute." He then proceeds to explain the nature of this unprecedented crime—the murder of a nation, of its body and soul.

> All have been murdered, many hundreds of thousands, a million Jews in Ukraine. This is not the death of armed people during the war, of people who left behind a home, a family, a field, songs, books, traditions, stories. This is the murder of a people, murder of a house, of a family, of books, of faith; this is the murder of the tree of life, this is the death of roots—not of branches and leaves; this is the murder of a people's soul and body, murder of great skilful experience created generation after a generation, by thousands of clever and talented craftsmen and intellectuals. This is the murder of a people's morality, of customs, humorous stories, passed on from grandfathers to their sons, this is the murder of memories, of a sad song, of people's poetry about a merry and bitter life, this is destruction of a hearth, of cemeteries, this is the death of a people, which lived for centuries beside the Ukrainian people, worked, sinned, and did good deeds, and was dying on the same land.

As Grossman emphasizes, Jewish communities had lived in Ukraine for generations: "Our grandfathers have lived here, our mothers have given birth to us here, the mothers of our sons were born here. So much sweat and tears were shed here that, it seems, only few could refer to a Jew as a stranger and say that this land—was not his land." It's impossible to forget the old Jewish men in prayer shawls walking to synagogues on Saturdays or the Jewish children running amid their Ukrainian peers. "Where are the Jewish people? Who will ask this severe question from a Cain of the twentieth century? Where's the Jewish people that has lived in Ukraine? . . . The people is killed, trampled into the ground." Mass executions of Jews took place in big cities and small towns alike. "One simply needs to say that if in a small town there were a hundred Jews, then all hundred were executed, not one less; if in a city there were fifty-five thousand Jews, all fifty-five thousand in this city were executed, not one less. One needs to say that these executions were conducted in accordance with accurately drawn up, detailed lists, that these lists did not omit one-hundred-year-old men and newborns, that all Jews remaining in Ukraine under the Germans were included in this death list, each and every one."

He discusses the Nazi ideology of race, which inspired and justified the mass murder of innocents, of elderly women, old men, the sick, and the children who comprised the majority of victims remaining under the occupation: "The Germans execute Jews solely because they are Jews. In their eyes there are no Jews who have the right to live. Being a Jew—is the greatest crime, and it's punishable by death." Grossman reveals the unprecedented nature of the Holocaust: "Humankind throughout its existence has not seen a slaughter of innocent and defenseless people that was so well organized, so extensive, and so brutal. This is the biggest crime in history, and human history has known many crimes, it is written in blood. . . . But here we are talking about the execution of an entire people, of millions of defenseless children, women, and elderly."

He writes on behalf of his generation, fated to live in "a cruel and terrible time" when the lives of individuals and whole nations have become devaluated. The rise of Fascism has been accompanied by the collapse of moral values and the destruction of principles of equality and individual rights; it has made murder and torture commonplace; it has crushed the value of personal freedom. Appealing to humanity as a whole, Grossman emphasizes the need to reject the Fascist philosophy of "complete amorality" and to establish high standards guaranteeing the rights of individuals and entire states.

He witnessed dozens of interrogations of captured Nazis. "These conversations took place amidst smoldering ruins, destroyed cities and villages, and focused on mass murder—executions of Ukrainian and Russian populations, total annihilation of the Jewish people—and not once have I observed remorse, horror, despair, the desire to renounce the shameful crimes linked with name of a German." Captured Nazis continued to preach superiority of their race and the notion that "the crime against humanity is not a crime if it's made for the benefit of Germany." In fact, many of the officers in the mobile killing units that conducted mass executions were educated professionals—lawyers, doctors, and architects. A commander of Einsatzgruppe C, Ernst Biberstein, was a Protestant minister who worked as a church official under the Nazis.[43]

The war tested Grossman's beliefs as a humanist, a pacifist, and an internationalist. At the time he perceived the war as a battle between internationalism and Fascism. Ehrenburg recalls a conversation they had in Moscow when Grossman was on furlough. "We sat until three in the morning; he talked about the front, and we were guessing what life would be like after the war. Grossman said, 'I now doubt many things. What I don't doubt is victory. Perhaps, this matters most.' "[44]

As the Nazis were erasing evidence of crimes, the Jewish Anti-Fascist Committee worked to document atrocities. In July 1943 the JAC's newspaper *Eynikayt* appealed to readers, soliciting their testimonies. After the liberation of Ukraine the JAC and its newspaper began to receive eyewitness accounts, which would form the basis of *The Complete Black Book of Russian Jewry*. The idea of producing this compendium was conceived almost simultaneously in America and in the USSR. In late 1942 Einstein and the Yiddish journalist Boris Goldberg, the son-in-law of Sholem Aleichem, proposed that the JAC gather material for such a book. Meanwhile, Ehrenburg, who wrote extensively about Jewish suffering, had accumulated his own archive of reader responses to his articles in the form of testimonies and diaries. As Ehrenburg recalls, "In late 1943, together with Grossman, I started working on a collection of documents to which we literally referred as the Black Book."[45] Both came to play a prominent role in this project and the work of the JAC. With that, Ehrenburg and Grossman believed in launching an edition of *The Black Book* for Soviet audiences.

The Kremlin was clearly uninterested in producing such an edition. It explicitly sanctioned only the JAC's participation in the international project, for example, sending materials on Nazi atrocities it had collected for publication in America. In spring 1943, on the heels of the Stalingrad victory, the Kremlin sent two prominent envoys, Solomon Mikhoels and Itsik Fefer, a Yiddish poet, on an unprecedented seven-month trip to North America and England. Their mission was to raise funds and political support for the Soviet war effort and opening of the second front. Helped by Jewish organizations in America, Mikhoels and Fefer raised millions of dollars for the Soviet Union. Some fifty thousand people assembled to hear them speak in New York's Polo Grounds stadium, decorated with American and Soviet flags that symbolized the wartime alliance.[46]

During their tour Mikhoels and Fefer received permission from the Sovinformburo to collaborate on *The Black Book* with the American side. After the war, during Stalin's secret trial of the JAC, this same collaboration was twisted as evidence of the Zionist and American-inspired plot against the USSR. Actually, Soviet official policy toward the Final Solution was duplicitous from the start. Stalin regarded information on Jewish suffering useful only as a propaganda tool. While the JAC had the Kremlin's permission to broadcast information abroad, references to Jews were suppressed at home. Soviet authorities acted according to Stalin's instruction not to divide the dead.[47] Newspapers had to report atrocities against undesignated "Soviet civilians."

Under such circumstances, Ehrenburg, Grossman, and members of the JAC, many of whom had lost families in the Holocaust, worked to produce an edition of *The Black Book* for Russian-speaking audiences. In 1944 Ehrenburg became chair of the JAC Literary Commission and recruited a number of prominent writers and journalists for the project. Grossman contributed his original articles "The Murder of the Jews of Berdichev" and "Treblinka." In 1945, when Ehrenburg resigned from the Literary Commission, Grossman took over as general editor, producing an introduction for *The Black Book* and fighting for its publication. But in the late 1940s the Russian edition would be banned. Despite frantic efforts by the JAC, Mikhoels, Ehrenburg, and Grossman to have their record published, the story of the Holocaust on Soviet soil was never told in the USSR.

Berdichev was liberated on January 5, 1944. Around this time, while in Kiev, Grossman searched for relatives who had lived there before the war. As he wrote Olga, he found no survivors: "My dear Lyusenka. . . . Yesterday I was in Kiev. It's hard to convey what I experienced in the few hours visiting the addresses of relatives and acquaintances. [There are only] graves and death. Today I'm going to Berdichev. My comrades have already been there; they say that the city is completely destroyed, empty, and that out of many thousands, tens of thousands of Jews who had lived there, only a few, perhaps ten people, have survived. I have no hope of finding Mama alive. The only thing I'm hoping for is to learn something about her last days and her death."[48]

Years later Grossman wrote two letters to his mother, reaching out to her beyond the grave. Even his family did not know these letters existed;

written on both sides of a single sheet, they were found after Grossman's death. He kept them in the same envelope as a photograph of a mass execution of Jewish women and girls. Their bodies are packed in an antitank trench as far as the eye can see. This photograph, taken by a Nazi officer, was the last link to his mother. By keeping it he made a commitment never to forget, to tell the truth about the war and the Holocaust. He told his mother's story in *Life and Fate*, the novel he dedicated to her. But of his personal pain he could speak only privately, addressing his mother.

He wrote the first letter to her in 1950, the ninth anniversary of the Berdichev massacre. In it he recalls arriving in the city in winter 1944.

> I arrived in Berdichev, entered the house where you lived—the house that had been home to Auntie Anyuta, Uncle David, and Natasha—and understood that you were no longer among the living. . . . But I did not know what a terrible death you had; I learned about this only when I . . . questioned people about the massacre that took place on September 15, 1941. I have tried dozens, perhaps hundreds of times to imagine how you died, how you walked to your death. I have tried to imagine the man who killed you. He was the last person to see you. . . . To me you are as alive as when we saw each other for the last time, as alive as when I was a little boy and you used to read aloud to me. And my pain is still the same as when one of your neighbors on Uchilishchnaya Street told me that you were gone and that there was no hope of finding you among the living.[49]

While in Berdichev Grossman had collected eyewitness accounts about the twenty thousand Jewish civilians who were slaughtered in the city.[50] Among others, he interviewed an Orthodox priest, Fr. Muromsky, who told about the Yatki ghetto. On August 26, fifty days after the city was occupied, the Jewish population was ordered to move into a ghetto in the oldest part of the city near the Yatki bazaar. Thousands of people were crammed into dilapidated old shacks with no sanitation. The ghetto, guarded by German troops and Ukrainian auxiliaries, was a step to total annihilation. The Ukrainian head of police, Korolyuk, took an active part in the selection and mass shooting of the Jewish population.[51]

In the article "The Murder of the Jews of Berdichev" written for *The Black Book* Grossman relates that several mass executions occurred in the city. First the Nazis liquidated everyone capable of resistance. On September 4 fifteen hundred people were rounded up, ostensibly for agricultural work, and shot. A fortnight later German troops surrounded the ghetto, forcing all inhabitants out on the market square, where selection began. Four hundred people—doctors and skilled workers—were taken aside and allowed to keep their families. As the privileged group shouted out the names of their family members, "hundreds of doomed mothers held out their sons and daughters to them, begging them to take the children as their own and thus save them from death." But these professionals would outlive the rest by only a few months.

On September 15 the doomed—around twelve thousand people— were marched to the field by the airport; small children and the elderly were driven on trucks. "The monstrous slaughter of the innocent and the helpless went on all day; all day the blood flowed. . . . All day people walking in an endless column past the execution site saw their mothers, sisters, and children already standing at the edge of the pit to which fate would bring them in an hour or two. And all day the air was filled with words of farewell."[52] Two boys survived the massacre. One was saved by his mother, who shouted that she knew the boy was Russian. Another boy, the ten-year-old Chaim Roitman, outwitted an SS officer: standing on the edge of the pit, he pointed to a shiny piece of glass and said, "Look, a watch." When the German gunman bent to pick it up, the boy ran off. He was hidden and adopted by a Ukrainian man.

There were other executions in Berdichev, but none involved as many victims as those on September 15, the day Grossman's mother perished. In 1946 Grossman received a letter from Rosalia Menaker, the Berdichev midwife who had assisted in his mother's labor. The Menakers had fled Berdichev before the Nazi occupation and survived. Rosalia reported to Grossman what she managed to learn about his mother's life in the ghetto. Ekaterina Savelievna settled with Berdichev's physician, Dr. Vurvarg, and taught French to his children, reading a French edition of *War and Peace*. Vurvarg was among the group of specialists spared during the first selection. His whole family later perished, except for one daughter, and it was she who witnessed Ekaterina Savelievna's final days.[53]

In March 1944, attached to the headquarters of the Third Ukrainian Front commanded by General Rodion Malinovsky, Grossman followed the army's push toward the Black Sea. In the piece "Thoughts on the Spring

Offensive," published by *Red Star* in late April, Grossman describes an unprecedented "sleepless advance that went on day and night." Roads were washed away by melting snow and rain. Unable to match the speed of the Soviet Army, German divisions had to abandon their vehicles and artillery in the mud. There was nowhere to rest, not a dry spot to sit down, but Soviet soldiers cheered themselves by saying that it must be "harder for the Germans." Advancing "under the eternal rain and the eternal, three times accursed, wet, melting snow," Soviet soldiers were pushing and pulling their heavy artillery and trucks, and there were days when even caterpillar-tracked transports would get stuck. They had to cross swollen rivers and build bridges, working in icy water up to the waist. But no task was more arduous than building a bridge over the Southern Bug. The sappers had to work in a marsh under enemy fire. They built that bridge in three days.[54]

Odessa was liberated on April 10, 1944. Grossman watched Soviet military equipment pour into the city, which had been occupied by the Third Romanian Army since mid-October 1941. Some scenes stuck in his memory. Scorched corpses, including that of a young girl with golden hair still intact, were carried from the Gestapo building. Before the war Odessa had a Jewish population of over two hundred thousand. About half of them managed to escape. The remaining one hundred thousand Odessa Jews, along with thousands of Jewish refugees from Transnistria, were forced to register with the Romanian authorities. Few of them lived to see liberation day: a report compiled in May 1944 by a Soviet Jewish lawyer, I. Leenzon, states that about one hundred thousand Jews were killed in Odessa.[55] Some seventy thousand of them perished in the ghettos and camps set up by the Romanians near Odessa— the killing grounds of Domanevka, Bogdanovka, and Akmechetka.[56] Ukrainian militiamen conducted the massacres in Domanevka, Grossman learned.

In Odessa he met a few Jewish survivors. Aisenshtadt Amnon, the son of a rabbi from the town of Ostrovets, north of Odessa, told Grossman that a Russian girl had hidden him for over a year in her room.[57] Grossman also learned from Amnon about the Warsaw Ghetto Uprising and the Treblinka extermination camp.

On June 6, 1944, while covering the advance of General Batov's Sixty-Fifth Army in Belorussia, Grossman learned about the opening of the second front. The news of the Allied landings in Normandy was met enthusiastically in the Soviet Army: that day there was spontaneous shooting and saluting.[58] At the end of June, two Soviet armies surrounded Bobruisk, trapping some five thousand German troops from the 383rd Infantry Division. After a thirty-hour battle, General Batov stormed the city set ablaze by the Germans. When Grossman and his company drove in, the fire was still raging. As Grossman writes in the piece "The Bobruisk 'Cauldron,' " German soldiers were told they had to fight to the death: deserters would be shot and their families purged.[59]

Grossman spoke with several German prisoners. The commander of their regiment, "a murderer with sky-blue eyes," had a set of "dreadful photographs" in his wallet. One showed a hanged Russian partisan and a woman clasping the dead man's feet. " 'It was in Poland,' said the German as if committing this in Poland would go unpunished. 'But why is the sign next to the body in Russian? . . . ' 'This doesn't mean anything; it was on the border between Russia and Poland.' "[60] Later that day Grossman witnessed the interrogation of Lieutenant General Adolf Hamann, the commander of the 383rd Infantry Division and a known war criminal. In the article "Good Is Stronger Than Evil" Grossman remarks:

> When you look at Hamann you're overcome with a horrible feeling. His appearance is like that of a human being. His hands, eyes, hair, speech—are the same as in other people. But in your mind's eye images stand out—of opened mass graves with hundreds, thousands of corpses of women and children who were buried alive: forensic anatomists found sand in their lungs; of the ruins of Orel he ordered liquidated on August 4, 1943, or of Karachev he erased from the face of the earth; of the burning and smoldering Bobruisk he set ablaze today. . . . And as a criminal should, he denies everything—the mass murder of Jews, mass killings of partisans . . . any violence at all.[61]

Hamann was convicted of war crimes against civilians and executed in December 1945.[62] In the same piece Grossman writes: "Sometimes you are so shaken by what you've seen, blood rushes away from your heart, and you know that the terrible picture you saw in a glimpse will haunt you forever, to your dying hour, and will press heavily on your soul."[63] His main message, however, is that the war failed to destroy humanity in people and that Nazism, the world's greatest evil, contains the seeds of its own destruction. He describes an incident that bolstered his faith in humanity's goodwill. A wounded German solder is sitting by the roadside near Bobruisk, watching

Soviet tanks and artillery stream into the burning city. A Red Army soldier approaches him and gives him some water. Moved by this, Grossman tells this story to remind the Red Army, soon to enter Germany, about an old tradition to take pity on the weak. In contrast, Ehrenburg in his columns expressed hatred of Germany and called for revenge, referring to the German people as "a colossal gang."[64]

At the end of July Grossman was reporting from eastern Poland. Plentiful fruit orchards along country roads, village boys selling cherries by the bucket for so little that even soldiers could buy fruit—such were his first impressions. Poland endured German occupation longer than other European countries. In Lublin the local university, theaters, museums, and schools had been shut down. The Poles suffered greatly under the Nazis, and Grossman heard many laments. But as he writes in "Cities and Villages of Poland," not a single lament came from Jews. There were no Jews left in Poland. "In Lublin, the city where there were more than forty thousand Jews before the war, I encountered neither a child nor a woman or an old person who spoke the language my grandfather and grandmother had spoken."[65]

Grossman had not yet read Julian Tuwim's lament and manifesto *We, Polish Jews*. Published in London in April 1944, Tuwim's forceful work about the fate of European Jewry was translated into scores of languages, including Russian. (Grossman kept the Russian translation of it.) "We Polish Jews. . . . We eternally living—that is those who died in the ghettos and the camps, and we specters—that is those, who have returned from beyond the oceans and the seas to our Homeland."[66] Written in New York for the first anniversary of the Warsaw Ghetto Uprising, Tuwim's words were eagerly read in many places from Palestine to Moscow.[67]

On July 23, 1944, the Soviet Army entered Majdanek, the first of the six killing centers in Poland to be liberated. Established in a suburb of Lublin as a concentration camp for civilians and prisoners of war, it later functioned as a death camp. The majority of Majdanek's inmates were Jews (120,000) and Poles (100,000).[68] Some 80,000 people perished in Majdanek; 60,000 of them Jews.[69] Unlike in Treblinka and other extermination centers, here the SS did not have time to destroy evidence of mass murder, enabling the Soviets to film Majdanek's premises. This newsreel was later shown at Nuremberg.

Grossman entered Majdanek with a group of correspondents and writers—Evgeny Dolmatovsky (a popular poet and songwriter), Simonov, Boris Gorbatov, Leonid Kudrevatyh, and Yakov Makarenko. Simonov, a fellow *Red Star* correspondent who had previously reported on Stalingrad's victory, was now commissioned to produce an article on Majdanek. His carefully worded piece, "Extermination Camp," appeared in *Red Star*. Simonov describes Majdanek as "a frightening case . . . of the crime against humanity," "too immense and too frightening to be comprehended in its entirety." In Majdanek they found gas chambers and crematoriums: their furnaces were filled with half-burned human remains. Majdanek's warehouses were crammed full of clothing and shoes. There were "Russian soldiers' boots, Polish soldiers' shoes, men's boots, women's slippers, rubber galoshes, and what is the most terrible sight of all—tens of thousands of pairs of children's footwear: sandals, small slippers and shoes from ten-year-olds, from eight-year-olds, six-year-olds, one-year-olds."[70] Majdanek's administration office held stockpiles of documents of the executed—passports and certificates from across Europe. These papers helped establish that Majdanek was a multinational camp; people of more than fifty nationalities had passed through it. There were Polish, French, German, Italian, Greek, Croatian, and even Chinese passports; "there were documents drenched in blood and washed out by water, torn in two and trampled on."[71] Simonov makes several references to Jews without saying they were the majority of the victims. He also presents the official Soviet version of the Katyn Massacre, stating that the slaughter of Polish officers was carried out by the Nazis in 1941, rather than by the NKVD in 1940. (In 1944 Alexei Tolstoy signed the report of the Special State Commission investigating the mass murder of Polish citizens in Katyn Forest. Tolstoy, among other nationally known figures, endorsed a report he knew to be false.)

About a thousand inmates, including some Russian citizens, lived to see the liberation of Majdanek. Soviet correspondents attended the interrogations of captured SS men and interviewed a Russian doctor who had managed the camp's infirmary. From these interviews Grossman learned, for example, that construction and management of the camp was handled by prisoners themselves and that the SS rarely appeared in the barracks. He would employ this information in *Life and Fate* where he describes a multinational German concentration camp managed by prisoners. But his research notes for the novel indicate that he is depicting Dachau, not Majdanek.[72]

Dolmatovsky, an ethnic Jew, later produced a memoir about his encounters with Grossman at the front. Majdanek had a stunning effect on both of them. After returning to Lublin from "the city of Death," they could neither sleep nor eat. Grossman was saying that humanity had crossed the final line, that "we'll never see anything as horrible as this." But they did: Grossman was assigned to write about Treblinka's death factory, and Dolmatovsky followed him there.

Arriving in Treblinka in early September, they witnessed the interrogation, carried out by Soviet prosecutors and investigators, of captured Ukrainian guards and an executioner. Later Dolmatovsky recorded this interrogation from memory:

> –How many people did you gas each day? . . .
> –Nine hundred, I think. –The word "people" is not used. After a pause: –Up to a thousand two hundred. . . .
> –How did you spend your time afterwards?
> –We sang songs.
> –What songs, for example?
> –"O Tannenbaum, O Tannenbaum."

> At this point Vasily Semyonovich [Grossman] literally jumped out of the bunker. I followed him. He stood in the cold wind, and tears were pouring from underneath his glasses. . . . Later he told me that it's because of the strong wind; he regained his composure, buttoned his greatcoat, and returned to the bunker where the interrogation was taking place.[73]

While Grossman's article about Treblinka makes no mention of this song, in *Life and Fate* German soldiers sing "O Tannenbaum" in Stalingrad as they unwrap Christmas gifts.

Dolmatovsky also recalls meeting Grossman on earlier occasions. In 1942, near Stalingrad, Grossman rescued him during a bombardment. Finding his fellow correspondent wounded in a bombed house, Grossman carried him on his back to a field hospital. To Dolmatovsky's surprise, Grossman never mentioned this episode to others. Also memorable was Grossman's ability to write with great speed; it contrasted with his otherwise unhurried, deliberate demeanor. In fact, Grossman would produce his comprehensive Treblinka article surprisingly quickly.

More than a decade would elapse before the world was prepared to deal with the ghastly evidence of the Nazi death camps. As Bettina Stangneth writes, in 1953 there was still not a single work on the Holocaust "aside from the Nuremberg judgment," and in 1957 literature on the Holocaust was still negligible.[74] But even at Nuremberg the focus was not on the fate of Jews: the first count, pressed by the Americans, was conspiracy to commit international crimes; the second charge, promoted by the British, was crimes against peace, and the third, brought by the French delegation, was "war crimes, including genocide."[75] It took decades for scholars and the public to grasp the hell of Treblinka and of the other death camps. Some memoirs of Treblinka took decades to emerge. The memoir by survivor Richard Glazer appeared only in 1992. Historian Raul Hilberg had difficulty finding a publisher for his major study of the Holocaust, *The Destruction of the European Jews*.[76] This silence only amplifies the value of Grossman's article about Treblinka.

First published in *Znamya* in November 1944, "The Hell of Treblinka" transcends its epoch and a single genre, being at once a work of investigative journalism, a historical and philosophical essay, and a requiem to the victims. His writing has the everlasting quality of genuine art, inviting comparison to Picasso's *Guernica*. Grossman is presenting evidence of unprecedented crimes "before the eyes of humanity, before the conscience of the whole world."[77]

The second major extermination camp after Auschwitz, Treblinka II was established by the Operation Reinhard authority in July 1942. Constructed a mile from the forced-labor camp Treblinka I, the killing center claimed around eight hundred thousand lives. "Himmler intended this camp to remain a profound secret: not a single person was to leave it alive," writes Grossman. It was located in a sparsely populated area east of Warsaw, between the villages of Treblinka and Małkinia.

Grossman arrived in Treblinka in early September 1944, thirteen months after an inmates' uprising on August 2, 1943. About three hundred inmates managed to escape; less than a third of them survived. Soon after the uprising, Treblinka's authorities started liquidating all evidence of mass murder along with the camp's structures. Pines and lupines were neatly planted at the sites of former mass graves. "For thirteen months from July 1942 the executioner's block had been at work—and for thirteen months from August 1943, the Germans had been trying to obliterate every trace of this work."

In July 1944, when the Red Army liberated Treblinka, forty survivors were found in the woods. Grossman was able to interview Jewish laborers and Sonderkommando members from Treblinka I and Treblinka II: "Everything written below has been compiled from the accounts of living witnesses; from the testimony of people who worked in Treblinka. . . . I have seen these people myself and have heard their stories, and their written testimonies lie on my desk before me." He also spoke with a captured Ukrainian guard, identified in his notebook as Ivan Shevchenko, who had served with the SS as a volunteer auxiliary. His notebook contains drawings of the death camp's layout—of the railway station, the road, the six-meter wall surrounding the camp, the "uniform rectangles" of the barracks, and facilities for the Germans including a bakery and barbershop. He recorded the hymn the SS men composed that Treblinka's laborers were forced to sing before execution.

The article pictures Treblinka from two parallel perspectives—of the victims and of the executioners. Having seen the killing grounds of Berdichev, Babi Yar, and Majdanek, Grossman was uniquely capable of reconstructing the entire picture of Treblinka's "vast executioner's block." Treblinka II was a camp for Jews, established to implement Hitler's Final Solution. "Nothing in this camp was adapted for life; everything was adapted for death."

Grossman explains how it was possible for a few SS and auxiliaries to lead hundreds of thousands to slaughter. "The SS psychiatrists of death" used deception to minimize attempts to resist or escape. Treblinka's new commandant, SS Captain Franz Stangl, previously in charge of Sobibor, turned it into the most "perfected" death camp.[78] He had the arrival area rebuilt to make it look like a regular railway station. Fake doors and windows were installed on what appeared to be a station building with a ticket office. False signs were posted: "Ticket Counter," "Waiting Room," "Information," and so on. There were even fake arrival and departure schedules to provide an illusion that trains were running to and from Treblinka in different directions, while in fact the single railway line ended there. (Captured in 1967 in Brazil, Stangl stood trial in Germany in 1970. He said that to him the Jewish deportees were "cargo" that must be destroyed. "I rarely saw them as individuals. It was always a huge mass.")[79] This deception helped the SS to minimize instances of escape and resistance. When the deportees were told they had arrived in a transit camp and had to proceed to the showers, they had hope for survival.

Grossman portrays Jewish deportees from Polish ghettos, packed tightly into freight cars, realizing "that the end is near," and unsuspecting

Jewish travelers from Western Europe who paid to be transported to a neutral country but were instead brought to Treblinka. "It is hard to say which is more terrible: to go to your death in agony . . . or to be glancing unsuspectingly out of the window of a comfortable coach just as someone from Treblinka village is phoning the camp with details of your recently arrived train."

He imagines the psychological condition of the new arrivals, whose thoughts and feelings alternate between hope and despair. As they stand in the reception area, they notice the camp's six-meter wall masked with yellowing pine branches, but dismiss the inner voice telling them they have fallen into a trap. Abrupt commands issued by the SS cloud their reason: the arrivals are instructed to leave their things in the square and proceed to the bathhouse with identification, valuables, and towels. People want to ask questions but "some strange force makes them hurry on in silence. . . . And everyone is overwhelmed by a sense of helplessness, a sense of doom." They walk through the gate, "an opening in a barbed-wire wall," from where "there is no escape, no way to turn back." All around them are the SS guards and Wachmänner (watchmen) armed with submachine guns, and heavy machine guns are directed at the deportees from the watchtowers. The Nazis use simple rules for operating a slaughterhouse, issuing a "never-ending sequence of abrupt commands" to break the arrivals' will. Grossman again contrasts the humanity and individuality of the victims with the inhumanity of the perpetrators whom he describes simply as "beasts." The SS men who prey on human beings are similar in their behavior and psychology. He speaks on behalf of the Jewish victims who begin to sense their imminent fate: "And all these thousands, all these tens and hundreds of thousands of people, of frightened, questioning eyes, all these young and old faces, all these dark- and fair-haired beauties, these bald and hunchbacked old men, and these timid adolescents—all were caught up in a single flood, a flood that swallowed up reason, and splendid human science, and maidenly love, and childish wonder, and the coughing of the old, and the human heart."

Nazi ideology excludes Jews from the realm of humanity. Belongings of the living dead, left behind, are being sorted and appraised: "Everything of value is to be sent to Germany." Letters, photographs, children's draw-ings, and "the thousands of little things that were so infinitely precious to their owners yet the merest trash to the masters of Treblinka" are gathered in heaps to be destroyed.

The order to undress reduces the deportees to helplessness. "We know from the cruel reality of recent years that a naked man immediately loses his powers of resistance. He ceases to struggle." Grossman was told that when families were separated and marched to different barracks, desperate scenes took place. "Love—maternal, conjugal, or filial love—told people that they were seeing one another for the last time." Deception was maintained almost to the end: the SS continued to pass "the regulations of death . . . as the regulations of life." When women's hair was cut, their hope was revived, says Grossman. Barbers told him that the "haircut of death did more than anything to convince the women that they really were going to the bathhouse." (But we know today that few believed this was being done for hygienic purposes. During the haircut the women often asked agonized questions about whether they were going to die. The Jewish barbers were either silent or tried to comfort them.)[80] Women's hair, along with valuables and everything else that could be used, was sent to Germany as raw material. Hitler's regime, Grossman writes, "harnessed" certain qualities of the German character, such as efficiency, to institute "a crime against humanity." The "brute beasts" of the SS make use of gold and valuables but discard "the most precious valuable in the world—human life."

The deportees are finally marched onto "the Road of No Return," a sandy path, 120 meters long, leading to the gas chambers. Now, forced to run to the execution place, people are beaten along the way, reduced to "a state of complete psychic paralysis." (Treblinka's commandant Stangl said that he sometimes "stood on the wall and saw them in the 'tube'—they were naked, packed together, running, being driven with whips.")[81]

The Nazis have condemned the Jewish nation to "the abyss of nonbeing," Grossman writes. Treblinka's inmates leave behind a "fresh imprint of bare feet: the small footprints of women, the tiny footprints of children, the heavy footprints of the old. This faint trace in the sand was all that remained of the thousands of people who had not long passed this way." Inside the gas chambers the plunder of human beings is complete: they were "robbed of the sky, the stars, the wind, and the sun." A few seconds is enough "to destroy what nature and the world had slowly shaped in life's vast and tortuous creative process." Grossman's biblical evocation is meant to elevate the doomed above their suffering and death: "The beasts and the beasts' philosophy seemed to portend the sunset of Europe, the sunset of the world, but the red was not the red of the sunset, it was the red blood of humanity—a humanity that was dying yet achieving victory through its death. People remained people. They did not accept the morality and laws of Fascism." (Grossman refers to Jews as "people" and "human beings" to refute their dehumanization by the Nazis.)

Grossman was an early chronicler of the Holocaust, and some factual mistakes were inevitable. He believed that Treblinka was "the SS's main killing ground," surpassing Auschwitz. His estimate of a total death toll ("around . . . three million people") was based on interviews with local peasants who told him, mistakenly, that on some days six trains arrived in Treblinka. He was also unaware of how long Treblinka's gas chambers had functioned at full capacity.

Grossman relied on his expertise as a chemical engineer to explain how Treblinka's death factory operated. "It was a conveyor-belt executioner's block; it was run according to the same principles as any other large-scale modern industrial enterprise." Treblinka used a variety of "murder experts," which Hitler's regime kept generating in abundance. In the gas chambers exhaust fumes were used as the main method of suffocation. Once the doors were sealed, an engine installed outside the building would pump in carbon monoxide.

Describing Himmler's visit to Treblinka, Grossman times it correctly: it took place in February–March 1943. Himmler arrived during the closing stage of Operation Reinhard to determine the camp's future. Grossman was mostly right about the purpose of Himmler's visit: "the minister of death" was concerned about erasing evidence of mass murder. The work of exhuming and cremating hundreds of thousands of bodies began immediately after.

Grossman's main source on this phase of Treblinka's operation was Yankel Wiernik's published memoir *The Year in Treblinka*. A Warsaw carpenter indispensable to the construction of the camp's facilities, Wiernik was kept alive for a whole year. During the Treblinka uprising he managed to escape and reach Warsaw, where he was persuaded to dictate his testimony. In May 1944 it was published clandestinely in Poland through the efforts of the Jewish National Committee and Polish Bund. Wiernik's memoir was smuggled to London and later appeared in English and in Yiddish in the United States. Grossman obtained a Russian translation, which today is to be found among his papers. A valuable witness to the camp's atrocities, Wiernik briefly handled disposal and incineration of bodies. In 1961 he testified during Eichmann's trial in Israel.

Wiernik describes scenes of inferno in Treblinka: "I . . . have seen a great deal in my life, but not even Lucifer could possibly have created a hell worse than this."[82] Grossman uses scenes from his testimony to depict the hellish summer of 1943 when the Sonderkommando cremated around a thousand bodies each day on gigantic grills. As Grossman writes, "More than eight hundred prisoners—more than the number of workers employed in the furnaces of even the largest iron and steel plants—were engaged in the work of burning the bodies." The story of how the bored SS men organized picnics by these grills also comes from Wiernik's testimony.

Grossman believes in the paramount importance of facing facts: "It is the writer's duty to tell the terrible truth, and it is a reader's civic duty to learn this truth. To turn away, to close one's eyes and walk past is to insult the memory of those who have perished." He points out that "it is not enough to speak about Germany's responsibility for what has happened. Today we need to speak about the responsibility of every nation in the world." The responsibility to "prevent Nazism from ever rising again" lies with all humanity.

"The Hell of Treblinka" is written with a deep emotional connection to the hundreds of thousands who perished there:

> We enter the camp. We tread the earth of Treblinka. The lupine pods split open at the least touch; they split with a faint ping and millions of tiny peas scatter over the earth. The sounds of the falling peas and the bursting pods come together to form a single soft, sad melody. It is as if a funeral knell—a barely audible, sad, broad, peaceful tolling—is being carried to us from the very depths of the earth. And, rich and swollen as if saturated with flax oil, the earth sways beneath our feet—earth of Treblinka, bottomless earth, earth as unsteady as the sea. This wilderness behind a barbed-wire fence has swallowed more human lives than all the earth's oceans and seas have swallowed since the birth of mankind.

Grossman's intention is to honor the nameless and to keep them in world's memory.

Upon returning to Moscow in September, he worked indefatigably to produce this article in a few weeks. "The Hell of Treblinka" was not easily accepted: he had to fight for its publication. However, for Soviet censors the murder of Jews in Poland was not as sensitive a topic as the fate of Jewry in

Ukraine, so Grossman succeeded in publishing the article in *Znamya*. In 1945, Voenizdat issued it as a separate publication. The article was translated into scores of languages and distributed by the Soviet delegation at Nuremberg as part of the evidence against the Nazis.[83]

After completing this article, Grossman suffered a nervous collapse. When Ehrenburg invited him to meet the French journalist and translator Jean Cathala, Grossman said he was too ill to come out. Cathala, who would translate Solzhenitsyn, was interested to know what Grossman had seen in the liberated death camps.[84] Gedda Surits, on the other hand, remembers that Grossman spoke frequently about Treblinka. He brought back a child's building block and a shoe from the death camp, later donating them to the Vilna Jewish Museum. Surits also remembers Grossman's stories about Polish ghettos where people continued to live their lives even as they knew that the end was near. Children attended school and adults gathered to discuss books. There was even a functioning music school. Surits recalls that Grossman brought home a graduation diploma issued by a music school in the ghetto. "Vasya spoke about this slowly, moved by human courage and inviting his listeners to grasp the true meaning of his words, to appreciate the genuine heroism of people who remained human in inhuman conditions."[85]

Upon returning to the front in January 1945, Grossman saw the Polish capital in ruins. Of its prewar population of 1.3 million only about 162,000 remained at the time of its liberation.[86] The Germans had bombed and shelled Warsaw mercilessly during the 1944 uprising by the Polish Home Army, and afterward razed large areas of the city as punishment. In the article "Moscow–Warsaw" Grossman mentions the tragedy of the participants in the uprising, "doomed from the start." (When Soviet troops approached Warsaw, Moscow encouraged the Home Army to rise up against the Germans. But far from helping the insurgents, the Soviet leadership ordered their troops to halt on the eastern bank of the Vistula River, allowing the Germans to crush the uprising.)

Warsaw's prewar Jewish population of more than 350,000 was the largest in Europe.[87] In November 1940 the Warsaw ghetto was sealed off from the rest of the city. The area, two square kilometers, was enclosed by a brick wall three meters high topped with barbed wire.[88] "Whose hands built this wall?" Grossman wondered in his notebook.[89] Over 300,000 Jews were crowded into this ghetto at one time, living more than seven to a room. More than a quarter of a million people were deported from here to Treblinka. Grossman met several survivors of the ghetto uprising. Among them was a stocking maker: he was carrying a child's wicker basket filled with Jewish ashes. "With these ashes he will be walking tomorrow to Łódź."[90]

When Soviet troops crossed the German border, Grossman thought of the hundreds of thousands who did not live to the end of the war. He writes about the German countryside without ill feelings: "Dark pine woods, fields, farmsteads, outbuildings, houses with pointed roofs. . . . There is a great charm in this landscape: its small but very thick woods are lovely."[91] Following the troops into the town of Schwerin, Grossman and his fellow reporter Efim Gekhman were billeted in one of the few houses unscathed by the fighting. The owners had fled in a hurry, leaving a warm kettle on the stove and cupboards full of provisions. Grossman "categorically" forbade his companions to touch anything in the house. When a colonel from the General Staff asked permission to stay, Grossman agreed: the man had such a "good Russian face." At night he heard strange noises from the colonel's room. By morning the colonel was gone and so were contents of the cupboards. "The colonel emptied the cupboards like a real looter."[92]

The end of the war was near; Germany's roads were crowded with POWs of all nationalities returning home from concentration camps. Grossman observed in his notebook: "French, Belgian, Dutch, all loaded with loot. Only Americans are walking light . . . they need nothing except drink. A few of them greet us, waving bottles. An international civilian multitude from across Europe travels on other roads. Women in pants, all pushing thousands of baby prams filled with stuff; the insane, joyous chaos. Where's East, where's West?"[93]

On April 20 Grossman and his companions set out from Moscow on their last trip to the front. During this journey he witnessed the Battle of Berlin and Germany's capitulation. They reached Berlin's outskirts on April 26. "The closer to Berlin, the greater the resemblance to the Moscow countryside," he wrote in his notebook.[94] Attached to Colonel General Nikolai Berzarin's Fifth Shock Army, Grossman arrived at a time when several Soviet armies competed for the honor of first reaching Berlin. The Battle of Berlin was one of the bloodiest and cruelest of the entire war. Many of the Soviet soldiers who survived Stalingrad and other campaigns would die during the last days in the ruins of Berlin.

Berzarin's headquarters were in Henning von Tresckow's castle. The owner, Lieutenant Colonel von Tresckow, had been a driving force of German resistance against Hitler. Involved in plots to assassinate the Führer, von Tresckow committed suicide the day after the failure of the last attempt on July 20, 1944. In his article "On the Brink of War and Peace" Grossman describes von Tresckow's castle, surrounded with an old park filled with sculptures. It felt surreal to sit by the fireplace in the ancestral home of the German nobleman, reading a book from his library.

On May 2 Germany capitulated and Grossman faced a flood of impressions—of Berlin, in ruins after Allied aerial bombardment, of "gigantic crowds of prisoners." Hundreds of dead lay on the streets amid smoke and ruined buildings; many were in brown shirts: those were Nazi activists who defended approaches to the Reichstag. The war correspondent and writer Alexander Bek recalled standing that day on the roof of the Reichstag next to Grossman. They saw columns of POWs, the city in smoke, and in the square below Soviet tanks and field kitchens. Grossman was silent, his usual reserved self. Then he said the words that became memorable to Bek: "Evil is overthrown."[95]

Elsewhere in the city, life was returning to normal: Grossman saw women sweeping sidewalks. He heard a local *Bürgermeister* ask Berzarin what the army would pay civilians mobilized for work. "Everyone here has a firm understanding of their rights," he thought.[96] There were "thousands of meetings" in Berlin with officers he recognized; he saw "thousands of refugees." Grossman had a comic encounter with a German woman dressed in an Astrakhan coat. After a pleasant chat, she asked: "But of course, you aren't a Jewish commissar?"[97]

The Reichstag struck him with its "enormity, power." Inside, soldiers were burning bonfires, opening cans of preserves with bayonets and warming up food. Grossman saw Goebbels's half-burned corpse. His scorched body was on display. "The enormity of victory. A spontaneous celebration." Grossman learned that a number of Soviet soldiers celebrating that day had accidentally drunk industrial alcohol from barrels in the Tiergarten. "The poison began to act on the third day, and killed without mercy."[98]

Grossman and Gekhman entered the new Imperial Reich Chancellery. In its vast lobby a young Kazakh soldier was learning to ride a bicycle. "Enormous crash of the regime, of ideology, of plans, of all, all. . . . Hitler's armchair and table. A huge metal globe, crushed and flattened." Parts of the ceiling had collapsed and the floor was strewn with plaster, papers, souvenirs, and books inscribed to the Führer. "Hitler's study, reception halls, offices of the fascist leaders designed to impress a visitor with their vastness. But what's the enormous size of Hitler's study compared to the enormity of crimes born in this damned place! What have these walls heard in the hours of horrible nocturnal discussions when Hitler and Goebbels sat at this table, amusing themselves with Himmler's stories about Poland, drenched in blood, Belorussia, Ukraine; about Oswiecim, Treblinka, Majdanek? . . . Blessed be the hands that destroyed this house."[99] Grossman picked up several seals in Hitler's office: "The Führer has confirmed," "The Führer has agreed," "The Führer's personal property."[100]

Grossman was among the few Soviet correspondents invited to attend the signing of Germany's capitulation in Karlshorst, Berlin, but he did not go. He gave his authorization to Vsevolod Ivanov, a writer and *Izvestia* correspondent who had collaborated on *The Black Book*. Dolmatovsky remembers Grossman saying that Ivanov hadn't seen much of the war and would be interested.[101] Ivanov was also a part of the Soviet press delegation at the Nuremberg trials. (Soviet press representatives at Nuremberg included Konstantin Fedin, Leonid Leonov, Vsevolod Vishnevskij, Boris Polevoj, Lev Sheinin, Boris Efimov, Grossman's fellow *Red Star* correspondent Pavel Troyanovsky, and the three cartoonists known collectively as Kukryniksy.)[102] According to his stepson Fedya, Grossman was invited to Nuremberg but gave his invitation to someone else. Ehrenburg traveled to Nuremberg, joining Soviet press representatives at one of the trials in 1945. Efimov recalls how Ehrenburg, by then the most celebrated Soviet journalist, with an international reputation as an anti-Fascist, entered the courtroom: "All eyes turned to him and there was movement even in the dock. I saw how the sinister gaze of Rosenberg turned toward [Ehrenburg], how Keitel moved his arrogant physiognomy ever so slightly, and how even Goering looked sideways at Ehrenburg with a swollen, blood-shot eye." Apparently even Hitler was familiar with Ehrenburg's articles calling for revenge on Germany; he referred to Ehrenburg as "Stalin's court lackey."[103] Ehrenburg wrote little about the Nuremberg trials. He considered the Nazis "petty criminals who have committed gigantic crimes."[104] Grossman shared this view. Although at Nuremberg Grossman could have seen General Paulus, one of the heroes of his future novel, he had his reasons not to attend. Grossman had witnessed many interrogations of Nazi criminals. It was painful for him to see the mass murderers once again. As for the glory of being at Nuremberg, this simply did not matter. As Surits tells in her memoir, Grossman spoke about the war without mentioning any of his feats. He considered himself a chronicler of events and was aware that at Nuremberg his testimony about Treblinka was available in both Russian and English. The American version of *The Black Book* published his abridged article alongside Ehrenburg's piece on Sobibor.

10. A Soviet Tolstoy

The hero of my tale—whom I love with all the power
of my soul, whom I have tried to portray in all his beauty, who
has been, is, and will be beautiful—is Truth.
—Leo Tolstoy, "Sebastopol in May"

In February 1945 the *Literary Gazette* published a photograph of Grossman at his desk to announce his work on a novel about Stalingrad. Grossman was quoted as saying that he had been writing this novel sporadically for a year and a half. Stalingrad's battle was won by the people, he continued, but "Stalingrad also determined human destinies and those of nations." He wanted his book to be worthy of the "nameless heroes" who must not be forgotten.[1]

Years later, in the second part of his novel about Stalingrad, *Life and Fate*, Grossman would dedicate pages to the impact of the victorious battle. It was achieved by the people but overseen by Stalin who, as a victor, created his own account of events and determined the destinies of Soviet nationalities and of peoples in Europe. "A people's war reached its greatest pathos at the time of the defence of Stalingrad; the logic of events was such that Stalin chose this moment to proclaim openly his ideology of State nationalism."[2] In *Life and Fate*, commenting on postwar Soviet politics of state nationalism and anti-Semitism, Grossman wrote that Stalin raised "the very sword of annihilation" over the heads of Jews "he had wrested from the hands of Hitler."[3] Mass arrests in the Jewish community and the secret executions of Jewish actors Mikhoels and Veniamin Zuskin and members of the Jewish Anti-Fascist Committee were followed by the highly publicized campaign against Jewish doctors.

Grossman's popularity peaked during the war, when his articles and stories were widely circulated. The influential newspaper of the writers' union, the *Literary Gazette*, continually interviewed him. In May 1945 the newspaper produced a special issue dedicated to the end of the war. Asked to contribute his thoughts, Grossman responded with a story: one day he was watching a battle, sitting next to a division commander at an observation post. The colonel seemed to forget all about Grossman. Then he smiled and said, "Well, I'm sweating now, but after the war it will be the writers' turn to sweat and describe it all." Grossman used the incident to appeal to contemporary writers: as eyewitnesses of events, "we are responsible" for truthfully depicting the war. "Is it possible that we will let writers of future generations have the honor of telling the world about this?" He called on his colleagues to be worthy "of the great literature of the past." So far "our attempts" have been "miserable . . . hasty, and superficial."[4] These remarks were certain to irritate a number of Soviet writers.

On June 22, 1946, the anniversary of the German attack, the *Literary Gazette* published Grossman's article "To the Memory of the Fallen." Grossman begins by mentioning the country's "tremendous losses" in the war. But millions of deaths cannot diminish the value of a single life: "There is nothing more precious than human life; its loss is final and irreplaceable." The loss of one person is the loss of a universe. "How many suns have become extinguished, how many worlds have descended into eternal darkness!" The Nuremberg Laws introduced by the Nazis erased the notion of "human being." The Soviet victory over Fascism asserts every person's "right to live, to think, and to be free" regardless of skin color, ethnicity, and income. Russia's greatest writers, Pushkin and Tolstoy, made it their mission to defend "basic and sacred human rights, the right of each individual to live on earth, to think, and to be free." This was literature's "eternal mission," Grossman concluded.[5]

Every word in this article argued against the regime. Remembering the fallen undermined Stalin's determination to wipe out the memory of the millions who had perished. Stalin never mentioned the fallen in his speeches or toasts. The price in human lives for victory had to be forgotten. After the war Stalinists created a victorious version of events that no one was allowed to challenge. When Stalin quoted Soviet military fatalities, it was a figure taken out of a hat—7 million. This was nowhere near the actual statistics.[6] In 1947 Stalin even prohibited celebrating Victory Day to discourage people from remembering and mourning the fallen. *Izvestia* published an official declaration making it a work day.[7]

Grossman's vocal defense of human rights and freedoms was unprecedented under Stalin. It came at a time of hope: a victorious nation expected the Party to relax its ideological pressure after the war. But liberal hopes for a better future would be dashed. The Party was about to launch a new round of ideological campaigns and purges. Less than two months after Grossman's article appeared, Stalin's main ideologist, Andrei Zhdanov, attacked freedom of expression and reestablished total Party control over literature and the arts.

The year 1946 began successfully for Grossman: his wartime prose appeared as a separate volume and was prominently reviewed. Ehrenburg praised the *Stalingrad* articles and quoted a passage from "The Hell of Treblinka." He believed these writings would have a profound impact on future novelists: they would see war "through Grossman's eyes."[8]

In July *Znamya* published Grossman's play *If You Believe the Pythagoreans,* which he had written before the war for the Vakhtangov Theater. The protagonist, Andrei Shatavskoi, is an old man and a talented military engineer who designed a new type of artillery weapon during World War I. The development of his invention had been hampered, however, first by the tsarist minister of war and later by Soviet bureaucrats. Despite these official obstacles, his ideas influence physicists and artillerists. With the onslaught of World War II and German armies advancing through Europe, Shatavskoi remembers the Great War: history is repeating itself. As an admirer of Pythagoras, Shatavskoi believes that all natural phenomena are cyclical, that life follows "a great circle" and things tend to recur.

Like Tolstoy, Grossman read philosophers and historians of antiquity; he was fascinated with the ideas of Aristotle, Lucretius (*On the Nature of Things*), Tacitus, and Plutarch.[9] But disseminating the ideas of Pythagoras, the legendary mathematician and philosopher of antiquity, brought Grossman much trouble. The Pythagorean idea of cyclical development contradicted the Marxist-Leninist view of social development as incessant progress. Although Grossman also included the conventional Soviet view, this did not shield his play from attacks.

The play appeared at a highly inopportune time. Only a few weeks later Zhdanov struck with his infamous Party resolution condemning the literary journals *Zvezda* and *Leningrad* for publishing apolitical works by Anna

Akhmatova and Mikhail Zoshchenko. Zhdanov, an administrator of socialist realism, reached the zenith of his power after the war. Stalin put him in charge of ideological and cultural policies for the Central Committee. The assault on the two writers and their subsequent expulsion from the writers' union was meant to bring all writers to heel. Zhdanov censured Akhmatova as "a leftover from the old aristocratic culture," a "half nun, half harlot, or rather harlot-nun."[10] Zoshchenko, a popular satirical writer who had published a story called "Adventures of a Monkey," was slammed for allegedly inserting "in the mouth of the monkey the nasty, poisonous, anti-Soviet maxim to the effect that it is better to live in the zoo than at liberty, and that it is easier to breathe in a cage than among the Soviet people." Zhdanov also attacked European and American "bourgeois culture."[11] This was the beginning of a new ideological campaign against "cosmopolitanism."

The *Literary Gazette* and *Pravda* attacked Grossman almost simultaneously. On September 4 *Pravda* published Vladimir Ermilov's article "A Harmful Play." Ermilov was known for his harassment of talented writers from Bulgakov to Platonov and the poet Nikolai Zabolotsky. Echoing Zhdanov's ideas and style, Ermilov denounced Grossman for straying from the method of socialist realism to broadcast ideas of "bourgeois decadence": "Perplexed and outraged we find convincing evidence that Vas. Grossman is flirting with a philosophy deeply alien to the Soviet people, with reactionary, archaic ideas. . . . Vas. Grossman is attempting to show Soviet reality in a crooked mirror of Pythagoreanism. . . . Vas. Grossman was so fond of his mystical perversion of Soviet reality he produced before the war that he decided to publish his bastardly product after the Great Patriotic War." Precisely like Zhdanov, who had recently condemned Leningrad's literary journals, Ermilov rebuked *Znamya* for printing Grossman's "reactionary anti-artistic play." Grossman was also disparaged for making Shatavskoi, an aristocrat, a central character. (This character was modeled on Prince Andrei Zvenigorodskij, a descendant of aristocracy and talented poet. He was Grossman's friend and a friend of Osip and Nadezhda Mandelstam. The latter mentions him in her memoirs.[12] Prince Zvenigorodskij would serve as inspiration for another of Grossman's characters—the nobleman and poet Shargorodskij in *Life and Fate*.)

On September 3 the *Literary Gazette* published an article by Johann Altman, "If One Believes the Author." Altman was a Jewish theater critic steeped in drama and Greek philosophy and an expert on Aristotle.

Participating in the assault on Grossman did not save him from becoming targeted in the course of Stalin's campaign against the Jews. On January 28, 1949, *Pravda* attacked all Jewish theater critics in an editorial which, in Grossman's words, marked "the beginning of a vast campaign to unmask 'cosmopolitans' in all areas of art and science."[13] The 1949 editorial was composed by Fadeev and revised by Stalin, who introduced the term "rootless cosmopolitans" along with variations, such as "rabid cosmopolitanism."[14] After this editorial appeared, Altman was expelled from the Party and arrested.

But in his 1946 review he accused Grossman of becoming trapped by Pythagorean "pessimistic philosophy" and of promoting anti-Marxist views. He quoted Stalin's 1938 article "On Dialectical and Historical Materialism," according to which "if the world is in a state of constant movement and development," the new and more progressive socialist system replaces the old and dying capitalist system. Altman's article effectively portrayed Grossman as a heretic who believed that the restoration of capitalism was not impossible.

These attacks took place at the critical time when Grossman was struggling for publication of *The Black Book* and was working on his major novel about Stalingrad. Fearing that Party bosses might signal to stop publishing him, as had happened with Akhmatova and Zoshchenko, Grossman asked his wife, "What should I do now?" Olga replied unsympathetically, "Write screenplays." According to Lipkin, Grossman was hurt by her indifference.[15] However, Boris Zaks, an editor at *Novy mir*, felt that Grossman was unperturbed by the press campaign: "The fate of the play, condemned by the Soviet press, did not upset Grossman's composure. At least, this is how it appeared to an outsider."[16]

Altman's criticism only inspired Grossman to argue his ideas more forcefully. In the novel *For the Right Cause* theoretical physicists Victor Shtrum and Dmitri Chepyzhin discuss the eternal cyclical nature of energy and the perpetual struggle between good and evil. The Soviet press would again attack Grossman for expressing this alternative view.

All of Grossman's projects of the period—his play, *The Black Book*, the novel *For the Right Cause*, and an idea for a book on Dostoevsky—were unacceptable to the regime. In July 1945 he had submitted a proposal to the State Literary Publisher (Goslitizdat) for the first Soviet biography of Dostoevsky. He wanted to examine Dostoevsky's life, work, and influence, promising to complete the book in time for Dostoevsky's 125th anniversary in November 1946. The product of "my many years of studying Dostoevsky, the book will illuminate him as an ingenious artist who created . . . a new type of novel, revered worldwide."[17] Grossman's remarkable project was turned down. During the Soviet era Dostoevsky remained the least recognized classic author: his work was excluded from school curriculums. The writer's preaching of Christianity and his absolute rejection of human sacrifice for the sake of building a paradise on earth made him unacceptable to the Soviet regime. As Grossman would write in *Life and Fate*, "Dostoevsky simply doesn't fit into our ideology."[18] While Tolstoy's teaching of nonviolence was "explained" by Lenin in the article "Lev Tolstoy as a Mirror of the Russian Revolution," Dostoevsky was "rehabilitated" by Soviet critics only in 1956.

Grossman's other major project, *The Black Book*, was mentioned in the Soviet press only once. In 1945 a young editor, Anna Berzer, interviewed him for the *Literary Gazette*, producing an article about the JAC's collaboration on the volume with the American Committee of Jewish Writers, Artists, and Scientists, headed by Einstein and the World Jewish Congress. Grossman spoke about this international project with pride. Berzer succeeded in publishing Grossman's explanation that Einstein had suggested the JAC produce a book "about fascist atrocities committed in the occupied territories where the Jewish population was entirely exterminated." As Berzer optimistically stated, *The Black Book* was to appear in 1945 and include documentary materials, diaries, final letters by "martyrs of the ghettos," excerpts from interrogations of captured Nazis, orders of the German military commanders, and photographs. "It will come out in the USSR, in England, the USA, and Palestine in Russian, English, Hebrew, Spanish, German, and in other languages."[19]

Two separate editions of this book, overseen by Sovinformburo, were launched in Moscow and in New York. In 1946 Grossman first read the American version of *The Black Book* for a review requested by Solomon Lozovsky. Only a small portion of Soviet documentary materials sent by the JAC to America was included in this edition. The American and the Soviet editorial boards had different agendas. Summarizing the differences, Grossman wrote that the American version elucidated on how the Final Solution was planned while the Soviet edition told how it was carried out.[20]

Initially the American edition included Einstein's introduction in which he stated that during the war Jews suffered proportionally greater losses than other nations; he also supported their immigration to Palestine.[21] This introduction was removed from the New York edition at the insistence of the

Sovinformburo. In 1952, during the JAC trial, Lozovsky testified that he sent telegrams to America to make sure Einstein's text was not included.[22] As he said in court, "The book contained a foreword by Einstein in which our commission discovered Zionistic tendencies."[23] Mikhoels, Fefer, and Grossman were forced to sign a letter saying that Einstein's remarks on the history and future of the Jewish people were superfluous to the project.[24] Einstein agreed to remove his introduction.[25] In 1946 several thousand copies of the American edition, entitled *The Black Book: The Nazi Crime against the Jewish People*, were published in New York and distributed at Nuremberg.[26] Einstein, Eleanor Roosevelt, Thomas Mann, and Stephen Wise were among the celebrities who sponsored and publicized this edition.

Sovinformburo and the Central Committee impeded publication of the Soviet edition prepared by Ehrenburg and Grossman. In February 1945 a commission appointed by Lozovsky assessed the entire manuscript. It produced a report stating that the manuscript had to undergo "scrupulous political and factual editing" to exclude information about "the abominable activity" of local collaborators "among the Ukrainians, Lithuanians, etc." Another major critique concerned the book's structure. Inclusion of articles by "prominent Soviet writers" alongside documents was unacceptable. Writers' articles should be issued as separate publications, mainly for distribution abroad.[27] As Lozovsky stated in court, "*The Black Book* was useful for the Soviet Union" during the Nuremberg trials. "But when the Central Committee prohibited publication of this book in the USSR, this was also the right thing to do, because Soviet people did not need such a book."[28]

By 1945 Ehrenburg sensed that there was no commitment to publish the Soviet edition of *The Black Book*. When after a rift with the JAC he distanced himself from the project, Grossman carried on as head of the Literary Commission and general editor. On April 25, 1946, at a meeting of the JAC, Grossman spoke about the commission's work soliciting testimonies of survivors and witnesses to the Jewish massacres in the formerly occupied territories. The creation of *The Black Book* could not be postponed "because the few survivors after the torments they've suffered are for the most part in delicate health. Often their days are numbered; besides, many of them are going away. The second task we have set for ourselves was collecting materials which would serve as the indictment against the German fascists. That's why I took it upon myself to carry out this difficult and, I should say, tormenting work."[29]

In August Grossman wrote his father that he was proofreading *The Black Book* and hoping it "will be published this winter."[30] Mikhoels was also optimistic, saying at the JAC's meeting in November that "*The Black Book* will come off the presses soon."[31] Members of the JAC presidium sent a letter to Zhdanov at the Central Committee asking to speed up publication.[32] This only prompted a further review of the manuscript, now by the Department of Agitation and Propaganda, which found publication "inexpedient." Its report alleged that *The Black Book* provided "a false picture of the true nature of Fascism," creating an impression that "the Germans fought against the USSR for the sole purpose of destroying the Jews."[33]

The Black Book was banned in early October 1947. By then the project was supervised by Mikhail Suslov, the new head of the Department of Agitation and Propaganda at the Central Committee. The member of Suslov's staff responsible for the publications branch reevaluated the manuscript, reporting that "the book contains serious political errors. . . . Accordingly, *The Black Book* cannot be published."[34] On February 13, 1948, Itsik Fefer made a desperate appeal on behalf of the JAC to print a limited edition of 150–200 copies for distribution to an approved list of libraries, anti-Fascist committees, and special collections.[35] Fefer's request was left unanswered. The Soviet edition was banned, its printed copies destroyed, and the plates broken up.[36] However, the authorities did not succeed in destroying all copies of the Russian text. In early 1946 the JAC sent copies of the Soviet edition to Jewish organizations in New York, London, Paris, Mexico City, Melbourne, Tel Aviv, Sofia, Budapest, Bucharest, Prague, and Rome.[37] In 1980 *The Black Book* was produced by the Israeli publishing house Tarbut. In 2001 it was translated and published in the United Kingdom and later in North America. But not until 2015 was a publicly funded edition issued in Russia.

In 1947 Grossman wrote a play based on the story "The Old Teacher." The Vakhtangov Theater was afraid to take it on after the attacks on Grossman's play about the Pythagoreans. Besides, after the war, stories about Jews were unwelcome. Mikhoels wanted to stage Grossman's play at the State Jewish Theater and sent it to be translated into Yiddish. Invited to discuss the script at Mikhoels's downtown apartment on Tverskoi Bulevard, Grossman arrived with his friend Lipkin. The latter recalls Mikhoels's fascinating suggestions for strengthening the play's structure and drama. They met a few times at Mikhoels's flat, drinking homemade cherry wine prepared by his second wife, Anastasia Pototskaya, a talented biologist. According to Mikhoels's daughter, Natalya Vovsi-Mikhoels, her father and Anastasia were close friends with the leading physicist Pyotr Kapitsa and prominent biologist and physiologist Lina Shtern, a member of the JAC. Both Kapitsa and Shtern (she would be arrested in January 1948 during Stalin's "secret pogrom") frequented the Mikhoels' apartment.[38] Kapitsa would become the prototype for Grossman's character of a leading physicist in his novel *For the Right Cause*.

On January 7, 1948, Grossman and Lipkin saw Mikhoels for the last time. He was leaving for Minsk to review local plays to recommend for government awards. Friends and colleagues from the Jewish Theater assembled at the station to see him off. Lipkin recalls that Mikhoels spoke again of staging Grossman's play. "I remember the Belorussian station platform, remember Mikhoels' face, beautiful and ugly, his eyes those of a wizard and cabalist, his lower lip pouted sardonically—and his unhurried words, uttered in splendid, dramatically articulate Russian: 'I'm sure, I'll play the part as the teacher. It will be my last role.' . . . He never had a chance to play this last part. . . . Like the character in Grossman's play he died at the hands of assassins. In Minsk, he was run over by a truck, killed by the same forces that killed the teacher Rosenthal."[39]

Mikhoels was killed in Minsk on Stalin's orders. On the night of January 12–13, Mikhoels and theater critic Vladimir Golubov-Potapov, who accompanied him, were murdered and later crushed by a truck. As Khrushchev writes in his memoir, Mikhoels's assassination was disguised as an accident. "They made it appear as though he had fallen in front of a truck, but in fact the truck ran over his dead body. . . . This operation was carried out with artistic skill, and who was it that did this? Beria and Abakumov's men, on orders from Stalin. . . . Everything was reported to Stalin, and Stalin personally decided who would be killed and who would be spared."[40] The official version of Mikhoels's death was widely disbelieved. Alexander Borshchagovsky, a playwright and writer who collaborated with Mikhoels's theater, remembers that within days of the director's demise there were rumors that he had been brutally murdered.[41] In May Fefer told Alec Waterman, a British Jewish Communist, that Mikhoels had been murdered.[42] Grossman had no doubt that Mikhoels was killed by the regime.

The purge of the Jewish intelligentsia associated with the JAC began before Mikhoels's murder.[43] Arrests were launched in December 1947, the

year that marked the start of the Cold War. Theater historian Lidiya Shatu-
novskaya and her husband, physicist Leonid Tumerman, a native of
Berdichev, were among the first to be detained, accused of association with
the JAC, by then described as a "Zionist-American espionage organization."
Two other JAC members purged that month were Isaak Goldshteyn, a senior
member of the Institute of Economics, and Zakhar Grinberg of the Institute
of World Literature. Following conveyor-belt interrogations and beatings,
both were forced to sign false accusations against Mikhoels (then alive) as
well as against Lozovsky, Fefer, and Markish. Members of the JAC were
accused of conducting anti-Soviet and Zionist activities and "maintaining
contacts with reactionary Jewish circles abroad." Grossman was witnessing
the disappearance of the Jewish elite including, in November 1948, the
simultaneous shutdown of the JAC and its Yiddish newspaper *Eynikayt*. The
Yiddish journals *Heymland* and *Der Shtern* were also closed.[44] Mikhoels's
State Jewish Theater ceased to exist in 1949. Yiddish culture in the Soviet
Union was effectively being destroyed.

From 1948 to mid-1949 five Yiddish writers and poets Grossman knew
closely and worked with—Markish, David Hofshteyn, Fefer, Leyb Kvitko,
and David Bergelson—and ten other people with links to the JAC vanished.
Arrests were made secretly; people simply disappeared, as had happened
during the Great Purge. Veniamin Zuskin, a celebrated actor who replaced
Mikhoels as the head of the State Jewish Theater, was taken away in December
1948. After Mikhoels's murder Zuskin suffered from severe insomnia and was
treated in hospital. MGB (state security) agents took the heavily sedated actor
from his hospital bed and carried him away despite doctors' protests.[45]

Lozovsky was arrested in January 29, 1949, near his apartment building.
Days earlier Lozovsky's grandson, who was married to the daughter of
Georgy Malenkov, a Politburo member, was forcibly divorced. Malenkov
presided over the destruction of the JAC and of Jewish cultural life in the
USSR. After distancing himself from his relative, Malenkov summoned
Lozovsky to announce he was being expelled from the Central Committee
and from the Party.[46] Lozovsky was one of the few remaining Old Bolshe-
viks. Molotov's Jewish wife Polina Zhemchuzhina was also arrested in
January. She took an interest in Mikhoels's theater and the work of the JAC.
Besides, the secret police had collected evidence of her "nationalistic
activity" in September 1948. Four months into the establishment of the State
of Israel, which the USSR had been the first to recognize, Golda Meir (then

Meyerson) arrived in Moscow with an Israeli delegation. Zhemchuzhina spoke in Yiddish with Meir at a diplomatic reception, and her "politically unworthy behavior" was reported to Stalin. When arrested, Zhemchuzhina firmly denied accusations of nationalism and her case was later separated from that of the JAC.[47]

It is generally believed that Stalin launched his secret pogrom when, after the establishment of the State of Israel and an outpouring of enthusiasm on the part of Soviet Jews, he suspected them of disloyalty. The Russian Jewish community had given a hero's welcome to the Israeli delegation in Moscow. Crowds gathered near the central Metropol Hotel to greet Meir and followed the visitors through the streets to the synagogue. The diplomats sensed they had unintentionally caused trouble for the Russian Jews: as Mordecai Namir writes, they felt they had "participated in a very tragic event."[48] After their visit to Moscow, the JAC was shut down and arrests began in the Jewish community.

But as Khrushchev suggests in his memoir, Stalin's retribution against the JAC may have been caused by its proposal to create a Jewish republic in Crimea, in the area vacant after the deportation of the Crimean Tatars. "Stalin's assessment of the matter was evidently that it was a proposal inspired by the American Zionists. The members of the Jewish Anti-Fascist Committee, he concluded, were agents of Zionism who wanted to establish their own independent state in the Crimea, to break away from the Soviet Union, establish a foothold for American imperialism, and serve as agents of American imperialism. Full and free rein was given to the imagination. . . . Stalin . . . literally went into frenzy. After a certain length of time arrests began."[49] Khrushchev also writes that Stalin always "supported and encouraged the bacillus of anti-Semitism."[50] Once Stalin even proposed that Khrushchev instigate a Jewish pogrom: "Some healthy elements among the workers need to be organized. Let them take clubs and when the workday ends give these Jews a beating."[51] Stalin's words revived Khrushchev's memory of a Jewish pogrom he witnessed in his youth in Donetsk.

Unleashed by Stalin after the war, anti-Semitism would take root in the public consciousness. It remained an undeclared government policy over the decades and in the 1990s, after the breakup of the Soviet Union, flared up with the establishment of Fascist organizations such as Russian National Unity. The 150 anti-Semitic newspapers published during this time also echoed Stalin's policies.[52]

In 1948 the writer Viktor Nekrasov met Grossman in Koktebel, Crimea. Nekrasov's honest novel *Front-line Stalingrad* had been awarded a Stalin Prize in 1947. The writer was told that Stalin himself decided the award, and this shielded his book from criticism. Nekrasov had read Grossman's articles while at the front and nearly met him in Stalingrad. Grossman's nephew Yura Benyash was the commander of Nekrasov's battalion. Grossman visited this battalion in December 1942, two months after Benyash was killed, and talked with people who knew him.

In Crimea Nekrasov first observed Grossman from a distance. Grossman looked gloomy and unapproachable; he took lonely walks and went for swims at a distant beach. Even for the sociable Nekrasov, a former actor, starting a conversation was not easy. One night he saw Grossman smoking on the lower verandah of their hotel and asked casually, "Can't sleep?" Grossman replied something "about the stars or about listening to cicadas—and this led to a conversation. We sat and talked for an hour. . . . Well, of course, the war, Stalingrad, Treblinka." After this encounter they met and talked daily.

> As it turned out, Vasily Semyonovich wasn't gloomy at all, but the look in his eyes from behind glasses was occasionally sad and pensive. But his eyes could also smile softly and ironically. He valued irony. . . . Like every shy person (and Vasily Semyonovich was shy, that is, he was afraid to appear bothersome, interfering) he would be more at ease after a drink. . . . He always spoke softly, disliked empty phrases and superlatives and, strange as it may seem, strongly disliked reminiscing . . . (only on the first night did we reminisce about Stalingrad); in his questions he was reserved and tactful. He disliked the apparatchiks and, when talking about them, was neither reserved nor delicate. He fervently hated lies, hypocrisy. Having endured critical attacks along with their repercussions, he never complained, although he was vexed and continued to believe what he believed before.[53]

Grossman called himself "a heretic" and was glad to find "a heretic-friend" in Nekrasov. A native of Kiev, Nekrasov would correspond with Grossman and was among the first to write him when his novel *For the Right Cause* was published.

Grossman completed this novel in late 1948, when Stalin's campaign against "rootless cosmopolitans" was picking up steam. Remembering "the moral and intellectual pogroms" of Stalin's final years, the distinguished Leningrad philologist Olga Freidenberg wrote to her cousin Boris Pasternak, "The purpose of the last campaign has been to cause concussion of the brain. . . . One should see the pogrom as carried out in our department. Groups of students rummage through the works of Jewish professors, eavesdrop on private conversations, whisper in corners. . . . Jews no longer receive an education, are no longer accepted at universities or for graduate study. . . . The finest professors have been dismissed. The murder of the remaining intelligentsia goes on without cease."[54] Freidenberg reported in her diary that any mention of foreign scholars was viewed as evidence of "cosmopolitanism" and had dire political consequences; that a professor was "mercilessly tortured" at university meetings for being a German; that an old professor, Mark Azadovsky, a specialist in folklore and an ethnic Jew, lost consciousness during one such meeting; that the atmosphere at the university was that "of slander, gossip, and lies."[55] During this time Jews were harassed across the country; Jewish war veterans were refused employment.

In Grossman's novel *For the Right Cause*, especially in its original version, the Jewish theme is conspicuous. The protagonist is Victor Shtrum, a Jewish physicist and an admirer of Einstein. In 1948 Shtrum's name alone could frighten editors out of their skin. Grossman's editors demanded he purge Shtrum from the book, but he did not comply. His central character remained. There is also a story of Shtrum's mother trapped in a Jewish ghetto of a Nazi-occupied town. The original text included her farewell letter to her son. Forced to remove it, Grossman incorporated the letter in *Life and Fate*. Such letters and notes were written by Jews before execution; several were included in *The Black Book* he edited. The powerful story of Sofya Levinton, a Jewish surgeon captured by the Nazis, made it into the published version of the novel *For the Right Cause*. And so did the scene of Hitler and Himmler discussing the Final Solution.

Grossman initially submitted his manuscript to *Znamya*, which had published his Treblinka article and other works. But when the influential Simonov, who had written about Majdanek, became editor of *Novy mir*, Grossman felt he had a better chance with this journal. In November 1948 he withdrew his manuscript from *Znamya* and returned the advance.[56] On August 2, 1949, he brought it to Simonov; that same day he started a diary to record his novel's passage to publication. Grossman realized his book would meet with obstacles but could not have imagined it would take him three years to publish it. Today his diary serves as a forceful illustration of the Party's interference in the arts.

At first the editors' reaction seemed too good to be true. On September 11 Simonov phoned to say that he liked the novel "very much. My recommendations only concern separate episodes and storylines."[57] Within days Simonov's deputy editor, Krivitsky, reported his positive impression: "Our suggestions are minimal. I'm more enthusiastic than Simonov." A fortnight later Simonov told Grossman that he had scheduled publication to begin in the January issue of the journal.

On September 20 Grossman attended an editorial board meeting to discuss his novel. Boris Agapov, whose film scripts had won two Stalin Prizes (one was about rebuilding Stalingrad), was alarmed by Grossman's focus on the "negative, dark sides" of the war. And how could Grossman take it upon himself to portray Hitler and claim that "Hitler made mistakes"? (According to Soviet thinking, discussing world leaders was the Party's prerogative.) In his diary Grossman recorded the exchange with Agapov:

> Grossman. "But these 'mistakes' resulted in the deaths of tens of millions!"
> Agapov. "I want to make your novel safe . . . from an ideological standpoint."
> Grossman. "Boris Nikolaevich, I don't want to make my novel safe."

At this point Simonov weighed in to say that he liked the novel and thought that Hitler and the Germans were "interestingly portrayed."[58]

The novel opens with Hitler and Mussolini's meeting in Salzburg in April 1942. Grossman depicts the relationship of the Fascist leaders: Mussolini's private dislike of Hitler, his thoughts about having to sit through five hours of Hitler's monologues. He drew such information from *The Ciano Diaries* kept by Mussolini's foreign minister and son-in-law Gian Galeazzo Ciano.[59] Grossman was the first Soviet writer to depict World War II as a global event. In the Soviet era it was known only as the Great Patriotic War, which began in 1941 with the German attack on the USSR. The Ribbentrop-Molotov Pact had to be forgotten. Grossman's opening chapters of the two dictators discussing world destinies and Hitler's summer advance of 1942 were slashed by editors. Grossman restored them in the post-Stalin era, in the 1956 edition of this novel.

Most Soviet writers could not access research material that became available to Grossman in the 1940s. It is possible that he obtained some books through Ehrenburg, who traveled abroad. Grossman did read the account of the British military strategist and war correspondent B. H. Liddell Hart, *The German Generals Talk: Startling Revelations from Hitler's High Command.*[60] Published in 1948 in the U.S. but not translated into Russian until 1957, Hart's book explores "inside the enemy camp." It was drawn from the author's conversations with German generals, including Rommel and Rundstedt, who survived Hitler's Reich. (Grossman had someone helping him with translation; all his research notes are in Russian.)

He also read the book by the American war correspondent Curt Riess, *The Self-Betrayal: Glory and Doom of the German Generals*, published in New York in 1942. A Jewish refugee from Nazi Germany, Riess settled in Manhattan, where he wrote for the *Saturday Evening Post*. Upon becoming an American war correspondent, he chronicled the demise of Hitler's Third Reich.[61]

In addition Grossman researched Heinz Guderian's chronicle *Erinnerungen eines Soldaten* (Memories of a Soldier), brought out by Kurt Vowinckel Verlag in 1950.[62] As is apparent from his notes, this reading did more than further his understanding of Hitler's inner circle and the Nazi regime. It inspired his heretical thoughts about the similarities between Nazism and Communism. In Nazi Germany, he wrote in his notes, "state power was passed into the hands of *Gauleiters*—party leaders. State institutions, jurisprudence lost all meaning and influence." (Grossman witnessed a similar situation in the Soviet Union with the Communist Party's disregard for the rule of law and human rights; the Party's total control; its ideology justifying crimes against humanity.)

In the novel *For the Right Cause* Grossman makes his first examination of Hitler's Germany governed by totalitarian ideology. As he wrote in his research notes, "Hitler called himself the Führer of the nation, Commander-in-chief of the armed forces, head of the government, the holder of the executive power, the chief judge, the Führer of the party." This idea surfaces in the novel *For the Right Cause,* where Hitler believes that he *is* Germany.[63] Hitler's order "Not a step back" inspired Grossman to remark in his notes, "But why would the lives of hundreds of thousands of German soldiers matter to Hitler?" (His thoughts that the lives of Russian soldiers did not matter to Stalin were then too dangerous to commit to paper.)

Grossman's major source on National Socialism was a handwritten summary of Hans Frank's legal and ideological views. (He could have obtained it from a Soviet translator who made notes at the Nuremberg trials where passages from Frank's diaries were read. Hitler's personal lawyer, Frank was executed as a war criminal.) The notebook included extracts from Frank's speeches on the purity of the German race and his statement that "National Socialism has abandoned the false principle of humanity."

The most diplomatic and tactful of Grossman's editors, Simonov never insisted; he always asked. Nonetheless, he proposed substantial changes—especially to the main character, Shtrum; he also asked Grossman to downplay the Jewish theme.[64] Having to cut eighty pages and write new parts, Grossman worked day and night to meet his December 10 deadline. But in the New Year he received a new batch of revisions. The editor was now avoiding him, and in February Grossman learned that Simonov was leaving *Novy mir* for the *Literary Gazette*.

The new editor of *Novy mir* was Tvardovsky, an old friend and the author of the genuinely popular poem *Vasily Terkin*. The story of an ordinary soldier, it was written without false heroics. In winter 1942 Grossman had visited Tvardovsky in Voronezh where he worked on the newspaper of the southwestern front, *Red Army*. In March, when Grossman was about to leave, Tvardovsky wrote his wife, Maria, that he was upset with his friend's departure: "He is my best companion, he understands and explains everything so nobly and well, and I have to admit I'll be quite lonesome here without him." And later, in April: "V. Grossman has gone away. . . . The man who was so dear to me has left; the man so perceptive, reliable, who knew when to say a kind word. That's one big loss."[65] Tvardovsky valued Grossman's truthful depiction of war from the battlefield but he had no sympathy for the Jewish theme. In March 1950 he summoned Grossman to say that "he can publish only the war parts." In his diary, Grossman reported that Tvardovsky spoke "sharply and crudely" about the rest. The Jewish physicist Shtrum, his mother's story, the old Bolsheviks Krymov and Mostovskoy, members of the Communist International dissolved by Stalin in 1943, and the Shaposhnikov family of intelligentsia had to go. Grossman told Tvardovsky that his revisions were "insulting, wrong, and entirely unacceptable" and he took them as a refusal to publish the novel. Tvardovsky asked him to wait until the editorial board had read the book.

The literary magazines were aware that Stalin anticipated a Soviet *War and Peace*. They were eager to publish an epic war novel, a potential winner of the Stalin Prize. Grossman's novel had many intentional parallels with Tolstoy's. Written with epic sweep, it also included war parts and peace parts. Like Tolstoy, Grossman depicted historical figures alongside fictional characters; his narrative switched between global events and family occurrences.

Back in 1943, when he was developing the plot for the entire novel, Grossman compared it against the structure of *War and Peace*. He drew up a list of protagonists from the first part of Tolstoy's epic. Some of Grossman's characters, for example, the three Shaposhnikov sisters, suggested a parallel with the Rostov sisters. Grossman was engaging in a dialogue with Tolstoy. As is apparent from his research notes, he intended to show "how life changed over 100 years." Grossman's protagonist Lieutenant Colonel Darensky, a descendant of Russian nobility, shared some personal qualities with Prince Bolkonsky from Tolstoy's novel, but what a different destiny! Far from being valued in the army, Darensky is arrested during Stalin's military purge. As Grossman writes in his notes, "You alone, prince, are a fragment of those who were Tolstoy's main characters. If he [Tolstoy] wanted to write his novel today, what a different slice [of life] he would have to choose."[66] Grossman's heroes fought in Stalingrad; were Soviet POWs in Dachau; were marched to Treblinka's gas chamber; and, like Shtrum and the physicists around him, worked on the Soviet nuclear program.

Tvardovsky would soon discover that even the war parts of Grossman's novel were unsafe to publish. Grossman failed to emphasize the role of the Party and Stalin in winning the war. Instead he wrote about Russia's indebtedness to ordinary soldiers who perished unknown. He wrote about the losses and chaotic retreat of 1941, of Soviet troops caught up in encirclements. Again and again he would bring up the theme of unknown heroes, both soldiers and officers. While Stalin regarded Soviet POWs as traitors, Grossman portrayed Mostovskoy and Sofya Levinton, captured by the Nazis, as unquestionably honest. Through the character of Darensky, falsely accused and imprisoned before the war, he addressed Stalin's military purge. Grossman had met and interviewed at least two of the formerly condemned military commanders, Rokossovsky, who survived beatings and torture, and Alexander Gorbatov, a survivor of the Kolyma gold mines. In 1941, when their experience and talents were needed, they were found in the Gulag and sent to the front. Grossman tells this story in *Life and Fate*, where he describes

Rokossovsky being taken from his barrack and flown "straight to the Kremlin in a Douglas."[67]

Boris Zaks, a junior editor at *Novy mir*, recalls that Grossman was regarded as an "exceptionally difficult author—obstinate and troublesome. . . . The novel proceeded to publication agonizingly slowly. Grossman hardly yielded to pressure. At times, I even felt that he was needlessly stubborn on small things."[68] For Grossman, though, telling the truth about the war was not a small thing: he considered it his duty as a writer. He was forced to compromise, to produce ten versions of the novel, to insert passages emphasizing Stalin's and the Party's organizing role in the war; he had to obscure the Jewish theme. But he succeeded in having some truth about the war published—at a time when none was being told. All the while he lived through high drama that nearly ended with his arrest.

In late March 1950 Tvardovsky and his deputy Tarasenkov visited Grossman at his home. They agreed that his central characters—the Shtrums, the Old Bolsheviks Mostovskoy and Krymov—would remain in the book. Grossman was told to make new extensive revisions, and he incorporated them by mid-April. The editorial board then voted unanimously to publish the novel. On April 28 Grossman received proofs. The next day he wrote in his diary that the printing of the novel was suspended owing to Mikhail Bubennov's denunciation. A member of the editorial board and a staunch Stalinist, Bubennov had participated in the press campaign against "rootless cosmopolitans." He dashed off a denunciation letter about Grossman's novel to the Central Committee. Publication was halted and the proofs were sent to Suslov, the head of the Department of Agitation and Propaganda, who was overseeing the closure of the JAC while directing the anti-cosmopolitan campaign.

In August 1950 Grossman's novel was sent for an additional assessment to the Marx-Engels-Lenin Institute (IMEL). The head of the Institute, Pyotr Pospelov, conveyed his "good impression" to Suslov at the Central Committee. The latter sent it for further appraisal to Malenkov, who was responsible, along with Beria, for the Soviet nuclear bomb program during the war. Malenkov was now occupied with a matter involving the JAC, according to which Jewish nationalists were planning to sell out Crimea and Birobidzhan, near China, to the Americans or Japanese.[69]

Until now, Grossman's inspiration for the central character, Shtrum, was believed to be the theoretical physicist Lev Landau, a future Nobel Prize laureate. In the 1930s Landau headed the theoretical physics department at the Kharkov Institute of Physics and Technology. In 1937 eleven leading researchers of the Kharkov Institute were arrested. The institute ceased to exist as the center for theoretical and experimental physics.[70] Landau fled to Moscow, joining Pyotr Kapitsa's Institute of Physical Problems. This did not save him: in 1938 he was arrested along with his collaborator Moisei Koretz and the theoretical physicist Yuri Rumer. The three physicists were denounced by an informer who alleged that they had discussed a leaflet comparing Stalin to Hitler and Mussolini. Landau spent one year in Lubyanka's prison. He was released after Kapitsa's appeal to the government describing him as indispensable to his research. When Stalin launched the atomic project during the war, Landau led a group of mathematicians at Kapitsa's institute, supporting atomic and hydrogen bomb development.

Recently it was discovered that the model for Grossman's central character was the nuclear physicist Lev Shtrum. The head of the theoretical physics department in Kiev's University, he liaised with Landau. In 1936 Shtrum was arrested and shot as "the enemy of the people." Grossman had known him well as a student. (On February 12, 1929, Grossman wrote his father of meeting Shtrum in Kiev and borrowing money from him.) Lev Shtrum was annihilated physically and spiritually: his name was erased, his publications destroyed in the USSR. Grossman used his name in the novel, thus resurrecting the memory of this physicist.[71]

The fictional Shtrum is invested with Grossman's personality: he is the author's alter ego. Grossman maintained his interest in science and tried to keep up with the latest publications. His notebook for 1944 contains a diagram of a nuclear chain reaction. But the brilliant Jewish scientist was too much for the editor Tvardovsky, who proposed to Grossman, "Well, make your Shtrum the head of a military retail shop." Grossman retorted, "And what position would you assign to Einstein?"[72]

In October Grossman found an unlikely supporter in Fadeev, the head of the writers' union. (Fadeev was among the authors of the infamous editorial in *Pravda* that launched Stalin's campaign against the "cosmopolitans." This was his public position but privately, he despised anti-Semitism. His support of Grossman was an atonement he badly needed.) Fadeev turned the tide for Grossman, speaking in favor of publishing the novel at a joint meeting of *Novy mir*'s editorial board with the writers' union. Yet Tvardovsky was still afraid to launch publication without explicit permission from the Central Committee.

On December 6 Grossman sent a letter to Stalin asking him to help resolve "the question about the fate of my novel." Grossman received no direct response. But Fadeev, now officially in charge of the project, was summoned to the Central Committee. In January 1951 Fadeev met with Grossman and Tvardovsky to report that the Central Committee had expressed a "high opinion on the novel" and proposed that the writer's union and *Novy Mir* jointly "decide the question of publication." Soon after Grossman received Fadeev's revision requests. He had to produce new chapters about the heroic wartime work in the rear, insert the current official view on the wartime alliance with England and America, and remove Shtrum. "I replied that I agree with everything, except Shtrum." Tvardovsky then proposed to introduce another Russian physicist, Shtrum's teacher Chepyzhin. This would downplay the Jewish theme. (As would become apparent from the second part of the novel, *Life and Fate*, Chepyzhin is modeled on Pyotr Kapitsa, the Nobel Prize laureate who founded and directed the Moscow Institute of Physics and Technology and was known for his independence. Kapitsa was a friend of Mikhoels, and possibly this connection was important to Grossman. In 1945 Kapitsa quarreled with Beria, who was in charge of the Soviet atomic bomb project, and had earlier intervened on behalf of Lev Landau.)

Fadeev sent additional detailed instructions from the hospital, where he was being treated for alcoholism: "Take out Malenkov"; "Take out Stalindorf" (the inhabitants of Stalindorf, a Jewish agricultural colony, were murdered by the Nazis); "Elevate Chepyzhin further"; "Enhance the end of the chapter—the Party, not only the people." Fadeev even provided his own passage for Grossman to insert, a marvelous example of socialist realism: "The Party of the Bolsheviks led millions of people to accomplish the great feat of defence production. The Party inspired people with its faith, word, and example. The Party became the organizing force in the fighting battalions, and workers' collectives; in giant plants and small workshops; in collective farms and state farms."[73] He also asked Grossman to write about German resistance under the Nazis. (This was necessary to help explain the Sovietization of East Germany.)

Grossman's chapter about German intellectuals and Social Democrats under Hitler is intriguing. The commander of the German Motorized Company, Lieutenant Bach, visits Berlin during a furlough. Some of his friends are arrested by the Gestapo while others are marginalized: "They had no future. Nobody needed their morality, painstaking honesty, and old-fashioned learning." These dissidents speak in whispers, afraid of being denounced. Bach's friend Maria confides her secret thoughts about the degradation of literature and the arts. "Most talented people have no opportunity to work—and if German physics lost the ingenious Einstein, then more or less the same is happening in every field of science and arts." Bach's friend Lunz whispers that the "Führer alone has the right to think; however, he relies on intuition rather than thinking. . . . But only, please, forget what I just said; don't tell anyone, even your mother."[74] National Socialism banished the notions of morality and humanity, says Lunz. This chapter makes an implicit parallel with the Stalinist regime.

In 1951 "Jewish nationalists" were ferreted out of every profession. In summer arrests were even conducted inside the Ministry for State Security (MGB). The ministry's Jewish personnel, including a senior interrogator in the JAC case, Lev Shvartsman, were purged. Shvartsman was forced to admit the existence of an anti-Soviet conspiracy within the MGB and the ministry's ties to the Jewish Anti-Fascist Committee. Investigation of the JAC was conducted in deep secrecy, with Stalin, Malenkov, and Beria receiving transcripts of the interrogations.[75] Lev Sheinin, a writer and legal adviser who aided the Soviet prosecution team during the Nuremberg trials, was arrested in October 1951 and accused of having ties to the JAC.[76] Jewish names were mentioned in the press only negatively. The writer Mikhail Bubennov chose this time to publish an article condemning Jewish writers who hid their origins behind Russian pseudonyms.

Lipkin recalls an anti-Semitic incident that took place around then. One night he and Grossman went to dine downtown. Because of some conference taking place in Moscow the only restaurant they could get into was the elite Metropol Hotel. A famous athlete, Grigory Novak, invited them to his table, the only available one. Just as they were about to raise a toast, a big man approached them chanting an anti-Semitic rhyme. Novak rose, "made a hardly perceptible movement," and the man went flying. "You found the only appropriate argument," said Grossman.[77]

When in March 1951 Grossman submitted another version of the novel with ninety pages of new text, Tvardovsky demanded he "remove all of the Shtrum chapters, every single line—otherwise the novel will not be published." Grossman rejected this ultimatum. The journal "anxiously" anticipated that

Bubennov would launch another denunciation to "undermine my work," Grossman wrote in his diary. Earlier, while preparing for an editorial meeting, he jotted down his thoughts: "Editing must have its limits. When a doctor and midwife assist in the birth of a baby, this is good business, but when twelve middle-aged men interfere in creative work, the resulting picture is bad. I categorically disagree with the view that novels and poems can be created collaboratively with editors—Communism has nothing to do with this. Just as Communism has nothing to do with childbirth. . . . The lifeless and miserable fruits of such misguided attempts in literature and in cinema are obvious." Grossman was determined to publicize Bubennov's semi-literate "resolutions" scribbled on the margins of his manuscript. Bubennov had applied his editorial pencil with such force that it ripped pages; on the basis of these remarks Grossman should be sent to Kolyma.[78] At the editorial meeting Grossman would also speak about the threshold for truth, the need to raise one's expectations of what is admissible and publishable. "[There is] fear that the unpublished is illegal. And then, upon being published it attains the status of legality. For example, 'The Hell of Treblinka' and many of my works [met with obstacles before publication]."[79]

In April Fadeev phoned from the Barvikha government sanatorium. He sounded cheerful. The novel had been approved by the Central Committee, the General Staff, and the Marx-Engels-Lenin Institute, said Fadeev. Who's left to object to its publication? With Fadeev's backing, the manuscript was again sent to the printers and Grossman received a new set of proofs. But Stalin's campaign against the Jews was moving full steam ahead. Over a hundred people connected to the JAC had been arrested across the country.[80] A longer list, comprising two hundred names, was being compiled; Grossman and Ehrenburg were on this new list.[81]

Fadeev continued to probe Suslov's opinion on the novel. "The gray cardinal" suggested that since Khrushchev was portrayed, his opinion should be sought. Grossman was at the end of his emotional rope: his nerves were shattered, his asthma had returned, and his heart was giving him trouble. He wrote Fadeev that his book had been edited four times over two years. "I got to the point when hope no longer helps—it torments. . . . After seven years of work, two years of editing, revising, rewriting, I want to tell the comrades . . . : 'I have no more strength, give me any reply, as long as it's final.' "[82] Now it was Fadeev's turn to appeal to Stalin and solicit his permission to publish the book. (The fate of this appeal is unknown.)

The situation deteriorated into farce. In the fall, in response to Gross-man's inquiry, Tvardovsky yelled hysterically, "I know nothing, ask Fadeev." The latter had lost his optimism. Citing an anonymous Party source, Fadeev told Grossman that the novel "doesn't properly reflect the working class, the peasantry, the Party, and . . . the wrong generals have been portrayed."

During the winter of 1952 Fadeev and Tvardovsky were hiding from Grossman. Then he learned that Fadeev was recovering from a three-week binge of heavy drinking and that Tvardovsky had also lost his nerve and taken to drink. Nevertheless, in spring the novel received Fadeev's blessing and the new title, *For the Right Cause*. (It was originally "Stalingrad."[83] The new title reflected Molotov's words at the start of the war, "Our cause is just.") The first installment was scheduled for July. In June Grossman read the new proofs without much hope. On July 1 he scribbled in his diary: "Morning post did not deliver the magazine."[84] But it was a false alarm: the magazine was delivered the next day. Published in four consecutive issues of *Novy mir*, the novel produced a sensation. The magazine issues sold out, people queued to read the novel in public libraries, and there were good reviews.

Soviet readers were thirsty for truth, for stories that allowed them to relive and fathom their experiences during the war. Compulsory and ubiqui-tous content about the Party was seen as inevitable and would not surprise anyone. Readers looked for episodes that evaded this official content and spoke to the heart. Grossman's novel inspired compassion for the most vulnerable—war orphans and refugees; it told about the unknown heroes of the first months of war, and of soldiers in Stalingrad who wanted to live, to be remembered, but had to die young. In August, the writer Yuri German wrote from Leningrad: "Your book made a tremendous impression on me. This is a first genuine book about the war, and not only about the war; it tells about things that are most important on this planet. . . . You opened the forbidden door, you wrote the truth." Nekrasov called the publication of Grossman's novel "a great and joyful event." His friends were fighting over copies of the magazine, "and I haven't met a person who wouldn't be glad that your novel came out." Many episodes impressed him; the story of Filyashkin's battalion, which perished while defending the railway station, was "unparalleled" in war literature.[85] Grossman's novel also enjoyed good official reception—for a few months.

Publication coincided with the secret trial of the Jewish Anti-Fascist Committee. The trial of fifteen Jewish defendants began on May 8, ironically the day celebrated worldwide for victory over Nazism. The hearings were held near the Lubyanka building in the former NKVD club. The Military Collegium, a rubber-stamp court chaired by Lieutenant General Alexander Cheptsov, received forty-two volumes of materials, the result of three years of interrogations. The defendants were forced to confess to four major crimes—bourgeois nationalism, creating an anti-Soviet nationalistic underground, treason against the Soviet Union, and espionage.[86] There was no evidence of wrongdoing apart from their confessions, extracted under torture. During the trial the defendants recanted, protesting that they had been beaten and forced to sign self-incriminations. Boris Shimeliovich, the medical director at the Botkin Clinical Hospital, received two thousand blows to his buttocks and heels; he had to be carried to the interrogations on a stretcher. Lina Shtern, the only female member of the USSR Academy of Sciences and the Academy of Medical Sciences, underwent eighty-seven interrogations. Shtern, in her seventies, was abused by the minister of state security, Victor Abakumov, who insulted her as "a Zionist agent" and "an old whore."[87] Lozovsky, also in his seventies, was beaten by his anti-Semitic interrogator, Colonel Vladimir Komarov, who referred to Jews as "dirty people" and "lousy bastards." Lozovsky said he signed his self-incrimination to live to the trial.[88]

The defendants were allowed to make long statements, which Lozovsky used effectively to dismantle the case. Despite torture and years of solitary confinement, he had the presence of mind to quote documents and letters exposing the baselessness of the accusations against the JAC. The fact that during the war the JAC had appealed to Jews around the world was now used as evidence of ties to "bourgeois nationalists." Collecting materials about Jewish suffering was twisted into an act of nationalism. Yet these same materials were presented by the Soviet prosecution team during the Nuremberg trials, said Lozovsky. "Let us say that this is nationalism, then I ask the court to take the following . . . into account: Did the Nuremberg trials take place under my supervision?"[89] Lozovsky's testimony was so convincing that the presiding judge interrupted the proceedings and appealed to Malenkov to reopen the investigation. Malenkov refused. On July 18 thirteen defendants were sentenced to death. (Solomon Bregman had died in prison. Shtern, whose research on longevity was of interest to Stalin, was sentenced to five years of exile.) The judge also made a request for clemency and sent Lozovsky's personal statement to Stalin, but to no avail. On August 12 thirteen members of the Jewish Anti-Fascist Committee were executed; their families were deported to Siberia or Kazakhstan. They were treated worse than Nazi war criminals: a number of Einsatzgruppen commanders, sentenced to death in Nuremberg, were released in the 1950s.[90]

In October 1952, when the last installment of the novel was published, Fadeev nominated it for the Stalin Prize. This was meant to defend it from ideological attacks. In late fall reviewers described *For the Right Cause* as "a Soviet *War and Peace*" and "an encyclopedia of Soviet life."[91] Two major publishers, the State Military Publishing House, or Voenizdat, and Sovetskij Pisatel' (Soviet Writer), wanted to launch separate editions of the novel. But this laudatory response was about to change.

In December 1952 Stalin declared during a meeting of the Presidium that "every Jew is a nationalist and an agent of American intelligence."[92] A campaign against Jewish doctors was launched. Yevgeniya Livshits, a well-known pediatrician, and Professor Miron Vovsi, a distinguished physician who worked in the Kremlin hospital and was Mikhoels's cousin, were arrested and tortured. On January 13, 1953, *Pravda* announced the "Doctors' Plot" on its front page. TASS, the country's major news agency, stated that "a group of doctors-saboteurs" had been arrested. Six out of nine doctors on the list were Jewish. Members of the "terrorist group" were accused of working to harm the health of major Soviet and military leaders. The Jewish doctors were singled out as the guiltiest:

> The majority of participants of the terrorist group (Vovsi M. S., Feldman A. I., Grinshtein A. M., Etinger Ya. G.) were linked to the international Jewish bourgeois-nationalist organization "Joint," ostensibly created by American intelligence to provide material aid to the Jews in other countries. In reality, this organization, guided by American intelligence, conducts wide spying, terrorist, and other subversive activity in a number of countries, including the Soviet Union. The arrested Vovsi told the investigation that he received a directive to "annihilate the USSR's leadership" from the American organization "Joint" via Moscow's doctor Shimeliovich and a well-known Jewish bourgeois nationalist, Mikhoels.[93]

This announcement was accompanied by an editorial headed "Foul Spies and Murderers in the Mask of Doctors and Professors." The editorial, revised by

Stalin, referred to the Jewish doctors as "monsters" and "vile traitors to the motherland." *Pravda*'s communiqué was reprinted across the country, an endorsement for anti-Semitic hatred and abuse, which had been on the rise since 1949.

In 1953 national newspapers daily published articles about the "killer doctors." Moscow was filled with all sorts of rumors—of the anti-Jewish pogroms in preparation and the imminent deportations of Jews to Biro-bidzhan, on the border with China, or to Central Asia. Grossman's editors and publishers distanced themselves from the Jewish author. Days after *Pravda*'s announcement, on January 16, the publisher Sovetskij Pisatel' held a board meeting to criticize *For the Right Cause*—which it had only recently consid-ered bringing out in book form. Grossman would later read the verbatim report from this meeting: his acquaintances were among the writers denouncing his novel. Dolmatovsky, a fellow war correspondent who had been with him in Majdanek and Treblinka, now objected to the Jewish theme, saying that Shtrum must be "surgically removed" from the novel. Editor and novelist Alexander Chakovsky, who was also Jewish, said that the depiction of Hitler "in connection with the Jewish question" was "historically . . . and politically incorrect." Author Ivan Aramilev compared Grossman with Lion Feucht-wanger, a known "Jewish bourgeois nationalist." A few had the courage to defend the novel—editor Klavdia Ivanova and writer Alexander Bek.[94]

Tvardovsky held a similar meeting at *Novy mir*, the only meeting Grossman attended, at the editor's insistence. Aramilev showed up there to claim that the Jewish theme took a disproportionately large part in the novel and that the "annihilation of the Jewish nation was not the Fascists' main plan." Grossman responded that the Final Solution was "a historical fact."[95]

In late January an incident took place that would haunt Grossman for the rest of his life. Acting on Stalin's initiative, *Pravda* editors drafted an open letter on behalf of the Jewish elite that denounced the Jewish doctors. A list of fifty-seven prominent Soviet Jews was compiled; their signatures were sought. Grossman received a call summoning him to *Pravda*, where "the future of the Jewish people" will be discussed. As he was heading to the newspaper Grossman was on edge. He called on Tvardovsky at *Novy mir* and accused him of failing to defend the novel he had just published. "You want me to resign my Party membership?" bellowed Tvardovsky. "I do," Grossman responded. Furious, Tvardovsky shouted, "I know where you must go from here. Go, go, it seems you didn't get it yet, they'll explain it to you there."[96] At *Pravda* Jewish artists, writers, and scholars sat in a meeting hall where historian Isaak Mintz, entrusted to collect signatures, read the open letter demanding severe punishment of the "killer doctors." Grossman sat in the hall next to the poet Margarita Aliger, a contributor to *The Black Book*. Both signed the letter.

Although the open letter was never published, Grossman did not forgive himself for acting against his conscience. He relives the affair in *Life and Fate* when Shtrum signs a similar letter denouncing the doctors.

> Victor felt overwhelmed by disgust at his own submissiveness. The great State was breathing on him tenderly; he didn't have the strength to cast himself into the freezing darkness. . . . He had no strength today, no strength at all. He was paralyzed, not by fear, but by something quite different—a strange, agonizing sense of his own passivity. . . .
>
> Victor did no work that day. There were no distractions, no telephone calls. He was simply unable to work. His work seemed dull, empty, pointless. Who else had signed the letter? . . . He wanted to hide behind someone's back. But it had been impossible for him to refuse. It would have been suicide. Nonsense, he could easily have refused.[97]

Also in January Ehrenburg was unexpectedly awarded the Stalin Peace Prize, which had been given only to foreign dignitaries in the past. On January 27, during the award ceremony at the Kremlin, Ehrenburg was asked to say a few words about the "criminal doctors." He responded that he didn't ask for the prize and was prepared to renounce it; he refused to speak about the doctors.[98] A few days later Ehrenburg was pressured to sign the collective Jewish letter to *Pravda*. When he refused, he was told that the letter had been drafted at Stalin's behest. Ehrenburg then appealed to Stalin, carefully explaining what prevented him from signing the open letter. A collective statement by Jewish individuals could "strengthen nationalistic tendencies" inside the country and "fuel anti-Soviet propaganda" abroad, Ehrenburg argued. But if Stalin believed publishing the letter was in the country's interest, "I shall at once sign it."[99] Stalin ordered the letter to be revised and demanded that Ehrenburg sign the softer version. Summoned to *Pravda* on February 20, Ehrenburg had no choice but to sign the repulsive letter. As Ehrenburg writes in his memoirs, "In the eyes of millions of readers I was a writer who could come to Stalin and tell him that I disagreed with him in this or that. But in reality, I was just the same 'cog' and 'screw' as my readers were. I attempted to protest. But it was fate, rather than my letter, which decided the outcome."[100] *Pravda* waited for Stalin's signal to publish the letter, but it did not come. Stalin's health was failing, and he retired to his nearby dacha. On February 17 he appeared in the Kremlin for the last time.[101]

But there was a signal to attack Grossman: in February newspapers launched their coordinated assault. Bubennov's article "On Grossman's Novel *For the Right Cause*" appeared in *Pravda* on February 13, occupying two large feuilletons. The article accused Grossman of a "historically inaccurate" depiction of Nazism, of failing to present the Party as the organizer of the victory, and of portraying too many Jewish characters. Shtrum is married into the Shaposhnikov family, which is "at the center of an epic novel about Stalingrad." On top of this, the Shaposhnikovs have befriended the Jewish doctor Sofya Levinton, "and that's a kind of family Grossman is trying to pass off for a typical Soviet family." Bubennov's article was followed with an avalanche of hostile reviews: "In a Distorting Mirror," "On a False Path," "Roots of Mistakes," and the like.

On March 2 the *Literary Gazette* published the statement of *Novy mir*'s editorial board, postulating that criticism of Grossman's novel reveals it was based on "a profoundly erroneous ideological conception." The editorial board admitted that publishing this work was "a grave mistake." On March 3 Fadeev held a meeting of the writer's union where speakers denounced the novel. Bubennov called it "a spit in the face of the Russian people." Voenizdat dissolved the contract and informed Grossman that he must return the advance.[102]

During this turbulent time, anticipating arrest, Grossman fled to his friend Lipkin's dacha. One day their village neighbor, a cleaning lady, asked, "Have you heard Stalin's ill?" Grossman and Lipkin did not believe her: the news seemed too good to be true. They walked to the station to buy a newspaper. The kiosk was closed, but a newspaper with a bulletin about Stalin's health was posted on the wall next to the train schedule. (Newspapers began to publish these bulletins on March 4.) Grossman and Lipkin spent a sleepless night wondering whether Stalin would die. "Of course, he will, otherwise they wouldn't have announced his illness in the newspaper. But, maybe he's already dead? What's to come next? Will things get better or worse?"[103]

Stalin had had a stroke at his nearby dacha; he remained prostrate on the floor for hours. The guards were afraid to enter, even though they realized that something was wrong. Eventually they alerted Beria and Malenkov; after the Politburo gathered at the dacha medical help was sought. A team of Russian doctors and nurses arrived; their hands shook when they examined Stalin. The Jewish doctors were in prison. Yakov Rapoport, an expert pathologist, was summoned by his interrogators; instead of beating him, they solicited his advice on how to treat a stroke patient and whether certain symptoms suggested a grave condition. Asked to recommend doctors who could treat "an important person," Rapoport named several. Every one he suggested was in prison.[104]

The anti-Semitic campaign did not cease with Stalin's death on March 5. The day after, Simonov, who edited the *Literary Gazette*, published a list of Jewish writers who should be expelled from the writers' union; he referred to them as "dead weight."[105] Then on March 19 the *Literary Gazette* published Simonov's editorial stating that Soviet writers had the task of portraying "the greatest genius of all time and all peoples—the immortal Stalin."[106] The collective leadership that replaced Stalin was upset with this piece. Khrushchev summoned Simonov, threatening to dismiss him from his post.[107]

On March 24, speaking at a meeting of the Presidium of the writers' union, Tvardovky called Grossman's novel "entirely absurd, entirely harmful, entirely false."[108] Fadeev denounced the novel and repented his mistakes. At the end of the month Fadeev published in the *Literary Gazette* a long blistering report on the meeting. After Stalin's death the campaign against the Jews proceeded without letup. But on April 4 the Kremlin publicly disavowed the "Doctors' Plot." Things were finally beginning to change.

11. Toward *Life and Fate*

> He was alive, he was free. What more did he need?
> —Vasily Grossman, *Life and Fate*

Stalin's death marked the end of an epoch that saw mass executions, deportations, deadly famine, and the bloodiest war in history. Incomprehensibly, after so much suffering under his rule, the country was shaken by Stalin's natural death at seventy-three. Nearly everyone cried during the days of mourning, but while many wept out of sorrow and anxiety, others cried for joy. Evgeniya Ginzburg, the writer and Kolyma survivor, recalls that on March 5 "the whole of Magadan was sobbing." Ex-prisoners of the deadliest Soviet camps "diligently wailed for the deceased." Across the country and in Magadan, Kolyma's capital, the radio played Bach: "Majestic musical phrases . . . rolled forth from all the loudspeakers in our building."[1]

In the novel *Everything Flows*, which he drafted in 1955, Grossman captures the impact of the announcement of the tyrant's death. "Stalin Had Died! In this death lay an element of sudden and truly spontaneous freedom that was infinitely alien to the nature of the Stalinist State. The State was shaken, just as it had been shaken by the shock of the German invasion of June 22, 1941." Stalin's totalitarian rule, lasting a quarter of the century, turned him into a cult figure, a deity, "a Russian god." The bulletins chronicling his failing health produced confusion and shock: people were discovering that the immortal Stalin had "weak and aging flesh." The death of "a great god, the idol of the twentieth century" devastated the nation.

> Stalin had died! Some were overcome by grief. There were schools where teachers made their pupils kneel down; kneeling down

themselves, and weeping uncontrollably, they then read aloud the government bulletin on the death of the Leader. Many people taking part in the official mourning assemblies in institutions and factories were overcome by hysteria. . . .

Others were overcome by joy. Villages that had been groaning beneath the iron weight of Stalin's hand breathed a sigh of relief.

And the many millions confined in the camps rejoiced.[2]

For three days lines of mourners streamed past Red Square into the House of Unions where Stalin had held his show trials and where his body was now lying in state. Even in death Stalin continued to inspire fanaticism and mass murder. "Millions of people wanted to see the deceased," writes Grossman in *Everything Flows*. "All of Moscow, all of the surrounding provinces, was flooding toward the House of Unions, toward the Hall of Columns."[3] Roads were jammed for hundreds of miles with vehicles and swarms of people walking to Moscow. Public transportation in the capital was halted. Large army trucks lined the main avenues and streets leading to Red Square. The authorities feared unrest.

The physicist Andrei Sakharov, then working with Igor Tamm on the construction of a thermonuclear bomb in a top-secret military facility outside Moscow, remembers that the announcement of Stalin's death came as a shock to all: "We realized that things would change, but in what direction? People feared that the situation would deteriorate—but how could it get any worse? Some, who harbored no illusions about Stalin and the regime, worried about a general collapse, internecine strife, another wave of mass repressions, even civil war."[4] Ehrenburg, who had to be present in the Hall of Columns as the mourners filed past, recounts that getting into the House of Unions was no easy matter, even though he lived within walking distance. Crossing the central Gorky Street was an ordeal, since all approaches to Red Square were fortified: "Huge trucks blocked the way and, if an officer would allow, I'd climb a truck and jump off on the opposite side, but in fifty paces I'd be stopped again, and everything would be repeated." Dense crowds were moving through Moscow's streets toward the House of Unions, and this human flood had to squeeze past the army trucks. "There were stories of a deadly crush on Trubnaya Square. . . . I don't think there's been another such funeral in history," Ehrenburg comments.[5] The poet Yevgeny Yevtushenko, who was on Trubnaya Square, the epicenter of the tragedy that ensued, describes "a monstrous whirlpool" that sucked people under. "I felt I was treading on something soft. It was a human body. I picked my feet up under me and was carried along by the crowd. For a long time I was afraid to put my feet down again. I was saved by my height. Short people were smothered alive, falling and perishing. We were caught between the walls of houses on one side and a row of army trucks on the other." People's heads were smashed against the steel panels of the trucks, but soldiers said they could not move the vehicles without instructions.[6]

Grossman, who was staying with Lipkin outside Moscow, would re-create the scene from witnesses' accounts: "Streams of people, like black, brittle rivers, clashed against one another, were squashed and flattened against stone walls; they twisted and crushed cars; they tore iron gates off their hinges. . . . The tragedy of Khodynka, on the day of the coronation of Nicholas II, paled into insignificance in comparison with the death of the earthly Russian god, the pockmarked cobbler's son from the town of Gori. People seemed to go to their deaths in a state of enchantment, in some kind of Christian, Buddhist, or mystical acceptance of doom."[7] Thousands are believed to have perished. Corpses were picked up at night, and the authorities never revealed the death toll. Khrushchev later claimed that 109 people had died in the Moscow crush, but others belive the number was much higher.[8]

The collective leadership, Stalin's closest collaborators—Malenkov, Beria, Molotov, Voroshilov, Bulganin, Khrushchev, Kaganovich, and Mikoyan, all those who bore personal responsibility for mass purges—had assumed power. With Stalin gone, the regime of terror was unsustainable; they realized the need for reform, but in Khrushchev's words, "We were scared—really scared. We were afraid the thaw might unleash a flood, which we wouldn't be able to control and which would drown us. . . . We wanted to guide the progress of the thaw."[9] The description *thaw* was coined by Ehrenburg. Written in the winter of 1953, his novella *The Thaw* gave the name to the new epoch.

In early April, soon after the Kremlin disavowed the "Doctors' Plot," announcing in *Pravda* that the case had been fabricated to incite "national antagonism," the regime also admitted that the imprisoned doctors had been subjected to "illegal methods of investigation," or torture. Upon reading this Ginzburg felt that "a new era" was beginning to dawn.

> "Illegal methods of investigation." Just think of it! They had come
> out with it at last. These four words became a vaccine injected under

the skin of millions of Kolyma deportees and prisoners and produced irrepressible excitement—in all of them together and in each one of them individually. People stopped sleeping. They grew haggard with the strain, with the expectation of unheard-of changes at any minute. They talked themselves hoarse, telling and retelling one another, as if in a sort of fever, the same old stories of interrogation that they had related a thousand and one times before now over those long, long years. All the wounds of '37 and '49 were reopened, tingled unbearably, and demanded relief.[10]

Reforms were conducted by hard-core Stalinists, all of them responsible for mass murder. Beria, the head of Soviet secret police since 1938 who had overseen the Gulag empire, handled the deportations of nationalities, and organized the Katyn Massacre, was also the one to introduce broad amnesty. By 1953 it was realized that the Soviet economy could not be sustained by slave labor in the Gulag. According to Beria, before the amnesty in late March 1953, over 2.5 million inmates were held in prisons and labor camps.[11] The Gulag's industrial and construction projects were controlled by the Ministry of Internal Affairs. Beria had them transferred to economic ministries, thus ending the use of Gulag labor in logging, manufacturing, mining, and construction. A number of Stalin's economically useless projects were discontinued. Among them was the infamous Salekhard-Igarka railway in northwestern Siberia, nicknamed the "Road of Death." Since 1949 the project had employed one hundred thousand prisoners, many of whom perished during the construction. As Grossman remarks in *Everything Flows*, "Men were building what no man needed. All of these projects—the White Sea canal, the Arctic mines, the railways constructed north of the Arctic Circle, the vast factories hidden in the Siberian taiga, the superpowerful hydroelectric power stations deep in the wilderness—were of no use to anyone."[12] These projects were abandoned for pragmatic reasons—not because they had claimed countless lives.

Beria's amnesty benefited 1 million prisoners, mostly common criminals. Contrary to expectation, it did not apply to political inmates. Hundreds of thousands of innocent people continued to suffer in prisons, forced labor camps, and special settlements, having to wait three more years until Khrushchev's secret speech at the Twentieth Party Congress in 1956.

After Stalin's funeral Beria created several commissions to review a handful of cases—the Doctors' Plot and Mikhoels's murder. (But the case of the Jewish Anti-Fascist Committee, related to the Doctors' Plot, was not reviewed. And not until 1955 were the victims' relatives even informed that their loved ones had been executed.) Beria, who had arranged Mikhoels's murder and whose men had tortured the imprisoned doctors, now liberated survivors. The review came late for the prominent Kremlin doctor Professor Yakov Etinger, arrested in 1950 for unguarded remarks about Stalin; he was tortured to death while in prison. The Jewish doctors were released because the Party elite wanted these highly qualified professionals back at their Kremlin hospitals.

When Beria emerged as the leading contender to power, Khrushchev, who knew him as "a butcher and a murderer," realized that this was a threat to the collective leadership. As he told Malenkov, "Beria is getting his knives ready for us."[13] On June 26, during a meeting of the Presidium of the Central Committee, Beria was arrested with the help of Marshal Zhukov and his military men. Placed under guard at the Council of Ministers, the mass murderer was later transferred to a bomb shelter in the Moscow Military District, from which he could not escape.

On July 10 Sakharov and other physicists working on the hydrogen bomb, the project supervised by Beria, noticed that "the signs on Beria Street had been replaced by cardboard markers reading: Kruglov Street." It turned out that Sergei Kruglov had been appointed the new minister of internal affairs.[14] Later that day the radio announced that Beria and his accomplices had been arrested. In the closed Soviet society, information about Beria's crimes, which affected millions, was revealed only to Party organizations and VIPs. Sakharov was included among the readers of the Beria document. (In the same way, in 1956, he was among the privileged few to be acquainted with Khrushchev's secret speech to the Twentieth Party Congress. Actually, this speech denouncing Stalin was only semi-secret: writers were also informed during official meetings of Khrushchev's revelations.) The document told about Beria's execution lists, which were endorsed by Stalin; it contained some information about "mass arrests, executions, the cruel tortures" Beria and his men had conducted.[15]

Roman Rudenko, the new procurator general appointed to investigate Beria and his henchmen, had been the chief Soviet prosecutor at the Nuremberg trials. Unlike those at Nuremberg, these proceedings were secret; moreover, the full transcript of Beria's trial has never been released.[16] The collective leadership feared that the evidence would undermine public trust in the Communist Party. So a long list of invented crimes was produced. On December 23, 1953, a special session of the Military Collegium of the Supreme Court of the USSR heard the indictment. It included accusations of treason, anti-Soviet conspiracy with the goal of restoring capitalism, and links to foreign intelligence services. Beria and his men were executed that same day.[17] In fact, this published indictment contained much of the same rhetoric used previously to accuse the Jewish doctors. One of the bloodiest henchmen of Stalin's regime, Beria was described as a "bourgeois degenerate" who sought "to weaken the defensive capacity of the Soviet Union."[18] Upon reading this, Grossman realized that the truth about Beria's actual crimes was being suppressed.

Nadezhda Mandelstam recalls her brother saying after Stalin's death, "We still do not realize what we have been through."[19] Someone had to shed light on the epoch that had produced Hitler and Stalin and destroyed all notions of humanity: "a wolfish time," as Grossman put it.[20] He felt his task was to capture his era and pose difficult questions: "Why has life been so terrible? Are you and I not to blame?"[21] He was not the only one to ponder the similarities between Hitlerism and Stalinism, to compare the regimes' brutal policies against their political opponents and against the Jews.

While living in Magadan as exiles, Ginzburg and her German husband Dr. Anton Walter, a Kolyma survivor, casually compared the Nazi and Soviet anti-Semitic policies. During Stalin's final campaign against the Jewish doctors, when authorities began expelling the Jewish hospital staff, Dr. Walter would joke darkly with Ginzburg: "Perhaps, I'd better send for a racial purity certificate from Germany."[22] Referring to the ulcers of the skin common among former Kolyma prisoners, himself included, Dr. Walter also told Ginsburg: "The inmates of Auschwitz and Dachau are known by the numbers branded on their wrists. The inmates of Kolyma can be recognized by this mark, tattooed on them by starvation." Dr. Walter was speaking of trophic ulcers, a sign of the disintegration of tissue he had observed in scores of Kolyma prisoners and on his own skin.[23]

As Shalamov observes in *The Kolyma Tales*, Stalin's "extermination camps" provided the "means of physical destruction of political enemies of the state." In 1937–38 prisoners were taken to Kolyma to die, he writes. Shalamov describes the Serpantinnaya interrogation prison in Kolyma as a death camp. Thousands were taken there in 1938 to be shot; nobody ever returned from Serpantinnaya.[24] There is dark irony in the fact that in 1946

Grossman's article "The Hell of Treblinka" was published as a separate booklet in Kolyma's capital, Magadan. In the Soviet Union his article was not widely published; issuing it in Magadan may have been necessary to put the regime in a better light by showing that the Nazi extermination camps were even deadlier.

Grossman's research for the first part of *Life and Fate* inspired his thoughts about the similarities between Hitler's and Stalin's totalitarian regimes. When the Gulag prisoners began returning from the camps, Grossman could finally collect evidence to compare the treatment of political enemies in Nazi Germany and in Soviet Russia.

In 1948 the distinguished poet and Gulag survivor Nikolai Zabolotsky became Grossman's neighbor and friend. He was the first ex-inmate of the labor camps in the Far East whom Grossman interviewed at length. From Zabolotsky's testimony, "The Story of My Imprisonment," committed to paper in 1956, we know precisely what Grossman was able to learn during his many conversations with the poet.

In 1947 Grossman and his family had received an apartment in a newly built housing complex for writers and composers in Moscow's outskirts. The inhabitants of "Begovaya village," as the settlement between Begovaya Street and Horoshovsky Highway was known, lived in suburban-type brick buildings two or three stories high shared by only several families. The land was generously allocated: the buildings were surrounded by orchards and vegetable gardens, cultivated communally. In summer the occupants would sit on benches near their houses dressed in their pajamas.

In summer 1948 Zabolotsky moved to this neighborhood with his wife Ekaterina and two children. While most Gulag survivors were unable to return to major cities until 1956, Zabolotsky was helped by such influential writers as Fadeev, Ehrenburg, Veniamin Kaverin, Samuil Marshak, Korney Chukovsky, Victor Shklovsky, and Alexander Stepanov, who petitioned for a review of his case. Although not officially rehabilitated, the poet was allowed to settle in Moscow and was granted a flat—an unimaginable luxury for most former inmates.

Zabolotsky's son Nikita recalls that his family and the Grossmans had quickly become close; the wives and children became friends, while Zabolotsky and Grossman found each other's company "most interesting." After the ordeal he had suffered, Zabolotsky lived in fear of denunciation and rear-rest. He understandably dreaded political discussions; however, "conversations with Grossman used to head towards the very topic that exacerbated Z's old inner wounds and disrupted the hard-won balance he needed in life and in his poetic work." Nikita's memoir captures Grossman interviewing Zabolotsky methodically and pitilessly as a professional journalist. "Grossman was always trying to uncover the authentic motives of the person he was talking to and find out what was going on inside them, without taking into account the pain he might be causing in so doing."[25] During these conversations Grossman would also make a "direct comparison between certain traits of German fascism and the system that had come into being under Stalin."[26] Such comparisons were inspired by Zabolotsky's own recollections. He would say, for example, that when he was tortured in the inner prison of the NKVD's headquarters in Leningrad, the Big House, he felt that he was in the hands of Fascists who had somehow penetrated the Soviet punitive system. When he shared this impression with his cellmate, an old Party member, the latter admitted that the same thoughts were also going through his mind.[27] If friends asked how hard it was in the camps, Zabolotsky would reply, "It's pretty hard, isn't it, when you work till you are dropping, take a quick breather, and they set the dogs on you?"[28]

Zabolotsky's misfortunes began in 1933 when his poem "Triumph of Agriculture" was attacked in the press. Critic Ermilov published an article in *Pravda* describing the poem as a lampoon on collectivization.[29] This political accusation was never forgotten and later served as part of the proof of Zabolotsky's anti-Soviet activity.

Zabolotsky was arrested on March 19, 1938, four days after Bukharin's execution. Following Bukharin's trial the NKVD moved to "unmask" Trotskyists among writers in Leningrad. Enemies of the state were sought in every sphere of professional activity: for the NKVD an anti-Soviet conspiracy among well-known writers would make for a promising case. Fortunately the secret police were unaware that Zabolotsky had sought Bukharin's help in publishing his poems. Bukharin had written him a note that the poet kept with a batch of manuscripts, but the NKVD failed to unearth it during the search. Later Ekaterina Zabolotskaya, realizing that any connection to Bukharin could mean a life sentence, destroyed this innocuous note.

After the poet's arrest Nikolai Lesyuchevsky, a writer and secret police informer, produced a report assessing Zabolotsky's work for the NKVD.

Like Pyotr Pavlenko, who "reviewed" Mandelstam's poems for the secret police, Lesyuchevsky dashed off a similar denunciation condemning Zabolotsky's poems as counterrevolutionary and anti-Soviet.[30] The Leningrad poet Boris Kornilov, whom Lesyuchevsky had previously denounced, was arrested and shot in February 1938. The denouncer was later promoted to head the major publishing house Sovetskij Pisatel'. Grossman would depict him in Pinegin, Ivan's denouncer in *Everything Flows*—a story that will be told later. Some episodes from Zabolotsky's testimony about his imprisonment and incidents he shared with friends are recognizable in *Life and Fate* and in *Everything Flows*.

In "The Story of My Imprisonment" Zabolotsky recounts being interrogated for four days and nights in Leningrad's Big House. Protesting the abuse, he referred to his rights under the Soviet Constitution, to which the interrogator responded: "The Constitution stops operating at our front door." Despite torture, Zabolotsky refused to incriminate himself or implicate others in anti-Soviet activity.

> During the first days they did not beat me, attempting to break me morally and physically. I was deprived of food. I was deprived of sleep. Interrogators worked in shifts, while I remained motionless on a chair before an interrogator's desk—day after day. My legs began to swell, and on the third day I had to rip my shoes, since I could no longer bear the pain in my feet. Consciousness began to dim, and I strained all my powers to answer rationally and not say anything unfair in relation to those I was questioned about. At times interrogation would halt, and we would sit in silence. The interrogator wrote something, I tried to nap, but he would wake me at once. . . . On the fourth day, as a result of nervous tension, hunger and sleep deprivation I gradually began to lose my reason. As I recall, I was by then shouting at the investigators and threatening them myself.[31]

This account is recognizable in Krymov's conveyor-belt interrogation in *Life and Fate*. During his incarceration in Lubyanka, Krymov spends several days and nights sitting on a chair in the interrogator's office. "The pain in his back and legs was crushing him. . . . All he wanted was to lie down on his bunk, stick his legs in the air, flex his bare toes, scratch his calves. 'Stay awake!' shouted the captain. . . . Time passed, slowly doing its work. . . . A dense grey fog filled Krymov's head. Past and future had disappeared; even the file with its curling pages had disappeared. There was only one thing left in the world—his need to take off his boots, have a good scratch and go to sleep. The investigator came back. . . . Krymov jumped up, grabbed the investigator's tie, and banged his fist on the table."[32] Krymov's Lubyanka interrogator threatens him by quoting Gorky: "If an enemy won't yield, he must be destroyed."[33] Grossman also borrowed this incident from Zabolotsky's memoir.

Zabolotsky's poem about Leningrad's NKVD headquarters likely inspired the image of Lubyanka's "sleepless building" in Grossman's novel. The poem does not survive, except for the summary; according to Ekaterina Zabolotskaya it told "about the evil Big House . . . about its windows that remained alight all night, and about the dark cells there in which innocent people were tortured." Zabolotsky let his wife read the dangerous poem before burning it.[34] In *Life and Fate* Krymov walks past the Lubyanka building in 1937, thinking about the fate of the many people who disappeared forever behind its doors. "A few windows were lit up; you could glimpse faint shadows through the white curtains. From the main entrance came the glare of headlights and the sound of car doors being slammed. The whole city seemed to be pinned down, fascinated by the glassy stare of the Lubyanka."[35] Ekaterina Zabolotskaya possibly told Grossman the story of her husband's poem about the Big House.[36] In 1955 she became Grossman's confidante and lover.

Zabolotsky lived through savage beatings and temporary loss of sanity, and was confined in an overcrowded cell where one hundred prisoners stood pressed against each other. At night when beatings began, they would hear screams from the investigators' offices. The screams could not be drowned out even by the roaring engines of the heavy trucks the NKVD left running in the courtyard. Upon receiving a five-year sentence in the labor camps for counter-revolutionary activity, Zabolotsky survived sixty days of winter transportation through Siberia in an unheated train. Packed together, suffering from cold and hunger, prisoners were also tormented by thirst. On one occasion they received almost no water for three days and had to lick "black sooty icicles" that had formed from their exhalations on the walls of the wagon. This was the first day of 1939, and for Zabolotsky that New Year Day's "feast" became only too memorable. Their destination was Komsomolsk-on-the-Amur, and it took so long to reach it because railway lines were jammed with prisoner trains.

Searchlights and machine guns were installed on the roofs of wagons; in addition the trains were heavily guarded by soldiers with German shepherds. This account informed Grossman when he depicted Gulag prisoner transportation in *Everything Flows*: "Searchlights were installed on each train. From the locomotive to the last wagon, their sharp beams pierced through the darkness—and if there was a man on the roof, the machine gun looking down the train knew only too well what to do."[37]

During his term in the Gulag Zabolotsky worked twelve-hour shifts cutting timber or quarrying in temperatures reaching minus fifty degrees Celsius. Along with extreme cold in winter and mosquitoes in summer, he suffered from hunger. Inmates lived in cold and damp barracks, sleeping on wooden planking around an iron stove. In the mornings, while their semiliterate guard counted them, they stood for hours facing a barbed-wire fence with slogans posted over the gate, such as "Labor is a matter of honor, glory and heroism." (Grossman, listening to this, would make an association with Dachau and Auschwitz where mottos on display read, "Work ennobles" and "Work sets you free.")[38]

The Gulag's purpose was the physical destruction of political inmates, who were regarded as the living dead. Criminals, on the other hand, were treated liberally; they reigned in the Gulag. Political prisoners, beaten and starved by the camp administration, compared their tormentors with the Gestapo.[39] In 1941 Zabolotsky had been a witness as camp authorities deliberately sank a barge with political prisoners on the Amur River, an act of ruthlessness that would haunt him all his life.[40] Grossman learned many such stories from Zabolotsky and from Ekaterina, who became entirely supportive of his determination to tell the truth about Stalinism.

As Nikita Zabolotsky wrote in his memoir, his mother became attracted to Grossman for his talent and charisma. In turn, Grossman valued Ekaterina's sensitivity and her moral support, particularly during Stalin's anti-Semitic campaign. At the time Ekaterina was his soul mate and intellectual companion, but not yet his lover. In *Life and Fate* Grossman describes their walks and conversations.

Ekaterina was a survivor in her own right, and her experiences impressed Grossman. In November 1938, after Zabolotsky was dispatched to the Gulag, where he would spend six years, Ekaterina was deported from Leningrad with the children. Allowed to choose a destination, she decided on the town of Urzhum (where Zabolotsky had once lived) some fifteen hundred kilometers east of Leningrad. Risking her safety, she took with her the very batch of Zabolotsky's manuscripts the NKVD had failed to find during the search. In 1939, upon learning that some political prisoners' cases were being reviewed, she sent a telegram to Beria asking for permission to return to Leningrad. From there she began petitioning for the review of her husband's case. She reached out to influential people and kept Zabolotsky's hope alive by sending him letters and parcels. Ekaterina achieved the high-level support essential for the review of his case; however, Zabolotsky's denouncer, afraid to lose his credibility with the NKVD, started working through his channels to prove that his assessment of Zabolotsky's writings was accurate. As a result, the poet remained in the Gulag until August 1944.

When the war began Ekaterina became trapped in Leningrad with her son and daughter. Almost a million people died of starvation during the siege; she and the children survived. In February 1942, suffering from dystrophy, they were evacuated over the frozen Ladoga Lake. In 1944, when Zabolotsky was released from the Gulag and settled as a semi-free worker in Kulunda, Altai, she ventured there with the children and the rescued manuscripts. Prior to his arrest Zabolotsky had been translating the twelfth-century Russian literary masterpiece *The Lay of Igor's Campaign*. Ekaterina brought this manuscript with her to Kulunda, and beginning in 1945 he worked nights to finish his translation. During the day he was employed as a draftsman, copying blueprints—stupefying mechanical work, as he wrote to his friend Stepanov in January. In a postscript to her husband's letter, Ekaterina described the poverty of their lives as exiles: "We are already getting used to living together with Kolya [the poet Nikolai Zabolotsky]. But our arrival hardly improved his life. In any case, I'm unable to provide proper conditions for his [creative] work. We live in a small hut along with sheep, chickens, and owners. In fact, we don't even have a corner to ourselves. But I'm happy with this, since fate has given me so much. . . . I'm trying to earn money as best I can. I'm knitting sweaters."[41]

While translating the medieval literary masterpiece, Zabolotsky remained a prisoner. His life in exile was only marginally better than in the Gulag. As he admitted to Stepanov, "My conditions—work, daily life, and rights—remain unchanged."[42] In June, upon completing a first draft of *The Lay of Igor's Campaign*, he described himself to Stepanov as half prisoner and half poet. While copying blueprints, he would passionately yearn for the moment when his day job ended and his creative work began. "Now, when I have penetrated into the spirit of this [literary] monument, I'm filled with the greatest awe, surprise, and gratitude to the fate that delivered this miracle to us from the depth of the centuries."[43] In his mid-forties, the poet regretted the lost time: "Years waste away, the art wastes away."[44] Zabolotsky and his family were finally able to return to Moscow in 1946, and two years later, with their friends' help, they moved into the same neighborhood as Grossman.

In 1953 Grossman drafted the short story "Tiergarten," which implies parallels between Hitlerism and Stalinism. During the last weeks of war in Berlin he had witnessed the battle for the city center during which the oldest zoo in Germany in the Tiergarten was devastated by the fighting. Grossman saw the zoo after the battle and talked to the keeper who had spent four decades overseeing the monkey house. Most of the animals had been killed by artillery fire. "A corpse of a gorilla in the cage," he wrote in his notebook.[45]

"Tiergarten" is a story about the old keeper, Ramm, and his caged animals, including the gorilla Frizzi who is killed during the battle by shrapnel. Ramm's story is told through flashbacks: three of his sons were killed in the war; the fourth, a Social Democrat, perished in Dachau. The state secret police arrived at night to arrest him and a while later Ramm received a black plastic box from Dachau with his son's ashes. "Black plastic urns containing feathery ashes came from Dachau and Mauthausen to many apartments," Grossman writes, relating events of 1933 when the Nazis were sending their political opponents to concentration camps. That year in Germany one hundred thousand political prisoners, mostly Social Democrats and Communists, were incarcerated in concentration camps. Dachau, opened by Himmler in 1933, was the first Nazi concentration camp intended for political opponents. As in Grossman's story, families would receive an urn filled with ashes to notify them of their relative's death. Grossman had apparently known that in 1933 many Germans were sent to Dachau by the Gestapo on the apprehension that they might present political problems in the future: "Police were merciless not only towards opponents who attempted to fight Hitler. The State secret police believed that no one in the world was innocent."[46] (In *Life and Fate* this same thought is expressed by a former Chekist, Katsenelenbogen: "The concept of personal innocence is a hangover from the Middle Ages.")[47]

In Nazi Germany fear of being denounced and sent to a concentration camp helped silence Hitler's opposition. In "Tiergarten" Ramm thinks that

Hitler's state was created on a foundation that entirely excluded freedom. In this story Grossman expresses another idea he would develop in *Life and Fate* and in *Everything Flows*: human nature is incompatible with slavery. "He felt: aspiration for freedom can be suppressed, but cannot be destroyed."[48] Unsurprisingly, Soviet censors in Glavlit found "Tiergarten" unpublishable. Although ashes of Gulag victims were never sent home—not even a death notice would arrive—the story about Hitler's Germany was read, correctly, as a story about Stalin's Russia.

After Stalin's death things began to look brighter for Grossman. On April 21, 1953, he won his civil suit against the State Military Publishing House, Voenizdat. The publisher had demanded he return the advance for the novel *For the Right Cause*, which it was afraid to issue. The judge took the author's side—unthinkable under Stalin. In June Voenizdat was back at Grossman's door, asking to reopen negotiations on publishing his novel. In September Fadeev phoned to say that his criticism of the novel "had been caused by the circumstances. The novel must be published [as a book]."[49] Fadeev was soon acting as a middleman, pressuring Voenizdat to speed up the book's publication and to produce it in time for the Soviet Writers' Second Congress in December 1954. Seizing on this opportunity Grossman restored some of his original text. It took the publisher more than a year to issue the book, but for Grossman things were happening surprisingly quickly.

In July 1954 he reported the latest developments to Lipkin. While he was staying at a rented dacha near Moscow, Grossman received Fadeev's telegram: *For the Right Cause* sent to printers, further discussions unnecessary, publication resolved. Grossman had a hard time believing that his book had finally received the green light. He thought the telegram was "someone's practical joke." In Moscow Fadeev confirmed the news: publication was settled once and for all. Fadeev, Grossman kidded in a letter to Lipkin, "decided to eclipse the Gospel miracle by taking part in both Lazarus's burial and Lazarus's resurrection."[50] That month Voenizdat sent Grossman a new contract: the publisher was planning to launch two regular editions in 1954, each with a run of fifteen thousand copies, and a mass-market edition with the run of seventy-five thousand copies. Voenizdat was already planning to reprint another regular edition the following year.[51] This was a moral victory for Grossman. He only regretted that his friend Lipkin was traveling and could not share the joy. Grossman recalled, nostalgically, how his friend had sheltered him at his dacha in March 1953 when the newspaper campaign against his novel could have ended in his arrest. "This book had a long, difficult road, and my friendship with you helped me travel through it; you shared this path with me, like a brother. But I'm far from thinking that the road has ended and the Park of Culture and Leisure has begun. I'm glad it hasn't ended and, if it's fated, let it be hard, but only let it continue. I remembered Ilyinskoe, our idyll at the dacha—the stove, playing *durak* [a card game], macaroni soup, our walks to the station, the thaw."[52]

A sociable man, Lipkin met many major writers and poets of his time; he liked to reminisce about his encounters with Mandelstam, Akhmatova, Babel, Bulgakov, Pasternak, and Marina Tsvetaeva. Actually, Lipkin's circle of friends was far more impressive than Grossman's. Lipkin had attempted to introduce Grossman to Akhmatova, but neither writer expressed enthusiasm, and the meeting never took place. Akhmatova was not interested in Grossman's subject matter and apparently did not read *For the Right Cause*. In turn, Grossman was indifferent to Akhmatova's poetry, although he read it and occasionally quoted her famous lines.

Despite the ultimate success of his book, which sold widely after it was published in 1954, Grossman's name was rarely mentioned in the press. Writers and journalists who had denounced him during the harassment campaign were now avoiding him. Grossman's old friend, the writer and Gulag survivor Yevgeniya Taratuta, who visited him in November 1954, recalls that his telephone never rang throughout the evening.

Taratuta had been released in April, earlier than most: she was helped by influential friends, including Fadeev. Arrested in 1950, at the height of Stalin's campaign against the Jews, Taratuta was incarcerated in Butyrskaya Prison, where she endured ten months of torture. Interrogated every night, deprived of sleep, threatened and beaten, she was pressed to denounce her friends the Jewish writers Lev Kassil and Leyb Kvitko. She refused to sign a false statement about their alleged ties to America and their anti-Soviet conspiracy. (Kassil remained free, but Kvitko, a member of the JAC's Presidium, was arrested in 1949 and executed in 1952.) For some reason her investigator also demanded that she admit her alleged friendship with Mayakovsky. Taratuta had been introduced to Mayakovsky at Mikhoels's theater after the premier of his satirical play *The Bathhouse* and shook hands with the famous poet, who also signed a copy of his book for her. It's unknown why Mayakovsky, who committed suicide in 1930, suddenly surfaced in her case, but nothing made sense in those days. (Taratuta's library was seized during her arrest. She also lost her notebooks in which she had recorded conversations with Pasternak. The NKVD never returned her papers: numerous writers' archives perished in Lubyanka.)[53] A year of physical and mental torture left Taratuta disabled at thirty-nine. Sentenced without a trial to fifteen years in the Gulag, she was dispatched to a secret labor camp for women invalids in the notorious Abez' settlement in the Komi Republic, south of the Arctic Circle. The fifteen hundred women in her camp were crippled by hard labor in Siberia or by torture. Peasants and scientists, old women and young, all were packed in barracks where by morning their hair would freeze to the bed boards. The average winter temperature in Abez' was minus fifty degrees Celsius. Inmates were fed frozen potatoes, which they had to peel with a piece of iron: knives were not allowed. Taratuta slept next to Lina Prokofieva, a former operatic soprano and Sergei Prokofiev's first wife. Lina, originally from Spain, was sentenced to twenty years for attempting to obtain an exit visa from the USSR in 1948. (She served eight years.) Prokofiev died on the same day as Stalin, but the inmates heard only about Stalin's death.

While in the camp Taratuta read Grossman's novel *For the Right Cause*. Several issues of *Novy mir* in which it was published ended up in Abez' in fall 1952. The novel was read there "with admiration." Newspapers were also delivered to her camp, so she followed the campaign against Grossman's novel: "This wonderful truthful novel was subjected to monstrous criticism." Taratuta told Grossman about the Party activists she met in her camp. One of them was the daughter of Commissar Verhotursky, whom Grossman depicts in the story "Four Days" under his real name.[54] Grossman was impressed when she told him how these Party activists cried when Stalin's death was announced. Each believed that she alone had been sentenced by mistake; the other inmates were real enemies of the people. Grossman spoke little that evening; he mostly asked her about the Gulag. He would produce a separate chapter about women in camps in *Everything Flows*.

In December 1954 Grossman met Konstantin Simonov at the writers' congress. Again appointed editor of *Novy mir*, Simonov asked Grossman to submit the second part of his novel to his journal. Grossman had been working on *Life and Fate* since 1952, but the closer he came to completing it, the less hopeful he felt about publication. In 1958 he wrote Olga, "I work systematically, but the prospects for my work, as you know, are more than uncertain."[55] By then *For the Right Cause* was regarded as a Soviet classic, but Grossman knew that *Life and Fate* was a completely different, uncompromising work. The action of the novel took place alternately in the Gulag, in a Nazi concentration camp, and at the front; in Nazi Germany and in Soviet Russia. It was structured to show the many similarities between Stalinism and Hitlerism that had become apparent to Grossman. He wrote *Life and Fate* without an eye on publication, or "without permission," to use Mandelstam's words. As Mandelstam remarks in "Fourth Prose," "I divide all the works of world literature into those written with and without permission. The first are trash, the second—stolen air."[56]

Grossman had initially expected to complete *Life and Fate* in 1954, but what he was learning about the camps affected his plot. In summer 1955 he wrote Lipkin that he was working hard on the novel, but that his work was taking him in a new direction.[57] That year Gulag survivors began to arrive in Moscow, where they had to apply to have their cases reviewed. They would meet with official impediments every step of the way: authorities did not even lift restrictions on their stay in Moscow. Arriving secretly from places of exile, they first had to line up at the USSR General Prosecutor's Office on Kirov Street. Ginzburg, who spent eighteen years in prison camps and exile, describes the reception hall at the prosecutor's office crammed full of ex-prisoners; the place was buzzing "like a transit camp." Everyone in the queue was gray-haired. She recognized many people in this line; one of the "graybeards" was Nikolai Mordvinov, a "former geologist, former inmate of the Verhneuralsk special political prison, former prisoner in the Ukhta camp, and formerly a handsome man." The final decision on their cases had to be made by the Supreme Court on Vorovsky Street. This is where hundreds of people lined up for days. In 1937 it had taken mere minutes to sentence them as traitors and spies; now, on their last legs, they had to stand in enormous queues to prove their innocence. Ginzburg recalls how they had to collect all sorts of papers by dealing with "sluggish bureaucrats, the best of whom were apathetic, while the worst scarcely concealed their resentment of these unforeseen, eccentric reforms." In 1955 the Supreme Court was still adorned with Stalin's portraits, and this inspired someone's angry remark, "Why did they hang him up there? So that people won't forget who caused all this?" This was said in front of an official who was no longer feared.[58] Grossman did not meet Ginzburg, but in the early 1960s he read her first memoir, *Into the Whirlwind.*

Zabolotsky did not apply for his rehabilitation certificate, naively thinking that the authorities would gradually issue rehabilitations and apologies to all victims of terror. He drafted an application, but did not mail it.[59] In fact, he was never free from fear of arrest and dreaded dealing with authorities; he kept warm clothing handy in case he would be again dispatched to a prison camp. After his release from the Gulag he was mostly occupied with translating work. To Ekaterina's distress, his fear of another arrest drove him to burn the batch of manuscripts with his poems that she had managed to save during the war.

In 1956 Grossman's stepson Fedya applied for his father Boris Guber's posthumous rehabilitation, which was granted later that year. But only in the early 1990s, when archives became open, was he able to read what his father had been accused of. In 1937 the family was told only that Guber was sentenced to "ten years without the right of correspondence," officialese for a death sentence. Nadezhda Mandelstam, among the first to apply for the rehabilitation of her late husband, recalls that officials at the Prosecutor's Office "had no illusions about the worth of all the records and 'confessions' in the files." Nonetheless, they refused to acquaint relatives with details of the case. "I thus never learned exactly what happened to M[andelstam] in 1938. Shielding it from me, the woman prosecutor quickly glanced through the very thin file in front of her . . . and told me that it was his 'second case' and was 'without basis.' Later I received by mail a document certifying that the case had been discontinued 'for lack of evidence.' "[60] Tens of thousands—both survivors and relatives of victims—received such documents with a few lines of standard text.

During Khrushchev's Thaw public discussion of mass purges remained strictly prohibited because every government member, including Khrushchev himself, took part in them. In February 1956 Alexander Yakovlev, a major Communist official who would become the key reformer of the Gorbachev era, attended the Twentieth Party Congress at the Kremlin. He heard Khrushchev deliver his emotional revelations about Stalin's crimes, a speech that mesmerized the audience. Yakovlev remembers a complete silence in the hall: "No one looked at anyone else; those in attendance were too overcome by the fear that seemed to have taken permanent root in the psychology of so-called Soviet Man and in the very core of his being."[61] Khrushchev's speech about Stalin's personality cult was not published in the Soviet Union until 1989. During Gorbachev's glasnost the nation first learned the full extent of the crimes committed by Stalin's regime.

✡

In September 1956, with rehabilitations under way, Grossman compiled a list of the writers destroyed during Stalin's purges. He was soon working on literary commissions of Guber, Kataev, Zarudin, Artyom Vesyolyj, and other purged writers, pressing for their posthumous rehabilitation and publication. He also struggled for posthumous publication of the work of his friend Andrei Platonov, who had been persecuted and rarely published under Stalin. Platonov and Grossman were particularly close during the war, when Grossman recommended the harassed writer as a correspondent for *Red Star*. Platonov's death from tuberculosis in 1951 was a blow to Grossman, who regarded him highly as a man and author. The writers' union and its newspaper barely acknowledged the demise of one of the greatest talents of their time. Grossman spoke at the funeral, attended by few, and later helped his friend's impoverished family obtain financial assistance from the Literary Fund. He headed the commission on Platonov's literary remains, arranging for the writer's vast archive to be deposited with the Literary Museum and struggling for posthumous publication. Grossman compiled a volume of Platonov's short prose, to which he wrote an introduction. But the slim volume took a long time to come out—not until 1958. "I'm reading Platonov's stories," wrote Grossman to Lipkin. "Could you really dislike them? There's a great power in 'Takyr,' 'Third Son,' and 'Fro.' I hear my friend's voice as though in a desert—it feels joyful and sad."[62] In 1960 Grossman also succeeded in publishing the first review of this volume in the recently founded newspaper *Literature and Life*. His piece opens with words applicable to Grossman himself: "A writer's recognition doesn't always . . . reflect his true importance and actual position in literature. Time is the chief judge in the affairs of undeserved literary glory. It's not a foe to genuine literary treasures, but a kind and clever friend, a calm and loyal curator."[63]

In 1956 Olga Adamova-Sliozberg, a former labor economist, received her rehabilitation certificate. Twenty years earlier she had been arrested as the wife of an enemy of the people. Her husband, a thirty-seven-year-old biologist, was shot in the basement of the Lubyanka; her children grew up as orphans; her friends were buried in Kolyma; she lost her profession and her home. In her memoir, *The Path*, she writes: "Everything is taken away from you, and no official paper will ever return your place in life. All that remains is within your soul. You are either a beggar or you are rich." In the camps she decided that she must survive to become a witness, and her life then acquired new meaning.[64]

Many survivors wanted to tell their stories, and Grossman began interviewing them around 1956. That year Uncle David's son, Victor Sherentsis, returned to Moscow from the Gulag. His apartment became the place where Grossman spoke with scores of former inmates. Among them was Lev Konson, a Gulag survivor who married Elena Surits, the daughter of Grossman's friends Gedda Surits and Alexander Nitochkin. Arrested in 1943 at sixteen, Konson was among a handful of people who actually had engaged in anti-Soviet activity—he distributed leaflets describing injustices of the Soviet system. Konson was incarcerated in the inner prison of the Lubyanka where, to break his will, he was kept in a tiny windowless isolation cell. He was sentenced to twenty-five years in the Gulag, of which he served six. He told Grossman of how political prisoners were abused by both criminals and guards. In 1950 they were gathered from several camps to build the Taishet-Bratsk railway in Siberia: "Extreme cold in winter, mosquitoes in summer; hunger and back-breaking work at all times." The hardest job was fetching logs from the freezing river. The guards chased them into the icy water with rifle butts. Konson's story surfaced in *Everything Flows* in the character of a schoolboy, Borya Romashkin, who receives a ten-year sentence for writing leaflets accusing the State of executing innocent people. As Grossman tells in the novel, the boy typed the leaflets and posted them on buildings in Moscow; his story became so famous that it "traveled all over Kolyma."[65] (Konson recorded his Gulag stories, which were published in Paris in 1983. He later immigrated to Israel.)[66]

In 1955 Grossman's work on the novel was interrupted by a family calamity. In May his daughter Katya was hit by a truck in Kharkov, where she lived with her mother and stepfather, Victor Baranov. The accident left Katya with multiple fractures and a head injury. Grossman flew to Kharkov and saw his daughter soon after her surgery. She was covered in bandages but was already speaking of various events in the hospital and "even attempted to joke." Grossman met Professor Tseitlin, "Kharkov's best surgeon," who had operated on Katya. The surgeon invited Grossman for supper. Grossman accepted but could not decide whether it was appropriate to buy him a present.[67]

Later that year Grossman helped Katya secure a job at the State Library for Foreign Literature in Moscow; father and daughter spent the next eight years in the same city. Their relationship was complex. Grossman wrote long, friendly letters to Katya, but she did not reply for months. As is apparent from Semyon Osipovich's letter to Grossman's first wife, Galya used Katya as a pawn to hurt Grossman. In 1953–54 Semyon Osipovich wrote Galya asking her "not to meddle" in Katya's relationship with her father. But Katya remained obedient to her mother's will even at twenty-one. Once, before her move to Moscow, she had agreed to spend a few days with Grossman in the city. When he came to meet her at the station, however, Katya told him that her mother had instructed her to return directly to Kharkov without stopping in Moscow. Grossman was deeply hurt.[68] Galya remained bitter about their divorce even after she remarried. It appears that she destroyed Grossman's letters to Katya along with the inscribed copies of his books that he had given her, and cut his face from family photographs.[69]

By 1955 Grossman's personal life had become more entangled: he was in love with Ekaterina Zabolotskaya, and his marriage with Olga was on the rocks. Over the years his interactions with Zabolotskaya had been "limited to family gatherings." Later, they began to take walks together in the Neskuchny Garden. As Nikita writes, Zabolotsky observed Grossman's friendship with his wife "growing into a deeper feeling." "At first, sure of her devotion to him, he was not much worried, but evidently began to realize in the first months of 1956 that danger was threatening him from the very quarter he least expected. His wife admitted that she was in love with Grossman. Z demanded that she should stop meeting him, but this proved not to be easy. Normally obedient to his will, Ekaterina showed firmness and said that there was nothing reprehensible in her relations with Grossman, and she could not break them off."[70] The depth of his wife's feeling for Grossman came as a shock to Zabolotsky, who declared that he and Ekaterina should get divorced, she could settle with Grossman, and he would find another wife. Shortly after, Zabolotsky phoned Natalya Roskina, an editor he barely knew. (She was the daughter of Grossman's friend the writer Alexander Roskin, who was killed in the war.) Zabolotsky invited the young woman to a restaurant and proposed marriage to her. They never married: although they had an affair, it lasted only several months, not least because Zabolotsky began to drink heavily.

Grossman's involvement with Ekaterina was deep and genuine. Gedda Surits recalls a conversation she had with Grossman in 1956, soon after he separated from his family. During a walk together Grossman, "in a rare instance of forthrightness," spoke about Ekaterina's kindness and femininity. " 'Do you see Lyusya [Olga]?' I asked about his wife. 'But of course,' he replied. 'This is not simple at all. We've been together for almost twenty years. I love Katya [Zabolotskaya], but Lyusya—is Lyusya, and there's a bit of me in her, too.' "[71] In fact, Grossman never completely broke with his family, visiting Olga and Fedya every week. In 1956 Fedya married and moved into Grossman's room in Begovaya village with his wife, Irina Novikova. A while later the writers' union gave Grossman one room in a communal apartment on Lomonosovsky Avenue; he settled there with Ekaterina. She repaired Grossman's relationship with his daughter: Katya would even stay overnight in their room, sleeping on the floor.

As Lipkin put it, Grossman's late love "brought him much happiness and suffering."[72] Analyzing these words, one may surmise that the two felt guilty about their happiness. Ekaterina realized that Zabolotsky's drinking, given his cardiac trouble and a previous heart attack, would end badly. Grossman felt remorseful about "ruining" his friend's life and letting Olga down. She wrote long tearful letters: Grossman's affair with Ekaterina, her close friend, had come as a blow. Yet Grossman was happy because he had a partner who understood him completely and who shared his determination to tell the truth about Stalinism. In *Life and Fate* he depicts his love triangle and Marya's spiritual affinity with Shtrum: "That perfect understanding of hers had seemed to him to be his only happiness." Shtrum's love for Marya "was the deepest truth of his soul."[73]

The union with Zabolotskaya benefited Grossman's work: he used her stories in *Life and Fate* and in *Everything Flows*. Beginning in 1955 he produced some of his best prose: that year he started *Everything Flows* and wrote a magnificent essay, "The Sistine Madonna." In her fifties, Zabolotskaya looked weary after her many tribulations. In *Everything Flows*, obviously referring to her, Grossman writes, "She was beautiful because she was kind. . . . She was kindness, all kindness, and he understood with the whole being that her tenderness, her warmth, her whispers were beautiful because her heart was full of kindness toward him, because love is kindness."[74] In *Life and Fate* Grossman portrays her thus: "Marya Ivanovna sat there, as thin and grey as a little sparrow. Her forehead was slightly protuberant, she had a hairdo like a village schoolteacher's and she wore a woolen dress patched at the elbows. To Victor [Shtrum] every word she spoke seemed full of intelligence, kindness and sensitivity; every movement she made was an embodiment of sweetness and grace."[75] In this novel Grossman also creates Olga's fictional double in Shtrum's wife, Lyudmila, depicting her as a good homemaker and Marya's opposite.

Unlike Zabolotskaya, Olga was difficult and domineering; Grossman referred to her as "a stone baba."[76] The nickname was a pun on her lack of sensitivity and her hobby of collecting stones. By then Grossman's bond with his wife had lasted two decades. She had witnessed his rise as a writer: she was his model and typist, and they had lived together through many trials. But nothing could undo a great wrong: Olga's indifference to his mother's fate became the major reason for their estrangement.

In August 1956 Grossman's father, his close companion over the years, died at eighty-six. On August 14 Grossman received a letter of sympathy from his friend Prince Zvenigorodskij: "Dear Vasily Semyonovich! Yesterday I learned of your father's death. Please accept, my dear, the deepest condolences for your painful loss. I know myself what it means to lose people who are close. May God help you live through this big sorrow! Loving you with my entire soul and my heart, A. Zvenigorodskij."[77]

Grossman's friendship with Lipkin helped him through the difficult year. In April they traveled in the Caucasus—through Georgia, Azerbaijan, and Abkhazia, where they were invited to a feast in a mountain village. Lipkin, who made a living as a literary translator, traveled across the Soviet Union to meet his authors; in 1961, at his friend's suggestion, Grossman would go alone to Armenia.

The affair with Zabolotskaya ended in 1958. In late summer Ekaterina returned home to be with her husband, whose health had deteriorated. Two months later, in October, the poet died of a heart attack. Afterward Grossman attempted to resume the relationship with Zabolotskaya, but she felt even guiltier about enjoying happiness after her husband's death; there was also family pressure against the relationship. Although Ekaterina rejected Grossman's proposal that they move in together, she remained his trusted friend. Grossman reunited with Olga, who wanted him back but never forgave his infidelity.

12. The Novel

The times provide the pictures, I merely speak the words
to go with them, and it will not be so much my own story I tell as that
of an entire generation—our unique generation, carrying a heavier
burden of fate than almost any other in the course of history.
—Stefan Zweig, *The World of Yesterday*

In 1945 the Red Army art-recovery teams brought trophy paintings from Dresden to Moscow. Ten years later Khrushchev's government decided to return some of this priceless art to Germany. But before sending back the paintings the authorities wanted to exhibit them. In May 1955 Raphael's *The Sistine Madonna*, kept in storage until then, was put on display in Moscow. This was a cultural event not to be missed, and Grossman stood in a long line stretching along Volkhonka Street to the Pushkin Art Museum. The painting captivated him, leaving him "stunned and confused." He elaborates his impressions in the magnificent essay "The Sistine Madonna." In summer, when he wrote the essay at Lipkin's dacha in Ilyinskoe, his friend Vyacheslav Loboda arrived unexpectedly with daughter Lyudmila. Decades later, she would recall Grossman and her father discussing their impressions of the painting at the dacha. Loboda soon left and Lyudmila, aged twelve, stayed with Grossman for two weeks. She describes an untypical Grossman, wearing an apron and cleaning pots; the room where he worked was strewn with papers.[1]

This simple life was completely unlike his complex vision and ideas. "As soon as you set eyes on this painting, you immediately realize one thing, one thing above all: that it is immortal. I realized that . . . for all the admiration I feel for Rembrandt, Beethoven, and Tolstoy—there was no work of art other than *The Sistine Madonna*, no other work created by brush, chisel, or pen, no other work that had conquered my heart and mind, that would continue to live for as long as people continued to live."[2]

A century earlier a spellbound Dostoevsky spent hours before the painting in the Dresden Art Gallery; he considered it "the highest manifestation of human genius."[3] But while Dostoevsky, a Christian, saw it as a symbol of religious faith and of beauty that would save the world, Grossman, a humanist, interpreted *The Sistine Madonna* as "a purely atheistic expression of life and humanity." As he writes in the essay, "What I saw was a young mother holding a child in her arms." This painting had been seen by twelve generations, and in each era people invested it with their contemporary understanding of human destiny. Grossman thought of a young mother "in the epoch of Fascism": bringing her child into the world, she would hear the roar of crowds welcoming Hitler. He imagined Hitler standing before the Madonna in the Dresden Art Gallery and deciding this young woman's fate. The Madonna revived Grossman's memory of Treblinka: "It was she, treading lightly on her little bare feet, who had walked over the swaying earth of Treblinka; it was she who had walked from the 'station' from where the transports were unloaded, to the gas chambers. I knew her by the expression on her face, by the look in her eyes. I saw her son and recognized him by the strange, un-childlike look on his face. This was how mothers and children looked, this was how they were in their souls when they saw, against the dark green of the pine trees, the white walls of the Treblinka gas chambers." The Madonna represents "the power of life, the power of what is human in man," the spiritual force that cannot be enslaved by any violence. This is why the faces of the Madonna and her child are calm: they are invincible. "Life's destruction, even in our iron age, is not its defeat."

Grossman perceived this painting as the contemporary symbol of suffering humanity; he repeats that the Madonna has suffered "together with us—for she is us, and her son is us." The painting's idea was universal and everlasting. It inspired his thoughts about the destinies of a young mother and child in the age of Stalin's total collectivization. "Here she is, barefoot, carrying her little son, boarding a transport train. What a long path lies ahead of her. . . . And where is your father, little one? Where did he perish? . . . Felling logs in the taiga?" His thoughts were of a young woman during Ukraine's famine: "I saw her in 1930, in Konotop, at the station. Swarthy from hunger and illness, she walked towards the express train, looked up at me with her wonderful eyes, and said with her lips, without any voice,

'Bread.' " In 1937 another young mother was holding her son for the last time, saying good-bye to him; "a black car was waiting for her below, a black seal had already been fixed to the door of her room." He also thought of a victorious Stalin standing in front of *The Sistine Madonna* in 1945 and gazing for a "long time at the faces of mother and son." Had he recognized this young woman and her child? "But we, we people, we recognized her, and we recognized her son, too. She is us; their fate is our own fate; mother and son are what is human in man. And if some future time takes the Madonna to China, or to the Sudan, people will recognize her everywhere just as we have recognized her today."

Grossman concludes the essay with thoughts of how the world has entered the nuclear age, the age of "atomic reactors and hydrogen bombs," and along with it prospects of a new global war. "Soon we will leave life; our hair is already white. But she, a young mother carrying her son in her arms, will go forward to meet her fate. Along with a new generation of people, she will see in the sky a blinding, powerful light: the first explosion of a thermo-nuclear bomb." Yet *The Sistine Madonna* also inspired Grossman's faith in humanity's eventual triumph over violence, in the power of life, in the irre-pressible human aspiration for freedom: "We preserve our faith that life and freedom are one, that there is nothing higher than what is human in man."

"The Sistine Madonna," unpublished during the writer's life, presents in concentrated form the major themes of *Life and Fate*. In this novel Grossman conflates the Gulag and the Holocaust to tell the story of his generation, which had witnessed the twin dictatorships in Europe during World War II. At the core of the novel is Grossman's message of the need to humanize European societies after an age of totalitarian violence. He believed that even the most "perfect violence"—of Fascism and of Stalinism—proved impotent to destroy human needs for love, compassion, and freedom. The novel expresses this idea in a letter of a former Tolstoyan, Ikonnikov, who has witnessed atrocities committed by both the Nazi and the Soviet regimes: "The more I saw of the darkness of Fascism, the more clearly I realized that human qualities persist even on the edge of the grave, even at the door of the gas chamber."[4] This idea is central to the novel.

In *Life and Fate* Grossman resumes the theme of an "earthly" Madonna. Sofya Levinton, a military doctor captured by the Nazis, has worked for three decades as a surgeon and has neither married nor had a child. In her fifties she experiences a maternal feeling toward David, a six-year-old boy whose parents were killed in a ghetto. They meet on a transport train taking them to a death camp like Treblinka. During selection in the camp, when doctors and surgeons are called, Sofya chooses to stay with the boy and share his fate. They walk together on the path of no return. Inside the gas chamber, Sofya hugs the boy to become inseparable from him in death; the boy dies first, and her heart aches for him as long as she lives. "I've become a mother."[5]

The Holocaust opened Grossman's eyes to the violence of totalitarian systems and their murderous ideologies; it became the prism through which he looked at the twentieth century's calamities. As he writes in the novel, "The first half of the twentieth century may be seen as a time of great scientific discoveries, revolutions, immense transformations, and two World Wars. It will go down in history, however, as the time when—in accordance with philosophies of race and society—whole sections of the Jewish population were exterminated."

The novel is structured to reveal similarities between Hitlerism and Stalinism. Both regimes have rejected the notion of humanity. Under Hitler and Stalin individual lives have been discounted; people are divided into categories—to be kept and to be destroyed. Yet totalitarian violence proved powerless to suppress the kernel of humanity in one's heart.

Anna Shtrum's farewell letter, written in the Jewish ghetto on the eve of its liquidation, becomes a source of spiritual strength to her son. Anna's final words are about her love and the power of life: "Remember that your mother's love is always with you, in grief and in happiness, no one has the strength to destroy it." Like the author himself, Shtrum believes that Fascism must perish "for the very reason that it has applied to man the laws applicable to atoms and cobble stones!"

The novel opens with a picture of the "camp-cities" in an enslaved Europe, "a world of straight lines," rectangular barracks and electrified barbed-wire fences. The image captures the essence of totalitarianism, which renders human life superfluous. "The wooden barracks stretched out in long broad streets. Their very uniformity was an expression of the inhumane character of this vast camp. . . . Everything that lives is unique."

Like Dachau, this fictional camp is first established by the Nazis for "enemies of the state." During the war the camp is expanded to hold POWs of various nationalities, criminals ("a privileged caste"), the "work-shy and asocial," émigrés, and other categories, which can be determined from the color of the badges prisoners wear. In this Nazi camp Russian inmates retain their political animosities toward each other. Thus, the Bolshevik Mostovskoy is antagonistic toward the Russian émigré Chernetsov, a former Menshevik. Mostovskoy detests him more than his actual enemies, the Nazis. Intolerance toward political opponents, typical of the Bolsheviks, was demonstrated by Lenin and Stalin in the course of their virulent campaigns. This same intolerance was also exhibited by the Nazis, who had incarcerated and destroyed their opponents in concentration camps. As Grossman writes, "In this hatred and lack of understanding between men who spoke the same tongue, you could see much of the tragedy of the twentieth century."

Similarities between the two regimes are revealed through the fate of the Tolstoyan Ikonnikov, persecuted and jailed both by the Communists and the Nazis for preaching compassion. During Stalin's collectivization Ikonnikov lives through the destruction of the peasantry as a class and the starvation imposed on millions in Ukraine. He preaches the Gospel, pleading for pity on the sick and the dying, but is arrested and later forced into psychiatric treatment. During the war, while in Belorussia, he witnesses the Nazi atrocities, the slaughter of twenty thousand Jews—experiences that make him lose his faith in God. He attempts to save Jewish women and children, but is arrested and ends up in a Nazi concentration camp.

In his conversation with Mostovskoy Ikonnikov rejects the contemporary social theories of National Socialism and Communism, which advocate violence as a means to attain their ideal of social good: "I saw the sufferings of the peasantry with my own eyes—and yet, collectivization was carried out in the name of Good. I don't believe in your 'Good.' I believe in human kindness. . . . You ask Hitler . . . and he'll tell you that even this camp was set up in the name of Good." Ikonnikov writes a letter rejecting state ideologies and organized religions alike for their demand of human sacrifices to attain universal harmony. "I have seen the unshakable strength of the idea of social good that was born in my own country. . . . I saw people being annihilated in the name of an idea of good as fine and humane as the ideal of Christianity. I saw whole villages dying of hunger; I saw peasant children dying in the snows of Siberia; I saw trains bound for Siberia with hundreds and thousands of men and women from Moscow, Leningrad and every city in Russia—men and women who had been declared enemies of a great and bright idea of social good." In this same letter Ikonnikov expresses his faith in the power of the human heart: "I have seen that it is not man who is impotent in the struggle against evil, but the power of evil that is impotent in the struggle against man."

He slips this letter under Mostovskoy's mattress. When it's unearthed during a search of the barracks, the Communist Mostovskoy is summoned by the SS officer Liss. The hypothetical conversation between the Nazi and the Communist is ironic: the SS officer explains to Mostovskoy that their two regimes are alike. Liss is a Baltic German who speaks Russian. Having read the letter preaching compassion, he remarks that neither a Nazi nor a Communist could have written it. An armchair philosopher, Liss tells Mostovskoy that "there is no divide" between their regimes: "When we look one another in the face . . . we are gazing into a mirror." Their "one-party States" similarly rely on terror, and both nations are led by the "great revolutionaries"— Stalin and Hitler. In fact, Nazi Germany "learnt many things from Stalin" when he liquidated millions of peasants to build socialism in one country. "Our Hitler saw that the Jews were the enemy hindering the German Nationalist Socialist movement. And he liquidated millions of Jews."

> "Just think for a moment! Who do you imagine fill our camps when there's no war and no prisoners of war? Enemies of the Party, enemies of the People! . . . Your prisoners are our prisoners!" He grinned. "The German Communists we've sent to camps are the same ones you sent to camps in 1937. Yezhov imprisoned them: Reichsführer Himmler imprisoned them. . . . Today you are appalled by our hatred of the Jews. Tomorrow you may make use of our experience yourselves. . . . I have been led by a great man down a long road. You too have been led by a great man; you too have traveled a long, difficult road. Do you really believe Bukharin was an agent provocateur? Only a very great man could lead people down a road like that. . . . What tortures me, though, is the thought that your terror killed millions—and we Germans were the only ones who could understand, the only men in the world who thought: 'Yes, that's absolutely right, that's how it has to be!' "

This conversation causes Mostovskoy to doubt his Bolshevik faith, if only briefly. The ideals of justice and equality for which revolutionaries fought are incompatible with terror. To maintain his revolutionary belief he "would have to hate the camps, the Lubyanka, bloodstained Yezhov, Yagoda, Beria! More than that . . .! He would have to hate Stalin and his dictatorship! More than that! He would have to condemn Lenin . . .! This was the edge of the abyss."

The Bolsheviks founded the socialist state promising equality and social justice, but they crushed freedom. The dictatorship of the proletariat established by Lenin had justified the destruction of entire classes and the establishment of concentration camps. Revolutionary goals freed the state from morality and justified the slaughter of both political opposition and the peasantry.

In the Gulag chapters, the Old Bolshevik Abarchuk intimates to a friend that he envies Soviet inmates in German concentration camps. It's easier to take beatings and death from the hands of the Fascists than your own people.[6] The revolution devours its children, and many of the Old Bolsheviks perish in the Gulag. Abarchuk retains his fanatical faith despite going through the circles of hell in Lubyanka and in Soviet labor camps, where he is harassed by criminals. But Abarchuk's friend and teacher Magar did not go through prisons and camps in vain. Magar imparts the truth to Abarchuk, who visits him in the infirmary, where he is dying. "We didn't understand freedom. We crushed it. Even Marx didn't value it—it's the base, the meaning, the foundation that underlies all foundations. Without freedom there can be no proletarian revolution." The Bolsheviks had committed a great crime—peasant genocide. Magar's neighbor in the infirmary, a dead peasant, is a silent witness to his words. He and millions of others were sacrificed to the cause of the revolution and, as Magar says, "No repentance can expiate what we've done."

Grossman's protagonists—in the Nazi concentration camps, in the Gulag, or living outside the barbed wire—yearn for freedom and suffer its loss. Historian Madyarov tells his friends the nuclear physicists Sokolov and Shtrum that throughout a millennium of Russian history, the country had never seen democracy and respect for human rights. "Our Russian humanism has always been cruel, intolerant, sectarian. From Avvakum to Lenin our conception of humanity has always been partisan and fanatical. It has always mercilessly sacrificed the individual to some abstract idea of humanity." This dangerous conversation liberates Shtrum from fear and stimulates his thought: it inspires his clear and beautiful nuclear theory. "And how strange, he thought suddenly, that this idea should have come to him when his mind was far away from anything to do with science, when the discussions that so excited him were those of free men, when his words and the words of his friends had been determined only by freedom, by bitter freedom."

In *Life and Fate* freedom is a main theme. The war is fought against enslavement by both the Nazis and the Bolsheviks, who destroyed freedom in their own land. During the worst bombardments of Stalingrad, living with an "acute sense of danger" and facing death, Red Army soldiers feel liberated from their fear of the Soviet state and its secret police. Stalingrad is "the only beacon of freedom in the kingdom of darkness." In the encircled Pavlov house, re-created in the novel as house 6/1 under Grekov's command, the fighters have "repelled thirty enemy attacks and set eight tanks on fire." They did not need the Party to lead them into battle; in fact, they were able to fight effectively because they felt free. But the Political Administration of the Front receives a report that in the doomed house Grekov and his people speak "the most appalling heresies." The house 6/1 has become "a state within a state," and even as they are fighting heroically, the Political Administration is alarmed. The battalion commissar Krymov is sent to the heavily shelled house to "establish Bolshevik order."

When Krymov arrives to "sort out unacceptable partisan attitudes," the fighters ignore him. His political threats are met with indifference: people who have seen death at close quarters cannot be intimidated. They casually discuss prohibited topics: "And what about the kolkhozes, comrade Commissar? Couldn't we have them liquidated after the war?" But questioning Party policy is a heresy that needs to be expurgated, so Krymov begins to work "with a surgeon's knife." Grekov is taunting him: "Why make such a fuss about the kolkhozes? It's true. People don't like them. You know that as well as I do." For Krymov, questioning Party strategies is like doubting faith. Sent by the Party to give Grekov's fighters "a taste of Bolshevism," he threatens to report Grekov to the authorities as "an alien and hostile element." At night Krymov is injured by a stray bullet (Krymov believes Grekov shot him) and is carried out from the house 6/1. By the time he submits his denunciation Grekov and his fighters are dead: the Germans have carpet-bombed their house. Now it's Krymov's turn to appreciate freedom: he has been denounced as a Trotskyist. (Much earlier, Trotsky has praised an article Krymov has written as "pure marble"; these words are enough to destroy a human life.) When Krymov is arrested his Lubyanka interrogator dismisses his Bolshevik past and treats him as an enemy, just as Krymov himself had treated Grekov. Krymov, who only recently believed himself immune to the fate of other Old Bolsheviks, is "deprived of freedom," and realizes there is no greater misfortune: "Life without freedom! It was an illness. Losing one's freedom was like losing one's health. There was still life, water still flowed from the tap, you still got a bowl of soup—but all these things were different, they were merely something allocated to you. Sometimes, in the interests of the investigation, it was necessary to deprive a prisoner of light, food and sleep. And if you were allocated them, that was also in the interests of investigation."

Grossman depicts perpetrators of state-sponsored violence as ordinary family men who regard their duties as mundane. Stalin's mock justice is carried out by the Lubyanka interrogators who routinely torture and kill innocent people. These officials receive salaries and benefits for extracting confessions under torture. At Lubyanka brutality and murder are justified by government campaigns. Krymov's interrogator is impervious to his sufferings, regarding the use of torture as simply a part of his duties. Before authorizing the beatings he makes a solicitous phone call to his pregnant wife to inquire about her health and discuss food orders, which they receive through a special distribution system.

Both regimes relied on ideological fanatics to conduct campaigns of destruction. The Stalinist Getmanov, who has denounced Krymov, and General Neudobnov, who has helped Yezhov conduct the military purge, have risen in the ranks by their actions. (Both are fictional characters.) Getmanov describes Neudobnov as a "fine fellow. A Bolshevik. A True Stalinist. A man with experience of leadership. . . . I remember him from 1937. Yezhov sent him to clean up the military district. Well, I wasn't exactly running a kindergarten myself at that time, but he really did do a thorough job. He was an axe—he had whole lists of men liquidated." Stalin's criminal regime rewards its perpetrators by allowing them to rob with impunity. In addition to a government dacha Neudobnov receives furniture, carpets, and porcelain, all confiscated in the course of arrests. A true Stalinist fanatic, he keeps talking about "enemies of the people who had been unmasked in the most unlikely places."

The question of personal responsibility for crimes is at the core of the novel, casting Stalin's henchmen against Nazi criminals. At the Nuremberg trials the Nazis argued that they were mere functionaries who executed government orders. Adolf Eichmann's claim during his 1961 trial in Jerusalem that he was obeying the law and "doing his job" inspired Hannah Arendt's famous expression "the banality of evil." Grossman, writing before Eichmann's arrest in 1960 and subsequent trial, understood his role, motivations, and place in history better than did Arendt, who had actually seen and heard him testify in Jerusalem. In *Life and Fate* Eichmann is shown touring construction sites and factories that produce equipment to increase the efficiency of crematoriums and gas chambers. In a scene depicting an apotheosis of evil Eichmann and the SS officer Liss are dining in the middle of a newly constructed gas chamber. This scene is based on fact. Grossman likely knew about Himmler's visit to Sobibor in 1943 where, according to survivors, Himmler and his retinue attended the gassing and cremation of a large group of young people. Afterward, Himmler and his generals went to the canteen where tables with food and flowers were set up for them.[7]

As is evident from this scene, Grossman perceived the mass murderer Eichmann differently than did Arendt, who describes him in her reports as an unthinking bureaucrat. In the novel Eichmann is one of the architects of the Final Solution. He tells Liss about the plan to exterminate millions of Jews, information known only to Hitler, Himmler, and Kaltenbrunner: "Just imagine! In two years' time, we'll be sitting at a comfortable table in this same office and saying: 'In twenty months we've solved a problem that humanity failed to solve in the course of twenty centuries.' " Grossman elevates Eichmann to the very top of the Nazi hierarchy with the masterminds of the Holocaust. Written before Arendt's reports, Grossman's portrayal of the "manager of the Holocaust" proved more accurate.[8]

Grossman also depicts an unthinking Nazi executive in Kaltluft, the commander of a death camp who takes pride in punctually performing his duties to the state. He is found at his desk even on Christmas Eve, an ironic allusion to the fact that his religion does not prevent him from carrying out the slaughter. Kaltluft and his employees regard murder as a "mundane" technical operation. If, on Judgment Day, Kaltluft will be called upon to explain how he became "the executioner of 590,000 people," he will mention "the war, fervent nationalism, the adamancy of the Party, the will of the State." Kaltluft's Soviet counterpart, the Chekist Katsenelenbogen, whom Krymov meets in Lubyanka, runs "a colossal camp construction project inside the Arctic Circle." He preaches the morality of the Soviet security organs and dreams of the entire country becoming one big Gulag. Katsenelenbogen "seemed to understand everything but feel nothing. Simple things like partying, suffering, freedom, love, grief, the fidelity of a woman, were mysteries to him. It was only when he spoke about his early years in the Cheka that you could sense any emotion in his voice. 'What a time that was! What people!' " Naturally, he also admires Stalin and Beria, who put him in charge of construction of the railway along the shores of the Arctic Ocean, "a strikingly beautiful project" that cost ten thousand lives.

Despite their different ideologies of race and of class, the two totalitarian systems functioned in similar ways. Both Hitler and Stalin orchestrated ideological campaigns inciting hatred of certain sections of the population. In both cases the slaughter of old men, women, and children was conducted in the name "of the motherland, world progress, the future happiness of mankind, of a nation, of a class." The Nazis relied on local populations to help exterminate millions of Ukrainian and Belorussian Jews. "And at an earlier date, in the same regions, Stalin himself had mobilized the fury of the masses, whipping it up to the point of frenzy during the campaigns to liquidate the kulaks as a class and during the extermination of the Trotskyist-Bukharinite degenerates and saboteurs."

Totalitarian systems, with their immense capacity for violence, wield "terrible power" over individuals, whom they turn into submissive tools: "Through propaganda, hunger, loneliness, infamy, obscurity, labor camps and the threat of death, this terrible power can fetter a man's will. But every step that a man takes under the threat of poverty, hunger, labour camps and death is at the same time an expression of his own will. . . . A man may be led by the fate, but he can refuse to follow." Grossman believes that "the highest thing" a person can do is to live in accordance with his or her own conscience. In a conversation with his fellow physicist Sokolov, Shtrum refers to Tolstoy's moral example: "Remember Tolstoy's words about capital punishment? 'I can't remain silent.' But we remained silent in 1937 when thousands of innocent people were executed. . . . And we remained silent during the horrors of general collectivization. . . . And if a man has the strength to listen to his conscience and then act on it, he feels a surge of happiness."

Shtrum, however, is coerced into participating in Stalin's campaign against the Jewish doctors. This happens during the harassment campaign against him, launched despite his recent scientific discovery, when he fears losing his job and his apartment as well. Instead, he suddenly receives a solicitous phone call from the dictator himself. Stalin had called Pasternak, Bulgakov, and Ehrenburg, but in the novel Grossman has him phoning Shtrum in the midst of the anti-Semitic campaign. This happens, of course, because Stalin is interested in the development of nuclear arms.

Stalin appreciates the importance of Shtrum's theory and inquires whether he needs anything for research. Does he need literature from abroad? (There is additional irony here since this is happening during an anti-cosmopolitan campaign when even the mention of a foreign book could land a scholar in prison.) Although Shtrum hasn't yielded to pressure or threats, the dictator's phone call breaks his will. He becomes an obedient servant of the state. After signing the notorious letter against the Jewish doctors he feels he has committed "a terrible sin," having betrayed his own people, his own mother. When Shtrum loses his integrity he also loses his inner freedom, feeling that his fear is beginning to transform him into a slave. "Then he realized that it still wasn't too late. He still had the strength to lift up his head, to remain his mother's son. And he wasn't going to try to console himself or justify what he had done. He wanted this mean, cowardly act to stand all his life as a reproach; day and night it would be something to bring him back to himself. . . . 'Well then, we'll see,' he said to himself. 'Maybe I do have enough strength. Your strength, Mother.' " We know that Grossman never forgave himself his lack of moral courage on this occasion. The novel gives a clue as to why he chose to reproach himself forever: this helped him resist becoming a slave. "Every hour, every day, year in, year out, he must struggle to be a man." Grossman writes here about his own struggle to preserve inner freedom in a state that crushed human liberty.

Life and Fate is a fearless work in which Grossman speaks out against dictatorship and oppression on behalf of millions of terror victims. The novel asserts his lifelong belief in democracy, the ideals of the February Revolution of 1917, which promised liberty, equality, and respect for human rights.

Upon reading *Life and Fate* in 1984, the German writer Heinrich Böll observed that the book captures historical events at their turning point, during the Battle of Stalingrad, and that it contains more than one novel. There are "several tightly intertwined novels" in it, a "multitude of lives and fates." During the war Böll, a soldier in the Wehrmacht, had experienced defeat, surrender to the Americans, and imprisonment in a POW camp. He was impressed by the humanity of Grossman's message in the novel and the fact that he depicts the defeated German soldiers with pity rather than glee.[9]

In 1958, in a letter to his friend Lipkin, Grossman wrote that he believed in the power of human kindness, in treating the fallen, the weak, the guilty ones with mercy.[10] Although this was not a new sentiment for Grossman (at the end of the war he reminded Soviet soldiers about a tradition to take pity on the weak), he had recently found confirmation of his beliefs in Churchill's writings. Grossman began reading Churchill's voluminous history *The Second World War* in March 1958. Each of the six volumes opens with a "Moral of the Work,"

Churchill's motto. "In war: resolution. In defeat: defiance. In victory: magnanimity. In peace: good will." After reading the first two volumes, Grossman remarked that there were many interesting facts, but that Churchill's personality interested him most. (The Russian edition of Churchill's six-volume history was first produced in 1954–55 by the Chekhov Publishing House in New York. Almost immediately, in 1955, all six volumes were issued in the Soviet Union. It was, however, a limited edition and not for sale. The volumes were distributed among the Soviet leadership and sent to *Spetshran* of major libraries, the book depositories for which readers were required to have special permission).[11]

With Lipkin, Grossman discussed anything from politics to world literature to the Bible, the former's most cherished book since childhood.[12] Reading the Bible helped Grossman discover new meaning in life after the age of Hitler and Stalin. Although Grossman rejected organized religion, his humanist ideals of love, mercy, forgiveness, and compassion are essentially the same as those at the core of many religious faiths.

In May 1957 Grossman attended a writers' conference in Moscow where Khrushchev gave the keynote speech. He made notes of Khrushchev's forthright remarks, which suggested that writers should not expect much from the Thaw: "Stalin's death came as a shock. We cried, like children, near Stalin's coffin." Khrushchev spoke sympathetically about Stalinist writers, artists, and musicians whose work glorified Soviet achievements: "They are accused of idealization. But they are the ones closest to the Party. . . . Idealists—are our people. We will not fire at our people. We will not betray you, for you and we are one. We are also idealists. . . . We do not support democracy without borders. . . . We will find strength to restrict it . . . and will arrest people if necessary." Khrushchev praised Stalinist writers such as Semyon Babaevsky, three times Stalin Prize laureate: "We must shield them with our bodies, and they will shield us."[13] The speech revealed the Party's determination to maintain its rigorous control of literature and the arts.

That year one Soviet novel was smuggled across the Iron Curtain and escaped Party control. *Doctor Zhivago* was the first book by a Soviet writer to be produced in the West after it was suppressed at home. Pasternak's work had been rejected by *Novy mir*. Khrushchev later regretted his failure to act and support this novel since its publication abroad during the Cold War was far more damaging to the Party.[14]

When the Italian Communist publisher Feltrinelli produced *Doctor Zhivago* in November 1957 it caused a political storm because of its criticism of the Soviet regime. As we know today, the CIA recognized the novel's "great propaganda value" and purchased thousands of copies, encouraging the book's publication throughout Europe. This helped it become an international sensation worthy of the author's Nobel Prize in Literature. As the CIA's declassified memo reveals, the agency perceived *Doctor Zhivago* as a weapon during the Cold War, "an opportunity to make Soviet citizens wonder what is wrong with their government."[15] A Russian edition was secretly produced and distributed in the Soviet Union, where many people read it.

Doctor Zhivago had circulated in samizdat since the early 1950s: Pasternak shared the manuscript with friends, and his book was read widely in the writers' milieu. Upon reading it in March 1958, months before Pasternak's nomination for the Nobel Prize, Grossman observed in a letter to his friend Lipkin that the novel's protagonist Zhivago seems too absorbed with his own talent and lacks an ability to love people and empathize with them. The Christian message in the novel serves only "to assert Zhivago's special, talented persona."[16] Grossman's dismissive remarks came months before the ugly anti-Pasternak campaign in the Soviet press.

Pasternak's prose and poetry did not appeal to Grossman, who valued clarity and social content above virtuoso style. In turn, Pasternak was critical of Grossman's novel *For the Right Cause*. After reading it in 1952, he wrote the poet Marina Tsvetaeva's daughter Ariadna Efron that he liked only some scenes, such as the part about evacuating the Stalingrad orphanage over the Volga and Grossman's "astute and profound" observations. But there were only sixty pages in the entire book of six hundred pages that struck Pasternak as genuine. "How could this happen to a man with his [Grossman's] wit and talent?" Pasternak went on to say that reading Grossman's novel gave him as much pain as his new dentures.[17] The two writers knew and respected each other, but their art was vastly different.

When in fall 1958 Pasternak was awarded the Nobel Prize the Soviets responded by launching a harassment campaign. National newspapers published abuse; Pasternak's colleagues and friends publicly denounced him as a traitor and demanded the poet's deportation. Pasternak was swiftly expelled from the writers' union. Grossman, who did not attend that meeting, was upset by the lack of decency on the part even of Pasternak's former acolytes. The most glaring example was the Leningrad writer Vera Panova, who readily joined in the campaign, although the walls of her apartment were covered with photographs of Pasternak. Grossman, who knew her, was appalled: "She came all the way from Leningrad," he thundered, "to help expel her dearest and most beloved poet, her idol!" Around this time, Grossman sent a warm letter to Pasternak, who was suffering from a number of ailments, to wish him good health and tranquility.[18] In May 1960, aged seventy, Pasternak died of lung cancer.

The *Zhivago* affair made it clear to Grossman what awaited his novel if he followed Pasternak's example. If published abroad *Life and Fate* would become a sensation; however, both sides would use it as a weapon in the Cold War. In his home country the book would be hopelessly compromised, presented as a bunch of lies, an anti-Soviet work. At public meetings across the country, people would be forced to denounce it even without reading it. This was not what Grossman wanted to achieve. He intended his novel for an audience at home, where it was most needed; he wanted political change to come from within.

Much later, when his daughter Katya asked Grossman why he did not send his novel abroad, which could be done clandestinely via foreign travelers, some of whom were his translators, he replied that it wasn't his way of doing things.[19] Of course, secrecy was against his nature. But Katya had a point: Grossman's prose was translated in a number of countries. His first novel about the war, *The People Immortal*, appeared in many languages in Eastern Europe and in Cuba; it was also published by Hutchinson in London in 1943. According to Grossman, some twenty editions of this novel appeared abroad. *Stalingrad Sketches* was translated into English, German, and French. His novels *Stepan Kolchugin* and *For the Right Cause* were published in countries of the Soviet Bloc as well as in England, France, and Denmark. In all, fifty foreign editions were produced during his life.[20] True, some of the translations were made in Moscow by the Foreign Languages Publishing House, which promoted the best of Soviet writings, but there were also translators living abroad.

Grossman had invested seven years in writing *Life and Fate*; it took sixteen years to produce both parts of the novel. He knew that publishing it at home was almost impossible, but after spending so many years with this book he did not feel that comparing Communism with Nazism was so explosive. In January 1959, upon receiving a clean copy from a typist (he wrote by hand), he experienced "what parents feel when they see their frightened children, raised at home, donning a school uniform for the first time. A strange feeling of pity and alienation: poor boy, what awaits him in life."[21] In October, while staying with Olga in a Crimean village near Koktebel, Grossman worked rigorously to revise *Life and Fate*. In the evenings he hiked in the mountains, walked along the seashore, played cards with Olga, and read. Among other books was a recently published volume of William Faulkner stories. Grossman valued Faulkner's prose, which he read in translation, and thought Faulkner "a powerful, talented writer." While in Crimea he also read *The Philosophy of Mahatma Gandhi* by Dhirendra Mohan Datta.[22]

His letter to Lipkin from the Crimea was filled with premonitions about his novel's future: "Will it have many readers, aside from the reader-writer? . . . These days [I feel how] the fate of this book is becoming separate from mine. It will realize itself without me, separately from me, when I may no longer be alive."[23] As is apparent from this letter, he felt that his novel might be banned from publication. Moreover, he realized he was ahead of his time in comparing Hitlerism and Stalinism. "I'm not experiencing joy, elation, excitement. I have some vague feeling of anxiety, of serious concern. Am I right [with the message]? That's the first and most important thing. Am I right before the people, and therefore—before God? And then comes the second, a writer's [concern], have I managed it well? And next—third—the book's fate, its road."[24] As Grossman has written in *Life and Fate*, "There is nothing more difficult than to be a stepson of the time. . . . Time loves . . . its own children, its own heroes, its own laborers."

Grossman read parts of this novel to friends, including Ekaterina Zabolotskaya and Gedda Surits. Lipkin, also among his first readers, recalls how Grossman read chapters aloud to him "in his quiet, slightly rasping voice." When reading Anna Shtrum's farewell letter to her son, Grossman was wiping away tears.[25] In winter 1960 Lipkin read the entire book for the first time. He felt at once that it was a "great . . . everlasting work."[26] But he also realized it would be impossible to publish it in the Soviet Union.

To Lipkin's surprise, Grossman decided to submit his novel to Vadim Kozhevnikov, the editor of *Znamya* and a Communist hard-liner. Lipkin felt it was dangerous to let Kozhevnikov read the book. In July Grossman asked his friend to reread the entire novel and mark the most precarious parts, those that should not be shown even to editors. In addition, Grossman sought Lipkin's opinion on whether there was any hope he could publish at least a revised, expurgated version. Lipkin reread it and told Grossman there was "no hope" and that handing over *Life and Fate* to *Znamya* was unsafe. "So, you think I'll be arrested after they read the novel?" asked Grossman. Lipkin thought Kozhevnikov could betray him.

Grossman chose *Znamya* rather than the liberal *Novy mir* not only because of his quarrel with Tvardovsky; he thought that as a liberal Tvardovsky was more vulnerable than the editor of *Znamya*, a known conservative. Grossman's story "Tiergarten," which subtly compared the two regimes, had recently been rejected by *Novy mir*. Tvardovsky was afraid to run it, but Kozhevnikov had accepted it in *Znamya*. When Glavlit censors refused to pass the story, Kozhevnikov defended it as long as possible. This inspired Grossman's hope that he would be unafraid to publish *Life and Fate*.[27] Of course, Kozhevnikov had edited *Pravda* during Stalin's anti-Semitic campaign. But in the early 1950s Tvardovsky also objected to the Jewish theme and demanded that Grossman purge Shtrum from the novel. There were no good options for Grossman.

In Lipkin's opinion, no Soviet editor, not even Tvardovsky of *Novy mir*, would publish *Life and Fate*. But it was safe to allow him to read it, as he was "a decent man." Grossman, although he valued Lipkin as a poet and had used his connections to help get his poetry published, responded with an outburst: "I'm not a coward, like you, I will not be writing for my desk drawer." Grossman's explosion "produced silence. Finally, Grossman, wheezing from asthma, asked, 'Did you mark the spots you propose to eliminate?' " Lipkin found some twenty episodes he thought could land Grossman in prison. He proposed removing the entire scene of SS officer Liss telling the imprisoned Bolshevik Mostovskoy that their two regimes were mirror images of each other.[28]

In 1960 Grossman succeeded in publishing a few extracts from *Life and Fate*. Lazar Lazarev (Lazar Shindel'), a literary critic and junior editor at the *Literary Gazette*, telephoned him and requested a piece for publication. Lazarev's call surprised the writer: editors rarely called him. The 1953 campaign against Grossman was not forgotten during the Thaw: he was still regarded as a politically untrustworthy writer. When in 1959 a Moscow publisher proposed issuing his collected works, Lipkin wrote to congratulate him. Grossman replied that his felicitations were premature. The publisher's proposal, which included the works of a number of authors, had yet to be officially approved, and "if they'll trim the plan, who will be thrown out if not me?"[29]

Lazarev was a fan: he had read and admired *Stepan Kolchugin* and *Stalingrad Sketches*. A decade Grossman's junior, he had participated in the war and spent the winter of 1942–43 at the Stalingrad front and in Kalmykia. While editors in his newspaper described Grossman as "a difficult man," Lazarev's impression was different. During their phone call Grossman invited him to his apartment in Begovaya village where they talked about Stalingrad over a bottle of wine. "I liked Grossman very much—he was kind, I felt at ease with him, and there was an aura of calm and wisdom about him."[30] Lazarev asked whether he was planning to complete *Stepan Kolchugin*, to which Grossman replied that it would be difficult for him to reenter the world of this novel after so many years. "Besides, Kolchugin's story ends in 1937 with prisons, labor camps, and executions. This is what my new novel is about." Grossman gave Lazarev three chapters of his new book to choose from. The first was about Sofya Levinton and David in the Polish death camp. The second dealt with an anti-Semitic incident in the Soviet Army during the war: fighter pilots discuss whether it's possible to be a good person and a Jew at the same time. (The *Literary Gazette* at once declined this chapter: the existence of anti-Semitism was officially denied.) The third was about a Ukrainian peasant woman, Khristya, and a Russian POW, Semyonov, so emaciated that the Nazis release him to die. This chapter was rejected because Khristya recalls the 1930s man-made famine in Ukraine.

The chapter about Sofya Levinton and David being marched to the gas chamber in a Polish death camp seemed like the safest option to junior editors. It was already in proofs when the editor in chief, Sergei Smirnov, killed it without giving a reason. Grossman was invited to meet the editor, and Lazarev witnessed the conversation. The editor claimed he had acted out of concern for Grossman. The latter retorted that if he, the author, was unafraid to publish the chapter, such talk about suppressing the work for Grossman's sake was hypocritical, and he pressed the editor to give the actual reason for his reluctance. The conversation went in circles: the editor never admitted the truth but simply asked Grossman to submit a different chapter. Eventually, the *Literary Gazette* published a chapter about the Soviet military headquarters in Stalingrad. In November–December 1960 three other extracts from *Life and Fate* appeared in the newspapers *Literature and Life*, the *Evening Moscow*, and *Soviet Soldier*. The last publication mangled Grossman's text beyond recognition. His letter of protest was ignored and remained unpublished.

The *Literary Gazette* also announced that *Life and Fate* would appear in *Znamya* in the new year. Later, many people expressed surprise with Grossman's choice of the conservative journal.[31] But Grossman had dealt with *Znamya* many times in the past; this magazine published "The Hell of Treblinka" and the play *If You Believe the Pythagoreans*.

Znamya received Grossman's manuscript in October 1960.[32] Also in October Grossman gave the novel to Tvardovsky simply to read.[33] That fall the two met during a family vacation in Koktebel, and their wives prevailed on them to make peace. In October Tvardovsky wrote in his diary that the novel gave him "the most powerful artistic impression . . . in many years" and compelled him to see "the most important things in life from a new perspective." Grossman's work "was so significant" that *Doctor Zhivago* seemed like "child's play" in comparison.[34] Publication of the novel could take contemporary Russian literature to a new level, restoring its lost importance.[35] But as Tvardovsky later told Grossman, he could publish only the war parts of *Life and Fate*.[36]

Grossman spent the fall of 1960 in great tension, anticipating the response from *Znamya*. Lipkin was able to learn the editor's opinion through a friend, fellow translator Nikolai Chukovsky, who was on *Znamya*'s editorial board. When Chukovsky asked the editor Kozhevnikov about the novel, the latter grumbled, "Grossman has let us down," and changed the subject.[37] Chukovsky said that the editor and his executives were hiding the manuscript from the staff. Arriving with this news at Grossman's apartment, Lipkin found himself in the middle of a party. Olga was entertaining her guests, the writers' wives Zinaida Pasternak and Berta Selvinkaya: they were sitting in Grossman's study, which served as the living room in the evenings, playing a variation of mahjong.[38] When Lipkin reported the news, Grossman's lips trembled; he asked him to repeat the account.[39] Grossman now realized it had been a mistake to submit his novel to *Znamya*.

13. An Unrepentant Heretic

I ask for my book's freedom.
—Vasily Grossman to Nikita Khrushchev

On December 16, 1960, days after Grossman turned fifty-five, *Znamya* sent a letter summoning him to an editorial meeting. Grossman telephoned the magazine's editor, Kozhevnikov, to suggest that they meet informally to discuss the novel. The editor declined, "absolutely and categorically," while claiming that he had not read the manuscript, even though he had received it over two months earlier. Grossman, realizing that the editor was lying and that the purpose of the meeting was to denounce him, refused to attend, explaining that he was having heart trouble. He promised, however, to read the transcript of the editorial meeting with "utmost attention."[1]

Kozhevnikov was acting on Party orders. Having read *Life and Fate* in the fall, he secretly sent Grossman's novel to the Central Committee. On December 9 he received a letter from Dmitry Polikarpov, head of the Central Committee's cultural section, describing Grossman's novel as a "dirty slander on Soviet society and the state." He directed *Znamya*'s editors to reject the manuscript and then conduct "an intense political conversation with Grossman." Polikarpov specified who should be present at the meeting: heads of the writers' union, the talentless literary functionaries Georgy Markov (active in the anti-Pasternak campaign), Sergei Sartakov, and Stepan Shchipachev (recipient of two Stalin Prizes). "It is important that writers themselves give Grossman to understand that any attempts to circulate his manuscript would be met with an irreconcilable attitude and utmost condemnation on the part of the literary community."[2] The Party was determined to prevent Grossman's novel from escaping abroad.

At the December 19 board meeting Kozhevnikov denounced *Life and Fate* as "a politically alien" book. Members of the board, none of whom had read the novel, and the heavyweights of the writers' organizations read quotations selected by the Central Committee's Department of Culture. According to the verbatim report, at the end of the meeting the editor phoned Grossman to say that the magazine had rejected his novel as "ideologically harmful." He demanded that Grossman keep copies of his manuscript out of circulation to make sure his novel did not "fall into enemy hands."[3] On December 28 Grossman was invited to *Znamya* where the editor, in the presence of senior staff, repeated his earlier political rhetoric. The magazine dissolved the contract but allowed Grossman to keep the advance he received in spring.[4]

The trio from the writers' union—Markov, Sartakov, and Shchipachev—later held a separate meeting with Grossman. They agreed that his novel "contained no defamatory material, that many things happened as he described." But they argued that "during the present difficult time [the Cold War] publication of the novel would be harmful to the state, and if it will be possible to ever publish it, then, perhaps, not for about 250 years."[5]

Earlier, preparing for the worst, Grossman had hidden a copy of his typescript, over one thousand pages, with Lipkin. Without telling his friend he also deposited the final draft of *Life and Fate* at the apartment of another friend, Lyolya Klestova. This woman, whom Grossman knew from his student years, had no connection to literary circles and lived in a communal apartment. She kept the novel until 1964, at which time Grossman's friend Loboda fetched it and hid it at his house outside Moscow.

In January 1961 Tvardovsky invited Grossman to *Novy mir*. They had a "long conversation." Tvardovsky undoubtedly knew by then that *Life and Fate* had met with strong disapprobation from the Party. He made it clear that he would not publish this novel or any further work Grossman might submit to *Novy mir*. As Grossman wrote to Lipkin, "It was a polite conversation but it left a difficult aftertaste."[6] (Tvardovsky was profoundly impressed with *Life and Fate*, having written in his notebook, on October 6, 1960, that the novel was among the few books that force the reader to change and "you feel day after day that something serious has taken place in you—your consciousness has evolved.")[7] Nonetheless, Tvardovsky distanced himself from the dissident novel and its author, a response he would later feel compelled to reconsider.

These developments were only a preamble to catastrophe. On February 14, at around noon, there was a ring at the door of Grossman's apartment. Olga and Fedya were out; the maid, Natalya Darenskaya, opened the door. "Some bad people have come," she told Irina, Grossman's daughter-in-law. Darenskaya, who had lived with the family for three decades and witnessed the 1937 arrest of Fedya's father, Boris Guber, told Irina: "These are the kind of people who had come for Boris Andreevich."[8] Three KGB officers in civilian clothes and two other men whom they had brought as witnesses walked into the apartment. One of the officers entered Grossman's study and showed his search warrant. Another knocked on Irina's door: "Are you related to Grossman? We are here to conduct a search, to arrest the novel. We are not asking you to sign the clause of silence, but we ask that you do not talk about this to anyone." The officers proceeded to Grossman's study, where they found him sitting by his desk, pale but composed. Irina was summoned to administer medicine: the officers thought Grossman had a heart condition. She stayed in the room, witnessing the arrest of the novel. The KGB officers removed folders from Grossman's desk—seven copies of the typescript and various drafts. The papers were put in sacks and carried to the car.

Lieutenant Colonel Prokopenko and two majors produced the report, which read, in part: "The following was confiscated during the search: Upon the agents' request to produce the manuscript and drafts for the novel 'Life and Fate' Grossman Iosif Solomonovich [his legal name] has voluntarily given the following copies. . . . 1. Manuscript of the novel 'Life and Fate,' part 1 on unattached sheets, in dark-blue folder, cardboard; 2. Manuscript of the novel 'Life and Fate,' part 2 on unattached sheets in dark-blue folder, cardboard; 3. Manuscript of the novel 'Life and Fate,' part 3 on unattached sheets in brown cardboard folder." A postscript to the protocol specified where the remaining copies of the typescript were located (the KGB was writing down Grossman's confession): "1. In editorial offices of *Znamya* journal—3 copies; 2. In editorial offices of *Novy mir*, 1 copy; 3. At my cousin Sherentsis Viktor Davydovich's place in Moscow, Nizhne-Syromyatinskaya, 5, Apt. 53, 1 copy; 4. In my study in Moscow, Lomonosovsky Avenue 15, Apt. 9, 2 copies and drafts." Grossman signed the report. The arrest of the novel took one hour and twenty minutes, from 11:40 a.m. until 1 p.m.[9]

As the KGB took Grossman away, Irina became "hysterical, shouting, 'Where are you taking him? What are you going to do?'" She described the scene: "It was winter. I helped Vasily Semyonovich put on his coat, a hat, and squeezed his wrist. I was in tears, and there were tears in his eyes, also." (In 1949, when she was fifteen, Irina witnessed the arrest of her father, a trained orientalist. Stanislav Novikov was sentenced to twenty-five years in the Gulag for "connections to foreigners." He was released as part of the clemency under Khrushchev and, beginning in 1957, Grossman frequently talked with Novikov about his imprisonment. The latter would say, "Never in my life have I met so many interesting people as in the camps!")[10]

The KGB agents drove with Grossman to the addresses he had given them. They also drove to his typists' offices, seizing even the carbon paper as a precaution. Upon returning home Grossman phoned Lipkin asking him to come at once. Lipkin recalls: "I realized something had happened. But it didn't occur to me that they had confiscated the novel. In my memory nothing like this happened before."[11] Manuscripts were usually seized from writers during their arrest. But there were exceptions. For example, in 1926 Bulgakov's novel *Heart of a Dog* and his diaries had been taken away during a search, but the writer had not been arrested and his papers had later been returned to him.

The Begovaya village was a small place, and writers were soon talking about the KGB's confiscation of the book. Tvardovsky came to see Grossman twice within a few days. He wrote in his diary that the arrest of a novel separately from its author "is, essentially, an arrest of a soul without a body. And what's a body without a soul? . . . I spoke with Grossman twice—he is depressed. This affair doesn't strike me as wise, not even to mention its coercive nature. . . . My copy, kept in the safe of N[ovy] m[ir] was seized also. Therefore, a share of that mistrust directed towards the author affects me, too. Oh, for pity's sake."[12]

Grossman discussed his options with Tvardovsky, who had contacts in the Central Committee. Tvardovsky advised meeting Polikarpov, the head of the Department of Culture, whom Grossman knew personally. Polikarpov had risen from a literary functionary in the bureaucracy of the writers' union to the top bureaucracy at the Central Committee. Grossman had talked to him on a beach by the Black Sea at a time when Polikarpov, temporarily out of favor with the Party, had been forced to vacation not at a rest home for Party officials but in one for writers. Polikarpov, however, was the very man who had instructed *Znamya* to punish Grossman; he also liaised with the KGB. Personal relations were now forgotten: Polikarpov spoke to Grossman severely. In the end he advised him to appeal to the Central Committee. In 1962 Grossman would petition Khrushchev.

The arrest of the novel sent shock waves through the writers' community and some were saying that all copies of the book had been seized, that the fruit of Grossman's labors was lost. Solzhenitsyn would write in *The Oak and the Calf* that he did not trust *Novy mir* to keep the manuscript of *The First Circle* in its safe: "I remember how Grossman's novel had been taken from that very safe at *Novy mir*."[13]

Grossman phoned Katya to tell her that the novel had been "arrested"; she thought he spoke in the same tone of voice he'd used on the day his father died. He also told her, "It would have been better if they killed me."[14] According to Fedya and Irina, after the novel's confiscation Grossman sank into depression. He felt remorseful that he had let down many people—from Tvardovsky to his cousin Sherentsis and the typists. And he thought incessantly about his novel's fate: his most important work, which told about the Holocaust and was dedicated to his mother's memory, was now in the hands of the KGB. During this time he could share his deepest sentiments with his mother alone: he felt closer to her than to anyone living. In September, on the anniversary of his mother's death, Grossman wrote her another letter.

> Dearest Mama,
>
> It is now twenty years since your death. I love you, I remember you every day of my life, and through all these twenty years this grief has been constantly with me. I wrote to you ten years ago. And ten years ago, when I wrote my first letter to you after your death, you were the same as when you were alive—my mother in my flesh and in my heart. I am you, my dearest. As long as I am alive, then you are alive too. And when I die, you will continue to live in this book, which I have dedicated to you and whose fate is similar to your own fate.[15]

Lipkin visited daily, taking Grossman out for walks. Around this time the writer Boris Yampolsky saw the two sitting on a bench in Alexandrovsky Garden near the Kremlin. Unaware of developments, Yampolsky asked Grossman whether he could give him a copy of *Life and Fate* to read. "Grossman replied curtly, 'Unfortunately I currently have no opportunity to do this.' Lipkin gave me a strange look. Only now did I notice that Grossman's head and hands shook."[16]

In the dreadful spring of 1961, when Grossman was unsure what to do with his life, Lipkin proposed that he take on a translation project. He had learned that the Armenian writer Hrachya Kochar was looking for a well-known Russian author and war participant to polish a word-for-word translation of his war novel *The Children of the Large House*. An abbreviated version of the novel had been translated and published in Moscow in the mid-1950s, but the author now wanted to produce the entire book, containing over fourteen hundred pages. The Russian author would be invited to Armenia and paid well. Grossman was hard up, as most people were after Khrushchev's monetary reform in early 1961, when the devaluation of the ruble caused savings to shrink to a tenth of their former value. And aside from money, Grossman badly needed a change of scene.

He liked the idea of traveling to Armenia and said that if Kochar's novel was not vile he would translate it. "I need money, and I have a heavy heart; perhaps daily toil would help."[17] Upon reading the literal translation and finding it morally acceptable he settled down to work. By fall Grossman had rewritten the draft, which he called "completely illiterate," and in early November he headed for Armenia to collaborate with the author on the final draft.[18]

From Armenia Grossman wrote Lipkin a few times a week: his friend's wife, Nina, recently diagnosed with cancer, was undergoing chemotherapy. Grossman's letters were filled with genuine concern and sympathy. These letters also became Grossman's travelogue in which he described Armenia's "biblical landscapes," thousand-year-old cathedrals, people, customs, and his backbreaking work as a translator.[19] His exuberant travel memoir *An Armenian Sketchbook* would emerge from these letters to Lipkin. Written as a first-person account, the memoir is unlike Grossman's other works: he takes center stage in it, confiding his impressions, thoughts, vulnerabilities, and even his physiological troubles, which he describes with irony. Humanity, love of life, desire for fellowship and goodness are recurrent themes. The original title of this memoir, "Dobro vam," employs the Armenian greeting, which literally translates as "Good to you." *An Armenian Sketchbook* captures the soul of the ancient country, built on rock.

As he writes in the memoir, "I first glimpsed Armenia from the train, early in the morning: greenish-gray rock—not mountains or crags, but scree, flat deposits of stone, fields of stone. A mountain had died, its skeleton had been scattered over the ground." Village houses were built of "large slabs of gray stone" with no greenery around—no grass, no flowers, no water in sight. "Sometimes a gray stone comes to life and begins to move. A sheep." Developing the theme, he writes that the sheep in Armenia eat the "powdered stone and drink the dust of stone." The gray color dominates the landscape: the peasants' wadded jackets and women's scarves are gray. Only Kurdish women wear red dresses and red head scarves, a "red mutiny against gray centuries amid gray stone."[20]

Upon arriving in Yerevan, the Armenian capital, Grossman stood alone on the platform: the author, Kochar, failed to meet him. Grossman felt rather humiliated by this: Kochar's forgetfulness seemed to emphasize his lack of importance in the eyes of the world. At the end of his writing career Grossman was making a fresh start—as a translator. From this moment on he would refer to himself as "translator Grossman" and an "elderly gentleman."[21]

It was a time when Stalin's portraits and statues still dominated the landscape. In Yerevan a gigantic bronze statue of Stalin stood on a hill. Sculpted by Sergei Merkulov, this was one of the biggest monuments to Stalin, so large that while it was being assembled workers could freely walk through Stalin's hollow legs. "If a cosmonaut from a far-off planet were to see this bronze giant towering over the capital of Armenia, he would under-stand at once that it is a monument to a great and terrible ruler." This statue conveyed two notions of power, religious and worldly, "so vast that it can belong only to God" and "a coarse, earthly power, the power of a soldier or government official."

Grossman arrived in Armenia during the Twenty-Second Party Congress, where Khrushchev's keynote speech called for continuing the process of destalinization. Soon afterward, Stalin's remains were removed from Lenin's Mausoleum and his statues taken down across the Soviet Union. The gigantic Stalin in Yerevan would also be removed, but it was still intact on November 7, an anniversary of the Bolshevik Revolution when Grossman watched the fireworks from the hill dominated by the statue. "With each salvo, long tongues of flame lit up the surrounding mountains and the titanic figure of Stalin would emerge from the darkness. . . . It was as if, for one last time, the Generalissimo were commanding his artillery. . . . Once again the command would be given and the terrible bronze god in a greatcoat would step out from the mountain darkness. No, no, it was impossible not to give this figure his due—this instigator of countless inhuman crimes was also the leader, the merciless builder of a great and terrible state."[22]

Grossman was appalled at the ease with which Armenians were now dismissing Stalin as *mama dʒoglu*, son of a bitch. They even refused to admit Stalin's role in creating the Soviet state and its industry; faced with this lack of objectivity, Grossman felt an urge "to stand up for Stalin." As he observes in the memoir, "hysterical worship of Stalin" and total "rejection of him sprang from the same soil." There was no attempt to understand what was wrong with the Stalinist state. In fact, the nature of the coercive state remained practically unchanged: there was no genuine public discussion of Stalin's crimes. The state issued a new directive—to dismantle Stalin's cult, rename the streets and cities, and take down his statues. Grossman felt these state measures would only produce the opposite effect, a desire to defend "one of the most terrible murderers in all human history." His words were prophetic; two years later, on November 7, 1963, there would be deadly riots in Sumbayit, Azerbaijan, when the authorities banned people from carrying Stalin's portraits. During the official demonstration marking the forty-sixth anniversary of the revolution crowds clashed with police, defending their right to carry Stalin pins and photographs.[23]

When Party officials in Armenia announced the plan to dismantle Stalin's colossal statue, local collective farmers grumbled. It was not the statue's loss they regretted, Grossman writes, but the money: the state had collected 100,000 rubles from them to erect the monument. If the state now wanted to take it down, it should give them their money back. Grossman heard a story about an old peasant who prudently proposed not to destroy but to bury the statue: "Who knows? If some new lot end up in power, the statue may come in handy." This was both practical and ironic. (The peasant was prescient. Stalin received partial "rehabilitation" under Brezhnev and in Putin's Russia the dictator is once again celebrated as a great leader.)

Grossman felt at home in Armenia, where anti-Semitism was absent. Armenians were genetically diverse, like Jews. He met Armenians who had black hair or blond, blue eyes or brown, hooked noses or small straight noses, "the thin lips of Jesuits and the thick protuberant lips of Africans." This diversity reflected thousands of years of Armenian history and the population's contact with different nations—numerous raids, invasions, enslavement, and liberation. The same genetic diversity was found among Jews, whose faces "look Asian, African, Spanish, German, Slav." Like Jews, the Armenians had experienced genocide, enduring "incalculable loss and suffering" in Turkey in 1915. They proved their resilience: "In spite of everything, life would go on."

Grossman had read Mandelstam's cycle of Armenian poems and likely read his travel memoir, published in 1933 in *Zvezda* journal. Nadezhda Mandelstam remembered that the poet referred to Armenia, connected to the Bible through Mount Ararat, as his "Sabbath Land."[24] In his travel account *Journey to Armenia* Mandelstam wrote, "There is nothing more pleasant and instructive than to immerse yourself in the society of people of an entirely different race, whom you respect, with whom you sympathize, of whom you are, though a stranger, proud."[25] Mandelstam perceived Armenians as the first Christians (they adopted Christianity as a state religion in about the year 300), pointing out that Christianity has a close relationship with Judaism.[26] In his poems Mandelstam calls Armenia a "younger sister of the land of Judea."[27] Grossman observed in his memoir: "I knew some sweet and touching details about Mandelstam's time in Armenia. . . . Mandelstam's poems are splendid. They are the very essence of poetry: the music of words." The Armenian journey had a similarly rejuvenating effect on Mandelstam's and Grossman's creativity.

To Grossman's disappointment the local literati did not remember that Mandelstam had visited Armenia. They also appeared unacquainted with Grossman's work—neither with his wartime articles in which he wrote about Armenians nor with his novels, though they had been translated into Armenian. He was likely correct in assuming that local writers avoided him because of his "recent troubles" with the authorities.

While in Yerevan Grossman could see from his window Mount Ararat, where Noah's Ark was supposed to have reached land. He wrote Lipkin: "What marvel, a biblical mountain. In the mornings it's pink, in the daytime it's snowy white, in the evenings it's pink again."[28] In his memoir he describes Ararat as "humanity's most important mountain—the mountain of faith." "Straight in front of me, shining in the sun, was the snowy peak of Greater Ararat. My feelings and thoughts became still more acute. . . . The Bible and the present day came together with astonishing ease, and I saw Mount Ararat through the eyes of people who lived on these mountain slopes before the birth of Christ. I saw the swift black waters of the great flood . . . the mountain was shining in its full glory. . . . From its stone foot to its white head it was lit by the morning sun. It belonged to today and to the life of past millennia. . . . Everything passes; nothing passes."[29]

At Lipkin's advice Grossman traveled to Echmiadzin, the central Armenian city that is the seat of the Catholicos, head of the Armenian Apostolic

Church. The Catholicos, Vazgen I, received Grossman in his residence: "We discussed literature and drank black coffee. A monk attended this, an astoundingly handsome young man. Vazgen I's favorite writer is Tolstoy, the one who was excommunicated by the Church. Vazgen is the author of a work about Dostoevsky; he told me that anthropology is impossible without Dostoevsky."[30] Back in Yerevan, Grossman toured the Institute of Ancient Manuscripts where he saw a rich collection of medieval manuscripts and books in a variety of languages, including Hebrew; "a millennium-old life of thought, word, color." Contemporary Yerevan also fascinated him; as he wrote Lipkin, "My Jewish heart delights at the bazaars—with heaps of fruit and vegetables."[31]

At the end of November Grossman and Kochar traveled to the writers' residence in the mountain village of Tsakhkadzor (translated as "the valley of flowers"), an hour's drive from Yerevan. Grossman soon made friends among the locals; he felt accepted even without speaking the language. *Barev dzez*, the greeting and wish of goodness, were the two words that helped establish understanding and trust. He watched a village woman make *lavash*, flattening the dough in the air, and her confident flowing movements "seemed like a beautiful ancient dance." He thought that "true brotherhood," the ties between different nations, is born not in offices, but "in peasant huts." Armenian bakers and craftsmen brought back his memories of Berdichev.

Grossman worked on the translation "from morning till night. . . . By evening, there are no thoughts, only fatigue."[32] At the height of his creative powers he was reduced to rewriting an illiterate word-for-word translation of a war novel. Kochar, his client, accepted the labors of "translator Grossman" with "sleepy indifference" and with no thanks. "I'm annoyed and saddened with my client's unresponsiveness; indeed, he could have thanked the worker."[33] Yet Grossman also felt the project was useful to him: "the rhythm, systematic nature" of this work had a calming and strengthening effect.[34] On December 2 he wrote Lipkin: "I'm happy to have respite— you know, I'm very tired. I sit at the desk so long that not only my head gets tired, but there are blotches in my face, and my back and shoulders hurt."

In late December Kochar took Grossman to a village wedding; of all his experiences of the journey, this made the deepest impression. The village on the slope of Mount Aragats was one of the poorest, and when the wedding coach drove down the stone street, amid stone hovels and stone walls, Grossman felt they were "still in the Stone Age." This impression was confirmed when he saw "basalt water barrels, basalt laundry tubs, basalt troughs for feeding the sheep." The Iron Age had not arrived here: ancient utensils, jugs and dishes, were also made of stone. He did see some steel: someone produced daggers, brought home as trophies from the war, engraved with the slogan, *"Alles für Deutschland"*—everything for Germany. As he wrote in the memoir, he felt at home among the Armenian peasants: "I could feel their immense labor, the poverty of their clothes and shoes, their wrinkles, their gray hair, the youthful mocking curiosity of the beautiful—and not so beautiful—young women, the mighty souls and wonderful straightforward-ness of the laborers. I sensed their honesty; I understood the hardship of their lives, how well disposed they were towards me. I was at home; I was among my own kind." Sitting among shepherds, craftsmen, and bakers, he thought that "these people are closely and durably linked by ties of kinship and commu-nity. These ties are eternal; their strength has been tested over millennia. Not even the wrath of Stalin would destroy them."

The wedding ritual, complex and "polyphonic," did not impress Grossman as much as "the smile of love" on the face of the bride when she looked at her younger brother. "My heart filled with joy, warmth, and sorrow." The sun was setting behind "the stone bones of the mountains," bathing them in red light, and "the biblical myth of Mount Ararat seemed entirely contemporary." The feast lasted into the night, with the guests sitting at tables in the open air under stars that had "shone above Mount Ararat before the Bible even existed." When toasts were made the guests did not address their words to the newlyweds but spoke "about good and evil, about honorable labor, about the bitter fate of the Armenian nation." A carpenter in an old soldier's shirt got up to speak. Grossman's host trans-lated: the carpenter spoke about the Jewish people and their tragic fate. He also spoke of Grossman's wartime articles with portrayals of Armenians: when reading them he thought that the author "was from a nation that had also suffered a great deal." At this point, everyone stood up and applauded, and then many of the guests spoke "about the Jews and the Armenians, about how blood and suffering had brought them together."

> Never in my life have I bowed to the ground; I have never pros-trated myself before anyone. Now, however, I bow to the ground before the Armenian peasants who, during the merriment of a village wedding, spoke publicly about the agony of the Jewish

nation under Hitler, about the death camps where Nazis murdered Jewish women and children. I bow to everyone who, silently, sadly, and solemnly, listened to these speeches. Their eyes and faces told me a great deal. I bow down in honor of their words about those who perished in clay ditches, earthen pits, and gas chambers, and on behalf of all those among the living in whose faces today's nationalists have contemptuously flung the words, "It's a pity Hitler didn't finish off the lot of you."[35]

Grossman began his Armenian memoir on December 29, 1961, the day after he finished his arduous translation project, on which he had worked diligently and as hard as a mule. As he wrote Lipkin, "Yesterday I finished this bone-breaking work—and today I've begun . . . recording my Armenian impressions. I'm like George Sand who finished a novel at 4 a.m. and, without going to bed, began another one. True, there's a difference—she was being published, but my actions are really hard to understand. Why should I hurry?"[36] He was habitually driving himself hard, realizing that his desire for work was "as irrational as the life instinct, and just as senseless and irrepressible."[37]

An Armenian Sketchbook is filled with love of life; yet this memoir was written by an ailing man. Grossman was unwell during the journey and sensed he was dying, although he was only fifty-six. He wrote Lipkin that the translating project was "an episode in my life, a life nearing the end."[38]

The local literati continued to avoid Grossman, leaving him alone in his hotel room on New Year's Eve. (Party officials likely advised writers to stay away from the dissident.) "I would have been glad to receive a phone call even from a dog."[39] Typically, Grossman made friends with ordinary people: his ability to connect with them, his curiosity about their lives never left him. *An Armenian Sketchbook* is filled with stories of people he met.

Thus, he interviewed "a sweet, asthmatic old man by the name of Sarkisyan" who had met Lenin before the revolution. This man first rose high in the Party, but during the purges was denounced as a Turkish spy, "beaten almost to death," and sent to a Siberian Gulag for nineteen years. While still in prison in Yerevan he shared his cell with eighty people—professors, old revolutionaries, famous doctors, sculptors, and artists. The guards were semi-literate and had a hard time counting this "human mass." So they invited an old shepherd who had "a phenomenal ability to count, almost instantaneously, flocks of several hundred, or even thousands, of sheep."

The shepherd would open the door to the overcrowded cell and estimate the number of prisoners at a quick glance. "This really was very funny—a shepherd counting a flock of professors, writers, doctors, and actors."[40]

His splendid Armenian memoir remained unpublished during his life. In 1962 Grossman gave it to his old acquaintance, Anna Berzer, who had interviewed him about *The Black Book*; she was now an editor at *Novy mir*. Tvardovsky accepted the manuscript, but censors demanded cutting the lines about Armenian peasants speaking of the Jewish nation and its tragic fate. Tvardovsky, of course, was prepared to sacrifice this passage, which he believed inessential. Both Berzer and Lipkin, who knew how important it was to get this memoir published, advised Grossman to accept this revision. But he refused to publish it without the passage that referred to the Holocaust and conveyed his belief about the need for love and unity among nations. Tvardovsky, who thought Grossman was being difficult, complained in his notebook: "Again a scandal over Grossman's piece about Armenia. The censors marked the ending (the Armenian and the Jewish peoples are juxtaposed to all the rest). That's a case when you need to go and petition on behalf of something you don't sympathise with. Grossman—a mad bull: kill it. That's as though his entire work was written for some [wedding] toasts between the chosen peoples."[41] Tvardovsky's words reflect a dislike of Armenians and the official Soviet anti-Semitic attitude, which qualified any mention of Jewish experience as nationalism. This is the opposite of Grossman's message in the memoir: "It is time we recognize that all men are brothers."[42]

Although Grossman's subject matter did not appeal to Tvardovsky, the latter met with a Party functionary to ask that the memoir be approved for publication. He did not try too hard, though. Tvardovsky was by then absorbed with his new author, Solzhenitsyn, and used his influence with Khrushchev to publish *One Day in the Life of Ivan Denisovich*. Curiously, Tvardovsky admired Solzhenitsyn for the very things he disliked in Grossman. "My god, what a writer. No kidding. The writer, who only cares to express what lies at the bottom of his mind and heart. No attempt to please, to ease the task of an editor or a critic."[43]

Ivan Denisovich took a year to come out in *Novy mir*; in November 1962 it appeared with Khrushchev's blessing. Grossman had read it earlier; his editor Berzer had given him the manuscript of the novella, which she had received from Solzhenitsyn's friends Lev Kopelev and his wife Raisa Orlova. The typescript was anonymous, and in place of a title, carried an inmate identification number, "Shch-854." Solzhenitsyn was then living in the city of Ryazan, southeast of Moscow, and had no connections in the literary world. Moreover, he was afraid to publish the novella. Kopelev, a distinguished linguist, had known Solzhenitsyn since 1947 when the two worked together in a *sharashka*, a special prison for scientists within the Gulag, near Moscow. A military translator during the war, Kopelev was arrested in 1945 for stating that it was wrong for Red Army soldiers to torture prisoners and pillage in Poland and Germany. Charged with "propaganda of bourgeois humanism and of pity for the enemy," he would spend ten years in the Gulag.[44] Kopelev would appear in Solzhenitsyn's *The First Circle* as Lev Rubin, the Jewish linguist who holds to his Communist beliefs even in prison.

In May 1961 Solzhenitsyn arrived in Moscow to show his novella to Kopelev and Raisa Orlova, a literary scholar. The couple circulated *Ivan Denisovich* among prominent writers and, assured of their support, worked out a strategy for publication. After the Twenty-Second Party Congress they persuaded Solzhenitsyn that it was time to submit the manuscript to *Novy mir*. Orlova delivered the novella to Berzer to pass on to Tvardovsky. The journal was then flooded with manuscripts written by former Gulag inmates, most of whom received refusals, which is why it was important that the novella land on the desk of the right editor.

Grossman was profoundly impressed with *Ivan Denisovich*. Upon reading the novella he phoned Lipkin asking him to come at once. Lipkin recalled: "It was a story printed single-spaced on onion skin. The story was anonymous. . . . I sat down to read—and could not tear myself away from these crinkled sheets. I read them with pain and delight. Grossman, time and again, came up to me, looked me in the eyes to share in my delight. That was 'One Day [in the Life] of Ivan Denisovich.' Grossman was saying, 'Do you realize that suddenly, over there, in the otherworld, in the realm of penal servitude, a writer is born. And not just a writer, but a mature, enormously talented one. Who can measure up to him here?' "[45]

Grossman expected that Solzhenitsyn might want to come and see him.[46] Had they met, he would have discovered that Solzhenitsyn's attitudes to freedom, democracy, science, Russian history, and "the Jewish question" were incompatible with his own. As Sakharov remarks in his memoir, "Solzhenitsyn's mistrust of the West, of progress in general, of science and democracy, inclines him to romanticize a patriarchal way of life . . . to expect too much from the Russian Orthodox Church. He regards the unspoiled northern region of our country as a reservoir for the Russian people where they can cleanse themselves of the moral and physical ravages caused by Communism, a diabolic force, imported from the West."[47]

In 2001–2 Solzhenitsyn produced a controversial two-volume study of Russian-Jewish relations, *Two Hundred Years Together*. A staunch defender of Russian Orthodoxy, he could not avoid bias when examining the sensitive topic of Jewish influence on Russian history. His lengthy 2003 article about Grossman's novels *For the Right Cause* and *Life and Fate* seems like an ironic follow-up to this study. In it Solzhenitsyn patronizingly explains what Grossman should have written about the war and the Holocaust. He even seems to know better than Grossman how Shtrum and his mother felt about their Jewishness before the war.[48]

Among his contemporary writers Grossman singled out Yevtushenko— mostly for civil courage. In 1961, upon reading his poem "Babi Yar," Grossman remarked, "Finally, a Russian man wrote there is anti-Semitism in our country. His poetry is so-so, but what matters is action—beautiful, even brave." According to Lipkin, Grossman "was distressed and insulted that writers who were ethnically Russian were not wounded by the horror" of the Holocaust.[49]

The Twenty-Second Party Congress in late 1961 demonstrated a significant change in government policy. Khrushchev's speech revived Grossman's hope for the democratization of Soviet society. Aside from various unrealistic claims, for example, that Communism in the USSR would be built in twenty years, Khrushchev spoke forcefully about serious violations of "Soviet democracy and revolutionary legality" and the need to tell the truth about the abuse of power under Stalin.[50] Tvardovsky, in one of the most promising speeches at the congress, called on writers to reveal the truth about the past, to write "the whole truth."[51]

Khrushchev's speech gave Grossman new hope. He believed that facing the truth about the Stalinist past was essential for moving forward and building a democratic society. When composing his appeal to Khrushchev, Grossman felt he had a chance to persuade him, if not to publish *Life and Fate*, then at least to return the work seized from him.[52] On February 26, 1962, in a letter to Khrushchev, Grossman wrote forcefully about the need to observe democratic freedoms and individual rights. His letter expressed his deepest held beliefs.

Dear Nikita Sergeevich!

In October 1960, I submitted the manuscript of my novel *Life and Fate* to the journal *Znamya*. Around the same time, A. T. Tvardovsky, the editor of the journal *Novy mir*, became acquainted with it as well.

In mid-February 1961, KGB operatives . . . seized from my home copies and drafts of *Life and Fate*. Copies of my manuscript were also confiscated from the editorial offices of the journals *Znamya* and *Novy mir*.

Thus ended my submission to the journals, which frequently published my writings in the past. . . .

After the manuscript's confiscation I appealed to Comrade Polikarpov at the Central Committee. D. A. Polikarpov severely disapproved of my work and suggested that I think things over, admit the fallacy and harmfulness of my book, and write a letter to the Central Committee.

One year has passed. I have thought long and incessantly about the catastrophe in my life as a writer, and about the tragic fate of my book.

I want to candidly share my thoughts with you. First of all, I have to say this: I did not come to the conclusion that my book contains untruth. I wrote in this book what I considered and continue to consider as truth, I described only those things that I have thought, felt, and suffered through.

My book is not a political book. I spoke in it, as best I could, about people, their grief, joy, prejudices, death; I wrote about love and about compassion.

My book contains bitter, difficult pages; it addresses our recent past, the events of the war. Perhaps, it's not easy to read these pages. But believe me that writing them wasn't easy, also. But I had to write them.

I began writing this book . . . when Stalin was still alive. Back then, it seemed there was not even a shadow of hope of publishing it. . . .

When submitting my manuscript [to *Znamya*], I expected there would be disagreements between the writer and the editor, that the editor would request cutting some pages, perhaps chapters.

The editor of the journal *Znamya*, Kozhevnikov, as well as the heads of the Writers' Union, Markov, Sartakov, Shchipachev, told me . . . that the book is harmful and cannot be published. But at the same time they did not accuse the book of being untruthful. One of the comrades said, "All this did happen or could have happened, and people similar to the ones that are depicted have lived or could have lived." The other said, "However, the book can be published only in 250 years."

Your report at the XXII Party Congress has shed new light on everything difficult and erroneous that took place in our country during Stalin's leadership; it made me realize even more that the book *Life and Fate* does not contradict the truth you have expressed, that this truth has become available today, and is not being postponed for 250 years.

It is even more terrible for me [to recognize] that my book was taken away from me by force. This book is just as dear to me as honest children are dear to their father. Taking away the book from me is like taking away a child from his father.

It's been a year since the book was seized from me. It's been a year since I started thinking incessantly about its tragic fate, searching for an explanation for what has happened.

Perhaps the explanation is in the fact that my book is subjective?

But all literary works, unless they are written by a hack, bear a personal, subjective mark. A book written by a writer does not directly illustrate the views of political and revolutionary leaders. Touching on these views, merging with them at times, contradicting them in some ways, a book always and inevitably expresses a writer's inner world, his feelings, images that are dear to him, so it cannot be anything but subjective. That's how it's always been. Literature is not an echo; it speaks about life and life's drama in its own way. . . .

I know that my book is imperfect, that it cannot compare in any way to the works of great writers of the past. But weakness of my talent is not the point. The point is in the right to write the truth that one has learned through long years of life and suffering.

So why is my book, which in some way may correspond to the spiritual needs of the Soviet people, a book which contains neither falsehoods nor slanders, but contains truth, pain, and love of people, banned; why is it taken away from me by means of administrative violence, hidden away from me and from the people, like a criminal or a murderer?

After a year I don't know whether my book is intact; has it been destroyed or burned?

If my book is a lie, then let people who want to read it learn this. If my book is slanderous, let that be announced. Let Soviet people, Soviet readers, for whom I've been writing for thirty years, judge what's true and what's false in my book.

But the reader is deprived of an opportunity to judge me and my book in the harshest trial of all—I mean the trial of heart, of conscience. I yearned and I yearn for this trial.

Also, when my book was rejected by the journal *Znamya*, it was recommended to me that I respond to the readers' requests by telling them that I hadn't yet completed my work on the manuscript and that this work would take a long time. In other words, I was asked to tell lies.

Furthermore, when my manuscript was confiscated, I was asked to sign a clause of silence, making me criminally responsible if I disclosed the fact of its confiscation.

The methods of concealing everything that happened with my book are not the methods of struggling with lies, slander. That's not how one struggles with lies. That's how one struggles against the truth.

So, what is happening? How's it possible to understand this in the light of the ideas of the XXII Party Congress? Dear Nikita Sergeevich! These days it's often being written and said that we are returning to Lenin's democratic standards. . . .

At the XXII Party Congress you unreservedly condemned the bloody lawlessness and brutal acts carried out by Stalin. The strength and courage of your speech give reasons to think that the norms of our democracy will grow just as production norms of steel, coal, and electricity grew after the days of economic collapse accompanying the Civil War. After all, the essence of a new society is even more [manifest] in the growth of democracy and freedom than in industrial development and economic consumption. I believe a new society is unthinkable without continuous growth of freedom and of democracy.

So, how can one understand that in this day and age a writer's home is searched, his book is seized from him . . . and the writer is threatened with imprisonment if he begins to speak about his grief. . . .

I ask you to give freedom to my book, I ask that my editors and not the KGB operatives discuss and debate my manuscript with me.

There is no logic, no truth in the present condition, in my physical freedom when the book, to which I have given my life, is in prison, for I wrote it, I have not renounced it, and I do not renounce it. . . . I ask for my book's freedom.

With deep respect,

V. Grossman.[53]

Grossman spent five months anticipating a response: in the daytime he stayed in his apartment so as not to miss a phone call from Khrushchev's office. In July, just as he gave up and went out for a walk, someone from the Central Committee phoned. Irina took the message: Grossman was to meet Mikhail Suslov on July 23.

Stalin's appointee to the Department of Agitation and Propaganda, Suslov was regarded as the chief Soviet ideologist. Grossman knew him from the days when he "supervised" the JAC's work on *The Black Book* and banned the project. Suslov spearheaded attacks on the Jewish Anti-Fascist Committee, accusing it of anti-Soviet actions and espionage.[54] Later, he did nothing to help publish *For the Right Cause*. Suslov went down in history for such deeds as supervising the deportation of ethnic minorities from the Caucasus during World War II and, after the war, deciding to deport Lithuanian dissidents to Siberia.

Grossman might have felt he had a chance of getting a sympathetic response from Khrushchev, but there was little hope that he would succeed in winning over Suslov. Khrushchev realized, as he would state in his memoirs, that "when dealing with creative minds, administrative measures are always most destructive and nonprogressive."[55] But Grossman's letter was passed down to Suslov, a Communist hard-liner who ran the Soviet ideological machine under both Stalin and Khrushchev and would continue to do so under Brezhnev.

Preparing for the meeting with the "gray cardinal," Grossman jotted down his thoughts. "I wrote things I felt and thought. . . . I wrote the truth." He would list what was seized from him—all materials related to the novel, even the published extracts. "I can't believe that forcible confiscation of the manuscript should be the only response to what I wrote in my book." He would seek to learn "the fate" of his manuscript: had it been "preserved, destroyed?" He would ask Suslov to convey his request to Khrushchev to read his book. He would also inquire about his own fate as a writer. "I want to say that I will not be intimidated by violence." Would he now be stopped from publishing altogether? He would talk about the campaign against his novel *For the Right Cause*, which had been denounced by many in 1952. He would mention the anti-Pasternak campaign as an example of excessive pressure. Yet, the authorities must have thought they were too lenient with Pasternak and should make up for this with Grossman. "They decided to crush me." He would end by repeating his request that Suslov convey to Khrushchev his plea to read his book.[56]

Grossman's meeting with the gray cardinal lasted three hours. When he returned home he recorded Suslov's main points from memory. He did not record his own words because, as he states in this document, "Grossman in his remarks mostly reiterated his letter to Khrushchev."

> Suslov: . . . Your novel cannot be published. . . . Your novel is a political book. You are wrong when you write that it's only an artistic work.
>
> Your novel is hostile not only to the Soviet people and the state, but also to everyone who struggles for Communism beyond Soviet borders, to all progressive laborers in the capitalist world, to everyone who struggles for peace.
>
> Your novel will serve only to benefit our enemies.
>
> You know as well as we do . . . about a great and intense struggle between our two systems. . . . We are restoring Leninist norms of democracy. But Leninist norms of democracy are not the bourgeois norms of democracy. . . . You think we have violated the principle of freedom in your case. Yes, that is so, if one interprets freedom in the bourgeois sense. But we have a different interpretation of freedom. We do not understand freedom the way they understand it in the capitalist world, as the right to do whatever you want without considering society's interests. Only imperialists and millionaires need such freedom.

Our Soviet writer must produce only what's necessary to the people and useful to society.

I did not read your book. But I read attentively numerous reviews and responses, which contain plenty of quotations from your novel. You can see here how many notes I made from these reviews.

Everyone who read your book is unanimous in evaluating it. Everyone who read it believes it is politically hostile to us. . . . Reviewers could be wrong in the artistic evaluation of the book, but they were unanimous in their political evaluation of it, and I have no doubt that their political assessment is accurate.

It is impossible to publish your book, and it will not be published.

No, it hasn't been destroyed. Let it rest. We will not change its fate. One shouldn't underestimate the harm from the potential publication of the book.

Why should we add your book to the nuclear bombs that our enemies are getting ready for us? Its publication will only help our enemies. . . .

Your book contains direct parallels between us and Hitlerism. Your book describes our people, Communists, incorrectly, falsely. How could we possibly win the war with the kind of people you describe? Your book speaks positively about religion, God, Catholicism. Your book defends Trotsky. Your book is filled with doubts about the legitimacy of our Soviet system.

You know what great harm Pasternak's book has inflicted upon us. For everyone who read your book, who is familiar with reviews of it, there's no doubt that the harm from *Life and Fate* would be incomparably greater than from Pasternak's book. Your book is incomparably more dangerous to us than *Doctor Zhivago*.

So why should we, after the forty years of triumphant existence of the Soviet regime, after the defeat of German Fascism . . . having one-third of humankind under our banners, why should we publish your book and launch a public discussion with you on whether people need Soviet power?

We have revealed the mistakes that accompanied Stalin's personality cult, but we will never criticize Stalin for fighting the enemies of the Party and the state. We criticize him for fighting our own people.

It is impossible to make any parallels between the fate of this novel and that of the book *For the Right Cause*. These books cannot be compared. A long time ago, Fadeev came to me asking me to read *For the Right Cause*. I read the book and found nothing politically offensive in it. But your novel *Life and Fate* is politically hostile to us. . . .

The Party and the people will never forgive us if we publish your book. . . .

We all read and discussed your letter, and you can see it here in front of me.

I highly value [*Stepan*] *Kolchugin*, *The People Immortal*, *For the Right Cause*—I haven't read your other books. I urge you to return to your former outlook, which you held at the time when you wrote these books. . . .

I recently read your story "The Road." This is not what is expected from you. I did not like the story. What is expected from you are the books similar to *The People Immortal*. . . .

I believe that you will renounce your current views and will continue writing from the positions that you held when writing your earlier books.

I will go on a vacation and will possibly read *Life and Fate*.[57]

The rhetoric of a Soviet apparatchik who divided people between "us" and "them" offered nothing new to Grossman. Suslov's remarks reflected the mindset of a high Party functionary, Stalin's appointee, which is why he wanted to document them. The journalist in Grossman continued to chronicle events. Undoubtedly he later reread these notes to reflect on them: the pages have cigarette burn holes.

During the meeting Suslov referred to internal reviews of *Life and Fate* and read "reprehensible" passages from the novel they quoted. These reviews, fifteen to twenty pages each, were written by Party apparatchiks. Years later, Lipkin learned that one of the reviewers was Igor Chernoutsan, a consultant in the Department of Culture of the Central Committee. This professional censor with a reputation as a liberal boasted it was his idea that instead of arresting the author, they seize the book.[58]

Grossman's story "The Road," which Suslov so disliked, was published in *Novy mir* in 1962. A moving story about a mule named Giu who pulls his load through the roads of Italy, Abyssinia, and Russia during World War II,

"The Road" is about loss of freedom, universal indifference to one's sufferings, and the need for compassion. One of Grossman's best animal stories, it
can be compared with Tolstoy's "Strider: The Story of a Horse" and Chekhov's "Heartache." In Chekhov's story, a coachman whose son has died and
who finds no human being with whom to share his grief confides it to his horse.

Grossman's story has the heart-rending quality of Chekhov's prose.
But his tale about the mule is also an allegory of his life as a writer. "The
Road" reflects Grossman's mood at the time, his nervous exhaustion and the
hopelessness he felt after his masterpiece, the labor of many years, was seized
by the KGB. "Giu stood there, hanging his head, as indifferent as before to
the question of whether to be or not to be, calmly indifferent to the world,
this flat world of the plains, that was indifferently, unconcernedly destroying
him."[59] The word *indifference*, often repeated in the story, describes a feature
of post-Stalinist society that was intolerable to Grossman.

There is a glimmer of hope at the end of his story: the mule is revived
by "the good kind warmth" of a mare on a collective farm who has "soft,
gently moving lips." Giu comes back to life, feeling that "the terrible labor,
the labor beyond labor that seemed to have destroyed him with its indifferent
weight . . . in the end, evidently had not quite destroyed him." The mule and
the mare, both crying, tell each other "of their life and fate."[60]

After the arrest of *Life and Fate* magazines were afraid to consider
publishing even Grossman's innocuous work. Each publication was now an
event. Berzer recalls that Grossman was as happy "as a child" when he saw
his story "The Road" in proofs. He told Berzer that a promise of publication
made him feel what Robinson Crusoe might have felt upon stepping on an
asphalt road.[61] "The Road" was published relatively swiftly, without much
hindrance from authorities. In 1963 *Novy mir* published another Grossman
story, "A Few Sad Days." It made a reference to Stalin's purges in which two
members of an extended family perish, leaving a young orphan, a disabled
boy. Adopted by a relative, the boy is treated with remarkable kindness, an
attitude that has become almost extinct in Soviet society. Censors thought
the story was pessimistic and halted its publication, but Tvardovsky
prevailed, and the story appeared in the December issue.

While in Armenia Grossman was constantly unwell, but despite back
pain and fatigue, he drove himself hard. Upon returning to Moscow in spring

1962, he noticed blood in his urine, but ignored his physician's advice to see a specialist. Later, when he was diagnosed with kidney cancer, an oncologist told Lipkin that had Grossman come sooner, his life could have been prolonged by a few years. As was customary in those days, the cancer diagnosis was not revealed to Grossman; however, he sensed that he was dying. He aged quickly: his asthma returned, his hair was turning gray, and his walk became a shuffle.[62]

His personal life was as tangled as ever. He lived with Olga, whom he no longer loved, while yearning to see Zabolotskaya. In January 1962, planning his return from Armenia, Grossman wrote Olga that he wanted to stop in Sochi to visit Zabolotskaya, who was staying there with her family. Olga was furious. "I received a very depressing letter from O.M.," reported Grossman to Lipkin. "Oh, this bitter misunderstanding."[63] Earlier, his daughter Katya, now thirty-one and married, sent a letter of congratulations on his fifty-sixth birthday that he found cold. Katya's letter was "written with such indifference. But it's still better than her silence during [the previous] five months."[64] His telephone was silent also. During his last years Grossman was thoroughly isolated and deprived of opportunity to publish his work. His health was waning. All that remained was his struggle "for the right cause." His last novel, *Everything Flows*, would become his political testament.

14. *Everything Flows*

How splendid freedom must be if a mere likeness of it,
a reminder of it, is enough to fill a man with happiness.
—Vasily Grossman, *Everything Flows*

During his last years Grossman said it didn't matter to him where he lived: he could even live at a railway station. But the family at the Begovaya village had grown; Fedya and his wife, Irina, had settled in his former study with their baby daughter, Lena. Grossman worked in the living room, which served as the guest room in the evenings. In 1962, upon returning from Armenia, he moved into a small flat in the writers' cooperative recently built in the northern part of Moscow.

In Soviet days writing was a hugely profitable business. In 1934 the newly created Union of Soviet Writers had fifteen hundred members. By 1959 its numbers swelled to almost five thousand. In 1989, near the end of Soviet era, there were almost ten thousand members of the prestigious writers' union of the USSR. To join one had to go through a rigorous process to qualify.[1] Soviet writers were in effect government propagandists, and the state rewarded them generously. As Grossman observes in *Everything Flows*, such writers were "most adept at passing off lies as truth."[2]

Back in October 1958 Grossman had read *The Brothers Yershov*, a novel about several generations of Soviet workers employed at a metallurgical plant. Filled with cardboard characters and improbable situations, it was written by the classic socialist realist and literary functionary Vsevolod Kochetov. In a letter to Lipkin, Grossman called this novel a "shameful, petty creation, structured on a template so alluring that it could arise in a head of a rooster, a pike-perch or a frog. The circulation is 500,000 copies. The only consolation—it's inept."[3] Kochetov had risen under Stalin and continued to prosper during the Thaw—Khrushchev even awarded him the Order of Lenin—and under Brezhnev, a granite monument in his memory would be erected in his native city of Novgorod. Because a great majority of Soviet writers were essentially state employees, their production was government subsidized. The Literary Fund, a rich and influential organization, provided members of the writers' union with essential services, and in the Aeroport district, where Grossman received a one-bedroom apartment, there was a separate polyclinic for writers and their families, special stores where they bought food, a tailor shop, and other quality services.

Grossman's new flat, which he used as an office, was on the sixth floor of the nine-story apartment house on Krasnoarmeiskaya Street 23. When moving in he kept saying, "How good! Nobody knows me here."[4] He knew only a handful of writers in this new neighborhood: his friend Lipkin lived nearby. The writer Marietta Shaginyan was one of the neighbors he did not want to meet. Best known for her biographies of Lenin, she had attacked Grossman's novel *For the Right Cause*. In March 1953 *Izvestia* published her long and abusive piece entitled "Roots of Mistakes."

Vyacheslav Loboda, who had recently returned from Chukotka with his family, helped Grossman move his library to the new flat. Continually harassed by the authorities as a brother of a "Trotskyist," Loboda found no peace even at the end of the earth. When in 1952 a former colleague denounced him to settle personal scores, another political case against him was in the making. Loboda and his wife Vera lost their jobs as school principals and were threatened with eviction from their home. The couple's younger daughter was then two years old. At this desperate time, in January 1953, Grossman helped arrange for the publication of an article in *Pravda*. Written by his journalist friend Ivan Ryabov, the piece described Loboda as a selfless ethnographer and educator and mocked his denouncer. Soon afterward Loboda and Vera were reinstated at work. Upon returning from Chukotka in 1961, they bought a house in the town of Maloyaroslavets, near Moscow, where Grossman visited them and where the manuscript of *Life and Fate* would be preserved.

Masha Loboda, the couple's younger daughter, became a model for the heroine of Grossman's 1963 story "In a Large Garden Ring." Masha was in hospital where she had undergone an appendectomy; full of impressions, she told her family about the old village women who shared her ward. When

Loboda related his daughter's stories to Grossman, he was unsatisfied with the retelling and asked that Masha be brought to his new flat. The eleven-year-old was surprised that Uncle Vasya, as she called him, treated her as a grown-up. Masha felt uncomfortable meeting Grossman's "serious, penetrating gaze" when he asked questions.[5] Grossman's curiosity in people was abounding: he wanted to produce a narrative employing a young girl's perspective. Typically, he was afraid to miss an interesting story. When he lived in Begovaya village Grossman would join in the conversation when Fedya and Irina's university friends visited.

After the confiscation of *Life and Fate* Grossman was placed under permanent KGB surveillance—an open secret to his friends and neighbors. His new flat was bugged. Before Grossman moved in, the KGB installed listening equipment in the apartment directly above. A construction engineer told this in confidence to an acquaintance in the house management. From there the news traveled to the writers' community and someone reported it to Grossman. When friends visited, Grossman would point to the light fixture on the ceiling and press an index finger to his lips. The writer Yampolsky recalled coming to see Grossman in his new flat. Without acknowledging his greeting, Grossman led him to his study, where he wrote on a sheet of paper: "Borya, remember that walls may have ears."[6] Grossman's friend Taratuta and Masha Loboda also report that he avoided speaking in this apartment, indicating with gestures that it was bugged.

Yampolsky, in his oft-quoted memoir of Grossman's last years, paints a picture of an impoverished, dejected, lonely, dying writer. Describing Grossman's study, he mentions a shabby sofa, a broken typewriter, a scratched writing desk, books with worn covers, a discolored old carpet, and a withered perishing palm in a corner. Yampolsky oddly adds to the list one feature that certainly was not there: the moth-eaten head of an elk hanging on the wall.[7] Both Masha Loboda and Grossman's family remember distinctly that there was no elk head in Grossman's flat. However, Grossman describes one in his story "The Elk" about a lonely, dying man, and this story so influenced Yampolsky that he remembered it as real. In 1962, after it appeared in *Moskva* literary journal, a reader sent Grossman her embroidery of an elk head. He kept it in his flat.

There were some things Grossman treasured and kept in his study over the years, such as a child's alphabet block from Treblinka and a miner's safety lamp, a present from the Donbass coal miners at Smolyanka–11. An elegant black inkwell set, covered with engravings, was a centerpiece on his desk. Grossman wrote with a fountain pen but also kept a typewriter, "Erica," which he used rarely. He kept an eagle's foot on a stand (he had acquired it before the war) and a porcupine needle he had picked up in a zoo where he would often go with family or friends. A small sculpture of a freezing man was a present from Olga's brother Nikolai Sochevets, whom Grossman depicts as Ivan in *Everything Flows*. Like Ivan in the novel, Nikolai had "a talent for sculpture" and made lifelike figures out of clay. (After seventeen years of exile Grossman's brother-in-law returned practically blind. His sculptures are still kept by Masha Loboda and Katya Korotkova-Grossman, among others, in Moscow.) Another keepsake in Grossman's study was a German barometer with an amusing drawing of a donkey and a tail attached to it. Grossman brought this barometer back from the war along with a German harmonica of the kind soldiers had at the front.[8]

When he was still working in Begovaya village Olga attempted to put on his desk a golden clock she had inherited from her sister Yevgeniya. Grossman told her, "Lyusya, as long as I live I will not own any gold things." Perhaps it was his modesty and democratic ways that inspired their maid Darenskaya's remark, "Vasily Semyonovich, although you are Jewish, you'll be in paradise." Grossman smiled at her and asked, "And what about Olga Mikhailovna?" The maid did not reply.[9]

In the new flat Grossman wrote a number of short stories, such as "The Elk," "In a Large Garden Ring," and "The Road," completed "Phosphorus," and worked on his Armenian memoir. He also worked to complete his final novel, *Everything Flows*, which he began in 1955 simultaneously with the essay "The Sistine Madonna."

Everything Flows is partly based on the story of Grossman's brother-in-law. In 1930, aged twenty-three, Nikolai Sochevets was deported with his elderly parents and sisters from Sochi by the Black Sea to a no-man's-land beyond the Urals. This was during Stalin's campaign against the kulaks: the family was dispossessed, accused of "slandering" the Soviet state, and branded as "kulaks"—all because they owned a small estate. The family (with the exception of the three eldest sisters, who lived separately) was transported in winter in an unheated cattle car. It was largely from Nikolai's words that Grossman describes deportations of kulak families in *Everything Flows*: "The journey lasted more than a month—peasants were being taken from all over Russia and the railway lines were jammed with transport trains. There were no bed-boards in the cattle wagons. Everyone just slept on the floor, packed together. The sick, of course, died before they reached their destination."[10] Upon arrival, the deportees were marched to a forest where they built makeshift houses. There was no employment, medical help, or adequate housing for the deportees, many of whom died from starvation and disease. Trained as an economist, Nikolai was able to find work as an accountant; he struggled to support the family on his tiny income. In 1947, the lone survivor of his deported family, he returned to Moscow; after that Grossman saw him every Sunday when he came for dinner. Nikolai was a talented man whose life had been shattered when he was still a student, before he had a chance to develop his many gifts as a sculptor, poet, economist, and historian. Nikolai's fascination with history and the Near East is reflected in the novel through Ivan's interest in Parthian manuscripts and monuments.

Nikolai's experiences helped Grossman create a collective portrait of their generation in *Everything Flows*. Ivan, considered "the most talented and intelligent" among his fellow students, is arrested following a political denunciation and spends much of his life in the Gulag. Through this story Grossman tells about the lives of young, able, and idealistic men and women whose lives and talents were senselessly destroyed by the Stalinist state, those "who had never had the chance to write their books and paint their paintings."

In this final novel Grossman also makes his strongest defense of human rights and liberty. Living under KGB surveillance, he felt the absence of freedom in the Soviet Union more acutely than before. His protagonist, Ivan, speaks out against dictatorship in a philosophy discussion group in the 1920s. "He had declared that freedom is as important and good as life itself." When a fellow student denounces him to the authorities, Ivan is expelled from university and exiled for three years to Kazakhstan. But it doesn't end there: during the following three decades Ivan did not spend "more than a year as a free man." In 1936, at the height of the purges, he is sentenced to nineteen years in the Gulag—such is his punishment for defending freedom in the Soviet state.

During his time in prisons and camps Ivan witnesses "a lot of deaths of talented people. . . . Young physicists and historians, specialists in ancient languages, philosophers, musicians, young Russian Swifts and Erasmuses— how many of them he had seen put on their 'wooden jackets' [coffins]." The cream of Soviet society was found in the camps—here one could meet the country's best scientists, politicians, military officers, engineers, Old Bolsheviks, and representatives of Russian prerevolutionary political parties. These people were arrested only because they belonged to a particular social stratum that the Party believed to be undesirable or potentially hostile. "There were Social Democrats and Social Revolutionaries in the camps. Most of them had been arrested after they had ceased their political activities and became ordinary, loyal Soviet citizens. They had been arrested not for opposing the Soviet state but because it was thought possible that they might oppose it." Similarly, peasants were sent to the camps because it was thought that they "*might*, under certain conditions, have opposed the collective farms."

Varlam Shalamov, whose story Grossman may have known, was a young Moscow writer and law student when he was first arrested. He belonged to a small minority of young people incarcerated for actual anti-Soviet activities. In 1927, on the tenth anniversary of the Bolshevik Revolution, Shalamov participated in a demonstration of Trotskyist opposition. He was also involved with an underground printing shop that produced leaflets entitled "Lenin's Testament."[11] Two years later, apprehended during a raid on this printing shop, Shalamov was sentenced to three years in a labor camp. Rearrested in 1937 he spent more than a decade as a prisoner in Kolyma working in horrendous conditions in gold and coal mines. What saved his life was getting employment there as a medical assistant. In 1953, returning to Moscow from the camps, Shalamov met Pasternak, with whom he had exchanged letters while still living in exile in the Far East. Pasternak recognized his poetic talent and navigated him through Moscow's literary circles. Shalamov's heavily edited poems about his time in Kolyma were first published in *Znamya* in 1957. Beginning in 1962 the future author of *Kolyma Tales* worked as an internal reviewer for *Novy mir,* where Grossman's prose was being published. Although the two are not known to have met, this is not the point. Grossman's novel captures the fate of Shalamov, a talented man whose life was broken when he attempted to resist the dictatorship.

The subject of *Everything Flows* is post-Stalinist Russia as seen through the eyes of "the man from the camps." The reader first meets Ivan on the train: he is returning from the Far East to Moscow, where only his cousin's family still remembers him. His fellow travelers on the train—an inspector of trade unions, an economist from the State Planning Committee, and a Siberian construction superintendent—are faces of post-Stalinist Russia.

The first two men work in state bureaucracies and when they discuss collective farms where peasants labor without pay, they express a government attitude, essentially that of slave owners toward their serfs: "And why should our dear friends be paid if they don't keep up with their grain deliveries?" The superintendent from Siberia supervises prisoners on his construction site. Such is the legacy of Stalinism.

Ivan's cousin, Nikolai, is a biologist, a senior researcher at the Moscow Institute of Genetics. He works under Trofim Lysenko, the pseudo-scientist who caused the downfall, arrest, and death of the prominent Soviet geneticist, plant breeder, and explorer Nikolai Vavilov. Here Grossman introduces the theme of the tragic destruction of biological sciences and genetics under Stalin. As director of the Institute of Genetics, Vavilov had built the first international seed bank of food plants, which had been called "a living library of the world's genetic diversity."[12] He aspired to end famine around the world, but was denounced and arrested in 1940, since Lysenko sought not merely to defeat his opponents but to destroy them. Three years later Vavilov was starved to death in a Saratov prison. Lysenko, whose political speeches earned Stalin's personal praise, led an assault on Mendelian genetics. Upon Vavilov's demise Lysenko replaced him as the institute's director, maintaining this position until 1965. Speaking out against Lysenko in 1964, Andrei Sakharov accused him of being "responsible for the shameful backwardness of Soviet biology and of genetics in particular, for the dissemination of pseudoscientific views, for adventurism, for the degradation of learning, and for the defamation, firing, arrest, even death, of many genuine scientists."[13] In fact, many of the opportunists and denouncers who drove talented people out of the sciences and other spheres of life maintained their key position in the post-Stalinist era.

In the novel Grossman sarcastically refers to Lysenko as "the famous agronomist" who resorted to "police methods" and denounced scientists for disagreeing with him. When Ivan's cousin, Nikolai, receives "a warm letter from Lysenko," it gives him "great pleasure." Nikolai is a mediocre biologist whose complacency with the regime has ensured his survival. But by the standards of the time, he is "seen as someone honorable, as a man of principle" since "he had never denounced anyone ... he had refused, when summoned to the Lubyanka, to provide compromising information about an arrested colleague." Yet he participated in Stalin's vile campaigns, voting in favor of Bukharin's execution and later, signing the notorious letter against the Jewish doctors. (Grossman partly portrays himself in Nikolai. In doing so, he seems to be confessing his feelings of guilt over his own political conformism in the past. He also seems to say that most people who managed to do reasonably well under Stalin had supported the regime and its horrid campaigns.)

Nikolai's soul searching is prompted by Ivan's return from the camps. A telegram from his cousin, whom he believed long dead, comes as a shock: "It made the whole of his own life, with its truth and untruth, appear before him." Khrushchev's revelations about Stalin's crimes were inconvenient to most people who had made their careers during the previous era. The idea is expressed through Nikolai's thoughts that the state "should have kept its mouth shut." While under Stalin the state took responsibility for its crimes "and had liberated people from the chimera of conscience"; now individuals have to grapple with the question of personal responsibility. Reviewing his life and complicity with the Stalinist regime, Nikolai remembers his many "despicable acts," such as voting in support of death sentences during the Moscow trials. As his conscience awakens he feels that "his entire life had been a single act of obedience." Many things are amiss in his life. Over the entire three decades Ivan was in the camps, he never wrote him a letter.

When Ivan and Nikolai meet, there is not much they can talk about. Nikolai attempts to discuss his career, but Ivan poses an uncomfortable question: "Did *you* sign the letter condemning the Killer Doctors? I heard about that letter in the camps." Ivan doesn't want to judge his cousin: the latter is judged by his own conscience. Nikolai feels that "deep inside him everything had gone cold with anguish." In fact, political inmates returning from the camps were the conscience of the nation, and it was inevitable that the corrupt society would ostracize them. As Akhmatova famously remarked in 1956, "Now the arrested are returning, and two Russias stare each other in the eyes: the ones that put them in prison and the ones who were put in prison."[14] Akhmatova's words express the essence of Grossman's novel.

After the painful meeting with his cousin, Ivan travels to Leningrad to see his former beloved, who stopped writing him eighteen years earlier. As Ivan learned from Nikolai, she married a physical chemist whose work has something to do with "nuclear matters." But Ivan merely stands by the entrance to her house: while he was in the camps she was "closer to his heart than . . . when he was standing beneath her window."

In Leningrad, where he spends three days, Ivan bumps into the very man who denounced him to the authorities when they were students. This key episode in the novel, the meeting between Ivan and Pinegin, is drawn from the poet Zabolotsky's encounter with his denouncer, the writer Lesyuchevsky. The latter was known to have written a "review" of Zabolotsky's poetry for the NKVD that helped it concoct its case. Upon release from the Gulag Zabolotsky, originally from Leningrad, settled with friends in Moscow. While at the restaurant of the writers' club the poet was approached by a man who asked permission to sit at the same table. The man turned out to be Lesyuchevsky, the very man who had "assessed" Zabolotsky's work for the NKVD. When Zabolotsky's friends arrived at the restaurant they were shocked to find the poet sharing a table with his denouncer. Later, when asked to explain what happened, Zabolotsky said, "Well, you can solve that psychological puzzle yourselves. Why did he have to come and sit down next to me? Evidently he wanted to see for himself that I wasn't a ghost, and not only that, but real enough to be eating soup!"[15]

In *Everything Flows* Ivan and Pinegin instantly recognize each other on the street, even though both of them have changed. Noticing a "stunned" expression on Pinegin's face, Ivan asks, "What is it? Did you think I was dead?" During their conversation the denouncer keeps wondering whether Ivan knows who betrayed him. When, to assuage his conscience, Pinegin offers money to Ivan, the latter looks into the Judas's eyes "with sad curiosity," his look suggesting that he knows all.

Through Pinegin's story Grossman shows the nature of post-Stalinist society once again. As was typical, the state has rewarded Pinegin for his services as a secret police informer with promotions, honors, and a position of power. He has a beautiful wife (it is implied that he married Ivan's beloved), and his "brilliant sons" are "studying nuclear physics." Yet he achieved his secure position by writing denunciations and helping the state destroy talented people like Ivan. Later, at an exclusive restaurant for foreign tourists, where Pinegin is a regular, he orders a lavish meal—not because he is hungry but because this helps settle the "confusion and horror that had suddenly been resurrected within him."

Stalinists preached loyalty only to the Party and demanded "thoughtless obedience" from all Soviet citizens: even children were expected to denounce their parents as class enemies. In the eyes of the Soviet state, informers were model citizens. Grossman shows a young Party follower's typical apprenticeship, designed to extinguish reason and turn the individual into an obedient tool: " 'Remember,' his mentors used to tell him, 'that you have neither father nor mother, neither brothers nor sisters. You have only the Party.' " At the height of the purges the NKVD was flooded with denunciations. Tens of thousands sent their reports to the secret police, condemning neighbors, friends, family members, and colleagues. Even during the Inquisition an accuser faced the person charged with heresy and was subject to legal reprisal if the charge was not upheld by the tribunal. In the Stalinist era sending a letter was sufficient to destroy someone's life.[16]

A separate chapter in the novel discusses the four "Judas" categories of the Stalinist era and the different motivations of these "informer-murderers." Reports to the secret police served as "the prelude to an arrest," helping the authorities to compile lists of "enemies of the people" and kulaks. People whose names were included on such lists would end up arrested, deported, or shot.

A Judas I informer would betray friends and colleagues out of fear. After days of conveyor-belt interrogations, broken by torture, he would sign the false confession demanded of him. Yet this doesn't save him from being sent to the Gulag: Judas I serves twelve years in the camps and returns "barely alive, a broken man, a pauper, on his last legs. But the fact remains: he committed slander."

Judas II is a type of denouncer who writes reports voluntarily. This is the case of Pinegin in the novel—a cultured and well-to-do man, he willingly becomes an informer for the secret police. "For many years he had conducted heart-to-heart conversations with his friends and then handed in written reports to the authorities." An opportunist, such an informer made a career by betraying friends.

The vilest type of informer, Judas III, helps the Party to conduct the Great Purge and to destroy the generation of Old Bolsheviks. "In 1937 he wrote more than two hundred denunciations at one go, without a second thought." In *Life and Fate* Grossman depicts this type in Getmanov, the Party official who betrays the Bolshevik Krymov. For Judas III the purges became a time of victory when his "thoughtless obedience" to the Party "endowed him with a terrible power."

Finally, Grossman introduces the most common type of traitor in Judas IV. Devoted only to his material interests, he denounces neighbors to seize their living space and property. In Grossman's analysis, the meanness of Soviet life, living in squalor in communal apartments, destroyed humanity in people.

There has never been a trial for Stalinists. In the novel Grossman contemplates whether such a trial would even be possible, given that the regime produced criminals en masse. A mock trial for the "informer-murderers" in the novel takes place in a courtroom with a judge, a prosecutor, and a defense counsel. Like the Nazis at Nuremberg, the Stalinists deny personal responsibility for their crimes, arguing that they "performed a service of use to the State." The state determined what categories of people had no right to live: "Those who belonged to particular social and ideological strata were scheduled for extermination. . . . We never informed against members of social strata that were healthy and not already marked for destruction." Like Nazi criminals, the Stalinist "informer-murderers" maintain that "only the State is to blame" and that judgment should be passed on the state alone.

Grossman then puts Stalin's regime on trial, charging it with committing crimes on a mass scale: "Could this really be socialism—with the labor camps of Kolyma, with the horrors of collectivization, with the cannibalism and the millions of deaths during the famine?" The strongest indictment of the regime comes from a woman who witnessed peasant genocide during collectivization and Stalin's Terror Famine.

Ivan makes his new home in a southern Russian town where he finds a job as a metalworker in a shop employing the disabled. For the first time in three decades he works "as a free laborer," and this feels "astonishingly good." His landlady, Anna Sergeevna, witnessed the Terror Famine in Kuban (a vast region in southern Russia between the Black Sea, the Don Steppe, and the Northern Caucasus) and later in Ukraine. She tells her story to Ivan during their first night of love. This woman who remembers the horrors of collectivization and the famine can share her story only with a Gulag survivor. Anna's account of the Terror Famine has the quality of a requiem.

The subject of the famine of the 1930s was among the strictest of Soviet taboos, so the story had to come from the West. In 1970 *Everything Flows* was smuggled abroad and published in Frankfurt. The famine chapter in Grossman's novel informed the British historian Robert Conquest: he uses it alongside eyewitness accounts in *The Harvest of Sorrow*. In Conquest's words, the famine chapter in *Everything Flows* belongs to "the most moving writing on the period."[17] More important, Grossman was one of the first to powerfully assert the deliberate nature of Ukraine's famine. His novel provided further evidence for Conquest's thesis that the famine was man-made.

Grossman's information about the Terror Famine came from several sources. Ekaterina Zabolotskaya helped him find a major eyewitness. (Zabolotskaya kept the manuscript of *Everything Flows* and it was through her efforts that the novel ended up in Frankfurt.)[18] The Zabolotskys were close friends of the writer Alexander Stepanov's family. The author of *Port Arthur*, a celebrated novel about the Russo-Japanese War of 1904–5, Stepanov lived in Begovaya village with his wife, Maria Alexandrovna. A former chemical engineer originally from Krasnodar (part of the Kuban region), she had witnessed the famine as a young woman.[19] The Stepanovs lived one floor above Grossman, who would definitely have taken an interest in his neighbor, a fellow engineer and former director of a chemical plant in Podolsk.[20] Talking about the famine was prohibited, so it is unlikely that Grossman would have learned the story without Ekaterina Zabolotskaya, who as Maria's friend knew about her harrowing experiences.[21]

Maria's Cossack family was from the Kuban area; the neighbors called her a "Cossack woman." During the civil war the Kuban Cossacks, most of whom were ethnic Ukrainians, fought against the Bolsheviks on the side of the Whites, and later resisted collectivization. Stalin deliberately starved them by ordering excessive grain requisitioning. In 1932–33, Kuban was among the areas most afflicted by the famine. By 1936 the Kuban Ukrainians were eliminated as the major group in this region through starvation, deportations, and forced registration as Russians. This seemed to be Stalin's plan from the start.[22]

The famine chapter is shaped as a first-person account, but this is not the story of a single eyewitness such as Maria. The chapter incorporates Grossman's other research, including accounts about the horrors of collectivization and the campaign to liquidate the kulaks that he heard during the war. In the novel Anna begins her story by telling Ivan about the anti-kulak campaign: it began in late 1929 and was "at its fiercest" in February–March 1930. The Party's relentless propaganda portrayed the kulaks as subhuman: "Everything about the kulaks was vile—they were vile in themselves, and they had no souls, and they stank, and they were full of sexual diseases, and worst of all, they were enemies of the people and exploiters of the labor of others." Young people were particularly vulnerable to government propaganda: many of them became Party activists, treating the kulaks and their families "as if they were cattle, or swine." Anna explains how she became one of those activists: "I was only a girl—and during meetings and special briefings, from films, books, and radio broadcasts, from Stalin himself, I kept hearing one and the same thing: that kulaks are parasites, that kulaks burn bread and murder children. The fury of the masses had to be ignited against them—yes, those were the words; it was proclaimed that the kulaks must be destroyed as a class." Here Grossman captures the typical experience of a generation of true believers.

Kopelev, who would become a prominent dissident, had participated in grain requisitioning as a young man. Later remembering those "plundering raids" with remorse, Kopelev would write, "With the rest of my generation I firmly believed that the ends justified the means. Our great goal was the universal triumph of Communism, and for the sake of that goal everything was permissible—to lie, to steal, to destroy hundreds of thousands and even millions of people, all of those who were hindering our work or could hinder it, everyone who stood in the way."[23]

In *Everything Flows* Anna witnesses the destruction of the kulaks in Cossack villages where the OGPU first rounded up heads of families capable of resistance: "Most of the men they took had fought for the Whites, in Denikin's Cossack units. . . . And everyone arrested was shot—to the last man." After killing the men the authorities moved in to round up families. Anna recalls how quotas for arrests were established: "The provincial Party committee would draw up a plan—that is, the total number of arrests to be made—and send it to each district party committee. The district committees would then decide on the number of kulaks to be arrested in each village— and the village soviets would then each draw up a list of names. It was on the basis of these lists that people were arrested. And who drew up the lists? A group of three—a troika. A group of three ordinary, muddle-headed people determined who was to live and who was to die." (The quotas for arrests were established in Moscow by the Politburo as well as locally. The original quotas sent from Moscow to the local authorities were overfulfilled.)[24]

Everything Flows remained unfinished. Whether intended or not, the famine chapter contains traces of an interview; Anna responds to an unseen interlocutor, whose questions are not included. She says: "No, there was no famine at the time of the dispossession of the kulaks. . . . The famine began in 1932, well over a year after what we called 'dekulakization.' " It was easy to set someone up as a kulak, she explains: "Just say that your neighbor owned three cows, or that he had hired hands working for him—and there, you've set him up as a kulak." People would denounce neighbors to settle scores or to enrich themselves by stealing the property of dispossessed kulaks.

Anna describes the deportation of the kulak families from her village. They were dispatched on foot in early spring, having to walk through deep mud with whatever possessions they could carry. As a whole column of them leaves, the women keep looking back at their huts. "The women were weeping, but they were too scared to howl. And what did we care? We were—activists. We could just as well have been driving a flock of geese down the road."

The famine chapter draws parallels between Stalin's campaign to liquidate the kulaks and Hitler's campaign to exterminate the Jews. Anna is speaking for the author in comparing the inhumanity and effectiveness of Stalin's and Hitler's propaganda: "In order to kill them, it was necessary to declare that kulaks are not human beings. Just as the Germans said that Yids are not human beings. That's what Lenin and Stalin said too: The kulaks are not human beings." After purging the villages of kulaks, the authorities proceeded with forced collectivization.

Although after the dispossession of the kulaks the area under cultivation dropped significantly, quotas for grain deliveries issued by Moscow were increased. It was assumed that without the kulaks agriculture would blossom. "And our village was given a quota it couldn't have fulfilled in ten years." When the collective farmers failed to meet the government target they were accused of hiding grain. Detachments, consisting mostly of local activists, were sent to expropriate every kernel, including the seed fund. "Who signed the decree? Who ordered the mass murder? Was it really Stalin? . . . The decree meant the death by famine of the peasants of the Ukraine, the Don, and the Kuban. . . . That was when I understood: what mattered to the Soviet authorities was the plan. . . . The State is everything, and people are nothing."

Relentless Soviet propaganda pictured the kulaks as subhuman, so there was no compassion for peasants and their families. When Kopelev worked as an activist requisitioning everything edible and of value in villages near Kharkov, he thought: "I mustn't give in to debilitating pity. . . . We were obtaining grain for the socialist fatherland. For the five-year plan. . . . Some sort of rationalistic fanaticism overcame my doubts, my pangs of conscience and simple feelings of sympathy, pity and shame."[25] He would later watch peasants die on the streets of Kharkov.

Stalin and the Politburo were well aware that their policies of excessive requisitioning were producing widespread famine. In 1932 Molotov visited the Ukrainian countryside where district officials told him that the population was starving. Khrushchev also admits in his memoirs that the Politburo knew that "people were dying in enormous numbers."[26] That same year, despite knowing about the starvation, Stalin ordered additional requisitioning. The decision to confiscate all foodstuffs led to unprecedented famine and the deaths of 3.9 million people in Ukraine alone and over 6 million people overall. In Kuban the famine was such that the dead could no longer be buried. The corpses were loaded on trains to be taken to old quarries and dumped. The OGPU closely guarded the secrecy of this operation.[27]

But the famine in the Kuban region is only briefly mentioned in the novel. As a young activist Anna is sent to a collective farm in Ukraine, said to be within a few hours' drive from her village. (Grossman was likely referring to the Dnepropetrovsk region in Ukraine, also among the most severely afflicted.) Activists requisitioned food, livestock, even clothing, making "a clean sweep" and leaving whole villages without means of survival.[28]

The regime made every effort to deny the existence of widespread famine. When trains passed through famine provinces, passengers were ordered to lower the blinds and then prohibited from approaching the windows. As Western newspapers began to report on the Soviet famine, some collective farms in Ukraine were reorganized into Potemkin villages to demonstrate the opposite. In the novel Anna relates that a French minister is taken to a collective farm in the Dnepropetrovsk region. At a nursery school he asks the children what they had for lunch. They reply: chicken soup, rice pudding, and pies. This brazen lie is later published in a Soviet newspaper. Anna comments: "Killing millions of people on the quiet and then duping the whole world."

According to Conquest, Grossman was referring to the French Radical leader Edouard Herriot, who visited Ukraine in 1933 when whole villages were dying. Brought to a model children's settlement near Kharkov, Herriot was duped into believing that Soviet famine did not exist. On September 13 *Pravda* announced that Herriot "categorically denied the lies of the bourgeois press about a famine in the Soviet Union."[29] Conquest also discusses preparations to receive Herriot at a collective farm in Brovary near Kiev. Ahead of the dignitary's visit local Communists and activists were mobilized to clean the farm; a dining hall was set up and decorated with furniture from

Brovary's regional theater. Collective farm workers, handpicked for the visit, were dressed up in clothes borrowed from Kiev's shops. They were told that a film studio from Odessa would be making a film at their farm. Steers and pigs were slaughtered to provide plenty of meat, and the collective farmers were instructed to eat slowly. In the end, the masquerade was for nothing: the dignitary's visit was cancelled, and the farmers had to return the clothes and shoes issued for the show.[30]

Grossman's friend Vyacheslav Loboda was another major source for the story about grain requisitioning and famine in Ukraine. As a student Loboda was sent to conduct requisitioning in villages around Kiev. He told Grossman that not only the grain but even baked bread was seized. His account surfaces in the novel: "One woman had some bread requisitioned, loaves that had already been baked." Later he learned and told Grossman of how the starving crawled to Kiev through woods and bogs because roads were cordoned off by police. In fact, the authorities prevented the starving peasants from leaving their area: army and police detachments were posted at train stations as well as on the roads. This alone proves the deliberate nature of the famine, which Grossman was among the first to expose. In the novel Anna accuses the Stalinist state of organizing mass murder.

> The stations were all condoned off, and the trains were constantly searched. There were army and OGPU roadblocks on every road. At the same time, people were getting to Kiev, crawling through fields and bogs, through woods and open country—anything to bypass the roadblocks. . . . The peasants could no longer walk— they could only crawl. . . . But it was only the lucky few, only one in ten thousand who managed to crawl as far as Kiev. Not that it did them any good—there was no salvation even in Kiev. . . . Every morning horses pulled flat-top carts through the city. Those who'd died in the night were taken away. I saw one cart, it was stacked with the bodies of children.[31]

In Kiev people had ration cards, but "there was not a gram for peasant children in the villages. It was the same as the Nazis putting Jewish children in the gas chambers: 'You're Yids—you have no right to live.' " The parallel between death by starvation imposed on Ukrainians and destruction of Jewish life in the Nazi death camps is made again in the novel. Soviet newspapers published photographs from the German camps, and the starved

Ukrainian children "looked just the same: heads heavy as cannonballs; thin little necks, like the necks of storks." But Soviet newspapers were forbidden to report on Stalin's "execution by famine," his policy of genocide.

As we know today, hundreds of corpses were being removed from Kiev's streets at the height of the famine; the dead and the dying were indiscriminately loaded on trucks.[32] In spring and summer of 1933 entire villages died. The regime would try to erase the evidence of mass murder by falsifying census results in the late 1930s. There was also an attempt to resettle Ukrainian villages with Russian peasants from Kursk. This attempt failed. The authorities first forced the Russians to bury the bodies and whitewash the huts. But nobody was able to live in these houses, which smelled of death, and the Russian peasants returned to Kursk. (In *Red Famine* Anne Applebaum gives her explanation of the regime's unsuccessful resettlement program in Ukraine. The government had promised not to impose taxes on new settlers; however, the authorities broke their promise, and thousands of Russian peasants fled as a result.)[33] The famine chapter ends with Anna's rhetorical question: "Is it really true that no one will be held to account for it all? That it will all just be forgotten without a trace?" Anna shares her story and her clarity of understanding of the man-made disaster weeks before she is diagnosed with lung cancer. (This was also Grossman's diagnosis when he was completing the novel.)

The book does not end with Anna's death. It is now Ivan's turn to make sense of everything he learned during his time in the camps, "time to see clearly, time to discern the laws of this chaos of suffering where . . . senseless absurdity—the murder of millions of innocent and loyal people— masqueraded as cast-iron logic."

The chapters devoted to Lenin and Stalin show how the People's State, founded on promises of liberty and equal rights, became one of the world's bloodiest dictatorships. The popular Revolution of February 1917 gave rise to a nascent democracy that lasted only eight months—until the Bolshevik coup. Under Lenin's leadership the Bolsheviks destroyed democratically established political parties that "had struggled against Russian absolutism." Lenin proclaimed that the Bolshevik Party alone was capable of taking the nation to the new socialist path. But socialism was being built in a predominantly peasant country with a legacy of slavery and "hundreds of years of Russian despotism." Most Russians had no notion of rights "except that of a master to do as he pleased with his serfs." For Lenin and the Bolsheviks, who held human rights and liberty in contempt, the purity of Marxist doctrine was paramount. The Bolshevik generation did not value individual freedom. By the end of the 1920s alternative political parties had been destroyed; former revolutionaries who fought against the tsar were back in prison. The Bolsheviks proclaimed a dictatorship in the name of laboring humanity, the proletariat, and "began to build a State such as the world had never seen." This fanatical generation "had no doubt that the new world was being built for the people." The trouble was that the Bolsheviks viewed people as the main "obstacle to the building of this new world."

Under Lenin and Stalin "the State became the master." Russia's legacy of despotism explains why they were able to succeed in building a new dictatorship. "During the thousand years of her history Russia had seen many great things. . . . There was only one thing Russia had not seen during this thousand years: freedom."

The Bolshevik fanatics were "the Party's dynamite": they helped destroy the old Russia; they were the very "people who made the earth stream with blood." Few of the Old Bolsheviks would die a natural death. "The fate of the generation of the Revolution now ceased to seem mystical and extraordinary and began to seem entirely logical. . . . Terror and dictatorship swallowed up their creators."

The Party fanatics continued to believe—even in the camps—that the needs of the Soviet state were paramount, whereas individual lives could be discounted. Ivan encounters this attitude in the Gulag where a former Party official, despite being tortured in the Lubyanka, thinks that a mistake was made in his case alone: "When a forest is being felled, splinters fly—but the truth of the Party still holds true. The truth is more important than my misfortune." This Party official is at a loss for words when Ivan remarks: "That's just it—they're felling the forest. Why do they need to fell the forest?"

Stalin destroyed the generation of Old Bolsheviks because the state no longer had any use for them and distrusted them as idealists who were motivated by more than their personal advancement. These revolutionary fanatics became potentially dangerous to the Stalinist state. They were replaced with petty-minded, obedient apparatchiks—functionaries—without initiative or talent. This was the only type of person who could thrive under Stalin: "The new people did not believe in the Revolution. They were the children not of the Revolution but of the new State that the Revolution had created." The totalitarian state eliminated freedom in every sphere to ensure its own survival. The workers lost their right to strike, the peasants their right to harvest what they sowed. Writers, artists, and scientists lost freedom to create, also becoming government employees.

Grossman's main message in the novel is that "there is no end in the world for the sake of which it is permissible to sacrifice human freedom." *Everything Flows* became his most radical anti-totalitarian work. However, his political views had not changed significantly: his early novel *Stepan Kolchugin* defends the ideals of freedom, human rights, and democracy.

Everything Flows ends with an allusion to the parable of the prodigal son. Ivan travels to his ancestral home by the Black Sea, the place where his house used to stand. "For a moment it seemed to him as if an improbably bright light, brighter than any light he had ever seen, had flooded the whole earth. A few more steps—and in this light he would see his home, and his mother would come out toward him, toward her prodigal son, and he would kneel down before her, and her young and beautiful hands would rest on his gray, balding head." But there is no house—"only a few stones shining white amid dusty grass that had been burned by the sun." This passage is Grossman's farewell to life, his final vision.

15. Keep My Words Forever

Keep my words forever for a taste of misfortune and smoke.
—Osip Mandelstam

In spring 1963, facing major surgery for kidney removal, Grossman brought a package of letters to Ekaterina Zabolotskaya. Explaining that it contained his mother's letters to his father, he asked her to destroy the package after he died. She promised to do as he asked, but kept postponing the unpleasant task.

> Years have gone by, Vasily Semyonovich was no more, and I was getting on in age—it was time to keep the promise. But it's not easy to strike a match and let the fire destroy a manuscript. I asked Semyon Izrailevich Lipkin [Grossman's friend] . . . for advice. He suggested reading the letters before burning them and extracting the lines concerning Vasily Semyonovich's creative work.
>
> And so, I opened the package. When I saw familiar handwriting, I was shocked: those were Vasily Semyonovich's letters to his father! All the letters and even insignificant notes had been lovingly collected and preserved. . . . Of course, I could not burn them.[1]

Zabolotskaya wrote this in 1990, after all of Grossman's major works had appeared in the Soviet Union, sparking controversy. She placed the collection of Grossman's two hundred letters in reliable hands: the Russian State Archive of Literature and Art accepted them with alacrity. However, her memoir does not give us a clue as to why Grossman wanted his letters destroyed—or whether he actually wanted them preserved. Whatever his true intentions were, he probably expected that the KGB would seize his personal correspondence after he died.

At the end of February 1963 Grossman wrote Lipkin that Zabolotskaya had returned from Leningrad where her brother-in-law, an oncologist and surgeon, had been diagnosed with cancer. The diagnosis was not revealed to him, but Grossman wondered how an oncologist would not realize he had cancer. Such stories now deeply interested Grossman in light of his upcoming surgery.

In early May Fedya walked him to the Botkin Hospital close to Begovaya village. Grossman shared his ward with the editor of the TASS news agency Yakov Khavinson, who wrote articles under the pseudonym M. Marinin. In 1953 this man and the historian Isaak Mintz had solicited signatures of prominent Soviet Jews, Grossman included, for the infamous letter against "the killer doctors." Meeting him would oblige Grossman to relive the affair once again. However, Lipkin recalls that Marinin's presence helped distract him from his disease.[2]

Before the surgery Lipkin visited his friend daily. Grossman was in a "meek, resigned" mood. The procedure, performed by a famous surgeon, Yakov Gudynsky, went without a hitch, but Lipkin and the family were told that Grossman's cancer was at an advanced stage and might have spread. When Lipkin reassured Grossman that his kidney had been removed only because of a cyst, he "listened warily." But perhaps he wanted to believe the white lie.[3] Soon afterward Lipkin left on a business trip to Central Asia; Zabolotskaya, who visited Grossman regularly, promised to write and keep Lipkin informed. Grossman's beloved and confidante, she watched him make his first steps through the ward. In mid-May she reported to Lipkin that Grossman came up to the window for the first time after the surgery; he told her that he wanted "to breathe fresh air and to look into the windows of the Oncological Institute."[4] This institute stood opposite his hospital, and Grossman's comment suggests he well knew what lay ahead of him.

In August Lipkin read the latest draft of *Everything Flows* and although Grossman would revise it further, the novel struck him as a finished work. As Lipkin later told the writer Vladimir Voinovich, Grossman used to say that there are no completed plots in life and that a literary work, like a human life, may end abruptly.[5]

When in fall 1963 Grossman's longtime editor Anna Berzer visited him at his family apartment in Begovaya village, he read aloud to her a chapter from *Everything Flows*. Next day he told her that it was careless of him, that he shouldn't have read it at his family flat, which he thought was also bugged. He "was unhappy with himself and with me, for failing to stop him." Berzer reassured Grossman that the radio behind the wall in the neighbor's apartment had been playing at full blast, drowning out the sound.[6] On another occasion, when she visited Grossman in the hospital in June 1964, he silently gave her the entire manuscript of the novel. " 'How good,' he told me in hospital after letting me read *Everything Flows*, " 'now I have four readers of this work, you are—the fourth.' "[7] During this last hospitalization Grossman kept the manuscript inside his bedside table; he let Berzer read it without saying what it was. The writer believed—whether rightly or not—that KGB surveillance did not stop at the hospital door, so Berzer had to speak like a conspirator. She said that a manuscript had arrived in the mail, and she had read it with fascination. Grossman was pleased, realizing she spoke about the novel, and encouraged her to say more. "I kept repeating that the author did an excellent job, that he succeeded in everything he was trying to achieve. . . . I knew I was his 'fourth reader' and last, and wanted to reward him for all his future readers."[8]

As an editor at *Novy mir*, Berzer worked indefatigably to get Grossman's prose published either in this journal or elsewhere. In September 1963 she placed a piece from the Armenian memoir with *Izvestia*'s supplement, *Nedelya*, a popular weekly. Grossman was then recuperating after the removal of his kidney at the Arkhangelskoe sanatorium near Moscow. The piece from the Armenian memoir, entitled "Sevan," occupied an entire newspaper page in proofs. But both Berzer and Grossman knew that publication remained uncertain. Their foreboding proved justified. In the morning of September 22 two versions of the paper were published—with Grossman's piece and without it. A deputy editor, Grigory Osheverov, arrived at the newspaper in the wee hours of the morning, halted the press, and replaced "Sevan" with another piece. Such things previously had happened under Stalin, Berzer recalls. There was nothing political in "Sevan," but Grossman's name could cause official displeasure, and the editor wanted to play it safe. Yet because some copies of the weekly had by then already been delivered to kiosks outside Moscow, there were two versions of that day's newspaper—one with Grossman's piece and one without it.

Grossman was pleased that "Sevan" managed to break through the wall of silence and reach some of his readers, albeit "illegitimately." He received several letters and phone calls from readers. In her letter the literary scholar Raisa Orlova, an acquaintance, called him "the creator of an everlasting world." She thought the Armenian memoir revealed "a genuine bond between people of different races and nationalities. . . . And it's not coincidental that these thoughts are born in Armenia."[9] This publication and the short story "A Few Sad Days," which appeared in *Novy mir* in December 1963, were Grossman's last opportunities to see his work printed and to connect with his readers. (Kopelev and Orlova would become Grossman's advocates abroad. In the early 1980s, as Soviet exiles living in Cologne, they recommended *Life and Fate* to German publishers.)

In September 1963, while in the sanatorium, Grossman worked to revise *Everything Flows*. As he wrote Olga, who was taking her usual two-month vacation in Koktebel, he was working, reading, and going for walks. The sanatorium, which belonged to the Ministry of Defense, was located on the former estate of Prince Nikolai Yusupov. The main palace, built in neoclassical style, was now primarily a museum; patients lived in the lesser buildings. Grossman liked to sit on a bench and read in the old terraced park decorated with statues. "There are tame squirrels in the park," he wrote Olga, "and if you tap one nut against another, they come down from the trees, jump on your shoulder, and take food from your hands. There is something very moving, saintly, in the trust of these little creatures." Solicitous of Olga's health, he advised her not to take excursions on hot days and to keep checking her blood pressure.[10]

While in the sanatorium Grossman did not make friends, even though he thought there were interesting people among the officers: "You can see it from their faces . . . but my contacts here are limited to conversations at the table in the dining hall. My day passes in work, reading, and walks. I watch movies in the evenings."[11] Grossman had visitors: his stepson Fedya, Efim Kugel, Berzer, and his brother-in-law, Nikolai Sochevets, came to Arkhangelskoe. Grossman was "very pleased" to see Nikolai. As he wrote Olga, Nikolai's sculptures were exhibited in several places, and one of his works was accepted at Moscow's Palace of Culture. Nikolai had aged; Grossman reported, "he's become as wrinkled as a crocodile."[12]

When he returned to Moscow in October Grossman felt somewhat stronger, but still did not risk travel to Maloyaroslavets where his friends Kugel, the Tumarkin brothers, Gedda Surits, and Nitochkin were celebrating Loboda's sixtieth birthday. Before his surgery Grossman had looked forward to such occasions, but now he had to observe a special vegetable diet.

After his sanatorium stay Grossman went to see his surgeon, Gudynsky, at the Botkin clinic. The hospital staff greeted him so cordially that he wrote Olga, "I wish they'd meet me so well in editorial offices."[13] The surgeon was pleased with Grossman's progress, but by winter his condition had deteriorated. The cancer spread to his lungs and in December Grossman was back in the hospital.

Loboda visited the ailing Grossman at the Begovaya village between his hospital stays. On the way he stopped to chat with Zabolotskaya and then relayed her latest news to Grossman. Overhearing this from another room, Olga burst out: "People who go *there* are unwelcome *here*!" Grossman was dying, and Olga's jealous reaction was so inappropriate that Loboda pretended not to hear. Grossman simply said, "Lyusya!"[14] Olga would reconcile with Zabolotskaya, her old friend; both took turns visiting Grossman in hospital.

In summer 1964 Grossman underwent chemotherapy at the First City Hospital, an old one-story wooden building. People close to him—Olga and Zabolotskaya, daughter Katya, Berzer, Nikolai Sochevets, Lipkin, and Efim Kugel—visited him during his final months. Berzer came daily after work. Grossman had a ward to himself now, a small narrow room; his hospital bed was also narrow and too short for him. There was no oxygen even for a patient with lung cancer, air-conditioning was then unheard of, and although the windows were kept open, Grossman was suffocating. The popular poet Mikhail Svetlov (Sheinkman), also dying of cancer, was in the neighboring room. Grossman and Svetlov had met during the war and worked at the same newspaper, *Red Star*. Now they often inquired about each other; Grossman would start a conversation by asking his visitor how Svetlov was doing.

During her visits Berzer would read aloud various samizdat works to Grossman. Thus she read the verbatim report from the poet Joseph Brodsky's trial. In February 1964 the Dzerzhinsky District Court in Leningrad heard Brodsky's case; Frida Vigdorova, the human rights activist and journalist, took notes in the courtroom. Brodsky, a future Nobel Prize laureate, was convicted of "social parasitism" and sentenced to five years of hard labor, a term he did not serve in full. Vigdorova's report, "The Trial of Joseph Brodsky," circulated in samizdat and was later published in the West. As Berzer read it, Grossman listened with sympathy.

JUDGE: What do you do for living?
BRODSKY: I write poetry. I translate. I suppose . . .

JUDGE: Never mind what you "suppose." Stand up properly. Don't lean against the wall. Look at the court. Answer the court properly. (To me [Vigdorova]) Stop taking notes immediately! Or else—I'll have you thrown out of the courtroom. (To Brodsky) Do you have a regular job?

BRODSKY: I thought this was a regular job.

JUDGE: Answer correctly!

BRODSKY: I was writing poems. I thought they'd be published. I suppose . . .

JUDGE: We're not interested in what you "suppose." Tell us why you weren't working.

BRODSKY: I had contracts with a publisher.

JUDGE: Did you have enough contracts to earn a living? List them: with whom, what dates, and for what sums of money?[15]

"'Poor boy,' commented Grossman. 'So many things are falling on him.' At this moment a nurse came in—big, gloomy, and cross. She said something abruptly to Vasily Semyonovich. When she left, he said: 'She talks to me like the judge to Brodsky.'"[16]

Grossman remained interested in people and events. He listened intently as Berzer read to him biologist Zhores Medvedev's book about Vavilov and Lysenko. *The Rise and Fall of T. D. Lysenko*, then unpublished, was circulated in samizdat. The destruction of genetic science under Stalin was one of the subjects Grossman covered in *Everything Flows*. Berzer recalls that Medvedev's book interested Grossman so much that he was trying to hold back his cough as she read. When she reached the parts about Vavilov's last days, Grossman listened with deep emotion, his eyes full of tears. Lysenko's betrayal and denunciations of various people were covered in exhausting detail, but Grossman said this "tormenting reading" was useful to him: it helped distract him from his own sufferings.[17]

The early 1960s was a successful time for many Soviet poets and writers who became internationally known. Readings by the poets Yevtushenko, Bella Akhmadulina, and Andrei Voznesensky drew enthusiastic crowds that could fill Moscow's Luzhniki Stadium. Yet for Grossman this was also a time when all opportunities were closed to him. Lying in his small narrow ward, he would say that he was "walled in," a remark that equally described his situation in literature.[18] Bearing his isolation with dignity, he would ask

Berzer to tell him about the authors of *Novy mir*, what they were writing, doing, what they looked like. He often inquired about Solzhenitsyn.

For quite some time Berzer had wanted to know whether Grossman had saved a copy of *Life and Fate*. Unable to ask directly, she resorted to hints. Grossman apparently took her meaning; once, when she came to visit, he introduced her to his friend Lyolya Klestova and the next day, pointing to the chair where this woman had sat, he implied that Lyolya had a copy of his novel.

In September 1964, during Grossman's last days, Olga asked Berzer to step outside to the hospital yard. She told her that Grossman wanted his friend Loboda to retrieve the manuscript of *Life and Fate* from Klestova's unsafe communal apartment. He asked that Berzer communicate this request to Loboda, which she did.[19]

Masha Loboda and her sister Lyudmila remember the day in September when their father brought the manuscript of the novel to their house in Maloyaroslavets.[20] He carried it home in his knapsack, the three heavy folders wrapped in Lyudmila's blue summer dress with flowers. Masha watched her parents whisper to each other in the kitchen; "then my father called me, showed the folders and said, 'This is the work Uncle Vasya has written. You shouldn't tell anyone that we're keeping it.' " She was later surprised that her father trusted her to know this, for she was only in her early teens.

> At one time, we kept the manuscript in the cellar, then in a shed where we had a closet. Both places were damp and weren't good for storing papers. Our neighbors kept reporting to the authorities that we had no residence permit in Maloyaroslavets. So, a militiaman would regularly come to check whether we got the registration. When my mother would spot him on the street, she would run to the shed and hang the bag with the manuscript on a nail, on the neighbor's side of the shed. Later the manuscript was kept in my bedroom cupboard. I read it at sixteen. It was a very painful reading; I was depressed by the novel because it told about concentration camps, the gas chambers. The strongest and most sobering impression was from the episode depicting the bombardment of Stalingrad when both a German and a Russian soldier hide in the same hole. It made me think of them as human beings rather than enemies.
>
> Both of my parents were strongly anti-Soviet. They would tell Grossman what was happening across the country and in the

camps. Frankly, my father did not hold a high opinion of Vasily Semyonovich as a writer. He disliked Stepan Kolchugin. But he valued Vasily Semyonovich's short stories and spoke about them enthusiastically. Grossman was offended when Father would criticize his works. Father never spoke about *Life and Fate*.[21]

Only Grossman's family knew that Loboda kept a copy of the novel in Maloyaroslavets. When Masha Loboda visited Grossman's widow, Olga would write on a sheet of paper: "How's the manuscript?" Then she would immediately destroy her note. Vyacheslav Loboda and his wife Vera risked their family's safety by hiding the illicit manuscript in their house. They had both experienced persecution from the authorities, yet they believed it important to preserve this work that told the truth about Stalinism.

Grossman's closest friends, Loboda and Lipkin, independently (and without knowing about each other) kept copies of the novel. Loboda had the final draft with handwritten revisions, invaluable for Grossman scholars today, and Lipkin safeguarded a copy of the typescript. (Lipkin did not keep it at his apartment, since the authorities knew he was Grossman's friend.) Without his friends' courage this masterpiece would have been lost.

During his final days Grossman told Lipkin and Zabolotskaya, "I want my novel to be published—at least abroad."[22] As the writer Voinovich would remark, Grossman suffered both physically and spiritually when dying. "There can be nothing more dreadful for a genuine writer than to die without seeing his main work published and, moreover, without knowing that this work would ever reach readers."[23] Voinovich thought that Pasternak was more fortunate as a writer, for although harassed and publicly insulted, he knew that his novel had been published and had become widely successful. Voinovich compared Grossman's fate with that of Bulgakov, who was denied publication and died in obscurity, never having seen his masterpiece, *Master and Margarita*, in print.[24] However, one needs to remember that the list of Soviet literary martyrs is extraordinarily long. It includes hundreds of writers killed during the purges and scores of others denied publication during their lifetime.

Grossman died on the evening of September 14, 1964, one day short of the anniversary of the massacre of Berdichev's Jews, including his mother.

He was fifty-eight. As Grossman has written in the Armenian memoir, "And when a man dies, there dies with him a unique, unrepeatable world that he himself has created—a whole universe with its own oceans and mountains, with its own sky."[25] Grossman created an everlasting world in his fiction; it survived him and continues to live on.

Within hours of his death the authorities conducted a search of his study. Boris Zaks, Grossman's neighbor in the Aeroport district who lived in the opposite wing of the building, described what he saw. It was late evening. He was standing on his balcony looking at the dark windows of Grossman's flat when he noticed circles of illumination from a flashlight here and there on the walls: it appeared that someone, without turning on the light, was walking through the apartment. This went on for about twenty minutes. The next morning the authorities placed a seal on Grossman's door.[26] For two months not even his widow was allowed to enter the flat.

As was customary in the police state, Soviet authorities controlled all postmortem arrangements for the dissident writer: from the text of the obituary to speeches at the funeral, which had to be printed and submitted in advance for approval. Literary functionaries at the writers' union determined where Grossman's obituary should be published, what it could say, and whether it would appear with or without a portrait. Lipkin, who collaborated on the obituary with Ehrenburg, was surprised to learn this text had to be edited. "I asked, 'Does Ehrenburg need editing?' " The official responded: "He most definitely does!"[27] In the end, Ehrenburg's words were distorted beyond recognition to exclude spontaneous and personal remarks. An impersonal obituary appeared without Grossman's portrait in the *Literary Gazette*.

Gedda Surits remembers that although information about the funeral was scarce, many people came to the conference hall of the writers' union. "Everyone who knew and remembered him [Grossman] was there," Surits recalls. According to Lipkin, there were about a hundred people—family, friends, and well-known writers such as Tvardovsky, Alexander Bek, Pavel Antokolsky, and Konstantin Paustovsky. As they waited for the ceremony to begin, the poet Antokolsky, who had contributed to *The Black Book*, observed: "All that should be said about Grossman—no one will say it. And lying—he hated lies more than anyone else."[28] Antokolsky referred to the fact that no one was allowed to speak off the cuff: all speeches at the funeral had to be printed to exclude anything spontaneous. But some speakers defied the official agenda. Evgeny Vorobyov, a novelist and war correspondent who had known and respected Grossman, spoke warmly about him. Ehrenburg made a fiery speech. Surits recalls: "He spoke about [Grossman's] last tragic years and months. He referred mockingly to the obituary, which was insulting to Grossman. He said that not everything Vasya has written is known and that time, this finest judge, will reveal what his best works have been. Ehrenburg spoke about [Grossman's] uncompromising honesty, which had not always helped him. 'He was a difficult man,' Ehrenburg said. 'His life was hard, and his death was hard, but he was honest to the end, and if it isn't necessary to learn from him *how* to write, it is necessary to learn *what* to write.' "[29]

Lipkin, who read his speech at the crematorium, also managed to squeeze in a few impromptu remarks. He spoke of Grossman as a man of great courage and expressed hope that "in the nearest future all of his writings, both published and unpublished, would become available to the reader."[30] The audience took the hint, and the literary functionary from the writers' union walked out.

Years later, war novelist Grigory Baklanov (Friedman), who regarded Grossman as his teacher, would remark: "Grossman spent the entire war at the front. I remember how at his funeral one of the speakers said, 'He was in Stalingrad during the whole battle, but just before the end they transferred him to another front. Everyone was being rewarded except Grossman because he wasn't there.' And it was the same in literature. He spent many years writing *Life and Fate*. When [the first part of this novel] *For the Right Cause* came out, a destructive campaign against this book and Grossman himself ensued. . . . He wasn't famous in his lifetime, he wasn't appreciated."[31] Baklanov, a generation junior to Grossman, brought his first fiction to him upon returning from the war.[32] He later participated in one of Grossman's creative seminars for young writers. (Since 1950 Grossman gave such seminars, organized by the union.) During Gorbachev's glasnost, when he became editor of *Znamya*, Baklanov published *An Armenian Sketchbook*, Grossman's short prose, and in 1989 issued his wartime notebooks as a separate edition. In fact, publication of Grossman's major works had to wait until the Gorbachev era.

When in 1964 a commission for Grossman's literary estate was formed, it accomplished little. The functionaries at the writers' union prevented the liberals Ehrenburg and Paustovsky from joining the commission. Tvardovsky and the writer Alexander Pismennyi, who knew Grossman, became part of it. They succeeded in having several short stories published, along with extracts from Grossman's wartime notebooks and a heavily edited version of the Armenian memoir. As Lipkin writes, "We didn't succeed with what was most important—publishing a five-volume edition of [Grossman's] collected works, or recovering the manuscript of *Life and Fate* from the Lubyanka to pass on to the TSGALI [future RGALI literary archive]."[33] The commission for Grossman's literary estate was dissolved in 1970. When an abridged edition of *Everything Flows* was issued in Frankfurt by the Russian émigré publishing house Posev, a political scandal broke out.[34] In the spirit of the Stalinist campaigns, the literary commission's chair, Georgy Beryozko, proposed that members write a collective letter to the *Literary Gazette* denouncing "the dirty alien work *Everything Flows*." When Lipkin asked whether he had read the novel (which would be illegal in the USSR), Beryozko looked frightened.[35]

While Party officials prevented readers from accessing the best of the twentieth century's works by Akhmatova, Bulgakov, Mandelstam, Pasternak, and others, they were often the first to buy limited editions of these books. The hypocrisy of the Soviet and Party elite can be gauged from a story in Tvardovsky's diary. In November 1969, Soviet best-selling author Yulian Semyonov told Tvardovsky about being at the wedding of the former head of the KGB, General Vladimir Semichastnyi. (This man led the harassment campaign against Pasternak, publicly abusing the writer as "a pig.") Semichastnyi's guests, including Alexander Shelepin, a member of the Politburo, danced to the music from the *Doctor Zhivago* film.[36] In 1974 Shelepin would propose the arrest of Solzhenitsyn. This clique suppressed freedom of the press and harassed dissident writers who threatened their regime.

Everything Flows was circulated in samizdat: Tvardovsky read the novel in 1969, having received it from the writer Yuri Trifonov, whose dacha was near his. Trifonov had a particular reason to appreciate Grossman's work as his own father, a former revolutionary and later a high official in the Council of People's Commissars, had been shot in 1938, and his mother, an economist, had spent years in the Gulag for having failed to denounce her husband. Trifonov had met Grossman in 1951 at the Second Congress of Young Writers and participated in his creative writing seminar. That same year he was awarded a Stalin Prize for his novel *Students*, a tendentious work of which he was later ashamed. Soon afterward, he came under fire for having concealed his status as "the son of the enemy of the people." Grossman had defended the young writer at a crucial meeting of the secretariat in the writers' union when Bubennov and other Stalinists attacked him.[37]

Unlike Trifonov, Tvardovsky disliked *Everything Flows*, which to him reflected the pessimism of a dying man. Although the novel tells of the sufferings of the dispossessed and deported kulaks, and Tvardovsky himself came from such a family, he was critical of the book. He described it in his diary as a "tract" and a "lampoon" that presented Russia's history as no more than a millennium-long reign of despotism and slavery. Stalin's violent epoch is seen as an extension of Lenin's. The novel conveyed "the deepest pessimism. . . . It's hard to read it because of the emphasis on 'crimes of revolution' and mainly because all this is undeniable."[38] A shrewd editor, Tvardovsky anticipated the main arguments against the novel that critics would raise in 1989 when it was published in the USSR.

Grossman would privately mock Tvardovsky's various failings. Back in 1961 he told Lipkin how Tvardovsky came to see him after the arrest of *Life and Fate*. "After a drink, he [Tvardovsky] cried out, 'It's impossible to write the truth in our country, there's no freedom.' " After a while, Tvardovsky said testily that Grossman, like a typical intellectual, cared only about Stalin's purges of 1937—and not about the destruction of millions of peasants during collectivization. "And here he begins retelling me what I myself wrote in *Life and Fate*," laughed Grossman.[39]

Lipkin never forgot his promise to help attain publication for *Life and Fate* in the West. In 1975 he approached his neighbor, the dissident satirical writer Voinovich, whose novel had come out abroad without the Soviet authorities' permission. Voinovich's book *The Life and Extraordinary Adventures of Private Ivan Chonkin* was circulated in samizdat and also had appeared in the émigré journal *Grani* in Frankfurt. Voinovich recalls how Lipkin first approached him on Grossman's behalf: "One day I walked through the yard and met my neighbor, Semyon Izrailevich Lipkin. I knew that Lipkin was Grossman's friend. I thought a great deal about the confiscated novel [*Life and Fate*] and suspected that not all copies were seized. I kept looking inquisitively at Lipkin, but never asked any questions. And here he suddenly approached me in the yard and said, 'I have a request. I know you have acquaintances among foreigners. Could you send one manuscript to the West?' I asked at once, 'Grossman's?' He said, 'Yes.' I responded, 'Of course I'll do this.' The following day Semyon Izrailevich brought me this manuscript."[40]

Voinovich invited a dissident friend who published samizdat literature, asking him to microfilm Grossman's novel. But instead of promptly and clandestinely handling this task, the man kept coming and going from Voinovich's home. Such carelessness threatened to wreck the entire undertaking: Voinovich lived under the KGB surveillance and if agents suspected illegal activity, his home would be searched and Grossman's manuscript confiscated.

In 1975 Voinovich himself photographed *Life and Fate* with his old Soviet camera. The result was poor. He then approached Sakharov and Elena Bonner for help: the home of the Nobel Peace Prize laureate was secure. At Sakharov's place the manuscript was photographed again. Both films—Sakharov's and Voinovich's—were smuggled to Paris, ending up in the hands of Vladimir Maksimov, the editor of the influential émigré journal *Kontinent*. In 1975–76, Maksimov published chapters from *Life and Fate* in several successive issues of *Kontinent*. Around this time, extracts also appeared in the émigré publications *Grani* and *Posev*, but the work failed to arouse attention. Grossman's novel was overshadowed by *The Gulag Archipelago*, released in December 1973, and Solzhenitsyn's deportation to the West the following year.

According to Voinovich, Maksimov also sent a copy of *Life and Fate* to Carl Proffer in Michigan. A famous professor of Russian languages and literatures, Proffer, with his wife Ellendea, founded Ardis publishing house in 1971. They had translated and produced dozens of Russian literary works, but rejected Grossman's novel. In 1985, in an open letter to Solzhenitsyn, Kopelev would explain that although Carl Proffer "passionately loved Russia, Russian literature," he had his literary preferences. "Thus, I did not share his admiration for [the memoirs of] N. Ya. Mandelstam, Sasha Sokolov's novels, and his high opinion of Maramzin's prose.[41] In turn, he did not share our regard for [Solzhenitsyn's] prose and Vasily Grossman's novel *Life and Fate* (he even refused to publish this novel, despite our persistent requests)."[42]

Unaware of these failures, Voinovich kept listening to the BBC and Voice of America in the hope of hearing news about the publication of *Life and Fate*. As he would later explain to Bonner, foreign radio was silent about it, so he decided to microfilm the novel and have it smuggled out again. In 1977 he invited a samizdat publisher from Leningrad, Vladimir Sandler, to his apartment. The typescript of *Life and Fate* had to be again retrieved from secret storage and delivered to Voinovich's flat. This task was entrusted to the poet Inna Lisnyanskaia, Lipkin's second wife: *Life and Fate* was hidden at her brother's apartment. Lisnyanskaia later described her taxi ride with the forbidden typescript as terrifying: "I can't remember anything more frightening. . . . It was a hugely responsible task. By then I knew it was a great novel and feared—what if its gets lost or what if they seize it from me, and then it'll be all over!"[43]

According to Voinovich, Sandler produced "an excellent quality" microfilm with his superior equipment. Voinovich summoned his acquaintance Rosemary Ziegler, a Slavic scholar from Austria, and gave her the film. "I explained to her . . . that this is an outstanding novel, that it's necessary not only to smuggle it to the West but also to find a publisher for it." An Austrian cultural attaché, Johann Marte, carried the microfilm across the border and passed it on to the Soviet philologist and émigré Efim Etkind and the literary scholar Shimon Markish (the son of the executed poet Peretz Markish).[44] The two worked indefatigably to prepare the novel for publication, which involved reading and comparing two separate copies of the microfilm now in their possession. Vladimir Dimitrijević, a political émigré from Belgrade as well as a literary scholar and founder of the publishing house L'Âge d'Homme in Lausanne, Switzerland, was also involved in deciphering the text. Dimitrijević spent two and a half months in a darkroom studing the microfilm: "Some parts were simply unreadable."[45] Finally, in 1980, L'Âge d'Homme published the novel in the original Russian. Because of technical problems some paragraphs and pages could not be reproduced; therefore, Grossman's original text was later compromised in translated versions.

It took another three years for *Life and Fate* to make a breakthrough. The French edition, launched in 1983, reached a broad audience: 120,000 copies of the novel were sold.[46] This sparked interest in the novel across Europe and in the United States. Robert Chandler's English translation appeared in 1985 in London and in New York. In September 2011 *Life and Fate* became a best seller in England after BBC Radio 4 aired an adaptation of the novel with Kenneth Branagh as Victor Shtrum.[47] *Life and Fate* was praised as one of the best war novels, ever "a moral monument, a witness-report in fiction from the heart of 20th-century darkness, an astonishing act of truth-telling."[48]

When in 1988 Etkind, who helped prepare the novel's publication in Lausanne, learned from a reliable source that a Moscow journal would soon launch *Life and Fate*, he dismissed the report as "fantasy." Likewise, Soviet dissidents in the West who read the novel felt sure, even at the height of Gorbachev's glasnost, that it could never appear in the USSR. Etkind explained later that he thought it more probable that the USSR would allow the formation of another political party. After all, the Communist Party with its 17 million members could easily control and marginalize an alternative party, if such was formed. But Grossman's novel (here Etkind concurred with the Soviet ideologist Suslov) actually threatened the regime's existence.[49]

A prominent dissident, Etkind had been deported from the USSR in 1974 for his ties to Solzhenitsyn. Previously he had been a witness at Brodsky's trial and worked to prepare the poet's samizdat collection in the Soviet Union. He risked his safety by hiding a copy of *The Gulag Archipelago*: it was buried near his Leningrad dacha. Known to the authorities as Solzhenitsyn's friend, Etkind was harassed after the release of *The Gulag Archipelago*. As Solzhenitsyn writes, Etkind had to "endure the shock of being publicly attacked and pilloried, then driven out of the country."[50] Etkind and his wife both lost their fathers in Stalin's prison camps—a typical background for Soviet dissidents.

In the end, it did not take 250 years to publish *Life and Fate* in the USSR—merely three decades. In 1988 the novel appeared in Moscow's literary journal *Oktyabr'*, which had a circulation of 250,000. In Etkind's view this publication alone suggested that "serious revolutionary changes" were taking place in the Soviet Union.

Grossman's calculation that only an editor known for conservative views would have the courage to accept and defend his novel proved accurate. The editor of *Oktyabr'*, the war novelist Anatoly Ananiev, was not a liberal: a former literary functionary in the writers' union, he had a solid reputation in the official world that helped him overcome the restrictions of Soviet censorship. But in 1988 he could succeed in publishing only a censored version of *Life and Fate*. Thus an entire chapter discussing anti-Semitism was cut. Passages discussing the absence of freedom in Russia were also missing, such as: "During an entire millennium Russia has been free for little more than six months. Your Lenin didn't inherit Russian freedom—he destroyed it."[51] But publication of even an edited version of the novel in the USSR was a major achievement: it opened the forbidden door. Two years later a comprehensive edition was launched in Moscow. The 1990 edition of *Life and Fate* appeared with Grossman's dedication, vital to the writer: "For my mother, Ekaterina Savelievna Grossman." (This dedication was absent from the versions used by early publishers in the 1980s. It was found, however, in the final draft Loboda and his family had preserved.)

The first publication in *Oktyabr'* produced a flood of reviews in the Soviet press. In the article "Grossman's Universe," a prominent critic, Lev Anninskij, wrote that although *Life and Fate* reached its Russian audience only three decades after it was written, it struck him as a "present day work. . . . The novel hasn't aged, and in a certain sense, it comes out at a right time. . . . We have matured to the point of being able to take in its message."[52] Pondering the words of Soviet literary functionaries that *Life and Fate* could not come out for 250 years, Anninskij quipped that they expressed confidence in the longevity of the novel. Anninskij had been a junior editor at *Znamya* when *Life and Fate* was arrested. The portrayal of the Holocaust in the novel affected him personally: during the war some of his family members perished in the gas chambers, and his grandmother was killed during a pogrom. Contemplating the novel's importance, Anninskij wrote that aside from capturing the epoch, the work exposed the basic principles of totalitarianism, the foundation on which Russia stood and might continue to stand.[53]

Life and Fate appeared at the height of glasnost, simultaneously with Pasternak's *Doctor Zhivago*. Under Gorbachev, the grandson of Gulag prisoners, Soviet newspapers and magazines were filled with revelations about Stalinism, and a flood of previously unpublished literary works appeared in quick succession. Given such circumstances Grossman's novel did not create the explosion of interest that might have been expected.

In 1987 Alexander Askoldov's brilliant film *Commissar*, based on Grossman's story "In the Town of Berdichev," was shown for the first time. The film had been produced twenty years earlier, but was immediately banned from screening—not in the least because of its prominent Jewish theme. Askoldov, then a young talented director, was expelled from the Party, fired from his job, and banished from Moscow; he was never allowed to produce another film. But in 1988 *Commissar* became the Soviet entry for the Best Foreign Language Film at the Academy Awards. The *Chicago Tribune* wrote: "A 1968 film up for a 1988 Oscar? How can this be? Well, as they used to say in vaudeville, timing is everything. . . . Deeply feminist and sympathetic to the plight of Soviet Jews (but not necessarily to their religion), the film was promptly banned by the Brezhnev regime."[54] *Commissar* had since become widely recognized internationally and won a number of awards, although not an Oscar.

In 1989 *Oktyabr'* published Grossman's most radical work, *Everything Flows*. One month before the novel was issued a group of nationalist writers associated with the conservative journal *Sovremennik* attempted to prevent its publication. They claimed that *Everything Flows* was insulting to their national dignity and threatened to sue *Oktyabr'* if the work came out.[55] When the novel did appear, this group of authors, among whom the internationally recognized mathematician Igor Shafarevich is best known, published a letter in the newspaper *Literary Russia* accusing *Oktyabr'* of Russophobia and calling for "administrative reprisal."[56] Shafarevich had long been preparing such an attack. In 1983 his essay "Russophobia" accused a number of Jewish writers, including Babel, Nadezhda Mandelstam, and Brodsky, of loathing Russia. He also expounded on a theory of a "small nation," or Jews, destroying the "large nation," or Slavs. The "small nation," he maintained, threatened to bring on "catastrophe" and extinction of the "large nation."[57] *Everything Flows* became the lightning rod for Shafarevich and his group.

These nationalists were outraged by Grossman's skeptical take on Dostoevsky's faith in the special "power of the Russian soul." In 1880 Dostoevsky had expressed his belief in Russia's messianic mission in Europe. Grossman argues that Dostoevsky was "tragically mistaken" when describing the "Russian soul" as "all-human and all-unifying." "Did Russia's prophets ever imagine," Grossman asks in *Everything Flows*, "that their prophesies about the coming universal triumph of the Russian soul would find their grating fulfillment in the unity of the barbed wire stretched around Auschwitz and the labor camps of Siberia?"[58] In Grossman's view that legacy of slavery would prevent Russia from assuming a moral leadership role: "However all-powerful you are, what can you give to the world if you have been a slave for a thousand years?"[59] In this novel Grossman sounds pessimistic about Russia's future, suggesting that the country's failure to face its past would prevent it from moving forward.

Grossman was following Russian writers' tradition of exposing the country's ills. From Alexander Radishchev to Pushkin, Lermontov, Chekhov, and Tolstoy, writers have decried Russia's slavery and violent past. In *Everything Flows* Grossman quotes from Pyotr Chaadayev's *Philosophical Letters*, written in the 1820s. Chaadayev views "the gradual enslavement" of the Russian peasantry as a "logical consequence of our entire history."[60] Grossman considers Chaadayev's remarks on Russia's past illuminating, especially his suggestion that Russians should make their contribution to the world by taking their place "among the nations . . . not only as battering rams but also through their ideas."[61]

Typically, the nationalists ignored the central chapter in Grossman's novel dealing with Stalin's famine and peasant genocide. By refusing to face the totalitarian past and re-creating the myth of Russia's greatness, they had invited this past to come back.

In 2013 the confiscated manuscripts of *Life and Fate* were finally returned to the public domain. That year the film director and journalist Elena Yakovich was shooting a television documentary about Grossman. At the time nobody knew whether Grossman's manuscripts had been preserved or destroyed. Deciding to find out, Yakovich approached Tatyana Goryaeva, the director of the Russian State Archive of Literature and Art (RGALI), suggesting that she send a formal inquiry to the FSB (the KGB's successor). In April 2013 Goryaeva sent a letter to the Central Archive of the FSB of the Russian Federation, explaining that RGALI was compiling a volume about Soviet writers who had participated in World War II and needed information about Grossman's manuscripts. Goryaeva sent this request without much hope: the KGB rarely returned writers' confiscated archives. But in June she received a positive response from Lieutenant General Vasily Hristoforov, then head of the central archives of the Federal Security Services of the Russian Federation. Hristoforov wrote that the FSB had decided to turn over all of Grossman's papers to RGALI.

The timing of Yakovich's and Goryaeva's request was opportune: this was before the Sochi Winter Olympics when the authorities were concerned about public relations. Yakovich believes there were also other factors at play. The FSB made the decision when interest in Grossman's work had been revived by Sergei Ursuliak's 2012 television film based on *Life and Fate*. Yakovich's documentary may also have helped prompt the FSB to release Grossman's papers from their secret depository.

In June 2013, upon receiving the news from the Lubyanka through RGALI, Yakovich got in touch with Lieutenant General Hristoforov. Already helpful to her project far beyond expectation, he puzzled her by asking, "Would you need something else?" Yakovich said, "Yes, I'd like to go with you to the FSB archive to retrieve Grossman's papers."[62] This wish was not granted, however: Grossman's file was held at a special facility outside Moscow where Hristoforov would not admit the filmmaker.

Fifty-two years after the arrest of the novel, Grossman's papers were returned to the public domain with much fanfare. On July 25 the FSB, one of Russia's most secretive institutions, held a public ceremony in a new building on Lubyanka. In the presence of the culture minister, Vladimir Medinsky, officials handed Grossman's file over to RGALI. The event was covered by national newspapers and television. The FSB cheerfully commented: "It is with pleasure that we are passing on the manuscript, it's now widely accessible, and literary scholars can begin researching this work."[63]

The FSB also hosted a smaller ceremony in its reading room on Kuznetsky Most, a street not far from Lubyanka, allowing Yakovich to film the event. Her documentary showed—for the first time—what was seized from Grossman during his novel's arrest. The FSB produced Grossman's papers in his original folders: 10,043 pages of typescripts and drafts. "How do I feel about this?" reacts Grossman's daughter, Katya Korotkova-Grossman in the film as she leafs through her father's draft of the novel with his multitude of handwritten revisions. "I regret that my father is not here to witness the moment." The title of Yakovich's documentary, *Vasily Grossman: I Understood That I Had Died*, employs the writer's words after the novel's confiscation.

An award-winning director, journalist, and scriptwriter, Yakovich has made a number of documentaries on topics ranging from the Holocaust to prominent Soviet émigrés such as Brodsky. *Vasily Grossman* was launched in 2014, in time for the fiftieth anniversary of the writer's death. As Yakovich told this writer, she couldn't imagine *Life and Fate* being published in the USSR in the 1960s or how Soviet society would have been affected by it. But the impact of concurrent publication in the West can be known, she says. If *Life and Fate* had appeared abroad in the 1960s, it would have "become an international cultural sensation" and impacted the discourse on Stalinism in the world. The postponement of its publication "stole" such momentum from Grossman and his novel.[64]

While *Life and Fate* appeared simultaneously with *Doctor Zhivago*, Grossman's last novel, *Everything Flows*, was published in Russia in 1989, in the same year as Solzhenitsyn's *Gulag Archipelago*. Printed in *Novy mir* at the height of glasnost, Solzhenitsyn's colossal work had less impact on the Soviet reader than his novella *Ivan Denisovich*. In the 1990s Russians began to lose interest in publications exposing the crimes of Stalinism.

Epilogue

After the confiscation of *Life and Fate* Grossman's name rarely appeared in the Soviet press. Few memoirs were written about him, and much of his correspondence was lost. This amplifies the importance of a recent discovery by the German-Ukrainian historian Tatiana Dettmer. She unearthed information about the nuclear physicist Lev Shtrum, the model for Grossman's principal character in *Life and Fate* and *For the Right Cause (Stalingrad)*. Grossman's 1929 letter to his father, found by the author of this book, mentions Shtrum, confirming that Grossman had known the physicist. Shtrum was shot in 1936 alongside thirty-six Ukrainian scientists. His early contributions to nuclear physics survive only in the West. Dettmer's discovery helps explain why Grossman resisted his editors' attempts to purge Shtrum from the novel. Lev Shtrum's tragic fate exemplifies that of a whole generation of Soviet physicists under Stalin.

The story of Georgy Demidov, a talented physicist, engineer, writer, and Kolyma survivor, may serve as a postscript to Grossman's subject matter. Demidov was still a student at Kharkov University when Lev Landau, his professor in theoretical physics, recruited him to work at his laboratory at the Kharkov Institute of Physics and Technology. This institute was at the cutting edge of science, exploring the field of nuclear and low-temperature physics. At the height of the purges the leading researchers of the Kharkov institute were arrested. In February 1938 Demidov, aged thirty, was thrown in jail, charged with "Trotskyist-terrorist activity," and dispatched to the Gulag, where he would spend fourteen years. His wife and baby daughter were kept in an overcrowded prison, temporarily released, and then, luckily, forgotten by authorities.

While in Kolyma Demidov worked as an engineer and for part of his term as a slave laborer in the gold mines. At the central Gulag hospital in the Far East where he underwent life-saving surgery, he met Shalamov, who would depict him in *Kolyma Tales* as the engineer Kipreev. In his reminiscences Shalamov describes Demidov as "the most intelligent and decent man I've ever met in my life."[1]

In 1951, when surviving physicists were sought in the Gulag for Stalin's atomic project, Demidov was transported under guard from Kolyma to Moscow. He was expected to work with other imprisoned scientists in a sharashka. By then he had fallen hopelessly behind in theoretical physics, and in any case, his prison sentence would soon expire, making him of no use to the sharashka's work. He was therefore sent back to the Gulag to finish his term in the Komi Republic in the far north. In "The Life of Engineer Kipreev," in which he tells Demidov's story, Shalamov observes that the authorities treated the man as a slave—an intelligent one, but still a slave.[2] Upon his release from the camps Demidov worked as an engineer at a factory where he still managed to make his mark, as the best inventor of the Komi Republic.

While in Kolyma Demidov became determined to survive so he could describe "all this hell" and "the conveyor belt of lies." He produced several books of prose and reminiscences in which he referred to Kolyma as "an Auschwitz without crematorium ovens."[3] As a dissident writer whose works circulated in samizdat, Demidov, like his friend and correspondent Shalamov, lived under KGB surveillance. In 1980 the KGB searched his home and the homes of his close friends and family, seizing all copies of his works along with typewriters. Demidov had lost his fingers to frostbite and was unable to hold a pen; aware of this, the authorities deprived him of the means to complete his testimony. As earlier with Grossman, the KGB considered it unnecessary to arrest the author, especially given that Demidov was seventy-two and not expected to live much longer. In 1987, after Demidov's death, his daughter Valentina appealed to Alexander Yakovlev, the chief ideologist under Gorbachev and the "godfather of glasnost," asking him to help arrange the return of her father's confiscated archive. Demidov's papers were returned to his daughter, who later succeeded in getting his works published in limited circulation. However tragic, Demidov's story was typical, and Grossman had known many such cases of the destruction of talented and independent-minded people whom the Soviet totalitarian state deemed dangerous.

While Grossman's writings were unacceptable in his lifetime, his ideas later helped lay a path for others to follow. The life of a prominent Soviet actor, Leonid Bronevoy, serves as an ironic comment to Grossman's comparison of the Soviet and Nazi systems. Bronevoy became a national celebrity for his role in the Soviet television series *Seventeen Moments of Spring*. The 1972 espionage drama about a Soviet spy operating in Nazi Germany was still wildly popular in the 1990s. The thriller became the most watched television series in Russia's history, with an estimated audience of between 50 million and 80 million. (According to the BBC Russian Service the production likely inspired Putin to become a Soviet spy in Germany.)[4]

Bronevoy, a Jew, played the part of the Gestapo chief Heinrich Müller. The staging makes an indirect parallel between the Gestapo and the NKVD. While Soviet intelligence is glorified, the Gestapo is also cast in a rather positive light: Bronevoy invests his character with human traits.

In later life the actor spoke out against Stalin's regime and the crimes of its secret police. In 2009 the BBC interviewed Bronevoy, asking why Russia was not ready to liken Stalinism to Fascism. The actor replied that in his view the Communist Party was even guiltier than the Nazi Party because it waged war against its own people. The Communist Party must be put on trial.[5]

The actor knew about Stalin's crimes firsthand. In the 1920s and the 1930s his father, Solomon Bronevoy (Factorovich), served as the OGPU/NKVD investigator in Kiev. "My father was one of the most brutal interrogators of Kiev's OGPU," the actor wrote in 2014. As deputy head of the so-called economic department of the OGPU his father extracted money and gold from his victims, beating them to a pulp.[6] (In his 1935 story "Four Days," employing the commissars' real names, Grossman depicts Factorovich as Kiev's fanatical Cheka investigator who arrests his own uncle during the civil war. The old man is sent to a concentration camp where he dies of typhus.)

Typically, Bronevoy's father ended up in the Gulag: arrested as a "Trotskyist" during the Great Purge, he was sent to Kolyma. His wife and son were deported from Kiev. As the son of an "enemy of the people," Bronevoy was refused university education and employment for many years. In 2014 he described the entire Soviet experiment as "an absurd horror film stretching for over 70 years." President Putin, of course, was promoting the opposite idea, having referred to the collapse of the Soviet Union as "the greatest geopolitical tragedy of the twentieth century." So Bronevoy was deliberately blunt in his public comments: "I wanted to be heard! [I wanted to say that] the system, which we are still praising and glorifying, persecuted its own people (it would kill them at best, and would force them to kill others at worst). We must remind ourselves of this to prevent repetition of the past, so that not even a thought would arise that life was good back then [under Stalin]! How can it be good if half of the country is incarcerated and the other half is incarcerating it?"[7]

Information about the true scale of Stalin's repressions was carefully guarded for decades. As is apparent from Alexander Yakovlev's book *A Century of Violence in Soviet Russia*, only the Politburo, people like Molotov, Khrushchev, Mikoyan, Kaganovich, Zhdanov, and Suslov, who personally participated in the purges, were thoroughly informed.

Although a major Communist Party official who served as head of the Propaganda Department at the Central Committee, Yakovlev was a maverick. In 1972 he published an article "on the dangers of chauvinism, nationalism and anti-Semitism in the USSR."[8] Because anti-Semitism remained an undeclared government policy, he was swiftly removed from Party work and sent to Canada as ambassador. Under Gorbachev, who brought him back, Yakovlev was appointed to the Politburo. From 1989 he chaired the Commission on the Rehabilitation of Victims of Political Repression. In the first year of its existence the commission reviewed 280,000 cases and cleared 367,690 names.[9] These archival documents revealed to Yakovlev that the Soviet regime had committed crimes against humanity. The documents told of mass executions without trial practiced routinely under Lenin and Stalin; of Soviet concentration camps, including those for children; of sweeping reprisals against the intelligentsia; of the destruction of peasantry, clergy, and non-Boshevik socialist parties; of brutal deportations of nationalities before, during, and after World War II; of Soviet POWs dispatched from Nazi concentration camps only to be sent directly to the Gulag. The history of the Soviet state was written in blood.

Reading these documents, Yakovlev pictured Russia as a vast cemetery, its land strewn with "the nameless graves of its citizens, felled in wars, killed by famine, or shot at the whim of the Leninist-Stalinist fascist regime."[10] "The practice of mass arrests has inflicted an incalculable loss on all the peoples of Russia, drained society of its lifeblood, and determined its moral collapse. During the seventy years of Bolshevism the forms of repression altered but the causes and nature of the despotism remained unchanged. The regime and its top leaders were ready to commit any crime against humanity to entrench their monopoly on power, ideology and property and to create a submissive herd."[11] Much like Grossman before him, Yakovlev realized that the Soviet and the Nazi regimes both conducted murder on an industrial scale. In Auschwitz, he writes, people had to die "for belonging to one of the 'inferior races.' In the prisons and camps of the Gulag, 'for class inferiority.' "[12]

In later years Yakovlev toured the country lecturing on history, economy, and Soviet repressions. He and his team published numerous volumes of declassified archival materials under the general title *Russia. XX Century. Documents*. "This is Russia's new history—an entirely different history," he said in his last interview in 2005. "It's impossible to read it without tears and rage. . . . We receive readers' response. You know what many people are writing? That this couldn't have happened."[13]

Yakovlev witnessed the return of Stalin's popularity and nostalgia for the Soviet Union. Explaining popular resistance to Gorbachev's democratic reforms, he pointed out in his book, "In trying to reform the country we . . . underestimated a great deal—above all, the psychological condition of the society, which turned out to be more inert, indifferent, and dependent than we had imagined. To this day, many people pin their hopes on some great man, some idol, and dream of slavery and 'stronger' leaders. There you are: the 'riddle' of the Russian soul. In actual fact, nothing more than a slave psychology." In turn, this mentality is responsible for Russia's curse, an almost "unbroken sequence of suffering . . . and crime."[14] The architect of glasnost and advocate of democracy, Yakovlev believed the vicious circle could be disrupted by making information accessible.

Three Soviet generations had been successively deceived about their past, and in Putin's Russia history is being revised once again. In 1996, years before becoming president, Putin declared that Russia's "return to a totalitarian past is possible." As he put it, "The danger is not from the organs of state power like the KGB, MVD, or even the army. It is a danger in the mentality of our people, our nation, our own particular mentality."[15] While Putin claimed that totalitarianism is not imposed from above, he cracked down on independent media upon coming to power.

Speaking to a French interviewer in 1974, Hannah Arendt elucidated on the connection between totalitarian regimes and political ignorance: "What makes it possible for a totalitarian or any other dictatorship to rule is that people are not informed; how can you have an opinion if you are not informed? If everybody always lies to you, the consequence is not that you believe the lies, but rather that nobody believes anything any longer. . . . And a people that no longer can believe anything cannot make up its mind. It is deprived not only of its capacity to act but also of its capacity to think and to judge. And with such a people you can then do what you please."[16]

In 2014 the late Arseny Roginsky, then head of the Russian human rights organization Memorial, dedicated to preserving the memory of Soviet repressions, remarked that Grossman's anti-totalitarian message "doesn't fit into official propaganda. Everything written today, including school text-books, aims to demonstrate that we must be proud of our past. . . . Grossman is now published, even included in the school curriculum [on a selective list]. On the surface everything is good, but this is not so. Grossman doesn't suit the existing regime."[17]

In Russia Grossman remains only marginally known; he is highly respected among intellectuals and human rights activists. In 2007 Lev Dodin of Petersburg's Maly Drama Theater staged a play based on *Life and Fate*. As the director told an interviewer, "I think our play helps popularize this novel in Russia, but, alas, this is a drop in a sea. In Russia Grossman is of interest to few—mainly because the entire energy of our society is directed today towards denying our own past. . . . We invest great efforts in preventing the nation from fathoming [its] tragic responsibility for what had happened, something Grossman had deeply realized and felt."[18] In contrast, when Dodin's stage adaptation of Grossman's novel premiered in London in May 2018, every major newspaper reviewed it. Headlines revealed an abiding interest in Grossman's subject matter. The *Guardian* referred to *Life and Fate* as "a remarkable epic of Soviet horror and hearbreak."[19] The *Independent* called the novel "the 20th century's *War and Peace*."[20]

In Russia history lessons have not been properly taught or learned. While Germans went through a denazification after the war, Soviet people continued to live under Stalin for almost another decade. Khrushchev's Thaw and de-Stalinization attempts were superficial and inconsistent. Khrushchev admitted Stalin's "mistakes" but suppressed information about mass purges and the regime's other crimes. Gorbachev became the first Soviet leader to publicly denounce Stalin's "enormous and unforgivable crimes"; however, he spared Lenin and the Communist Party. In post-Soviet Russia there was no full indictment of the Communist system. Stalin's henchmen, who personally signed execution lists, were not put on trial. In Germany monuments to the victims of Nazism are ubiquitous; they keep reminding citizens that the past must not be repeated. In Russia the extent of Stalin's crimes have never become public knowledge and only a few monuments to the victims of Stalinism have been built. Gulag survivors lived out their days in poverty and isolation while millions of the regime's victims vanished from official records and public memory.

For Putin, who is striving to re-create the Soviet police state, rehabilitating Stalin has become expedient. Russian bookstores and the internet are filled with titles praising Stalin as a great statesman: *Stalin the Great*; *Stalin: Father of a Nation*; *The Great Slandered Leader: Lies and Truth about Stalin*; *"Stalin's Repressions": The XX-Century's Great Lie*, among others.

In 2009, when the Communist Party pompously celebrated Stalin's 130th birthday, over a thousand adherents laid flowers at the dictator's tomb by the Kremlin wall. In the past decade monuments to the dictator have been rebuilt in many places; Stalin posters, buses covered with the dictator's portraits, and plaques commemorating him have become a familiar sight. One can see a new Stalin bust in the heart of Moscow in the Leaders' Alley. This is where the busts of all Russia's rulers before Putin are exhibited, promoting an image of a strong state and an uninterrupted succession of great leaders. This proud history in stone endorses Putin's Russia as the heir of both the Russian Empire and the Soviet Union.

Modern-day Stalinists campaign for the return of the dictator's name to geographical places, for example, renaming Volgograd as Stalingrad. They organize Stalin's private museums and promote their views on state television and in student auditoriums. Recently the head of the Russian Orthodox Church, Patriarch Kirill, called on Russians to remember not only Stalin's "villainies," but also his successes in modernizing the country.[21] This explains the steady rise of Stalin's popularity. In 2017, according to polling conducted by the Russian Levada-Center, Stalin was named the most outstanding person of all time, followed only by Putin and Alexander Pushkin.[22]

In 2016 academician Andrei Vorobyov (the former minister of health of the Russian Federation) stated the obvious: "De-Stalinization in our country is halted. The most dreadful murderer of all times and of all peoples is widely publicized in new films where he receives a clearly positive evaluation."[23] Vorobyov was orphaned at eight when in 1936 his parents, participants in the October Revolution, were arrested.

Memorial, Russia's oldest human rights organization, campaigns to ban glorification of Stalin and Stalinism. In 2015 its proposal caused an uproar in the State Duma. (Politicians rejected it as a presumed attempt to limit freedom of speech.) In 2017, the year marking the centennial of the Bolshevik Revolution and eighty years since the beginning of Stalin's Great Purge, a public petition supporting the ban was launched.

As Grossman predicted in *Life and Fate*, Stalin's name has become linked with the Soviet victory in World War II. The victory, he writes, would help Stalin wipe out the past, along with the memory of the millions who perished during collectivization, the famine, and the purges. Putin has employed the myth about Stalin winning the war to bolster his own political power.

In 2015, during the seventieth anniversary of V-Day, central bookstores in Moscow displayed numerous war novels in their windows, but none of Grossman's. His main argument that both the Nazi and the Soviet totalitarian regimes had committed genocide, war crime, and crimes against humanity is officially denied in Russia. Under Putin the memory of Communist terror has been overlaid with the myth of the country's great history. "Russia has never recognized the crime of the Soviet regime, the crimes of the Stalin regime and the millions that died—there was no repentance," says Lev Ponomarev, one of the founders of Memorial.[24] In recent years this organization has been continually harassed and threatened with shutdown. Its historian Yuri Dmitriev, who spent two decades working in the FSB archives and locating the secret killing grounds of Stalin's terror victims in Karelia, was imprisoned in December 2016 on trumped-up charges. Dmitriev had uncovered mass graves in the forests in Sandarmoh and Krasnyi Bor, turning these places into public memorials. Since 1998 relatives have traveled annually to Sandarmoh, the main killing ground, to pay tribute. Having resurrected the identities of seventy-five hundred victims of political repression, Dmitriev published Memory Books containing the names of the executed and brief biographical information.[25] In the 1930s Gulag prisoners—many of those who worked on the construction of the White Sea Canal—were transported to Sandarmoh at night for secret mass executions. People of sixty ethnicities and different walks of life—scholars, priests, tsarist military officers, engineers, and peasants—were shot by the NKVD in this pine forest. According to Dmitriev there are over fifty such killing grounds in Karelia.

Dmitriev and his cause have united two generations of Russian dissidents. As his closed trial drags on, writers, artists, and public figures release video addresses in support. Natalya Solzhenitsyna, in her address, called Dmitriev "an honorable man who did much to commemorate the innocent victims." In December 2017 an evening of solidarity with Dmitriev filled the auditorium of Moscow's Sakharov Center. Lyudmila Ulitskaya, an internationally acclaimed writer and the granddaughter of a Gulag prisoner, called Dmitriev "the pride of our people, of our generation."[26] In April 2018 Dmitriev was aquitted of criminal charges and released; soon after, he was imprisoned again.

In Petersburg the historian Anatolij Razumov invested three decades in resurrecting the names of fifty thousand people shot by the secret police in Leningrad. The names and brief biographies of the victims fill sixteen volumes of the *Lenigrad Martyrology* he has compiled. Razumov had previously worked for Solzhenitsyn, producing an index to *The Gulag Archipelago*. His family history did not influence him: Razumov lost one distant relative to Stalin's purges. Razumov's father, a military officer, served in East Germany, and the son was inspired by German memorials to the victims of Nazism. When in 1991 post-Soviet Russia opened archives for research he began collecting information about Soviet repressions. This led to his discovery, for example, of the methods the NKVD had used to conduct mass executions of its own citizens. The bodies of the people they shot filled gigantic trenches. The truth was hidden from the victims' families for many decades.[27]

In October 2017 Putin unveiled the Wall of Sorrow, the first state-sponsored monument to the victims of Soviet terror. But in December the state celebrated the centenary of the creation of the Cheka, the Bolshevik secret police, responsible for the mass murder of Soviet citizens. The head of the FSB, Alexander Bortnikov, declared that his agency was a proud successor of the Cheka-OGPU-NKVD; that although some "excesses" in the work of the NKVD had existed locally, in 1938 Beria improved the quality of investigative work.[28] There are two versions of Soviet history in modern Russia, which means that the state has never taken responsibility for murdering millions, has never admitted its crimes once and for all; the story can be turned either way.

But glasnost did not fail. Publications in the Gorbachev era helped form the nucleus of civil society, and today such groups resist government pressure and assaults by neo-Stalinists. Although Russian society at large is afflicted with historical amnesia, thousands have committed themselves to remembrance. In 1990 a symbolic monument to the victims of Soviet repressions, the Solovetsky Stone, was installed across from the Lubyanka building.

The rock was transported from Solovetsky Island, the site of the first Soviet concentration camps. During the years of terror forty thousand people were shot in Moscow alone. On October 30, the Remembrance Day of the Victims of Political Repressions, geneticist Galina Muravnik comes to the Solovetsky Stone. Joining a sizable crowd, she waits her turn to read the names of terror victims. These names, drawn from execution lists and distributed by Memorial, are read across the country for two days, the idea inspired by a line in Akhmatova's poem "Requiem": "How I wish I could name them all." Akhmatova's words are inscribed on the Solovetsky Stone in Petersburg, another such monument. Muravnik's large family, including her revolutionary grandfather who helped establish the Bolshevik regime, perished at the height of the purges; her father, then an adolescent, was the lone survivor.

Muravnik and her father read Grossman's novels in the late 1980s. "If I previously believed that Stalin distorted Lenin's ideas, Grossman persuaded me that Lenin established the mechanism for mass repressions." This important idea works like a catalyst. It helps one to rid oneself of illusions about the Soviet past. Muravnik is among a number of Russian individuals who believe in the need for national atonement. In the fall of 2017 she spoke publicly about her family and repented on her grandfather's behalf.[29] But few are capable of such acts: it requires courage to face the truth.

Grossman remains unpopular in Russia for the same reason. It's easier to believe in a glorious past than to admit that Stalinism and Nazism were mirror images of each other.

Notes

Preface

1. Patrick Finney, introduction to "Vasily Grossman: Ruthless Truth in the Totalitarian Century," special issue, *Journal of European Studies*, 43 no. 4 (2013), http://journals.sagepub.com/doi/full/10.1177/0047244113501746, accessed July 22, 2018.

Introduction

1. Vasily Grossman, *Everything Flows*, trans. Robert Chandler and Elizabeth Chandler (New York: New York Review Books, 2009), 67. Translation copyright belongs to Robert Chandler for this work and all other Chandler translations cited.
2. Vasily Grossman, "The Hell of Treblinka," in *The Road: Stories, Journalism, and Essays*, trans. Robert Chandler, Elizabeth Chandler, and Olga Mukovnikova (New York: New York Review Books, 2010), 123.
3. Vasily Grossman, *Life and Fate*, trans. Robert Chandler (New York: Harper & Row, 1985), 581.
4. Grossman, *Everything Flows*, 164.
5. Ibid., 153.
6. Robert Conquest, *The Harvest of Sorrow: Soviet Collectivization and the Terror-Famine* (New York: Oxford University Press, 1986), 9.

1. In the Town of Berdichev

1. Vasily Grossman, "Berdichev ne v shutku, a vser'yoz," *Ogonyok*, nos. 51–52 (1929). Unless otherwise specified, translations are by the author.
2. *Favorite Tales of Sholom Aleichem*, trans. Julius Butwin and Frances Butwin (New York: Avenel Books, 1983), 1.

3. Marie Waife-Goldberg, *My Father, Sholom Aleichem* (New York: Simon and Schuster, 1968), 127.

4. Natan M. Meir, *Kiev, Jewish Metropolis: A History* (Bloomington: Indiana University Press, 2010), 1, 45.

5. Robert Service, *Trotsky: A Biography* (Cambridge, MA: Belknap Press, Harvard University Press, 2009).

6. Elie Wiesel, *Souls on Fire*, trans. Marion Wiesel (New York: Random House, 1972), 90.

7. Vasily Grossman, *Stepan Kolchugin* (Moscow: Sovetskij pisatel', 1947), 2:292.

8. "Berdychiv," in *Encyclopedia Britannica*, last modified August 12, 2016, http://www.britannica.com/place/Berdychiv, accessed July 22, 2018.

9. Meir, *Kiev*, 110–11.

10. Yuri Slezkine, *The Jewish Century* (Princeton: Princeton University Press, 2004), 122.

11. Ibid., 119–21.

12. *The Memoirs of Count Witte*, trans. Sydney Harcave (London: M. E. Sharpe, 1990), 93.

13. Slezkine, *Jewish Century*, 115.

14. Joshua Rubenstein, *Tangled Loyalties: The Life and Times of Ilya Ehrenburg* (New York: Basic Books, 1996), 10.

15. Slezkine, *Jewish Century*, 105, 116.

16. Ekaterina Korotkova-Grossman, *Vospominaniya: Rasskazy bez vymysla* (Moscow: Novyi hronograf, 2014), 11–12.

17. Slezkine, *Jewish Century*, 125.

18. *Memoirs of Count Witte*, 377–79.

19. Ibid., 715.

20. Service, *Trotsky*, 199.

21. Slezkine, *Jewish Century*, 148.

22. Ibid., 169.

23. Grossman, *Life and Fate*, 300.

24. Grossman, *Stepan*, 1:104.

25. Grossman, "In the Town of Berdichev," in *The Road*, 24, 18.

26. Grossman's (VG) letter to Semyon Osipovich (SO), November 3, 1929, Russian State Archive of Literature and Art (hereafter RGALI), F. 1710. Unless otherwise indicated, all Grossman's letters to his father come from this source. Translation is by the author.

27. Semyon Lipkin, *Zhizn' i sud'ba Vasiliya Grossmana* (Moscow: Kniga, 1990), 41.

28. Slezkine, *Jewish Century*, 127.

29. Ibid., 129. The expression belongs to Vladimir Iokheleson.

30. Gregory Freidin, ed., *The Enigma of Isaak Babel: Biography, History, Context* (Stanford: Stanford University Press, 2009), 34.

31. Osip Mandelstam, *Shum vremeni,* in *Sochineniya v dvuh tomah* (Moscow: Khudozhestvennaya literatura, 1990), 2:13.

32. Grossman, *Life and Fate,* 210–11.

33. Lipkin, *Zhizn',* 30.

34. Quoted in Slezkine, *Jewish Century,* 137.

35. Author's interview with Ekaterina Korotkova-Grossman, 2015.

36. Vasily Grossman, "Chetyre dnya," in *Vsyo techyot . . . Povesti, rasskazy, ocherki* (Moscow: Eksmo, 2010), 14.

37. Ibid., 34, 17–18.

38. Slezkine, *Jewish Century,* 124.

39. Service, *Trotsky,* 37.

40. Meir, *Kiev,* 109.

41. Grossman, *Stepan,* 1:299–300.

42. Ekaterina Savelievna's (ES) letter to VG, April 9, 1941, in Fyodor Guber, *Pamyat' i pis'ma* (Moscow: Probel, 2007), 73–74.

43. Grossman, "Four Days," in *Vsyo techyot,* 28.

44. Michael Hamm, *Kiev: A Portrait, 1800–1917* (Princeton: Princeton University Press, 1993), 221.

45. Grossman, *Stepan,* 2:222.

46. Yitzhak Arad, *The Holocaust in the Soviet Union* (Lincoln: University of Nebraska Press; Jerusalem: Yad Vashem, 2009), 11.

47. Information comes from David MacKenzie and Michael M. Curran, *A History of Russia, the Soviet Union, and Beyond* (Belmont, CA: West/Wadsworth, 1999), 375.

48. Dominic Lieven, *Nicholas II, Emperor of All the Russias* (London: John Murray, 1993), 204.

49. Grossman, *Stepan,* 2:235.

50. Hamm, *Kiev,* 221.

51. Natan Meir, "Beilis, Mendel," in *YIVO Encyclopedia of Jews in Eastern Europe,* http://www.yivoencyclopedia.org/article.aspx/Beilis_Mendel, accessed April 25, 2018.

52. Mikhail Kalnitskij, "Yushchinskij Andrei," 2013, http://www.m-necropol.ru/yushinskiy-andrei.html and "Pamyat' otroka-muchenika Andreya Yushchinskogo," http://zembin.by/pravoslavnyie-novosti/pamyat-otroka-muchenika-andreya-yushhinskogo.html, both accessed April 25, 2018.

53. Grossman, *Stepan*, 1:303.

54. "Anti-Semitism: History of the 'Protocols of the Elders of Zion,' " in *Jewish Virtual Library*, http://www.jewishvirtuallibrary.org/the-ldquo-protocols-of-the-elders-of-zion-rdquo, accessed April 25, 2018. See also Arad, *The Holocaust*, 6–7.

55. Grossman, *Stepan*, 1:205.

56. Antoine Prost, "War Losses," in *International Encyclopedia of the First World War*, http://encyclopedia.1914–1918-online.net/article/war_losses, accessed April 25, 2018.

57. New-style according to the Gregorian calendar will be used here. Russia, unlike Western Europe, was then using the old-style dates of the Julian calendar, which explains the term "February Revolution." The revolution occurred on March 8–12, 1917 (February 23–27 old style).

58. There were three successive Provisional Governments. In the third, the Mensheviks and the Socialist Revolutionaries made up the majority.

59. Semion Lyandres, *The Fall of Tsarism: Untold Stories of the February 1917 Revolution* (Oxford: Oxford University Press, 2013), 238, 220.

60. Stéphane Courtois et al., *The Black Book of Communism: Crimes, Terror, Repression*, trans. Jonathan Murphy and Mark Kramer (Cambridge, MA: Harvard University Press, 1999), 44.

61. Grossman, *Everything Flows*, 181.

62. Arad, *The Holocaust*, 12.

63. Grossman, *Stepan*, 2:369–70.

64. Grossman, *Everything Flows*, 177.

65. Oliver Radkey, *Russia Goes to the Polls: The Election to the All-Russian Constituent Assembly, 1917* (Ithaca: Cornell University Press, 1989), ix–x, 87–96.

66. Alexander N. Yakovlev, *A Century of Violence in Soviet Russia*, trans. Anthony Austin (New Haven: Yale University Press, 2002), 66.

67. Stephen Kotkin, *Stalin: Paradoxes of Power, 1878–1928* (New York: Penguin, 2014), 1:440.

68. Grossman, *Everything Flows*, 172, 181.

69. Courtois et al., *Black Book of Communism*, 68.

70. Service, *Trotsky*, 357.

71. Grossman, *Everything Flows*, 181.

72. Courtois et al., *Black Book of Communism*, 78.

73. Conquest, *Harvest of Sorrow*, 46–48.

74. Ibid., 53–54.

75. Yakovlev, *Century of Violence*, 234.

76. David Bullock, *The Russian Civil War, 1918–22* (Oxford: Osprey, 2008), 133.

77. ES letter to SO, June 1941, Ekaterina Korotkova-Grossman's archive.

78. Evan Mawdsley, *The Russian Civil War* (Edinburgh: Birlinn, 2011).

79. Slezkine, *Jewish Century*, 173.

80. Arad, *The Holocaust*, 13.

81. Nadezhda Mandelstam, *Hope Abandoned*, trans. Max Hayward (New York: Atheneum, 1974), 515.

82. Grossman, *Stepan*, 2:403.

83. Grossman, "In the Town of Berdichev," 30–31, 29.

84. Grossman, "Four Days," in *Vsyo techyot*, 27, 16.

85. Ivan Bakalo et al., "Education," in *Internet Encyclopedia of Ukraine*, reproduced from *Encyclopedia of Ukraine*, edited by Volodymyr Kubijovyc (Toronto: University of Toronto Press, 1984), vol. 1. http://www.encyclopediaofukraine.com/display.asp?linkpath=pages%5CE%5CD%5CEducation.htm, accessed April 28, 2018.

86. "Institutes of People's Education," in *Internet Encyclopedia of Ukraine*, reproduced from *Encyclopedia of Ukraine*, edited by Volodymyr Kubijovyc (Toronto: University of Toronto Press, 1988), vol. 2, http://www.encyclopediaofukraine.com/display.asp?linkpath=pages%5CI%5CN%5CInstitutesofpeopleseducation.htm, accessed April 28, 2018.

87. Estimate by the American Commission on Russian Relief in 1922. Conquest, In *Harvest of Sorrow*, 56.

88. Grossman, *Stepan*, 1:304.

2. From Science to Literature and Politics

1. Grossman, *Stepan*, 1:204.

2. Ibid., 1:310, 204–6.

3. Author's interview with Korotkova-Grossman.

4. Grossman, *Stepan*, 2:135.

5. Author's interview with Korotkova-Grossman.

6. J. A. E. Curtis, *Manuscripts Don't Burn: Mikhail Bulgakov, A Life in Letters and Diaries* (London: Bloomsbury, 1991), 48.

7. Grossman, *Stepan*, 2:102–3. Wilhelm Bölsche (1861–1939) was a German writer on natural history and instigator of humanistic naturalism in Germany. Ernst Heinrich Philipp August Haeckel (1834–1919) was a German biologist, naturalist, philosopher, and artist. Herbert Spencer was an English philosopher, biologist, anthropologist, and prominent classical

liberal political theorist of the Victorian era. He is best known for his expression "survival of the fittest," inspired by his reading of Darwin.

8. Nadezhda Mandelstam, *Hope Abandoned*, 206.

9. Grossman, *Life and Fate*, 524–25.

10. Varlam Shalamov, "Moskva 20h–30h godov," in *Novaya kniga. Vospominaniya, zapisnye knizhki, perepiska, sledstvennye dela* (Moscow: Eksmo, 2004), http://www.booksite.ru/fulltext/new/boo/ksh/ala/mov/5.htm, accessed July 22, 2018.

11. Bulgakov, quoted in Curtis, *Manuscripts*, 36, 37, 45.

12. Grossman, "Phosphorus," in *Vsyo techyot*, 374.

13. Author's interview with Maria Karpova, née Loboda, 2017.

14. "Surits Yakov," in *Elektronnaya evreiskaya entsiklopediya*, reproduced from *Kratkaya evreiskaya entsiklopediya* (Jerusalem: Biblioteka–Aliya, 1996), 8:655–56, http://www.eleven.co.il/article/13977, accessed April 25, 2018.

15. Ilya Ehrenburg, *Lyudi, gody, zhizn'*, in *Sobranie sochinenij* (Moscow: Hudozhestvennaya literatura, 1962–67), 9:711–12.

16. Author's interview with Sergei Nitochkin, 2017.

17. Gedda Surits, "Neliteraturnye druz'ya. Iz vospominanij," in *Dialog* 2 (1997–98): 422.

18. Grossman, *Everything Flows*, 156.

19. Yevgeniya Taratuta, *Kniga vospominanij* (Moscow: Yanus, 2001), 96, http://www.sakharov-center.ru/asfcd/auth/?t=page&num=7719, accessed April 25, 2018.

20. VG letter to Taratuta, December 10, 1961, *Ogonyok* 40 (1987).

21. Grossman, *Stepan*, 2:340.

22. VG letter to SO, October 8, 1927.

23. VG letter to SO, December 2, 1925.

24. VG letter to SO, October 8, 1927.

25. VG letter to SO, September 21, 1928.

26. VG letter to SO, April 10, 1929.

27. VG letter to SO, December 2, 1925.

28. VG letter to SO, January 22, 1928.

29. Grossman, *Stepan*, 2:125.

30. VG letter to SO, October 8, 1927.

31. VG letter to SO, April 12, 1928.

32. VG letter to SO, January 22, 1928.

33. Yuri Bit-Yunan and David Feldman, *Vasily Grossman v zerkale literaturnyh intrig* (Moscow: Forum, 2016), 44.

34. VG letter to SO, March 30, 1928.

35. VG letter to SO, March 30, 1928.

36. Grossman, *Everything Flows*, 150–51.

37. VG letter to SO, April 12, 1928.

38. VG letter to SO, April 25, 1928.

39. VG letter to SO, June 1, 1928.

40. VG letter to SO, June 27, 1928.

41. VG letter to SO, January 22, 1928.

42. VG letter to SO, April 25, 1928.

43. VG letter to SO, May 26, 1929.

44. ES letter to SO, May 12, 1930, Fyodor Guber's private archive.

45. ES letter to SO, April 27, 1929.

46. VG letter to SO, September 21, 1928.

47. VG letter to SO, October 6, 1928.

48. VG letter to SO, November 3, 1929.

49. VG letter to SO, September 21, 1928.

50. VG letter to SO, 1929.

51. VG letter to SO, January 26, 1929.

52. VG letter to SO, January 30, 1929.

53. VG letter to SO, 1929.

54. VG letter to SO, January 26, 1929.

55. VG letter to SO, March 14, 1929.

56. VG letter to SO, February 27, 1929.

57. VG letter to SO, March 14, 1929.

58. VG letter to SO, May 8, 1929.

59. VG letter to SO, fall 1929.

60. Ibid.

61. Bit-Yunan and Feldman, *Vasily Grossman*, 82.

62. VG letter to SO, 1929.

63. VG letter to SO, May 19, 1929.

64. "Revelations from the Russian Archives: Collectivization and Industrialization," Library of Congress, https://www.loc.gov/exhibits/archives/coll.html, accessed April 25, 2018.

65. Conquest, *Harvest of Sorrow*, 97.

66. Donald Rayfield, *Stalin and His Hangmen: An Authoritative Portrait of a Tyrant and Those Who Served Him* (London: Viking, 2004), 159.

67. VG letter to SO, 1929.

68. VG letter to SO, January 7, 1941.

69. VG letter to SO, fall 1929.

70. Grossman, "Phosphorus," 372.

71. VG letter to SO, April 10, 1929.

3. Facts on the Ground

1. Grossman, "Phosphorus," 372.

2. Vasily Grossman, *Glückauf* (Moscow: Sovetskij pisatel', 1935), 17.

3. Anne Applebaum, *Red Famine: Stalin's War on Ukraine* (Toronto: Signal, 2017), 114–15.

4. MacKenzie and Curran, *History of Russia*, 474.

5. Barbara Freese, *Coal: A Human History* (New York, Penguin Books, 2003), 3, 48–50.

6. Grossman, *Glückauf*, 229–30.

7. Ibid., 37.

8. Vasily Grossman, "The Safety Inspector," in *Great Soviet Short Stories*, trans. Sam Driver (New York: Dell, 1962), 155–56.

9. VG letter to SO, August 27, 1931.

10. Grossman, "Phosphorus," 373.

11. Ibid., 380.

12. Grossman, *Glückauf*, 259.

13. VG letter to SO, July 10, 1931.

14. Rayfield, *Stalin and His Hangmen*, 119.

15. VG letter to SO, 1931.

16. Ibid.

17. VG letter to SO, July 10, 1931.

18. Conquest, *Harvest of Sorrow*, 151.

19. Ibid., 152.

20. Applebaum, *Red Famine*, 280.

21. For a short biography of Gareth Jones by his niece, Margaret Siriol Colley, reproduced from Margaret Siriol Colley, *Gareth Jones—A Manchukuo Incident* (CD-ROM, 2001–2), http://www.garethjones.org/overview/mainoverview.htm, accessed April 25, 2018. The site includes links to Jones' newspaper articles.

22. Applebaum, *Red Famine*, 315.

23. Conquest, *Harvest of Sorrow*, 312.

24. Applebaum, *Red Famine*, 306.

25. Nadezhda Mandelstam, *Hope against Hope*, trans. Max Hayward (New York: Modern Library, 1999), 159.

26. Vasily Grossman, "The Sistine Madonna," in *The Road*, 171. Konotop is a city in Ukraine's northeast, the region bordering Russia.

27. VG letter to SO, August 1, 1931.

28. Korotkova-Grossman, *Vospominaniya*, 46.

29. VG letter to SO, August 1, 1931.

30. Conquest, *Harvest of Sorrow*, 185.

31. Osip Mandelstam, *Journey to Armenia*, trans. Sidney Monas (San Francisco: George F. Ritchie, 1979), 54.

32. VG letter to SO, winter 1932.

33. Ibid.

34. Ibid.

35. RGALI, F. 1710/1/70.

36. RGALI, F. 1710/1/94.

37. RGALI, F. 1710/1/98.

38. Grossman, *Glückauf*, 11–13.

39. Author's interview with Elena Surits, 2016.

40. ES letter to SO, 1930s, Fyodor Guber's private archive.

41. VG letter to SO, August 26 (13?), 1932.

42. Conquest, *Harvest of Sorrow*, 248.

43. VG letter to SO, August 13, 1932.

44. Ilya Zemtsov, *Encyclopedia of Soviet Life* (New Brunswick: Transaction, 1991), 297–99.

45. VG letter to SO, July 6, 1932.

46. Grossman, *Glückauf*, 5.

47. Curtis, *Manuscripts*, 52.

48. VG letter to SO, August 26 (13?), 1932.

49. Alexander Sharov, "Iz vospominanij o Vasilii Grossmane," in *Okoyom: povesti, vospominaniya* (Moscow, Sovetskij pisatel', 1990), 400. It's unknown whether the original manuscript of *Glückauf* survives. In any case, it is not found at the Russian State Archive of Literature and Art where Grossman's papers are deposited.

50. Bit-Yunan and Feldman, *Vasily Grossman*, 176–77. Grossman was bending the truth when he said he'd worked in the mines for three years, exaggerating his work record to impress Gorky.

51. Maxim Gorky's letter to VG, October 7, 1932, in Maxim Gorky, *Sobranie sochinenij* (Moscow: Goslitizdat, 1955), 30:261–63.

52. Grossman, *Glückauf*, 5.

53. Ken Howard and Rauf Israfilov, eds., *Current Problems of Hydrogeology in Urban Areas, Urban Agglomerates and Industrial Centers* (Springler: NATO Science Series, 2002), 4:366.

54. "Ecology," in *Visit Donetsk*, http://visitdonetsk.com/ecology-donetsk-has-reputation-city-roses%E2%80%A6, accessed April 28, 2018.

55. *Vospominaniya o Babele* (Moscow, 1989), http://www.lib.ru/PROZA/BABEL/about_wospominaniya.txt, accessed April 25, 2018.

4. Great Expectations

1. Conquest, *Harvest of Sorrow*, 124, 170.

2. Grossman, *Life and Fate*, 122.

3. VG letter to SO, April 21, 1933.

4. Ibid.

5. VG letter to SO, May 16, 1933.

6. Sheila Fitzpatrick, "Memoirs of a Revolutionary by Victor Serge," *Guardian*, August 17, 2012, https://www.theguardian.com/books/2012/aug/17/memoirs-revolutionary-victor-serge-review, accessed April 25, 2018.

7. Chandler, introduction to *The Road*, 7.

8. Bit-Yunan and Feldman, *Vasily Grossman*, 133.

9. VG letter to SO, February 2, 1933.

10. Vasily Grossman, "Tseilonskij grafit," 1935, http://lib.ru/PROZA/GROSSMAN/r_grafit.txt, accessed April 25, 2018.

11. Ceylon's or Sri Lanka's unique deposits of vein-type, or lump, graphite had a carbon content of more than 90 percent.

12. Conquest, *Harvest of Sorrow*, 248.

13. VG letter to Olga Rodanevich, June 11, 1933, RGALI, F. 1710/3/73.

14. Grossman, *Everything Flows*, 134–35.

15. VG letter to SO, 1933.

16. VG letter to SO, February 19, 1934.

17. VG letter to SO, July 19, 1933. See Chekhov's phrase in A. P. Chekhov, *Polnoe sobranie sochinenij i pisem* (Moscow: Nauka, 1987), 17:177.

18. VG letter to SO, August 3, 1933.

19. Edelweiss, a rugged alpine flower. It has been used as a symbol for alpinism and is the national symbol of Austria, Switzerland, Bulgaria, and Romania.

20. Yuri Slezkine, *The House of Government: A Saga of the Russian Revolution* (Princeton: Princeton University Press, 2017), 428.

21. Conquest, *Harvest of Sorrow*, 237.

22. Applebaum, *Red Famine*, 197.

23. VG letter to SO, November 17, 1933.

24. VG letter to SO, 1933.

25. VG letter to SO, January 8, 1934.

26. VG letter to SO, January 24, 1934.

27. Ibid.

28. VG letter to SO, April 17, 1934.

29. VG letter to SO, January 8, 1934.

30. VG letter to SO, March 26, 1934.

31. VG letter to SO, April 3, 1934.

32. Lipkin, *Zhizn'*, 5.

33. Freidin, *The Enigma of Isaak Babel*, 70.

34. Guber, *Pamyat'*, 40–41.

35. Grossman, "In the Town of Berdichev," 16.

36. Ibid., 25, 26.

37. VG letter to SO, April 17, 1934.

38. Maxim Gorky, "Russia and the Jews," trans. A. Yarmolinsky, http://www.online-literature.com/maxim-gorky/4430/, accessed April 25, 2018.

39. Quoted in Slezkine, *Jewish Century*, 164–65.

40. Freidin, *The Enigma of Isaak Babel*, 30.

41. Slezkine, *Jewish Century*, 134.

42. VG letter to SO, May 8, 1934.

43. VG letter to SO, June 11, 1934.

44. Rayfield, *Stalin and His Hangmen*, 220.

45. Surits, "Neliteraturnye druz'ya," 428.

46. VG letter to SO, April 26, 1934.

47. VG letter to SO, 1933.

48. Mass executions of Gulag prisoners were conducted in Prokopievsk. See "Spisok lagerei gulaga," http://chort.square7.ch/Pis/Gulag.pdf, accessed April 25, 2018.

49. Korotkova-Grossman, *Vospominaniya*, 201–2.

50. Natalya Semyonova, "Verili v pobedu svyato," in *Institut russkoi literatury Rossijskoi Akademii Nauk* (St. Petersburg: Pushkinskij Dom, 2015), 71.

51. Flat and resembling blinis, or pancakes, these pies with savoury or sweet stuffing were fried in oil. Apparently they are still sold at the Konotop junction railway station.

52. Evgeny Dobrenko, *Political Economy of Socialist Realism* (New Haven: Yale University Press, 2007), 60.

53. Régine Robin, *Socialist Realism: An Impossible Aesthetic*, trans. Catherine Porter (Stanford: Stanford University Press, 1992), 212.

54. Guber, *Pamyat'*, 30.

55. Applebaum, *Red Famine*, 136.

56. Guber, *Pamyat'*, 31.

57. Rayfield, *Stalin and His Hangmen*, 239.

58. Slezkine, *House of Government*, 717.

59. VG letter to SO, June 30, 1934.

60. VG letter to SO, 1934.

61. Ibid.

62. VG letter to SO, December 16, 1934.

63. VG letter to SO, September 23, 1934.

64. VG letter to SO, September 8, 1934.

65. Ibid.

66. VG letter to SO, November 23, 1934.

67. VG letter to SO, February 5, 1935.

68. VG letter to SO, April 15, 1935.

69. "Alexei Stakhanov," *Russiapedia*, http://russiapedia.rt.com/prominent-russians/history-and-mythology/aleksey-stakhanov/, accessed April 25, 2018.

70. Dobrenko, *Political Economy of Socialist Realism*, 169.

71. Grossman, *Glückauf*, 16.

72. VG letter to SO, August 4, 1935.

73. Guber, *Pamyat'*, 29.

74. Grossman was in love with Gedda Surits. In the mid-1950s he became involved with a younger woman, of whom we know only that she was a scientist and she was Jewish. Grossman wanted to introduce his daughter to his new companion, but something interfered. In 1998 Katya wrote a short memoir about this mystery woman she never met: "I was already married, and my father was in his fifties. I felt his whole life was consumed with this last strong and deep feeling. . . . I was very curious about this woman. . . . My father told me quite a bit about his new companion. She wasn't domestic at all. She's made a brilliant career, held a doctorate in chemistry, and her name was well-recognized. She was an audacious driver. She was audacious in everything." Korotkova-Grossman, "Iz tsikla 'Okruzhenie,' " *Dialog* 2 (1997–98).

75. Olga Matvienko, "Ostat'sya chelovekom," *Sochinskij kraeved*, February 21, 2016.

76. Author's interview with Elena Kozhichkina, 2015.

77. John Garrard and Carol Garrard, *The Bones of Berdichev: The Life and Fate of Vasily Grossman* (New York: Free Press, 1996), 121.

78. ES letter to SO, November 3, 1935.

79. VG letter to SO, November 27, 1935.

5. The Dread New World

1. Grossman, *Life and Fate*, 457.

2. Courtois et al., *Black Book of Communism*, part 1.

3. Nadezhda Mandelstam, *Hope against Hope*, 161.

4. Varlam Shalamov, "Vospominaniya," https://www.booksite.ru/fulltext/new/boo/ksh/ala/mov/5.htm, accessed June 20, 2018.

5. Boris Andronikashvili-Pilnyak, "Dva izgoya, dva muchenika: Boris Pilnyak i Evgeny Zamyatin," *Znamya* 9 (1994): 126.

6. Vitaly Shentalinsky, *Arrested Voices: Resurrecting the Disappeared Writers of the Soviet Union*, trans. John Crowfoot (New York: Free Press, 1993), 24.

7. Quoted in Cynthia Ozick, introduction to *The Complete Works of Isaak Babel*, ed. Nathalie Babel, trans. Peter Constantine (New York: Norton, 2002), 23.

8. VG letter to SO, November 12, 1936.

9. Guber, *Pamyat'*, 35.

10. Grossman, *Life and Fate*, 117, 116.

11. Simon Sebag Montefiore, *Stalin: The Court of the Red Tsar* (London: Weidenfeld and Nicolson, 2003), 166.

12. Korney Chukovsky, *Diary, 1901–1969*, trans. Michael Henry Heim (New Haven: Yale University Press, 1991), 326.

13. Grossman, *Everything Flows*, 135.

14. Anne Applebaum, *The Gulag: A History* (New York: Doubleday, 2003), 564–65.

15. Quoted in Tovah Yedlin, *Maxim Gorky: A Political Biography* (London: Westport, 1999), 203–4.

16. Montefiore, *Stalin*, 167.

17. Rayfield, *Stalin and His Hangmen*, 270.

18. Grossman, *Life and Fate*, 526.

19. Quoted in Oleg Khlevniuk, *The History of the Gulag: From Collectivization to the Great Terror*, trans. Vadim Staklo (New Haven: Yale University Press, 2004), 141.

20. Alexander N. Yakovlev's Archive, "Lubyanka," document 152, July 31, 1937, http://www.alexanderyakovlev.org/fond/issues-doc/61134, accessed April 25, 2018.

21. Oleg Khlevniuk, *Stalin: New Biography of a Dictator*, trans. Nora Seligman Favorov (New Haven: Yale University Press, 2015), 150–51.

22. According to the data released by Memorial, in 1937, at the height of the purges, 860,160 people were convicted of political crimes and of those approximately half received capital punishments. In 1938, when arrests began to subside, there were 625,680 convictions and 372,210 executions. See N. G. Ohotin and A. B. Roginsky, "O masshtabe politicheskih repressij v SSSR pri Staline: 1921–1953," *Demoscop* 313–14, December 10–31, 2007, http://demoscope.ru/weekly/2007/0313/analit01.php#1, accessed April 25, 2018.

23. Robert Conquest, *The Great Terror: A Reassessment* (Oxford: Oxford University Press, 2008), 205.

24. Alan Bullock, *Hitler and Stalin: Parallel Lives* (Toronto: McClelland and Stewart, 1993), 717.

25. Grossman, *Life and Fate*, 627.

26. *The Road*, 301.

27. Guber, *Pamyat'*, 31–33.

28. Ibid., 33.

29. Khlevniuk, *History of the Gulag*, 169.

30. Ibid., 147.

31. Grossman, *Life and Fate*, 288.

32. The Moscow geneticist Galina Muravnik told this author how her grandparents, active during the Bolshevik Revolution, were charged with Trotskyist activity and physically annihilated at the height of the purges. Her father, aged ten in 1937, asked to be admitted to an orphanage: his grandmother was afraid to shelter him.

33. Quoted in Bit-Yunan and Feldman, *Vasily Grossman*, 251.

34. Lipkin, *Zhizn'*, 8.

35. Shentalinsky, *Arrested Voices*, 192–93.

36. Grossman, *Life and Fate*, 621–22.

37. Shentalinsky, *Arrested Voices*, 27.

38. Quoted in Bit-Yunan and Feldman, *Vasily Grossman*, 247.

39. Grossman, *Life and Fate*, 623.

40. Author's interview with Elena Kozhichkina, 2016. Grossman called Olga by the pet name Lyusenka.

41. In *Vasily Grossman* Bit-Yunan and Feldman speculate that Grossman was helped by Yezhov's wife, Yevgeniya. However, she had no influence with her husband and had refused even Babel's request to intercede on behalf of a friend.

42. Rayfield, *Stalin and His Hangmen*, 319.
43. Shentalinsky, *Arrested Voices*, 187–93.
44. See *Svyato-Ekaterininskij muzhskoi monastyr'*, http://www.ekaterinamon
    .ru/index.php3?id=128, accessed April 25, 2018.
45. Nadezhda Mandelstam, *Vospominaniya* (Moscow: Soglasie, 1999), 382–83.
46. Lipkin, *Zhizn'*, 77.
47. Vasily Grossman, "Mama," in *The Road*, 206.
48. Ibid., 211.
49. Grossman, *The Road*, 213–14.
50. Vasily Grossman, "A Young Woman and an Old Woman," in *The Road*, 47.
51. Ibid., 48.
52. Bit-Yunan and Feldman, *Vasily Grossman*, 240, 256.
53. Vera Ivanovna Dan'ko, "Reminiscences." Vera's unpublished reminiscences
    were given to the author by her daughter, Maria Loboda (Karpova).
54. Grossman, "Mama," in *The Road*, 211.
55. Grossman, *Life and Fate*, 174–75.

6. The Inevitable War

1. Arad, *The Holocaust*, 36–37.
2. Bullock, *Hitler and Stalin*, 608.
3. Arad, *The Holocaust*, 38.
4. Ilya Ehrenburg, *Memoirs, 1921–1941*, trans. Tatania Shebunina and Yvonne
   Kapp (Cleveland: World Publishing, 1964), 474.
5. Nikolai Sokolov, "Sovetskie gazety 1939 goda: Mesto 'fashistov' zanyali
   'germanskie voiska,'" September 1, 2009, http://ria.ru/politics
   /20090901/183144226.html, accessed April 25, 2018.
6. Ehrenburg, *Memoirs*, 475.
7. Timothy Snyder, *Bloodlands: Europe between Hitler and Stalin* (New York:
   Basic Books, 2010), 119.
8. Sokolov, "Sovetskie."
9. *Izvestia*, January 9, 1939.
10. Snyder, *Bloodlands*, 153.
11. VG letter to SO, April 12, 1940.
12. Ehrenburg, *Memoirs*, 498.
13. Ibid.
14. Ibid.
15. Vasily Grossman, *If You Believe the Pythagoreans*, Znamya 7 (1946).

16. Tigre-singe (tiger-monkey) was Voltaire's epigrammatic definition of his countrymen during the Reign of Terror.

17. Grossman, *Stepan*, 2:308.

18. RGALI, F. 1710/3/54.

19. VG letter to SO, 1939.

20. VG letter to SO, January 12, 1941.

21. Yevgeniya Taratuta, "Chestnaya zhizn' i tyazhkaya sud'ba," *Ogonyok* 40 (1987).

22. Lipkin, *Zhizn'*, 10.

23. See Maxim D. Shrayer, ed., *An Anthology of Jewish-Russian Literature: Two Centuries of Dual Identity in Prose and Poetry* (Armonk, NY: M. E. Sharpe, 2007), 1:539.

24. Solomon Volkov, *Shostakovich and Stalin: The Extraordinary Relationship between the Great Composer and the Brutal Dictator*, trans. Antonina Bouis (New York: Knopf, 2004), 160.

25. Lipkin, *Zhizn'*, 6.

26. Anatoly Bocharov, *Vasily Grossman: Zhizn', tvorchestvo, sud'ba* (Moscow: Sovetskij pisatel', 1990), 12.

27. ES letter to VG, December 1940, Korotkova-Grossman's archive.

28. VG letter to SO, December 1940.

29. Lipkin, *Zhizn'*, 8.

30. VG letter to SO, April 12, 1940.

31. Grossman, "Alexander Roskin," RGALI, F. 1702/2/933.

32. Ibid.

33. Vasily Grossman, *Za pravoe delo* (Moscow: Voenizdat, 1954), 117.

34. N. G. Okhotin and A. B. Roginsky, "O masshtabe politicheskih repressij v SSSR pri Staline: 1921–1953," December 10–31, 2007, http://demoscope.ru/weekly/2007/0313/analit01.php#1, accessed April 25, 2018.

35. Quoted in Bullock, *Hitler and Stalin*, 685.

36. Ibid., 689.

37. Ehrenburg, *Memoirs*, 506.

38. ES letter to VG, April 9, 1941.

39. Molotov's speech at the Extraordinary Eighth Congress of Soviets of the USSR, November 25, 1936. *Pravda*, November 30, 1936. Also http://www.yadvashem.org/yv/ru/education/learning_environments/families/memory.asp, accessed July 23, 2018.

40. Arad, *The Holocaust*, 532–33.

41. Lipkin, *Zhizn'*, 59.

42. Grossman, *Life and Fate*, 72.

43. Grossman, *Za pravoe delo*, 116.

7. 1941

1. Bullock, *Hitler and Stalin*, 701.

2. Ibid., 713.

3. Grossman, *Za pravoe delo*, 68–69.

4. Bullock, *Hitler and Stalin*, 716.

5. Ibid., 717.

6. Ehrenburg, *Memoirs*, 507.

7. Ilya Altman and Joshua Rubenstein, eds., *The Unknown Black Book: The Holocaust in the German-Occupied Soviet Territories*, trans. Christopher Morris and Joshua Rubenstein (Bloomington: Indiana University Press, 2008), 6.

8. Arad, *The Holocaust*, 80.

9. Ilya Ehrenburg and Vasily Grossman, eds., *The Complete Black Book of Russian Jewry*, translated by John Glad and James Lavine (New Brunswick, NJ: Transaction, 2002), 12–20.

10. According to Yitzhak Arad, one-third of a total of twenty-four thousand Berdichev Jews managed to escape. Arad, *The Holocaust*, 80.

11. ES letter to SO, June 25, 1941.

12. Ekaterina Savelievna's letters to her son come from Ekaterina Korotkova-Grossman's private archive.

13. VG letter to SO, September 9, 1941.

14. VG letter to SO, October 1, 1941.

15. VG letter to SO, May 15, 1942.

16. Arad, *The Holocaust*, 347.

17. Grossman, *Za pravoe delo*, 120. I am quoting Robert Chandler's translation of this passage from the 2019 translation of *Stalingrad* (Grossman's initial title for the novel *For the Right Cause*).

18. VG letter to SO, November 1, 1942.

19. David Ortenberg, *Vremya ne vlastno: Pisateli na voine* (Moscow: Sovetskij pisatel', 1979), 314.

20. Grigory Baklanov, *Sobranie sochinenij* (Moscow, 2003), 5:32.

21. MacKenzie and Curran, *History of Russia*, 528.

22. Bullock, *Hitler and Stalin*, 703.

23. Baklanov, *Sobranie*, 5:34.

24. Vasily Grossman, *Notebooks*, in *Gody voiny* (Moscow: Pravda, 1989), 244, 251. Unless otherwise specified, information from Grossman's *Notebooks* comes from this edition.

25. Ibid., 247.

26. Ibid., 249.

27. Ibid., 253.

28. Bullock, *Hitler and Stalin*, 726.

29. Altman and Rubenstein, *The Unknown Black Book*, 6.

30. Snyder, *Bloodlands*, 182, 184.

31. Bullock, *Hitler and Stalin*, 726–28.

32. Anthony Beevor, ed., *A Writer at War: Vasily Grossman with the Red Army, 1941–1945*, trans. Anthony Beevor and Luba Vinogradova (London: Harvill, 2005), 38.

33. Grossman, *Notebooks*, 277.

34. Grigory Baklanov, "Vse knigi o voine," *Delovoi vtornik*, May 6, 2003.

35. Grossman, *Notebooks*, 279.

36. Ibid., 280.

37. Ibid., 281.

38. Ibid., 287.

39. Ibid., 289.

40. Ibid., 290–91.

41. Bullock, *Hitler and Stalin*, 728.

42. Grossman, *Notebooks*, 290.

43. Tvardovsky's letter to Maria Tvardovskaya, December 13, 1941, in Alexander Tvardovsky, *"Ya v svoyu hodil ataku . . ." Dnevniki. Pis'ma. 1941–1945* (Moscow: Vagrius, 2005), 51.

44. VG letter to OM, October 14, 1941, *Voprosy literatury* 3 (2005).

45. Ilya Ehrenburg, *Vospominaniya* (Moscow: Sovetskij pisatel', 1990), 2:348.

46. Bullock, *Hitler and Stalin*, 691.

47. Ibid., 730.

48. VG letter to Olga Guber (OM), December 20, 1941. Unless otherwise specified, Grossman's letters to his wife come from Guber, *Pamyat'*.

49. Ibid.

50. Ilya Ehrenburg, *The War, 1941–45*, in *Men, Years, Life*, trans. Tatania Shebunina and Yvonne Kapp (London: Macgibbon and Kee, 1964), 5:38.

51. Beevor, *A Writer at War*, 63.

52. Grossman, *Notebooks*, 314.

8. The Battle of Stalingrad

1. VG letter to SO, February 25, 1942.
2. Ibid.
3. Beevor, *A Writer at War*, 98.
4. Vasily Grossman, *Zhizn' i sud'ba* (Moscow: Slovo, 1999), 129.
5. VG letter to SO, March 7, 1942.
6. Grossman, *Notebooks*, 294.
7. VG letter to SO, February 1, 1942.
8. Catherine Merridale, "Stalin's Order No. 227: 'Not a Step Back,' " July 28, 2011, http://www.thehistoryreader.com/modern-history/stalins-order-227-step-back/, accessed April 25, 2018.
9. Grossman, *Notebooks*, 296.
10. Michael Geyer and Sheila Fitzpatrick, *Stalinism and Nazism Compared* (Cambridge: Cambridge University Press, 2009), 387. Also see Merridale.
11. VG letter to SO, March 1 (6?), 1942.
12. Maria Tvardovskaya's letter to Tvardovsky, April 29, 1942 in *"Ya v svoyu hodil ataku,"* 92–93.
13. VG letter to SO, June 17, 1942.
14. Bullock, *Hitler and Stalin*, 771–72.
15. Vasily Grossman, *Narod bessmerten,* in *Gody voiny* (Moscow, 1946), 137–38.
16. Ibid., 30.
17. Ibid., 26–31.
18. Ibid., 25.
19. David Ortenberg, *God 1942*, http://militera.lib.ru/memo/russian/ortenberg_di2/07.html, accessed April 25, 2018.
20. VG letter to SO, July 12, 1942.
21. VG letter to SO, August 18, 1942.
22. Beevor, *A Writer at War*, 124.
23. Bullock, *Hitler and Stalin*, 777.
24. Grossman, *Life and Fate*, 382.
25. In 1925 Tsaritsyn was renamed after Stalin.
26. Bullock, *Hitler and Stalin*, 773.
27. Beevor, *A Writer at War*, 150.
28. Grossman, *Life and Fate*, 388.
29. Grossman, *Notebooks*, 340.
30. Ibid., 343.
31. Reina Pennington, "Women and the Battle of Stalingrad," in *Russia: War, Peace and Diplomacy; Essays in Honour of John Erickson*, eds. Ljubica

Erickson and Mark Erickson (London: Weidenfeld and Nicolson, 2005), 169–211.

32. Grossman, *Notebooks*, 344.

33. Ibid., 344–45.

34. Grossman, *Za pravoe delo*, 361.

35. Beevor, *A Writer at War*, 119.

36. Bullock, *Hitler and Stalin*, 775.

37. Grossman, "Stalingradskij front," in *Gody voiny* (1946), 280.

38. Grossman, *Notebooks*, 345.

39. Antony Beevor, *Stalingrad: The Fateful Siege, 1942–43* (London: Penguin Books, 1999), 174–75.

40. Beevor, *A Writer at War*, 168–69.

41. Grossman, "Stalingradskaia bitva," in *Gody voiny* (1946), 194.

42. Beevor, *A Writer at War*, 151.

43. Ibid., 155.

44. Grossman, *Life and Fate*, 430–31.

45. Ibid., 436–37.

46. Grossman, "Glazami Chekhova," in *Gody voiny* (1946), 227.

47. Grossman, *Za pravoe delo*, 258.

48. Ortenberg, *Vremya ne vlastno*, 317.

49. VG letter to OM, June 28, 1943.

50. Guber, *Pamyat'*, 54.

51. VG letter to OM, September 10, 1942.

52. Grossman, "Stalingradskoe voisko" in *Gody voiny* (1946), 269.

53. Beevor, *A Writer at War*, 171.

54. Grossman, *Life and Fate*, 39.

55. Beevor, *A Writer at War*, 174.

56. Grossman, "The Axis of the Main Offensive," in *Gody voiny* (1946), 233.

57. Ibid., 240.

58. Ibid., 238.

59. http://zema.su/blog/mamaev-kurgan-i-rodina-mat-v-volgograde-opisanie-i-fotoekskursiya-foto, accessed April 25, 2018.

60. Grossman, *Life and Fate*, 440.

61. Ibid., 435–36.

62. Beevor, *Stalingrad*, 195.

63. Beevor, *A Writer at War*, 175.

64. Grossman, *Life and Fate*, 427.

65. Grossman, "Napravlenie glavnogo udara," in *Gody voiny* (1946), 242.

66. Grossman, "Po dorogam nastupleniya," in *Gody voiny* (1946), 248.

67. Ibid., 246.

68. Grossman, "The New Day," in *Gody voiny* (1946), 251–55.

69. Erich Maria Remarque, *All Quiet on the Western Front*, trans. A. W. Wheen (Boston: Little, Brown, 1929), 74.

70. Ecclesiastes 1:5, King James Bible.

71. VG letter to OM, November 15, 1942.

72. Grossman, *Notebooks*, 400.

73. Grossman, *Gody voiny* (1946), 258.

74. Ibid., 264.

75. Ibid., 278.

76. This vigorous song was rearranged in Soviet Russia. Andrei Globa (1888–1964), a Russian playwright, poet, and translator who composed the lyrics, disregarded the original poetry. Moreover, Beethoven's music was played in slow tempo, making the Irish Feast Song sound like a melancholy Slavic ballad. The Russian version of the song begins with the words: "A snowstorm is howling." In Grossman's day the song was highly popular.

77. Grossman, "Stalingradskoe voisko," in *Gody voiny* (1946), 267–68.

78. A German socialist, Liebknecht co-founded with Rosa Luxemburg the Communist Party of Germany; he was best known for his opposition to World War I in the Reichstag. Grossman idealized him in his youth and mentions his name in *Stepan Kolchugin*.

79. Ehrenburg, *Vospominaniya*, 2:349.

80. Grossman, *Life and Fate*, 372, 376.

81. Ehrenburg, *Vospominaniya*, 2:350.

82. Grossman, *Notebooks*, 365.

83. Beevor, *A Writer at War*, 205.

84. Guber, *Pamyat'*, 56.

85. VG letter to OM, August 17, 1943.

86. VG letter to OM, December 5, 1942.

87. David Ortenberg, *Iyun'– dekabr' sorok pervogo* (Moscow: Sovetskij pisatel', 1984), http://militera.lib.ru/memo/russian/ortenberg_di1/01.html, accessed April 25, 2018.

88. Ehrenburg, *Vospominaniya*, 2:349.

89. VG letter to OM, August 17, 1943.

90. David Ortenberg, *Sorok tretij* (Moscow: Politizdat, 1991), 217.

91. Guber, *Pamyat'*, 64.

92. Beevor, *A Writer at War*, 225.

9. Arithmetic of Brutality

1. Altman and Rubenstein, *The Unknown Black Book*, xvii.

2. Ibid., 3.

3. Shimon Redlich, *War, Holocaust and Stalinism: A Documented History of the Jewish Anti-Fascist Committee in the USSR* (Luxembourg: Harwood Academic, 1995), 96.

4. Altman and Rubenstein, *The Unknown Black Book*, xxi.

5. Redlich, *War*, 95.

6. Altman and Rubenstein, *The Unknown Black Book*, 21.

7. Beevor, *A Writer at War*, 105.

8. Grossman, *Notebooks*, 367.

9. Arad, *The Holocaust*, 289.

10. Ibid., 287–88.

11. VG letter to SO, March 20, 1943.

12. Lawrence Langer has established the term "choiceless choices" in *Versions of Survival: The Holocaust and the Human Spirit* (1982), https://www.jewishvirtuallibrary.org/langer-lawrence-l, accessed June 27, 2018.

13. Vasily Grossman, "The Old Teacher," in *The Road*, 90.

14. Ibid., 93.

15. Ibid., 109.

16. Ibid., 111.

17. Ibid., 102, 109.

18. Ibid., 114.

19. Ibid., 104.

20. Ortenberg, *Sorok tretij*, 399.

21. Rubenstein, *Tangled Loyalties*, 205.

22. Altman and Rubenstein, *The Unknown Black Book*, 18.

23. Bullock, *Hitler and Stalin*, 794.

24. Beevor, *A Writer at War*, 236–37.

25. Quoted in ibid., 234.

26. Grossman, "Iyul' 1943 goda," in *Gody voiny* (1946), 327.

27. Ortenberg, *Sorok tretij*, 357.

28. Bullock, *Hitler and Stalin*, 794.

29. Grossman, "Iyul' 1943 goda," in *Gody voiny* (1946), 319.

30. Grossman, preface to Ehrenburg and Grossman, *The Complete Black Book of Russian Jewry*, xxix.

31. Grossman, "Orel," in *Gody voiny* (1946), 332.

32. Grossman, "Ukraina," in *Gody voiny* (1946), 346.

33. Ibid., 345.

34. Ibid.," 345–54.

35. Arad, *The Holocaust*, 175.

36. Ehrenburg and Grossman, *The Complete Black Book of Russian Jewry*, 11.

37. Grossman, "Ukraina," in *Gody voiny* (1946), 354.

38. Arad, *The Holocaust*, 350.

39. Ibid., 347.

40. Ibid., 347–48.

41. The full text of "Ukraina bez evreev" is found in RGALI, F. 618/14/355. In 2011 Polly Zavadivker published her translation of this article, assuming that Riga's journal *VEK: Vestnik Evreiskoi Kultury* 4 (1990) had reproduced the complete Russian version. This was not so. A comparison of Zavadivker's translation with Grossman's original version reveals that *VEK* did not reproduce it faithfully and cut paragraphs. Previously, "Ukraine without Jews" appeared in the 1985 Russian back-translation from the Yiddish by Rokhl Baumvol'. See Shimon Markish, ed., *Na evreiski temy: Primer Vasiliya Grossmana* (Jerusalem: Biblioteka–Aliya, 1985), 2:333–40. "Ukraina bez evreev" is yet to be translated in full.

42. Arad, *The Holocaust*, 190.

43. Altman and Rubenstein, *The Unknown Black Book*, 5.

44. Ehrenburg, *Vospominaniya*, 2:347.

45. Redlich, *War*, 97.

46. Altman and Rubenstein, *The Unknown Black Book*, xx.

47. Beevor, *A Writer at War*, 251.

48. Guber, *Pamyat'*, 77.

49. Grossman's letter in Robert Chandler's translation is published in *The Road*, 265–66.

50. Ehrenburg and Grossman, *The Complete Black Book of Russian Jewry*, 12–20. According to the Jewish Museum in Moscow, over sixteen thousand Jews were killed in Berdichev.

51. RGALI, F. 1710/1/110.

52. Ehrenburg and Grossman, *The Complete Black Book of Russian Jewry*, 12–20.

53. Rosa Menaker's letter to VG, June 2, 1946, in Guber, *Pamyat'*, 77–78.

54. Grossman, "Mysli o vesennem nastuplenii," in *Gody voiny* (1946), 357–71.

55. Ehrenburg and Grossman, *The Complete Black Book of Russian Jewry*, 59.

56. Altman and Rubenstein, *The Unknown Black Book*, 14.

57. The name in Grossman's *Notebooks* is Amnon rather than Simon, as in Beevor, *A Writer at War*. See Grossman, *Notebooks*, 433.

58. Beevor, *A Writer at War*, 271.

59. Grossman, "Bobruiskij 'kotyol,' " in *Gody voiny* (1946), 380.

60. Ibid., 388.

61. Grossman, "Dobro sil'nee zla," in *Gody voiny* (1946), 397. Karachev is an ancient Russian town in the Bryansk region. Most of its architecture was destroyed during World War II.

62. Beevor, *A Writer at War*, 272.

63. Grossman, "Dobro sil'nee zla," in *Gody voiny* (1946), 390.

64. Rubenstein, *Tangled Loyalties*, 221–22.

65. Grossman, "V gorodah i selah Pol'shi," in *Gody voiny* (1946), 406.

66. Julian Tuwim, *We, Polish Jews*, trans. Krystyna Piórkowska, August 1944, http://www.polish-jewish-heritage.org/Eng/RYTM_Tuwim_Eng.htm, accessed April 25, 2018. Tuwim's manifesto is also found in Grossman's file in RGALI, F. 1710/1/147.

67. Michał Sobelman, "Zionists and 'Polish Jews': Palestinian Reception of *We, Polish Jews*." *Folia Litteraria Polonica* 6, no. 36 (2016).

68. Judith Tydor Baumel, "Extermination Camps," in *The Holocaust Encyclopedia*, ed. Walter Laqueur and Judith Tydor Baumel (New Haven: Yale University Press, 2001), 177.

69. *Majdanek*, http://www.majdanek.eu/en/history, accessed April 25, 2018.

70. Konstantin Simonov, "Extermination Camp," in Ilya Ehrenburg and Konstantin Simonov, *In One Newspaper: A Chronicle of Unforgettable Years*, trans. Anatol Kagan (New York: Sphinx, 1985), 419.

71. Ibid., 411–12.

72. RGALI, F. 1710/3/10.

73. E. A. Dolmatovsky, *Ochevidets: Kniga dokumental'nyh rasskazov o zhizni avtora i ego sovremennikov v XX veke, v sovetskoe vremya* (Nizhnij Novgorod: DEKOM, 2014), 122–26.

74. Bettina Stangneth, *Eichmann Before Jerusalem: The Unexamined Life of a Mass Murderer*, trans. Ruth Martin (London: Bodley Head, 2014), 142, 175–76, 269.

75. Philippe Sands, *East West Street: On the Origins of "Genocide" and "Crimes against Humanity"* (New York: Knopf, 2016), 271.

76. *The Destruction of the European Jews* was first published in 1961.

77. All quotations from "The Hell of Treblinka" come from Grossman, *The Road*, 116–62.

78. Itzhak Arad, *Bełżec, Sobibor, Treblinka: The Operation Reinhard Death Camps* (Bloomington: Indiana University Press, 1987), 37.

79. Ibid., 186.

80. Ibid., 212.

81. Ibid., 186.

82. Yankel Wiernik, *A Year in Treblinka* (New York: American Representation of the General Workers' Union of Poland, 1945), http://www.zchor.org/treblink/wiernik.htm, accessed April 25, 2018.

83. Bocharov, *Grossman*, 116.

84. Rubenstein, *Tangled Loyalties*, 425.

85. Surits, "Neliteraturnye druz'ya."

86. Beevor, *A Writer at War*, 319, 311.

87. United States Holocaust Memorial Museum, "Warsaw," in *Holocaust Encyclopedia*, https://www.ushmm.org/wlc/en/article.php?ModuleId=10005069, accessed April 25, 2018.

88. Ibid.

89. Grossman, *Notebooks*, 438.

90. Ibid.

91. Ibid., 447.

92. Beevor, *A Writer at War*, 326.

93. Grossman, *Notebooks*, 447.

94. Ibid., 452.

95. Alexander Bek, "O Vasilii Grossmane" (remarks at the funeral on September 17, 1964), RGALI, F. 2863/1/176.

96. Grossman, *Notebooks*, 453.

97. Ibid.

98. Ibid., 456.

99. Vasily Grossman, "Na rubezhe voiny i mira," *Znamya* 7 (1945).

100. Ortenberg, *Vremya ne vlastno*, 328.

101. Dolmatovsky, *Ochevidets*, 127.

102. A. I. Poltoratskij, *Nurnbergskij epilog* (Moscow: Voenizdat, 1965), 37.

103. Rubenstein, *Tangled Loyalties*, 220–21.

104. Ibid.

10. A Soviet Tolstoy

1. Vasily Grossman, "Budushchie knigi," *Literary Gazette*, February 3, 1945.

2. Grossman, *Life and Fate*, 665.

3. Ibid., 646–47.

4. Anna Berzer, *Proshchanie* (Moscow: Kniga, 1990), 122.

5. Vasily Grossman, "To the Memory of the Fallen," *Literary Gazette*, June 22, 1946.

6. This number grew to 20 million under Khrushchev and 27 million under Gorbachev. In May 2017 Putin's Duma quoted declassified information from the Soviet State Planning Committee (Gosplan): 19 million military deaths and 23 million civilian deaths. This raises the overall Soviet death toll in World War II to 42 million. Pavel Gutiontov, "Pobeda pred'yavlyaet schyot," March 22, 2017, https://www.novayagazeta.ru/articles/2017/03/22/71864-pobeda-pred-yavlyaet-schet, accessed April 28, 2018.

7. The Declaration of the Presidium of the Supreme Soviet of the USSR to make May 9 a work day appeared in *Izvestia* on December 24, 1947.

8. Ilya Ehrenburg, "Glazami Vasiliya Grossmana," *Literary Gazette*, February 23, 1946.

9. Guber, *Pamyat'*, 40.

10. Roberta Reeder, *Anna Akhmatova: Poet and Prophet* (New York: Picador USA, 1994), 292.

11. Andrei Zhdanov, "On the Errors of the Soviet Literary Journals, *Zvezda* and *Leningrad*," August 20, 1946, http://soviethistory.msu.edu/1947–2/zhdanov/zhdanov-texts/the-zvezda-affair/, accessed April 28, 2018.

12. Elena Ilyinskaia, "Zabytyi Poet," February 14, 2012, https://www.proza.ru/2012/02/14/1654, accessed April 28, 2018.

13. Grossman, *Everything Flows*, 18.

14. Alexander N. Yakovlev's Archive, "Stalin i kosmopolitism," document 100, January 28, 1949, http://www.alexanderyakovlev.org/fond/issues-doc/69512, accessed April 28, 2018.

15. Lipkin, *Zhizn'*, 80.

16. Boris Zaks, "Nemnogo o Grossmane," *Kontinent* 52 (2013).

17. RGALI, F. 613/7/841.

18. Grossman, *Life and Fate*, 281.

19. Berzer, *Proshchanie*, 126–27.

20. RGALI, F. 1710/1/123.

21. Redlich, *War*, 103.

22. Joshua Rubenstein and Vladimir Naumov, eds., *Stalin's Secret Pogrom: The Postwar Inquisition of the Jewish Anti-Fascist Committee*, trans. Laura Esther Wolfson (New Haven: Yale University Press, 2005), 225–26.

23. Altman and Rubenstein, *The Unknown Black Book*, xxxi.

24. Redlich, *War*, 103.
25. Rubenstein and Naumov, *Stalin's Secret Pogrom*, 225–26.
26. Ibid., 226–27.
27. RGALI, F. 1710/1/123.
28. Rubenstein and Naumov, *Stalin's Secret Pogrom*, 227.
29. Guber, *Pamyat'*, 72.
30. VG letter to SO, August 14, 1946.
31. Altman and Rubenstein, *The Unknown Black Book*, xxxii.
32. Ibid.
33. Ibid., xxxii–xxxiii.
34. Ibid., xxxiii–xxxiv.
35. Ibid.
36. Ibid., xxxvii.
37. RGALI, F. 1710/1/123.
38. N. S. Vovsi-Mikhoels, *Moi otets Solomon Mikhoels: Vospominaniya o zhizni i gibeli* (Moscow: Vozvrashchenie, 1997), https://www.sakharov-center.ru/asfcd/auth/?t=page&num=2310, accessed April 28, 2018.
39. Lipkin, *Zhizn'*, 80.
40. Nikita Khrushchev, *Memoirs of Nikita Khrushchev*, ed. Sergei Khrushchev, trans. George Shriver (University Park: Pennsylvania State University Press, 2006), 2:53, 55.
41. Alexander Borshchagovsky, "Obvinyaetsya krov,' " *Novy mir* 10 (1993), http://magazines.russ.ru/novyi_mi/1993/10/borsh.html, accessed April 28, 2018.
42. Redlich, *War*, 129.
43. Ibid., 128–29.
44. Ibid., 148.
45. Rubenstein and Naumov, *Stalin's Secret Pogrom*, 43.
46. Ibid., 45.
47. Ibid., 46–47.
48. Rubenstein, *Tangled Loyalties*, 257–58.
49. Khrushchev, *Memoirs*, 2:54–55.
50. Ibid., 2:52.
51. Ibid., 2:47.
52. Yakovlev, *Century of Violence*, 210.
53. Viktor Nekrasov, "Vas. Grossman," in *Viktor Nekrasov v zhizni i v pis'mah* (Moscow: Sovetski pisatel', 1971), 150–52.

54. Elliott Mossman, ed., *The Correspondence of Boris Pasternak and Olga Freidenberg, 1910–1954,* trans. Elliott Mossman and Margaret Wettlin (New York: Harcourt Brace Jovanovich, 1982), 295.

55. Ibid., 279.

56. RGALI, F. 1710/1/115.

57. RGALI, F. 1710/2/1. Unlike otherwise specified, information about the passage of *For the Right Cause* for publication comes from Grossman's diary kept at RGALI.

58. RGALI, F. 1710/1/106.

59. The *Diaries* were first published in Bern in 1946.

60. Information on Grossman's research comes from RGALI, F. 1710/1/149.

61. Wolfgang Saxon, "Curt Riess, Author and Journalist, 90; Expert of Nazi Era," *New York Times,* May 21, 1993, http://www.nytimes.com/1993/05/21/obituaries/curt-riess-author-and-journalist-90-expert-on-nazi-era.html.

62. Guderian's memoir appeared in Russian in 1954.

63. Grossman, *Za pravoe delo,* 585.

64. RGALI, F. 1710/1/152.

65. Tvardovsky, *"Ya v svoyu hodil ataku,"* 83, 85.

66. RGALI, F. 1710/3/10.

67. Grossman, *Life and Fate,* 342.

68. Zaks, "Nemnogo o Grossmane."

69. Redlich, *War,* 146, 150.

70. M. Shifman, ed., *Physics in a Mad World,* trans. James Manteith (Hackensack NJ: World Scientific, 2016), 18–19.

71. Tatiana Dettmer, "Fizik Lev Shtrum. Neizvestnyi geroi znamenitogo romana." Radio Svoboda, September 30, 2018. https://www.svoboda.org/a/29512819.html. Accessed October 3, 2018. Grossman's letter to his father is found in RGALI, F. 1710/3/65.

72. Lipkin, *Zhizn',* 22.

73. RGALI, F. 1710/1/154.

74. Grossman, *Za pravoe delo,* 352–54.

75. Redlich, *War,* 147–48, 150.

76. Ibid., 142.

77. Lipkin, *Zhizn',* 31.

78. RGALI, F. 1710/1/111.

79. Ibid.

80. Redlich, *War,* 145.

81. Ibid., 152.

82. RGALI, F. 1710/1/114. Grossman's letter to Fadeev, a draft, dated July 12, 1951.

83. Grossman's initial title for the whole novel was "Life and Fate." Later, the first part received the title "Stalingrad." Soviet editors, however, feared that such a title carried a weight of responsibility, so a "safer" one was sought.

84. RGALI, F. 1710/2/1.

85. Fyodor Guber, "Iz arhiva Vasiliya Grossmana," *Voprosy literatury* 4 (1997).

86. Rubenstein and Naumov, *Stalin's Secret Pogrom*, 50–51.

87. Ibid., 52.

88. Ibid., 229, 231.

89. Ibid., 204.

90. Altman and Rubenstein, *The Unknown Black Book*, 42–43.

91. Bocharov, *Grossman*, 172.

92. Altman and Rubenstein, *The Unknown Black Book*, 62.

93. Alexander N. Yakovlev's Archive, "Stalin i kosmopolitism," document 262, January 13, 1953, http://www.alexanderyakovlev.org/fond/issues-doc/69982, accessed April 28, 2018.

94. RGALI, F. 1710/1/111.

95. Lipkin, *Zhizn'*, 178.

96. Ibid., 32.

97. Grossman, *Life and Fate*, 835, 837.

98. Ehrenburg, *Sobranie sochinenij*, 9:729.

99. Rubenstein, *Tangled Loyalties*, 274–75.

100. Ehrenburg, *Sobranie sochinenij*, 9:730.

101. Boris Frezinsky, *Pisateli i sovetskie vozhdi* (Moscow: Ellis Lak, 2008), 577.

102. RGALI, F. 1710/2/1.

103. Lipkin, *Zhizn'*, 34.

104. Joshua Rubenstein, *The Last Days of Stalin* (New Haven: Yale University Press, 2016), 15–16.

105. Ibid., 95.

106. Berzer, *Proshchanie*, 208.

107. Rubenstein, *Last Days of Stalin*, 136.

108. RGALI, F. 1710/1/111.

11. Toward Life and Fate

1. Eugenia Ginzburg, *Within the Whirlwind*, trans. Ian Boland, (New York: Harcourt Brace Jovanovich, 1981), 357.

2. Grossman, *Everything Flows*, 25–26.

3. Ibid., 26–27.

4. Andrei Sakharov, *Memoirs*, trans. Richard Lourie (New York: Knopf, 1990), 163–64.

5. Ehrenburg, *Sobranie sochinenij*, 9:731.

6. Rubenstein, *Last Days of Stalin*, 109.

7. Grossman, *Everything Flows*, 27.

8. Rubenstein, *Last Days of Stalin*, 109.

9. Nikita Khrushchev, *Khrushchev Remembers: The Last Testament*, ed. and trans. Strobe Talbott (Boston: Little, Brown, 1974), 79.

10. Ginzburg, *Within the Whirlwind*, 363.

11. Rubenstein, *Last Days of Stalin*, 137.

12. Grossman, *Everything Flows*, 153.

13. Khrushchev, *Memoirs*, 2:189.

14. Sakharov, *Memoirs*, 166–67.

15. Ibid., 167–68.

16. Rubenstein, *Last Days of Stalin*, 225.

17. Ya. Etinger, "Beria: palach v roli 'reformatora'?" *Mezhdunarodnaya evreiskaya gazeta*, nos 25–26 (2003), in *Historicus*, http://www.historicus.ru/beriya_palach/, accessed April 28, 2018.

18. Rubenstein, *Last Days of Stalin*, 225.

19. Nadezhda Mandelstam, *Hope against Hope*, 301.

20. Grossman, "The Sistine Madonna," in *The Road*, 170.

21. Ibid., 173.

22. Ginzburg, *Within the Whirlwind*, 346.

23. Ibid., 248.

24. Varlam Shalamov, *Kolymskie rasskazy, stikhotvoreniya* (Moscow: Slovo, 2000), 568.

25. Nikita Zabolotsky, *The Life of Zabolotsky*, trans. R. R. Milner-Gulland and G. G. Bearne (Cardiff: University of Wales Press, 1994), 321.

26. Ibid., 282.

27. Nikolai Zabolotsky, "Istoriya moego zaklyucheniya," http://www.lib.ru/POEZIQ/ZABOLOCKIJ/istoriya.txt, accessed April 28, 2018.

28. Zabolotsky, *Life of Zabolotsky*, 168–82.

29. Ibid., 135.

30. Ibid., 342.

31. Zabolotsky, "Istoriya."

32. Grossman, *Life and Fate*, 783, 786.

33. Ibid., 786.

34. Zabolotsky, *Life of Zabolotsky*, 166.

35. Grossman, *Life and Fate*, 627.

36. Natalya Zabolotskaya, the poet's daughter, gave the author this information.

37. Grossman, *Everything Flows*, 95.

38. Peter Fritzsche, *Life and Death in the Third Reich* (Cambridge, MA: Harvard University Press, 2008), 101.

39. Zabolotsky, *Life of Zabolotsky*, 203.

40. Ibid., 202.

41. The Zabolotskys' letter to Stepanov, January 26, 1945, RGALI, F. 3112/1/93.

42. RGALI, F. 3112/1/93.

43. Zabolotsky's letter to Stepanov, June 20, 1945, RGALI, F. 3112/1/93.

44. "Gody uhodyat, uhodit iskusstvo." From Zabolotsky's letter to Stepanov, July 4, 1945, RGALI, F. 3112/1/93.

45. Grossman, *Notebooks*, 457.

46. Grossman, "Tiergarten," in *Vsyo techyot*, 285.

47. Grossman, *Life and Fate*, 635.

48. Grossman, "Tiergarten," in *Vsyo techyot*, 87.

49. RGALI, F. 1710/2/1.

50. VG letter to Lipkin, July 22, 1954. Grossman's correspondence with Lipkin comes from *Znamya* 6 (2016). Translation is by the author.

51. RGALI, F. 1710/1/125.

52. VG letter to Lipkin, July 22, 1954.

53. Yevgeniya Taratuta, *Kniga vospominanij* (Moscow: Yanus, 2001), vol. 2, http://www.sakharov-center.ru/asfcd/auth/?t=page&num=7721, accessed April 28, 2018.

54. Ibid.

55. Quoted in Darya Kling, *Tvorchestvo Vasiliya Grossmana v kontekste literaturnoi kritiki* (Moscow: Dom-muzei Mariny Tsvetaevoi, 2012), 37.

56. Osip Mandelstam, *The Noise of Time: The Prose of Osip Mandelstam*, trans. Clarence Brown (San Francisco: North Point, 1986), 181.

57. VG letter to Lipkin, July 16, 1955.

58. Ginzburg, *Within the Whirlwind*, 404–12.

59. Zabolotsky, *Life of Zabolotsky*, 313.

60. Nadezhda Mandelstam, *Hope Abandoned*, 573–74.

61. Yakovlev, *Century of Violence*, 7.

62. VG letter to Lipkin, January 25, 1959.

63. Quoted in Lazar Lazarev, *Zapiski pozhilogo cheloveka: Kniga vospominanij* (Moscow: Vremya, 2005), 167.

64. Olga Adamova-Sliozberg, *Put'* (Moscow: Vozvrashchenie, 2002), 7, 59.

65. Grossman, *Everything Flows*, 91–92.

66. L. F. Konson, *Kratkie povesti* (Paris: La Presse Libre, 1983), http://www.sakharov-center.ru/asfcd/auth/?t=book&num=1510, accessed April 28, 2018.

67. VG letter to Lipkin, May 18,1955.

68. SO letter to Galya, 1953–54, V.I. Dahl State Museum of the History of Russian Literature, F. 76/1/10.

69. According to Korotkova-Grossman, her father's letters and photographs were destroyed in her absence. She discovered this in 1955 in Kharkov, where she lived with her mother and stepfather. Grossman's books with his endorsement were also destroyed. This could have been done either by her mother or her stepfather, Victor Baranov; however, Victor was on good terms with Grossman while Galya remained bitter about their divorce and often tried to hurt Grossman.

70. Zabolotsky, *Life of Zabolotsky*, 321.

71. Surits, "Neliteraturnye druz'ya."

72. Lipkin, *Zhizn'*, 52–53.

73. Grossman, *Life and Fate*, 825.

74. Grossman, *Everything Flows*, 115.

75. Grossman, *Life and Fate.*, 703.

76. Surits, "Neliteraturnye druz'ya."

77. Fyodor Guber's private archive.

12. The Novel

1. Author's interview with Lyudmila Loboda-Efremova, October 2017.

2. Vasily Grossman, "The Sistine Madonna," in *The Road*, 163–74.

3. Anna Dostoevsky, *Dostoevsky: Reminiscences*, trans. Beatrice Stillman (New York: Liveright, 1975), 117.

4. Grossman, *Life and Fate*, 410.

5. Ibid., 554. Unless otherwise specified, all quotations in this chapter come from *Life and Fate*.

6. Grossman, *Zhizn' i sud'ba*, 146.

7. Arad, *Belzec*, 166.

8. Bettina Stangneth's *Eichmann Before Jerusalem* is written as a dialogue with Arendt, who was misled by Eichmann's testimony that he was "a small cog"

in Hitler's extermination machine. Stangneth provides overwhelming evidence that Eichmann was a fanatical National Socialist and the man behind the Holocaust.

9. Heinrich Böll, "Sposobnost' skorbet': O romane Vasiliya Grossmana 'Zhizn' i sud'ba,' " in Böll, *Sobranie sochinenij* (Moscow: Hudozhestvennaya literatura, 1996), 5:615–24.

10. VG letter to Lipkin, March 29, 1958.

11. http://www.litfund.ru/auction/63s1/300/, accessed July 16, 2018.

12. Lipkin, *Zhizn'*, 72–73.

13. Guber, *Pamyat'*, 88.

14. Khrushchev, *Khrushchev Remembers*, 76.

15. "CIA Declassifies Agency Role in Publishing *Doctor Zhivago*," Central Intelligence Agency, April 14, 2014, https://www.cia.gov/news-information/press-releases-statements/2014-press-releases-statements/cia-declassifies-agency-role-in-publishing-doctor-zhivago.html, accessed April 28, 2018.

16. VG letter to Lipkin, March 29, 1958.

17. Pasternak's letter to Ariadna Efron, October 19, 1952, http://magazines.russ.ru/znamia/2003/11/paster.html, accessed April 28, 2018.

18. Lipkin, *Zhizn'*, 73–74.

19. Author's interview with Korotkova-Grossman, 2016.

20. Bit-Yunan and Feldman, *Vasily Grossman*, 302.

21. VG letter to Lipkin, January 25, 1959.

22. VG letter to Lipkin, October 24, 1959.

23. Ibid.

24. Ibid.

25. Lipkin, *Zhizn'*, 42, 40.

26. Ibid, 42.

27. Lazarev, *Zapiski*, 165.

28. Lipkin, *Zhizn'*, 57–58.

29. VG letter to Lipkin, January 25, 1959.

30. Lazarev, *Zapiski*, 162.

31. Ibid.

32. Guber, *Pamyat'*, 93.

33. Alexander Tvardovsky, *Novomirskij dnevnik*: 1961–1966 (Moscow: Prozaik, 2009), 1:528.

34. Ibid., 1:529.

35. Ibid.

36. Lipkin, *Zhizn'*, 60.

37. Ibid., 59.

38. Berta Selvinkaya was the poet Ilya Selvinsky's wife.

39. Lipkin, *Zhizn'*, 59.

13. *An Unrepentant Heretic*

1. VG letter to Kozhevnikov, December 19, 1960, in Guber, *Pamyat'*, 95–96.

2. Quoted in Elena Yakovich's Russian 2014 documentary *Vasily Grossman: I Understood That I Had Died*, http://www.liveinternet.ru/users/rinarozen/post315826030/, accessed April 28, 2018.

3. Bocharov, *Grossman*, 178–79.

4. Vyacheslav Katinov's letter to VG, January 5, 1961, in Guber, *Pamyat'*, 96.

5. Lipkin, *Zhizn'*, 63.

6. VG letter to Lipkin, February 1, 1961.

7. Quoted in "Vasily Grossman, Pis'ma Semyonu Lipkinu," publikatsiya Eleny Makarovoi, *Znamya* 6 (2016).

8. Guber, *Pamyat'*, 97.

9. RGALI, F. 1710/2/17.

10. Author's interview with Irina Novikova, 2016.

11. Lipkin, *Zhizn'*, 61.

12. Tvardovsky, *Novomirskij dnevnik*, 18.

13. Alexander Solzhenitsyn, *The Oak and the Calf*, trans. Harry Willetts (London: Collins and Harvill, 1980), 101.

14. The author's interview with Ekaterina Korotkova-Grossman, 2016.

15. Grossman's letter to his dead mother, September 15, 1961, in *The Road*, 267.

16. Boris Yampolsky, "Poslednyaya vstrecha s Vasiliem Grossmanom," *Kontinent* 8 (1976): 138–39.

17. Lipkin, *Zhizn'*, 81.

18. VG letter to Lipkin, December 11, 1961.

19. VG letter to Lipkin, November 4, 1961.

20. Vasily Grossman, *An Armenian Sketchbook*, trans. Robert Chandler and Elizabeth Chandler (New York: New York Review Books, 2013), 3. All quotations from Grossman's memoir come from this edition.

21. VG letters to Lipkin, November 22 and December 11, 1961.

22. Grossman, *An Armenian Sketchbook*, 7.

23. More on this in V. Kozlov, *Neizvestnyi SSSR: Protivostoyanie naroda i vlasti, 1953–1985* (Moscow: Olma-Press, 2006).

24. Nadezhda Mandelstam, *Hope Abandoned*, 549.

25. Osip Mandelstam, *Journey to Armenia*, 42.

26. Ibid., 7–8.

27. Ibid., 11.

28. VG letter to Lipkin, November 15, 1961.

29. Grossman, *Armenian Sketchbook*, 102.

30. VG letter to Lipkin, November 9, 1961.

31. VG letter to Lipkin, November 15, 1961.

32. VG letter to Lipkin, November 22, 1961.

33. VG letter to Lipkin, December 2, 1961.

34. VG letter to Lipkin, October 13, 1961.

35. Grossman, *Armenian Sketchbook*, 113.

36. VG letter to Lipkin, December 29–30, 1961.

37. VG letter to Lipkin, January 11, 1962.

38. VG letter to Lipkin, December 2, 1961.

39. Grossman, *Armenian Sketchbook*, 30.

40. Ibid., 44–45.

41. Tvardovsky, *Novomirskij dnevnik*, 134.

42. Grossman, *Armenian Sketchbook*, 15.

43. Tvardovsky, *Novomirskij dnevnik*, 129.

44. Lev Kopelev, *To Be Preserved Forever*, trans. Anthony Austin (Philadelphia: J. B. Lippincott, 1977), 13–14.

45. Lipkin, *Zhizn'*, 70–71.

46. Ibid., 71.

47. Sakharov, *Memoirs*, 408–9.

48. Alexander Solzhenitsyn, "Dilogiya Vasiliya Grossmana," *Novy mir* 8 (2003).

49. Lipkin, *Zhizn'*, 41.

50. Marxist Internet Archive / Soviet Archives, http://marxism.halkcephesi.net/soviet%20archives/Congre%20reports/congress%2022.htm, accessed April 28, 2018.

51. Hans Björkegren, *Alexandr Solzhenitsyn: A Biography*, trans. Kaarina Eneberg (New York: Third Press, 1972), 43.

52. Lipkin, *Zhizn'*, 67.

53. RGALI, F. 1710/2/17. Translation is by the author.

54. Redlich, *War*, 69–70.

55. Khrushchev, *Khrushchev Remembers*, 76.

56. Guber, *Pamyat'*, 103–4.

57. RGALI, F. 1710/2/17.

58. Lipkin, *Zhizn'*, 69.

59. Vasily Grossman, "The Road," in *The Road*, 232.

60. Ibid., 234.

61. Berzer, *Proshchanie*, 253.

62. Lipkin, *Zhizn'*, 69–70.

63. VG letter to Lipkin, January 11, 1962.

64. VG letter to Lipkin, December 1961.

14. Everything Flows

1. "Soyuz pisatelej SSSR–soyuz fal'sifikatorov istorii i rastlitelej sovetskogo naroda," *LiveJournal*, July 25, 2016, http://cat-779.livejournal.com/89447.html, accessed April 28, 2018.

2. Grossman, *Everything Flows*, 89. Unless otherwise specified, all quotations in this chapter come from *Everything Flows*.

3. VG letter to Lipkin, October 2, 1958.

4. Author's interview with Maria Loboda, 2017.

5. Ibid.

6. Yampolsky, "Pospednyaya vstrecha," 146.

7. Ibid., 138.

8. Information about Grossman's study comes from Elena Kozhichkina. One of the rooms in Elena's apartment is turned into Grossman's memorial study.

9. Author's interview with Irina Novikova, 2015.

10. Grossman, *Everything Flows*, 122.

11. Varlam Shalamov, "Biografija," https://shalamov.ru/biography/, accessed April 28, 2018.

12. Peter Pringle, *The Murder of Nikolai Vavilov: The Story of Stalin's Persecution of One of the Great Scientists of the Twentieth Century* (New York: Simon and Schuster, 2008), 2.

13. Sakharov, *Memoirs*, 234.

14. Reeder, *Anna Akhmatova*, 318.

15. Zabolotsky, *Life of Zabolotsky*, 230.

16. Leonid Rybakovskij, *Politicheskij terror 1937–38 godov* (Moscow, 2013), http://rybakovsky.ru/demografia5a8.html, accessed April 28, 2018.

17. Conquest, *Harvest of Sorrow*, 9.

18. Maria Loboda (Karpova), who met Zabolotskaya, gave this information to the author.

19. Natalya Zabolotskaya's letter to the author, January 18, 2017. The Stepanovs' son-in-law, Gennady Grigorievich, told the author about Maria Alexandrovna's career as a chemical engineer.

20. During the war Maria was trapped in Krasnodar and nearly perished there with her daughter, Inga, when the area was occupied by the Nazis. Like everyone who lived in the occupied territories, Maria was later under suspicion by the Soviet authorities and lost her career.

21. Contrary to what was previously believed, Grossman did not interview the Zabolotskys' maid about the famine. The maid, Polina Semyonova, came from the village of Likhodeevo near the city of Kalinin (or Tver), about 180 kilometers northwest of Moscow, and had lived neither in Kuban nor in Ukraine during the famine. Information comes from Natalya Zabolotskaya's letter to the author, 2017.

22. Michael Ellman, "Stalin and the Soviet Famine of 1932–33 Revisited" in *Europe-Asia Studies* 54, no. 4 (June 2007): 663–93, http://www.paulbogdanor .com/left/soviet/famine/ellman1933.pdf, accessed April 28, 2018.

23. Kopelev, *To Be Preserved Forever*, 11.

24. Khlevniuk, *History of the Gulag*, 10–12.

25. Lev Kopelev, *The Education of a True Believer*, trans. Gary Kern (New York: Harper and Row, 1980), 235.

26. Khlevniuk, *History of the Gulag*, 324.

27. Ibid., 279–80.

28. Kopelev, *Education*, 234.

29. Conquest, *Harvest of Sorrow*, 314.

30. Ibid., 314–15.

31. Grossman, *Everything Flows*, 134–35.

32. Applebaum, *Red Famine*, 201.

33. For more on this, see ibid., 300–302.

15. Keep My Words Forever

1. RGALI, F. 1710/3/64.

2. Lipkin, *Zhizn'*, 105.

3. Ibid.

4. Ibid., 106.

5. Yakovich, *Vasily Grossman: I Understood That I Had Died.*

6. Berzer, *Proshchanie*, 249.

7. Ibid., 259.

8. Ibid., 268.

9. Guber, *Pamyat'*, 115–16.

10. VG letter to OM, September 17, 1963.

11. VG letter to OM, September 20, 1963.

12. VG letter to OM, September 30, 1963.

13. VG letter to OM, October 9, 1963.

14. Information comes from the author's 2017 interview with Maria Karpova (née Loboda).

15. Frida Vigdorova, "The Trial of Joseph Brodsky," trial transcript translated by Michael R. Katz, 2014, http://www.nereview.com/files/2014/01/NER-Vigdorova.pdf, accessed April 28, 2018.

16. Berzer, *Proshchanie*, 255.

17. Ibid., 256–57.

18. Ibid., 251.

19. Ibid., 268–69.

20. Both sisters believe this happened in September 1960 rather than in September 1964. This author relied on Anna Berzer's memoir.

21. Author's interview with Maria Loboda (Karpova), 2017.

22. Lipkin, *Zhizn'*, 119.

23. Vladimir Voinovich, "Zhizn' i sud'ba Vasiliya Grossmana i ego romana," *Posev* 11 (1984): 54.

24. Ibid., 55.

25. Grossman, *Armenian Sketchbook*, 21.

26. Zaks, "Nemnogo o Grossmane," 362.

27. Lipkin, *Zhizn'*, 110.

28. Surits, "Neliteraturnye druz'ya," 439.

29. Ibid., 440.

30. Lipkin, *Zhizn'*, 111.

31. Quoted in Natalya Kochetkova, "Vasya, ty zhe Hristos," *Izvestia*, December 13, 2005.

32. Grigory Baklanov's novel *July 1941* (*Iyul' 41 goda*) was published in 1964 and later banned for over a decade. His novels in English translation include *Forever Nineteen* and *The Moment between the Past and the Future*.

33. Lipkin, *Zhizn'*, 113.

34. Extracts also appeared in the émigré journal *Grani*.

35. Lipkin, *Zhizn'*, 113.

36. Tvardovsky, *Novomirskij dnevnik*, 2:427.

37. Yuri Trifonov, *Zapiski soseda. Vospominaniya*, December 3, 2014, http://www.litmir.me/br/?b=226906&p=6, accessed April 28, 2018.

38. Tvardovsky, *Novomirskij dnevnik*, vol. 2, November 9, 1969.

39. Lipkin, *Zhizn'*, 60.

40. Quoted in Kochetkova, "Vasya, ty zhe Hristos," *Izvestia*, December 13, 2005.

41. Sasha Sokolov is known for his paradoxical novel *A School for Fools*. Vladimir Maramzin, a Soviet dissident writer, was arrested in 1974 in Leningrad for compiling Joseph Brodsky's samizdat edition. Maramzin's books include the short story collection *City-Dwellers* and the novel *The Country Called Emigration*.

42. Lev Kopelev, "Letter to Solzhenitsyn," Cologne, January 30–February 5, 1985, *Syntaxis* 37 (2001), 87–102, http://imwerden.de/pdf/syntaxis_37_pismo_kopeleva_solzhenicynu.pdf, accessed April 28, 2018.

43. Yakovich, *Vasily Grossman: I Understood That I Had Died*.

44. Vladimir Voinovich, *Avtoportret: Roman moei zhizni* (Moscow: Eksmo, 2010), 843–44.

45. Yuri Bit-Yunan and David Feldman, "Istoriya sohraneniya i publikatsii romana *Zhizn' i sud'ba*: protivorechiya v istochnikah," in *Grossman Studies: The Legacy of a Contemporary Classic*, eds. Maurizia Calusio, Anna Krasnikova, and Pietro Tosco (Milan: EDUCat, 2016).

46. Efim Etkind, "Zhizn' i sud'ba knigi," *Vremya i my* 101 (1988).

47. Blake Eskin, "Vasily Grossman's *Life and Fate*," *New Yorker*, December 13, 2011, http://www.newyorker.com/culture/culture-desk/the-year-in-listening-vasily-grossmans-life-and-fate, accessed April 28, 2018.

48. Francis Spufford, "*Life and Fate* by Vasily Grossman," *Guardian*, August 31, 2011, https://www.theguardian.com/books/2011/aug/31/life-fate-vasily-grossman, accessed April 28, 2018.

49. Etkind, "Zhizn' i sud'ba knigi," 198–99.

50. Alexander Solzhenitsyn, *Invisible Allies*, trans. Alexis Klimoff and Michael Nicholson (Washington, DC: Counterpoint, 1995), 186.

51. Grossman, *Life and Fate*, 301.

52. Lev Anninskij, "Mirozdan'e Vasiliya Grossmana," *Druzhba narodov* 10 (1988): 253–63.

53. Ibid., 263.

54. Johanna Steinmetz, "1968 Film *The Komissar* a Timely Oscar Entry for USSR." *Chicago Tribune*, November 18, 1988, http://articles.chicagotribune.com/1988-11-18/entertainment/8802180029_1_soviet-jews-san-francisco-film-festival-commissar, accessed April 28, 2018.

55. Kling, *Tvorchestvo*, 166–67.

56. Ibid., 166–67.

57. Igor Shafarevich, "Russofobia," 1999, https://malchish.org/lib/politics/shaf_rusofobia.htm, accessed April 28, 2018.

58. Grossman, *Everything Flows*, 184.

59. Ibid., 176.

60. Ibid., 175.

61. Ibid.

62. Author's interview with Elena Yakovich, 2017.

63. Rossijskij gosudarstvennyi arhiv literatury i iskusstva, "Arhiv novostej," July 31, 2013, http://www.rgali.ru/object/262403205#!page:1/o:262403205/p:1, accessed April 28, 2018.

64. Author's interview with Elena Yakovich, February 2017.

Epilogue

1. Varlam Shalamov, "Vospominaniya. Dvadtsatye gody," https://shalamov.ru/library/30/, accessed April 28, 2018.

2. Varlam Shalamov, "Zhitie inzhenera Kipreeva" in V. T. Shalamov, *Sobranie sochinenij* (Moscow: Vagrius, 1998), 2:150–63, https://shalamov.ru/library/5/14.html, accessed April 28, 2018.

3. Georgy Demidov, *Ot rassveta do sumerek: Vospominaniya i razdum'ya rovesnika veka* (Moscow: Vozvrashchenie, 2014), 8.

4. "BBC ispugalos': Rossiyane schitayut Putina nastoyashchim Shtirlitsem," *Pravda*, May 11, 2017, https://www.pravda.ru/news/society/11-05-2017/1333508-putin-o/, accessed April 28, 2018.

5. Leonid Bronevoi, "KPSS vinovata ne men'she, chem natsistskaia partiia v Germanii i dazhe bol'she," *LiveJournal*, December 9, 2017, https://philologist.livejournal.com/9868340.html, accessed April 28, 2018. See also Leonid Bronevoy, "Ya stal aktyorom ponevole," *BBC News*, Russian service, November 4, 2009, https://www.bbc.com/russian/interactivity/2009/11/091103_bronevoy_interview, accessed July 23, 2018.

6. Leonid Bronevoi, "Ya, ch'yo detstvo ispoganeno . . .," *Bul'var Gordona* 48, no. 500 (December 2014), http://bulvar.com.ua/gazeta/archive/s48_66997/8889.html, accessed April 28, 2018.

7. Ibid.

8. Yakovlev, *Century of Violence*, 211.

9. Masha Gessen, *The Future Is History: How Totalitarianism Reclaimed Russia* (New York: Riverhead Books, 2017), 143.

10. Yakovlev, *Century of Violence*, 233.

11. Ibid., 25.

12. Ibid., 22.

13. Alexandra Samarina, "Rodonachal'nik glasnosti–o kontrreformah," *Nezavisimaya gazeta*, April 19, 2005, http://www.ng.ru/ideas/2005-04-19/1_yakovlev.html, accessed April 28, 2018.

14. Yakovlev, *Century of Violence*, 24.

15. Karen Dawisha, *Putin's Kleptocracy: Who Owns Russia* (New York: Simon and Schuster, 2014), 2007.

16. Thomas B. Edsall, "The Self-Destruction of American Democracy," *New York Times*, November 30, 2017, https://www.nytimes.com/2017/11/30/opinion/trump-putin-destruction-democracy.html, accessed April 28, 2018.

17. Roginsky's remarks at the 2014 International Grossman Conference in Moscow.

18. Galina Yuzefovich, "Vspomnit' vsyo," *Itogi*, October 3, 2011, http://www.itogi.ru/literatura/2011/40/170349.html, accessed April 28, 2018.

19. Michael Billington, "*Life and Fate* Review—A Remarkable Epic of Soviet Horror and Heartbreak," *Guardian*, May 9, 2018, https://www.theguardian.com/stage/2018/may/09/life-and-fate-review-a-remarkable-epic-of-soviet-horror-and-heartbreak, accessed July 27, 2018.

20. Paul Taylor, "*Life and Fate,* Theatre Royal Haymarket, London, Review: Maly Drama Theatre Stage 'the 20th Century's *War and Peace*,'" *The Independent*, May 10, 2018, https://www.independent.co.uk/arts-entertainment/theatre-dance/reviews/life-and-date-review-maly-drama-theatre-russian-theatre-royal-haymarket-vasily-grossman-a8344646.html, accessed July 27, 2018.

21. Boris Vishnevskij, "Vynesti Stalina iz obshchestvennoi zhizni," *Novaya gazeta*, November 10, 2015, https://www.novayagazeta.ru/articles/2015/11/10/66310-vynesti-stalina-iz-obschestvennoy-zhizni, accessed April 28, 2018.

22. Levada-Tsentr, "Vydayushchiesya lyudi," June 26, 2017, https://www.levada.ru/2017/06/26/vydayushhiesya-lyudi/, accessed April 28, 2018.

23. Andrei Vorob'yov, "V Rossii est' pytki, a pravosudie v strane otsutstvuet," *LiveJournal*, December 14, 2016, http://philologist.livejournal.com/8932900.html, accessed April 28, 2018. Originally published as Andrei Vorob'yov, "Poka est' pytki, pravosudiya v strane net," *Novaya gazeta*, December 14, 2016, https://www.novayagazeta.ru/articles/2016/12/14/70897-poka-est-pytki-pravosudiya-v-strane-net, accessed July 23, 2018.

24. Michael Birnbaum, "Russia's Justice Ministry Targets Memorial, a Human Rights Defender," *Washington Post*, October 13, 2014, https://www.washingtonpost.com/world/europe/russias-justice-ministry-targets-memorial-a-human-rights-defender/2014/10/13/8d20755a-52e0-11e4-b86d-184ac281388d_story.html?utm_term=.90eb248a0a9f, accessed April 28, 2018.

25. Shura Burtin, "Delo Hottabycha," May 30, 2017, https://les.media/articles/406627-delo-khottabycha, accessed April 28, 2018.

26. Otkrytaia Rossiia, "Vecher solidarnosti s Yuriem Dmitrievym v Sakharovskom tsentre," December 9, 2017, https://www.openrussia.org/notes/717134, accessed April 28, 2018.

27. Irina Tumakova, "Tridtsat' let s pravom perepiski," *Novaya gazeta*, December 21, 2017, https://www.novayagazeta.ru/articles/2017/12/21/74999-tridtsat-let-s-pravom-perepiski, accessed April 28, 2018.

28. Vladislav Fronin, "FSB rasstavlyaet aktsenty," interview with Alexander Bortnikov, *Rossijskaya gazeta*, December 19, 2017, https://www.rg.ru/2017/12/19/aleksandr-bortnikov-fsb-rossii-svobodna-ot-politicheskogo-vliianiia.html, accessed April 28, 2018.

29. Galina Muravnik, "Moi dedushka ne mozhet prinesti pokayanie. Ya prinoshu," October 6, 2017, https://s-t-o-l.com/istoriya/moj-dedushka-ne-mozhet-prinesti-pokayanie-ya-prinoshu/, accessed April 28, 2018.

Bibliography

Archival Collections

Russian State Archive of Literature and Art (RGALI), Moscow
    F. 613–State Literary Publishing House
    F. 618–*Znamya* magazine
    F. 631–The Union of Soviet Writers
    F. 1702–*Novy mir* magazine
    F. 1710–Vasily Grossman
    F. 2863–Alexander Bek
    F. 3112–Alexander N. Stepanov
V. I. Dahl State Museum of the History of Russian Literature (Russian State Literary Museum), Moscow
    F. 76–Vasily Grossman
Fyodor Guber's private archive
Maria Karpova's (Loboda) private archive
Ekaterina Korotkova-Grossman's private archive
Elena Makarova's private archive
Kornely Zelinsky's private archive

Primary Sources

Ehrenburg, Ilya, and Vasily Grossman, eds. *The Complete Black Book of Russian Jewry*. Translated by John Glad and James Lavine. New Brunswick, NJ: Transaction, 2002.

Grossman, Vasily. "Alexander Roskin." RGALI, 1702/2/933.

———. *An Armenian Sketchbook*. Translated by Robert Chandler and Elizabeth Chandler. New York: New York Review Books, 2013.

———. "Berdichev ne v shutku, a vser'yoz." *Ogonyok* 51–52 (1929).

———. *Esli verit' pifagoreitsam. Znamya* 7 (1946).

————. *Everything Flows*. Translated by Robert Chandler and Elizabeth Chandler. New York: New York Review Books, 2009.

————. *Glückauf*. Moscow: Sovetskij pisatel', 1935.

————. *Gody voiny*. Moscow: OGIZ, 1946.

————. *Gody voiny*. Biblioteka zhurnala *Znamya*. Moscow: Pravda, 1989.

————. *Life and Fate*. Translated by Robert Chandler. New York: Harper and Row, 1985.

————. "Na rubezhe voiny i mira." *Znamya* 7 (1945).

————. "Pis'ma Lipkinu." *Znamya* 6 (2016).

————. *The Road: Stories, Journalism, and Essays*. Translated by Robert Chandler, Elizabeth Chandler with Olga Mukovnikova. New York: New York Review Books, 2010.

————. "The Safety Inspector." In *Great Soviet Short Stories*, translated by Sam Driver. New York: Dell, 1962.

————. *Sobranie sochinenij*. 4 vols. Moscow: Agraf, 1998.

————. *Stepan Kolchugin*. 2 vols. Moscow: Sovetskij pisatel', 1947.

————. "Ukraina bez evreev." RGALI, 618/14/355.

————. *Vsyo techyot . . . Povesti, rasskazy, ocherki*. Moscow: Eksmo, 2010.

————. *Za pravoe delo*. Moscow: Voenizdat, 1954.

————. *Za pravoe delo*. Moscow: Sovetskij pisatel', 1989.

————. *Zhizn' i sud'ba*. Moscow: Slovo, 1999.

Secondary Sources

Adamova-Sliozberg, Olga. *Put'*. Moscow: Vozvrashchenie, 2002.

Aleichem, Sholom. *Favorite Tales of Sholom Aleichem*. Translated by Julius Butwin and Frances Butwin. New York: Avenel Books, 1983.

Altman, Ilya, and Joshua Rubenstein, eds. *The Unknown Black Book: The Holocaust in the German-Occupied Soviet Territories*. Translated by Christopher Morris and Joshua Rubenstein. Bloomington: Indiana University Press, 2008.

Andronikashvili-Pilnyak, Boris. "Dva izgoya, dva muchenika: Boris Pilnyak i Evgeny Zamyatin." *Znamya* 9 (1994).

Anninskij, Lev. "Mirozdan'e Vasiliya Grossmana." *Druzhba narodov* 10 (1988).

Applebaum, Anne. *Gulag: A History*. New York: Doubleday, 2003.

————. *Red Famine: Stalin's War on Ukraine*. Toronto: Signal, 2017.

Arad, Yitzhak. *Belzec, Sobibor, Treblinka: The Operation Reinhard Death Camps*. Bloomington: Indiana University Press, 1987.

————. *The Holocaust in the Soviet Union*. Lincoln: University of Nebraska Press; Jerusalem: Yad Vashem, 2009.

Baklanov, Grigory. *Sobranie sochinenij*. 5 vols. St. Petersburg: Propaganda, 2003.

Beevor, Antony. *Stalingrad. The Fateful Siege, 1942–43*. London: Penguin Books, 1999.

———, ed. *A Writer at War: Vasily Grossman with the Red Army 1941–1945*. Translated by Anthony Beevor and Luba Vinogradova. London: Harvill, 2005.

Berzer, Anna. *Proshchanie*. Moscow: Kniga, 1990.

Bit-Yunan, Yuri, and David Feldman. *Vasily Grossman v zerkale literaturnyh intrig*. Moscow: Forum, 2015.

Björkegren, Hans. *Alexandr Solzhenitsyn: A Biography*. Translated by Kaarina Eneberg. New York: Third Press, 1972.

The Black Book: The Nazi Crime against the Jewish People. New York: Jewish Black Book Committee, 1946.

Bocharov, Anatoly. "Bolevye zony." *Oktyabr'* 2 (1988).

———. "Pravoe delo Vasiliya Grossmana." *Oktyabr'* 1 (1988).

———. *Vasily Grossman: Zhizn,' tvorchestvo, sud'ba*. Moscow: Sovetskij pisatel', 1990.

Böll, Heinrich. *Sobranie sochinenij*. 5 vols. Moscow: Hudozhestvennaya literatura, 1996.

Borshchagovsky, Alexander. "Obvinyaetsya krov,'" *Novy mir* 10 (1993).

Brent, Jonathan, and Vladimir Naumov. *Stalin's Last Crime: the Plot against Jewish Doctors, 1948–1953*. New York: HarperCollins, 2003.

Bulgakov, Mikhail. *A Dead Man's Memoir. A Theatrical Novel*. Translated by Andrew Bromfield. London: Penguin Books, 2007.

Bullock, Alan. *Hitler and Stalin: Parallel Lives*. Toronto: McClelland and Stewart, 1993.

Bullock, David. *The Russian Civil War, 1918–22*. Oxford: Osprey, 2008.

Calusio, Maurizia, Anna Krasnikova, and Pietro Tosco, eds. *Grossman Studies: The Legacy of a Contemporary Classic*. Milan: EDUCat, 2016.

Chekhov, A. P. *Polnoe sobranie sochinenij i pisem*. 17 vols. Moscow: Nauka, 1987.

Chukovsky, Korney. *Diary, 1901–1969*. Translated by Michael Henry Heim. New Haven: Yale University Press, 1991.

Cohen, Stephen. *Bukharin and the Bolshevik Revolution: A Political Biography, 1888–1938*. New York: Vintage Books, 1975.

Conquest, Robert. *The Great Terror: A Reassessment*. Oxford: Oxford University Press, 2008.

———. *The Harvest of Sorrow: Soviet Collectivization and the Terror-Famine*. New York: Oxford University Press, 1986.

———. *Reflections on a Ravaged Century.* New York: Norton, 2000.

———. *Tyrants and Typewriters: Communiqués from the Struggle for Truth.* Lexington, MA: Lexington Books, 1985.

Courtois, Stéphane et al. *The Black Book of Communism: Crimes, Terror, Repression.* Translated by Jonathan Murphy and Mark Kramer. Cambridge, MA: Harvard University Press, 1999.

Curtis, J.A.E. *Manuscripts Don't Burn: Mikhail Bulgakov, A Life in Letters and Diaries.* London: Bloomsbury, 1991.

Daniel, Alexander, and Arseny Roginsky. "Arestu podlezhat zheny." In *Uznitsy "Alzhira": Spisok zhenshchin zaklyuchennyh Akmolinskogo i drugih otdelenij Karlaga.* Moscow: Zven'ya, 2003.

Dawisha, Karen. *Putin's Kleptocracy: Who Owns Russia.* New York: Simon and Schuster, 2014.

Dedkov, Igor. "Zhizn' protiv sud'by." *Novy mir* 11 (1988).

Demidov, Georgy. *Ot rassveta do sumerek: Vospominaniya i razdum'ya rovesnika veka.* Moscow: Vozvrashchenie, 2014.

Dobrenko, Evgeny. *Political Economy of Socialist Realism.* New Haven: Yale University Press, 2007.

Dolmatovsky, E. A. *Ochevidets: Kniga dokumental'nyh rasskazov o zhizni avtora i ego sovremennikov v XX veke, v sovetskoe vremya.* Nizhnij Novgorod: DEKOM, 2014.

Dostoevsky, Anna. *Dostoevsky: Reminiscences.* Translated by Beatrice Stillman. New York: Liveright, 1975.

Dwork, Deborah, and Robert Jan Van Pelt. *Flight from the Reich: Refugee Jews, 1933–1946.* New York: Norton, 2012.

Ehrenburg, Ilya. *Lyudi, gody, zhizn'.* In *Vospominaniya.* 3 vols. Moscow: Sovetskij pisatel', 1990.

———. *Memoirs, 1921–1941.* Translated by Tatania Shebunina and Yvonne Kapp. Cleveland: World Publishing, 1964.

———. *Sobranie sochinenij.* 9 vols. Moscow: Hudozhestvennaya literatura, 1962–67.

———. *The War, 1941–45.* In *Men, Years, Life,* translated by Tatania Shebunina and Yvonne Kapp. London: Macgibbon and Kee, 1964.

Ehrenburg, Ilya, and Konstantin Simonov. *In One Newspaper: A Chronicle of Unforgettable Years.* Translated by Anatol Kagan. New York: Sphinx, 1985.

Elina, Nina. *Vasily Grossman.* Jerusalem, 1994.

Ellis, Frank. *Vasily Grossman: The Genesis and Evolution of a Russian Heretic.* Oxford: Berg, 1994.

Ellman, Michael. "Stalin and the Soviet Famine of 1932–33 Revisited." *Europe-Asia Studies* 4 (2007).

Erickson, Ljubica, and Mark Erickson, eds. *Russia: War, Peace and Diplomacy: Essays in Honour of John Erickson*. London: Weidenfeld and Nicolson, 2005.

Etkind, Efim. "Zhizn' i sud'ba knigi." *Vremya i my* 101 (1988).

Fitzpatrick, Sheila. *The Russian Revolution*. Oxford: Oxford University Press, 1994.

Freese, Barbara. *Coal: A Human History*. New York: Penguin Books, 2003.

Freidin, Gregory, ed. *The Enigma of Isaak Babel: Biography, History, Context*. Stanford: Stanford University Press, 2009.

Frezinsky, Boris. *Pisateli i sovetskie vozhdi*. Moscow: Ellis Lak, 2008.

Fritzsche, Peter. *Life and Death in the Third Reich*. Cambridge, MA: Harvard University Press, 2008.

Garrard, Carol, and John Garrard. *The Bones of Berdichev: The Life and Fate of Vasily Grossman*. New York: Free Press, 1996.

Gessen, Masha. *The Future Is History: How Totalitarianism Reclaimed Russia*. New York: Riverhead Books, 2017.

Geyer, Michael, and Sheila Fitzpatrick. *Stalinism and Nazism Compared*. Cambridge: Cambridge University Press, 2009.

Ginzburg, Evgenia. *Within the Whirlwind*. Translated by Ian Boland. New York: Harcourt Brace Jovanovich, 1981.

Gorelik, Gennady. "The Top-Secret Life of Lev Landau," 1997. https://www.scribd.com/document/167244875/The-Top-Secret-Life-of-Lev-Landau. Accessed April 28, 2018.

Gorky, Maxim. *Sobranie sochinenij*. 30 vols. Moscow: Goslitizdat, 1955.

Goryaeva, Tatyana. *Politicheskaya tsenzura v SSSR, 1917–1991*. Moscow: ROSSPEN, 2009.

Guber, Fyodor. *Pamyat' i pis'ma*. Moscow: Probel, 2007.

Hamm, Michael. *Kiev: A Portrait*. Princeton: Princeton University Press, 1993.

Hellbeck, Jochen. *Stalingrad: The City That Defeated the Third Reich*. New York: Public Affairs, 2015.

Jones, Michael. *Stalingrad: How the Red Army Triumphed*. Barnsley: Pen and Sword, 2007.

Kershaw, Ian, and Moshe Lewin, eds. *Stalinism and Nazism: Dictatorships in Comparison*. Cambridge: Cambridge University Press, 1997.

Khlevniuk, Oleg. *The History of the Gulag: From Collectivization to the Great Terror*. Translated by Vadim Staklo. New Haven: Yale University Press, 2004.

————. *Stalin: New Biography of a Dictator*. Translated by Nora Seligman Favorov. New Haven: Yale University Press, 2015.

Khrushchev, Nikita. *Memoirs of Nikita Khrushchev*. 3 vols. Edited by Sergei Khrushchev. Translated by George Shriver. University Park: Pennsylvania State University Press, 2004–2007.

————. *Khrushchev Remembers: The Last Testament*. Edited and translated by Strobe Talbott. Boston: Little, Brown, 1974.

Kling, Darya. *Tvorchestvo Vasiliya Grossmana v kontekste literaturnoi kritiki*. Moscow: Dom-muzei Mariny Tsvetaevoi, 2012.

Kopelev, Lev. *The Education of a True Believer*. Translated by Gary Kern. New York: Harper and Row, 1980.

————. *To Be Preserved Forever*. Translated by Anthony Austin. Philadelphia: J. B. Lippincott, 1977.

Korotkova-Grossman, Ekaterina. *Vospominaniya: Rasskazy bes vymysla*. Moscow: Novyi hronograf, 2014.

Kotkin, Stephen. *Stalin: Paradoxes of Power, 1878–1928*. Vol. 1. New York: Penguin, 2014.

Kowalski, Ronald. *The Bolshevik Party in Conflict: The Left Communist Opposition of 1918*. London: Macmillan, 1991.

Kozlov, V. *Neizvestnyi SSSR: Protivostoyanie naroda i vlasti, 1953–1985*. Moscow: Olma-Press, 2006.

Laqueur, Walter, and Judith Tydor Baumel, eds. *The Holocaust Encyclopedia*. New Haven: Yale University Press, 2001.

Lazarev, Lazar. "Duh svobody." *Znamya* 9 (1988).

————. *Zapiski pozhilogo cheloveka: Kniga vospominanij*. Moscow: Vremya, 2005.

Lieven, Dominic. *Nicholas II, Emperor of All the Russias*. London: John Murray, 1993.

Lipkin, Semyon. *Kvadriga*. Moscow: Knizhnyi sad–Agraf, 1997.

————. *Zhizn' i sud'ba Vasiliya Grossmana*. Moscow: Kniga, 1990.

Lyandres, Semion. *The Fall of Tsarism: Untold Stories of the February 1917 Revolution*. Oxford: Oxford University Press, 2013.

MacKenzie, David, and Michael Curran. *A History of Russia, the Soviet Union, and Beyond*. London: West/Wadsworth, 1999.

Mandel, David. *The Petrograd Workers and the Soviet Seizure of Power: From the July Days 1917 to July 1918*. London: Macmillan, 1984.

Mandelstam, Nadezhda. *Hope Abandoned*. Translated by Max Hayward. New York: Atheneum, 1974.

————. *Hope against Hope*. Translated by Max Hayward. New York: Modern Library, 1999.

Mandelstam, Osip. *Journey to Armenia*. Translated by Sidney Monas. San Francisco: George F. Ritchie, 1979.

————. *The Noise of Time: The Prose of Osip Mandelstam*. Translated by Clarence Brown. San Francisco: North Point, 1986.

————. *Sochineniya*. 2 vols. Moscow: Khudozhestvennaya literatura, 1990.

Markish, Shimon. *Na evreiskie temy: Primer Vasiliya Grossmana*. 2 vols. Jerusalem: Biblioteka–Aliya, 1985.

Mawdsley, Evan. *The Russian Civil War*. Edinburgh: Birlinn, 2011.

Meir, Natan M. *Kiev, Jewish Metropolis: A History*. Bloomington: Indiana University Press, 2010.

The Memoirs of Count Witte. Translated by Sydney Harcave. London: M. E. Sharpe, 1990.

Merridale, Catherine. "Stalin's Order No. 227: 'Not a Step Back,'" July 28, 2011. http://www.thehistoryreader.com/modern-history/stalins-order-227-step-back/. Accessed April 28, 2018.

Montefiore, Simon Sebag. *Stalin: The Court of the Red Tsar*. London: Weidenfeld and Nicolson, 2003.

Mossman, Elliot, ed. *The Correspondence of Boris Pasternak and Olga Freidenberg, 1910–1954*. Translated by Elliot Mossman and Margaret Wettlin. New York: Harcourt Brace Jovanovich, 1982.

Nekrasov, Viktor. "Vas. Grossman." In *Victor Nekrasov v zhizni i v pis'mah*. Moscow: Sovetskij pisatel', 1971.

————. *Zapiski zevaki*. Frankfurt: Posev, 1976.

Novikova, Irina. "O stat'e G. Kalihmana 'Vasily Grossman, pisatel' i chelovek.'" *Partnyor* 4 (2011).

Nyurnbergskij protsess: voennye prestupleniya i prestupleniya protiv chelovechnosti. 8 vols. Moscow: Gosudarstvennoe izdatel'stvo yuridicheskoi literatury, 1958.

Ortenberg, David. *God 1942*. Moscow: Politizdat, 1988.

————. *Iyun'– dekabr' sorok pervogo*. Moscow: Sovetskij pisatel', 1984.

————. *Sorok tretij*. Moscow: Politizdat, 1991.

————. *Vremya ne vlastno: Pisateli na voine*. Moscow: Sovetskij pisatel', 1979.

Pennington, Reina. "Women and the Battle of Stalingrad." In *Russia: War, Peace and Diplomacy. Essays in Honour of John Erickson*, edited by Ljubica Erickson and Mark Erickson. London: Weidenfeld and Nicolson, 2004.

Poltorak, A. I. *Nyurnbergskij epilog*. Moscow: Voenizdat, 1965.

Pringle, Peter. *The Murder of Nikolai Vavilov: The Story of Stalin's Persecution of One of the Great Scientists of the Twentieth Century*. New York: Simon and Schuster, 2008.

Radkey, Oliver. *Russia Goes to the Polls: The Election to the All-Russian Constituent Assembly, 1917*. Ithaca: Cornell University Press, 1989.

Rajchman, Chil. *Treblinka: A Survivor's Memory, 1942–1943*. Translated by Solon Beinfeld. London: Maclehose, 2011.

Rayfield, Donald. *Stalin and His Hangmen: An Authoritative Portrait of a Tyrant and Those Who Served Him*. London: Viking, 2004.

Redlich, Shimon. *War, Holocaust and Stalinism: A Documented History of the Jewish Anti-Fascist Committee in the USSR*. Luxembourg: Harwood Academic, 1995.

Reeder, Roberta. *Anna Akhmatova: Poet and Prophet*. New York: Picador USA, 1994.

Robin, Régine. *Socialist Realism: An Impossible Aesthetic*. Translated by Catherine Porter. Stanford: Stanford University Press, 1992.

Ro'i, Yaacov, ed. *Jews and Jewish Life in Russia and the Soviet Union*. Ilford, UK: Frank Cass, 1995.

Roskina, Natalya. *Chetyre glavy: Iz literaturnyh vospominanij*. Paris: YMCA-Press, 1980.

Rubenstein, Joshua. *The Last Days of Stalin*. New Haven: Yale University Press, 2016.

———. "The Night of the Murdered Poets," 1997. http://web.archive.org/web/20070827145945/http://www.joshuarubenstein.com/stalinsecret/intro.html. Accessed April 28, 2018.

———. *Tangled Loyalties: The Life and Times of Ilya Ehrenburg*. New York: Basic Books, 1996.

Rubenstein, Joshua, and Vladimir Naumov, eds. *Stalin's Secret Pogrom: The Postwar Inquisition of the Jewish Anti-Fascist Committee*. Translated by Laura Esther Wolfson. New Haven: Yale University Press, 2005.

Sakharov, Andrei. *Memoirs*. Translated by Richard Lourie. New York: Knopf, 1990.

Sands, Philippe. *East West Street: On the Origins of "Genocide" and "Crimes against Humanity."* New York: Knopf, 2016.

Sarnov, Benedikt. *Imperiya zla. Sud'by pisatelei*. Moscow: Novaya gazeta, 2011.

Segev, Tom. *Simon Wiesenthal: The Life and Legends*. New York: Doubleday, 2010.

Service, Robert. *Trotsky: A Biography*. Cambridge, MA: Belknap Press, Harvard University Press, 2009.

Shalamov, Varlam. *Kolymskie rasskazy, stikhotvoreniya*. Moscow: Slovo, 2000.

Sharov, Alexander. "Iz vospominanij o Vasilii Grossmane." In *Okoyom: Povesti, vospominaniya*. Moscow: Sovetskij pisatel', 1990.

Shentalinsky, Vitaly. *Arrested Voices: Resurrecting the Disappeared Writers of the Soviet Union*. Translated by John Crowfoot. New York: Free Press, 1993.

Shifman, M., ed. *Physics in a Mad World*. Translated by James Manteith. Hackensack, NJ: World Scientific, 2016.

Shrayer, Maxim, ed. *An Anthology of Jewish-Russian Literature: Two Centuries of Dual Identity in Prose and Poetry*. Armonk, NY: M. E. Sharpe, 2007.

Sisir, Kumar Das, ed. *The English Writings of Rabindranath Tagore*. New Delhi: Sahitya Academi, 1994.

Slezkine, Yuri. *The House of Government: A Saga of the Russian Revolution*. Princeton: Princeton University Press, 2017.

———. *The Jewish Century*. Princeton: Princeton University Press, 2004.

Snyder, Timothy. *Bloodlands: Europe between Hitler and Stalin*. New York: Basic Books, 2010.

Solzhenitsyn, Alexander. "Dilogiya Vasiliya Grossmana." *Novy mir* 8 (2003).

———. *Invisible Allies*. Translated by Alexis Klimoff and Michael Nicholson. Washington, DC: Counterpoint, 1995.

———. *The Oak and the Calf*. Translated by Harry Willetts. London: Collins and Harvill, 1980.

Stangneth, Bettina. *Eichmann Before Jerusalem: The Unexamined Life of a Mass Murderer*. Translated by Ruth Martin. London: Bodley Head, 2014.

Surits, Gedda. "Neliteraturnye druz'ya. Iz vospominanij." *Dialog* 2 (1997–98).

Svirsky, Grigory. "Vosem' minut svobody." *Grani* 136 (1985).

Taratuta, Yevgeniya. "Chestnaya zhizn' i tyazhkaya sud'ba." *Ogonyok* 40 (1987).

———. *Kniga vospominanij*. Moscow: Yanus, 2001.

Tvardovsky, Alexander. *Dnevnik: 1950–1959*. Moscow: Prozaik, 2013.

———. *Novomirskij dnevnik: 1961–1966*. 2 vols. Moscow: Prozaik, 2009.

———. *"Ya v svoyu hodil ataku . . ." Dnevniki. Pis'ma. 1941–1945*. Moscow: Vagrius, 2005.

Voinovich, Vladimir. *Avtoportret: Roman moei zhizni*. Moscow: Eksmo, 2010.

———. "Zhizn' i sud'ba Vasiliya Grossmana i ego romana." *Posev* 11 (1984).

Waife-Goldberg, Marie. *My Father, Sholom Aleichem*. New York: Simon and Schuster, 1968.

Wiernik, Yankel. *A Year in Treblinka*. New York: American Representation of the General Workers' Union of Poland, 1945. http://www.zchor.org/treblink/wiernik.htm#chapter1. Accessed April 28, 2018.

Wiesel, Elie. *Souls on Fire*. Translated by Marion Wiesel. New York: Random House, 1972.

Yakovlev, Alexander. *A Century of Violence in Soviet Russia*. Translated by Anthony Austin. New Haven: Yale University Press, 2002.

Yampolsky, Boris. "Poslednyaya vstrecha s Vasiliem Grossmanom." *Kontinent* 8 (1976).

Yedlin, Tovah. *Maxim Gorky: A Political Biography*. London: Westport, 1999.

Zabolotsky, Nikita. *The Life of Zabolotsky*. Translated by R. R. Milner-Gulland and C. G. Bearne. Cardiff: University of Wales Press, 1994.

Zabolotsky, Nikolai. "Istoria moego zaklyucheniya." http://www.lib.ru/POEZIQ/ZABOLOCKIJ/istoriya.txt. Accessed April 28, 2018.

Zaks, Boris. "Nemnogo o Grossmane." *Kontinent* 52 (2013).

Zemtsov, Ilya. *Encyclopedia of Soviet Life*. New Brunswick: Transaction, 1991.

Zola, Émile. *Germinal*. Translated by Peter Collier. Oxford: Oxford University Press, 1993.

Zweig, Stefan. *The World of Yesterday*. Translated by Anthea Bell. Lincoln: University of Nebraska Press, 2009.

Index

In this index "VG" stands for Vasily Grossman.